Resources of Hope

D1382949

Resources of Hope

Culture, Democracy, Socialism

RAYMOND WILLIAMS

Edited by Robin Gable

With an Introduction by
Robin Blackburn

VERSO

London · New York

First published by Verso 1989
Second impression 1989
© the estate of Raymond Williams
All rights reserved

Verso
UK: 6 Meard Street, London W1V 3HR
USA: 29 West 35th Street, New York, NY 10001-2291

Verso is the imprint of New Left Books

British Library Cataloguing in Publication Data

Williams, Raymond, *1921-1988*
    Resources of hope : culture, democracy,
    socialism.
    1. Socialism. Theories, 1800-1985
    I. Title
    335.009′034

    ISBN 0-86091-229-9
    ISBN 0-86091-943-9 Pbk

US Library of Congress Cataloging in Publication Data

Williams, Raymond.
        Resources of hope: culture, democracy, socialism/Raymond Williams.
        p.   cm.
        Bibliography: p.
        Includes index.
        ISBN 0-86091-229-9 : $42.50.   ISBN 0-86091-943-9 (pbk.) : $14.95
        1. Political culture—Great Britain.   2. Socialism—Great Britain.
    3. Great Britain—Politics and government—20th century.   I. Title.
    JA75.7.W55 1989
    306′.2′0941—dc19

Typeset by Leaper & Gard, Bristol
Printed in Great Britain by Bookcraft (Bath) Ltd

Contents

Acknowledgements

The essays collected in this volume were first delivered in lecture form or published as follows: 'Culture is Ordinary' in *Convictions*, ed., Norman Mackenzie, MacGibbon and Gee 1958; 'Communications and Community' is the text of the William F. Harvey Memorial Lecture, given at Bedford College, University of London on 8 April 1961; 'The Idea of a Common Culture' (originally titled 'Culture and Revolution: A Comment') in *From Culture to Revolution: The Slant Symposium 1967*, eds, Terry Eagleton and Brian Wicker, Sheed and Ward 1968; 'The Arts Council' in *Political Quarterly* 50, 1979; 'Why Do I Demonstrate?' in *The Listener* 79, 25 April 1968; 'You're a Marxist, Aren't You?' in *The Concept of Socialism*, ed., Bhiku Parekh, Croom Helm 1975; 'The Writer: Commitment and Alignment' in *Marxism Today*, June 1980; 'Art: Freedom as Duty' in *Planet* 68, April/May 1988, originally a contribution to the symposium, 'Art: Duties and Freedoms' at Gregynog Hall, Newtown, Powys on 8–10 September 1978, and first published by the Department of Extramural Studies, The University College of Wales, Aberystwyth, in conjunction with The Welsh Arts Council 1979; 'Welsh Culture' in *Culture and Politics: Plaid Cymru's Challenge to Wales*, Plaid Cymru 1975, originally a talk on BBC Radio 3, 27 September 1975; 'The Social Significance of 1926' in *Llafur* 2:2, 1977, originally an address to the commemorative conference, 'The General Strike and the Miners' Lockout of 1926' organized jointly by Llafur and the National Union of Mineworkers at Pontypridd on 9–11 April 1976; 'The Importance of Community' in *Radical Wales* 18, Summer 1988, originally a lecture given to the Plaid Cymru Summer School at Llandudno on 13 July 1977; 'Mining the Meaning: Key Words in the Miners' Strike' in *New Socialist* 25, March 1985; 'The British Left' in *NLR* 30, March–April 1965, an amended version of an article written for the French journal *Esprit* 32, 1964; 'Ideas and the Labour Movement' in *New Socialist* 2, November/December 1981; 'An Alternative

Politics' in *The Socialist Register 1981*, Merlin Press 1981; 'Problems of the Coming Period' in *NLR* 140, July–August 1983, originally a talk given to the Socialist Society on 11 May 1983; 'Socialists and Coalitionists' in *The Future of the Left*, ed., James Curran, Polity Press and New Socialist 1984, originally published as 'Splits, Pacts and Coalitions', *New Socialist* 16, March/April 1984; 'The Politics of Nuclear Disarmament' in *NLR* 124, November–December 1980, and subsequently in *Exterminism and Cold War*, eds, E.P. Thompson et al., Verso 1982; 'Socialism and Ecology', in SERA pamphlet 1982, originally a talk given to the Socialist Environment and Resources Association; 'Between Country and City' in *Second Nature*, eds, Richard Mabey et al., Jonathan Cape 1984; 'Decentralism and the Politics of Place' in *Society and Space* vol. 2, 1984, an interview conducted by Philip Cooke of Plaid Cymru, first published in a slightly shorter form as 'Nationalisms and Popular Socialism' in *Radical Wales* 2, Spring 1984; 'The Forward March of Labour Halted?' in *The Forward March of Labour Halted?*, eds, Martin Jacques and Francis Mulhern, Verso 1981; 'Democracy and Parliament' in Socialist Society pamphlet 1982, and subsequently in *Marxism Today*, June 1982; 'Walking Backwards into the Future' in *New Socialist* 27, May 1985; 'Hesitations before Socialism' in *New Socialist* 41, September 1986; 'Towards Many Socialisms' in *Socialism on the Threshold of the Twenty-first Century*, ed., Miloš Nikolić, originally a contribution to The Tenth Round Table International Conference 'Socialism in the World' at Cavtat, Yugoslavia on 21–26 October 1985; 'The Practice of Possibility', an interview conducted by Terry Eagleton, in the *New Statesman*, 7 August 1987.

****

The writings republished in this volume have received only a necessary minimum of editorial intervention. Obvious errors and omissions have been corrected; punctuation has been normalized only where required by sense; superfluous headings have been omitted or amended. As a collection of lectures, articles, essays and interviews spanning thirty years and originally addressed to specific audiences or readerships, there inevitably exists a degree of overlap and repetition in the volume. In particular a decision was made to publish all the available work on Labour strategy and socialist democracy rather than introduce arbitrary criteria for editing or exclusion. The title *Resources of Hope* takes up a phrase used on a number of occasions by Raymond Williams; most significantly in the final chapter of *Towards 2000*, 'Resources for a Journey of Hope'. We thank Joy Williams for her help and advice in preparing this volume.

Robin Gable
October 1988

Introduction

Raymond Williams, who died on 26 January 1988, was the most authoritative, consistent and original socialist thinker in the English-speaking world. The loss to the British Left of a spokesman at the height of his powers remains deeply felt. Tributes to Williams appeared in many newspapers and periodicals, testifying to a widespread sense that the established culture had lost its most acute critic.[1] Williams approached literature, cultural studies, communications and adult education in such radically new ways that he revolutionized their study and practice. While this cultural work was linked to his conception of a democratic 'long revolution', its validity and importance were nevertheless recognized by many who had no prior commitment to his anti-capitalist politics. Similarly Williams's drama and novels explore profoundly political themes but, like all his writing, are couched in a language far removed from received political discourse. Part of the value of Williams's work to the Left is that it does not belong to the Left alone.

Yet for a full understanding of Williams's work it is essential to attend to its political meanings. An understanding of, and commitment to, a radically transformed social order were integral to his vision and

1. Among tributes to Williams were those by Bill Webb, *The Guardian*, January 27; Terry Eagleton and Frank Kermode, *The Independent*, January 28; Francis Mulhern, *The Guardian*, January 29; Blake Morrison, *The Observer*, January 31; Anthony Barnett, *The Listener*, February 3; Tony Benn, *The Morning Star*, February 4; Fred Inglis, *The Times Higher Education Supplement*, February 5; Anthony Arblaster, *Tribune*, February 5; Stuart Hall, *The New Statesman*, February 5; Patrick Parrinder, *London Review of Books*, February 12; Judith Williamson, Anthony Barnett, Stuart Hall and Dafydd Ellis Thomas, Channel 4, February 28; Margot Heinemann, *Marxism Today*, March 1988; Kevin Davey, *Interlink*, March 1988. In April the New York weekly *The Nation* also published tributes by Edward Thompson and Edward Said.

achievement. Williams's directly political interventions were a natural outgrowth of his concern for a democratic culture, just as the experience and commitments they reflect themselves helped to inform his major critical studies. The writings and lectures brought together in this book share a political theme even when they do not directly engage with politics as such – they can all be seen as expressing and developing his conception of that 'long revolution' whereby full equality and citizenship could be extended to the whole population.

The idea that Western societies do not embody the democratic values · they proclaim is not, of course, in itself peculiar to Williams, but few have pursued this theme at once in such rigorous detail and into so many areas of life. Whether Williams is writing about the mass media or the educational system, the British State or the structure of the Labour Party, or indeed the functioning of the economy, he is concerned to specify the institutional and material conditions for democratic participation. The essays assembled here concern such diverse subjects as the culture of consumption and the politics of culture, the roots and character of political commitment, the values of community and resistance, mass communications and the challenge of ecology and anti-militarism. A number have not been widely available before and in different ways each sheds a fascinating light on Williams's life and work. Informal talks before a variety of audiences are included together with deliberate reactions to burning questions of the day. The book is intended to reflect both the range and the intensity of Williams's work as a public intellectual – his insistence on confronting the most demanding issues and his ability to bring together the personal and the political. Interestingly enough, Williams's insistence on rooting his political ideas in personal experience mean that there are many autobiographical passages here, as he reflects on his childhood in the Welsh border country, his student days as a Communist at Cambridge, his wartime role as tank commander, his work as WEA tutor or as Professor of Drama at an ancient university.

The present book can thus be seen as a complement to the interviews of *Politics and Letters* which ranged over his whole life and work up to the date of publication (1979), as well as to the two previous collections of Williams's writings published by Verso – *Problems in Materialism and Culture* and *Writing in Society*. A further volume will collect Williams's writings on modernism and cultural theory, including previously unpublished work. The prefatory remarks which follow are intended simply to signal some of the themes explored in the present collection and to suggest certain links with the wider work. Some readers will prefer to read Williams himself first and they can do no better than start with the first essay, which has been long out of print – with great eloquence and immediacy it introduces themes which Williams was to elaborate in the most diverse and fruitful ways in his later cultural and political writings, including those to be found here.

Whether personal, programmatic or polemical the writings in this book reflect Williams's longstanding involvement with the project of building a 'New Left'; one which would contest the paternalism, insularity, short-sightedness, and philistinism of the postwar British labour movement while encouraging its critical and educational faculties. His work was an inspiration to the first wave of the New Left in the 1950s; he helped found *New Left Review* in 1960; he was the main drafter of the *May Day Manifesto* published by Penguin in 1968; and was a founder of the Socialist Society in 1981. In many less formal ways Williams was sponsor, contributor and guide to a host of radical educational, cultural and political ventures, across more than three decades, which sought to go beyond the narrow and elitist assumptions of the Labour establishment.

While British culture and politics furnished the occasion for many of the reflections, initiatives and proposals to be found here, the work often enabled a wider inspiration and application, as Williams saw the project of a New Left taken up and modified in particular ways by the anti-war movement and student revolt of the sixties, by the re-birth of women's movements, by the Greens in the seventies, and by the emergence of a socialist opposition in Eastern Europe. In 'Culture is Ordinary' (1958) Williams pays tribute to both Marx and Leavis, and thereafter his criticism and his politics nourish one another and draw on an increasingly diverse range of historical and national sources: Strindberg and Brecht, Lukács and Timpanaro, Goldmann and Bahro. Williams's deep, lifelong engagement with British culture was assisted by his ability to view it, as it were, from the outside as well as the inside, and to discern within the British pattern general problems of late twentieth-century civilization. In the sixties and the seventies Williams wrote regularly for the New York weekly *The Nation* while his essay on 'The British Left' (1965), reprinted in Section 5, was first written for the French monthly *Esprit.*

The natural transition from *Culture and Society* (1968) to *The Long Revolution* (1961) already showed Williams's refusal to respect a boundary dividing high culture and popular culture, or separating art and politics – for him both of the latter were broad human concerns rather than special preserves of privileged minorities. Williams's work was always controversial within the Left but these controversies, though sometimes sharp, were nevertheless constructive as his critics found themselves acknowledging his rare combination of integrity and boldness, originality and scholarship.[2]

The generosity of Williams's approach to pre-socialist, or even anti-socialist traditions was to be disconcerting to critics on the left. Yet it allowed him to tap neglected sources of social critique and to construct a socialist commitment that was to prove robust and weatherproof through several changes in the political climate. His insight into the formation of ruling-class hegemony, and the ability of his own work to challenge it, stemmed from his decision to examine the formations of established culture at their strong points and not to content himself with the comforts of a purely radical lineage. The main impulse of Williams's work in the fifties was to (re)construct a critique of industrial capitalism as a human order rather than to pursue its specifically economic failures, or alleged failures, in the area of productivity. While his work was subsequently to develop many new concerns, this theme was in no way abandoned as the reader will readily see in essays such as 'The British Left' (1965) and 'Socialism and Ecology' (1982).

In *The Long Revolution*, Williams went on to elaborate new conceptual tools able to identify hidden dimensions of political transformation and deep structures of the social formation. The insistence that political and economic institutions excluded vital areas of experience and social practice, the attention paid to whole forms of life and *longue durée*, suggested at least the title and perhaps something of the overall method of Juliet Mitchell's pioneering feminist analysis, 'Women: The Longest Revolution' in *New Left Review* 40 (1966). In his theoretical work as much as in his novels Williams paid attention to patterns of 'generation and nurture' as well as to those of production and communication.[3]

Williams's abiding concern even with conservative tradition went together with the boldest espousal of new practices and institutions. The patterns whereby culture is produced and reproduced were a central preoccupation for him, as were the democratic possibilities opened up by transformations in communications technology. Williams's work on education and communications was to create a climate of discussion and

2. There are far too many assessments of Williams's work, both critical and otherwise, to attempt a bibliography here. But I would like to mention the most significant discussion of Williams's work to appear in *New Left Review*. See, in particular, the articles by E. P. Thompson in *NLR* 9, 10 and 99; Terry Eagleton in *NLR* 96; Anthony Barnett in *NLR* 99; Francis Mulhern in *NLR* 148.

3. Williams was later to be both puzzled and self-critical when considering the paradox that while he made conceptual allowance for the realm of 'generation and nurture' in his early work, he nevertheless failed to address many vital issues later raised by the women's movement. See *Politics and Letters*, pp. 147–50.

expectation which could not be wholly ignored even by officialdom. In his much reprinted Penguin Special, *Communications,* first published in 1962, he made detailed proposals concerning the public management of the communications media. Those responsible for setting up the Open University or Channel 4 did not directly involve Williams; yet the power of his advocacy remains visible in the better features of these institutions. In the conclusion to *Communications* he also outlined the need for a new arts and education policy aimed at diffusing civic skills and democratic access to cultural resources as widely as possible. Because of these concerns Williams agreed to join the Arts Council in the late seventies; but he found himself fundamentally at odds with a structure whose mode of 'administered consensus by cooption' effectively prevents genuine democratic participation and thereby strengthens ruling interests. The reader will find his critical reflections on this experience in Section 2.

Williams's rejection of both the commercial and the bureaucratic tutelage of culture remains distinctive and exemplary. In *Politics and Letters* Williams explained in the following way the approach that he had adopted in his work on communications:

> The traditional answer on the left to everything was public ownership. But no one had ever worked out what public ownership should mean in a field as sensitive as this. The prospect of bureaucratic monopoly was rightly feared, given the examples of state-controlled media, as just jumping out of the frying pan into the fire. The result was to induce resigned acceptance among people working in the media of the existing capitalist arrangements. The essence of my proposals was that public ownership of the basic means of production should be combined with leasing of their use to self-managing groups, to secure maximum variety of style and political opinion and to ensure against any bureaucratic control. This principle is perfectly practicable in every field from the newsprint industry through to broadcasting facilities and cinema.[4]

A powerful indictment of the capitalist organization of newspapers will be found in 'Why Do I Demonstrate?', written for *The Listener* in April 1968 and reprinted in Section 3. Williams had recently taken part both in demonstrations against the Vietnam War and in a demonstration outside the German Embassy to protest at the attempted assassination of Rudi Dutschke, the German student leader; in the weeks before the attempt on his life was made the Springer press empire had vilified Dutschke in the most provocative manner. This article exemplifies Williams's ability to make the most pointed of interventions, to situate present problems in a new and unexpected context, and to explain to a new generation of radicals the full meaning of their actions.

4. Ibid., p. 370.

Williams drew certain fundamental values from his own background and early experience that enabled him to share a deep sympathy with anticolonial struggle and peasant resistance. While Williams's father was a railway worker, his family belonged to an agricultural Welsh border community near Pandy, comprising farmers, agricultural labourers, teachers and preachers as well as a few trade unionists. When Williams spoke of his earliest political experiences he recalled the Left Book Club group established in Pandy, and its campaigns of solidarity with China and Spain, mentioning the impression made on him by Edgar Snow's *Red Star over China* or a talk by Konni Zilliacus.[5] One has a sense of a nascent 'structure of feeling' – internationalism reinforced by local attachments and a discursive model of political culture – that was to endure. In 'You're a Marxist Aren't You?' (1975), reprinted in Section 3 here, Williams explains how his wartime experience in Normandy fighting the SS also shaped his later response to popular revolt in the Third World. Military rule, landlordism and imperialism demanded resistance and revolution: 'I have never been able to say that the use of military power to defend a revolution is something that I am against.'

Williams knew enough of revolution in the twentieth century for these not to be easy affirmations. As he explains in the 'Afterword' (1979) to a new edition of *Modern Tragedy* he particularly detested those who turned the avoidable and unavoidable suffering of revolution into a terrifying dumb show while remaining oblivious to the violence of imperialism. In *Modern Tragedy* (1966) he had reflected upon these themes and on the suffering caused by the 'disordered struggle against disorder' in the twentieth century:

> We have to recognize this suffering in a close and immediate experience, and not cover it with names. But we follow the whole action: not only the evil, but the men who have fought against evil; not only the crisis but the energy released by it, the spirit learned in it.[6]

In 'You're a Marxist Aren't You?' Williams categorically opposed any resort to physical violence in 'societies with functioning political democracies'. Such violence, unless in defence of democracy itself, would itself defeat the aspiration to build more generous forms of

---

5. Ibid., p. 31. The Left Book Club, which seems to have been formative for so many of the outstanding British socialists and Marxists of the postwar years, should not, on this evidence, be assimilated to the stereotype of an accommodating Popular Front – Williams here remembers how, aged eighteen or nineteen and fresh from the Pandy Left Club, he told the first Communist organizer he met at Cambridge: 'I want to be with the reddest of the reds.' (Ibid., p. 41)

6. Raymond Williams, *Modern Tragedy* revised edn, p. 83.

human solidarity. But demonstrations and strikes, sit-ins and boycotts could all help, depending on their precise goals and the extent of popular participation, to extend a democracy that was atrophying at the centre.

It is characteristic that directly political reflections on contemporary issues are to be found in the main body of Williams's critical work in a way that would perhaps not have been so appropriate for a historian. All of Williams's books have a historical dimension. But this history is brought to bear on the present; and there contemporary experience is characteristically invoked as a crucial test of cultural theory. In Williams's hands the Leavis-influenced touchstones of authenticity and experience enfranchise a world that had been barely acknowledged by criticism before. Hence in a work like *Modern Tragedy* Williams can observe 'I am writing on a day when British military power is being used against "dissident tribesmen" in South Arabia.' These were the actions of a Labour government and lead to the conclusion:

> I know this pattern and its covering too well, from repeated experiences in my lifetime, to be able to acquiesce in the ordinary illusion. Many of my countrymen have opposed these policies and in many particular cases have ended them. But it is impossible to believe that as a society we have yet dedicated ourselves to human liberation, or even to that simple recognition of the basic humanity of all other men which is the impulse of any genuine revolution. To say that in our affairs we have made this recognition would also be too much, in a society powered by great economic inequality and by organized manipulation. But even if we had made this recognition, among ourselves, it would still be a travesty of any real revolutionary belief. It is only when the recognition is general that it can be authentic, for in practice every reservation, in a widely communicating world, tends to degenerate into actual opposition.[7]

Williams not only appeared on the platforms of the Vietnam Solidarity Campaign; he also studied the general implications of rural resistance and overseas aggression for a socialist understanding of culture and civilization. *The Country and the City* (1973) shows the process of capitalist despoliation at home and colonial slavery abroad behind the culture of the English 'country house' and the conventions of a pastoral mode that conjured them away. Likewise in establishing a precise social context Williams situated but did not diminish the work of writers whose critical moral sensibility transcended the pastoral. He urged his British readers to consult such contemporary Third World authors as Wilson Harris and Ngugi if they were to understand the past of their own

7. Ibid., p. 79.

society. Against the 'new metropolis', etched in terms foreshadowing debates on the 'postmodern city', Williams discerned a new 'sense of society', prepared to take responsibility for the whole 'human ecology'.[8]

In a conversation in 1987 about the recent spate of fictional dystopias – books like Paul Theroux's *O-Zone* and Pete Davis's *The Last Election* – Williams remarked sardonically that these doom-laden prophecies and satires were no longer set a generation or two in the future but were just a few years off. If *Modern Tragedy* had situated itself in a world gripped by imperialism and revolution, *The Country and the City* prepared the ground for a thoroughgoing ecological critique of capitalism and of 'productivist' distortions of socialism. In the late seventies Williams became a sponsor of the Socialist Environmental Resources Association. He was also amongst the first to respond to Edward Thompson's theses on the escalating danger of the nuclear arms race. In 'The Politics of Nuclear Disarmament', reprinted in Section 6, he argued that 'to build peace, now more than ever, it will be necessary to build more than peace'; since there were essential links between nuclear militarism and the alienations of modern nation-states, with their corrupted media of communications, their increasingly remote and incompetent representative assemblies and their ruthless and irresponsible concentrations of economic power. In Williams's view the lasting threat of modern weapons systems came from their embeddedness within antagonistic social relations.

While Williams consistently attacked the brittle unrealities of a pastoral or consumerist culture which concealed the labour sustaining it, he could not subscribe to the notion of a progressively unfolding class subject. His search for social meaning focused on intersubjectivity, and its material preconditions, and he always argued that social consciousness was formed between as well as within classes and class fractions. The ambiguous international legacy of the sixties, the deeply contested British conjuncture of the seventies, or the *trompe l'oeil* of the 'postmodern' eighties were all illuminated by this relational approach, with its attention to a complex social totality, to generational shifts, and to the bonds of locality.

Williams's characteristic mode of piling qualification upon complexity, to be found in many of the essays and lectures in this book, was not prompted by any reflex of moderation but by a search for accuracy and realism, and by his awareness that human social capacities were cumulative and developmental. On the one hand his work spoke of a developing crisis of capitalist civilization and of the main forces arrayed against it; on the other hand it was informed by an acute sense of the

8. Raymond Williams, *The Country and the City*, p. 329.

variety of forms of culture and association that would be required to assert human control over processes of economic and military competition run amok. Williams's references to ecological crisis were sober and empirical because he wished to foster deliberate and effective forms of social counteraction. If his socialism could sometimes seem to echo and renew Morris's tremendous indictments of capitalist waste and destruction, he never succumbed to the latter's tempting simplification either of the problems or of the solutions. Socialism was neither a ready-made nor an easy way out of the impasse of capitalism and imperialism. In absorbing the implications for socialism of the ecological critique he saw that this made at once more urgent and more difficult the construction of a global 'collective consciousness'. The political core of Williams's preoccupations is nowhere more evident than in *Towards 2000* (1983) in which he sought to reconcile the legacy of class-rooted politics with the necessary corrective offered by the 'new social movements'. He saw the latter as essential to reconstituting a sense of the 'general interest' rising above particular corporate class interests. On the other hand he insisted that the vital issues put on the agenda by the social movements would, if followed through, 'lead us into the central system of the industrial capitalist mode of production and . . . its system of classes'.[9]

While attentive to the weight of the mode of production Williams drew attention to its link to a specific 'mode of consumption'. His critique was in no sense a disguised lamentation that working people could now afford consumer durables which had formerly defined middle-class lifestyles. His point was rather that in capitalist society the sphere of consumption was dominated by a wasteful, destructive and irresponsible system of accumulation. Consumption itself was ill-informed or misinformed and in many ways manipulated, subordinate and passive. While hostile to the prevailing ethos of 'consumerism', Williams urged the need for agencies which would inform and protect consumers in quite new ways. In fact Williams's ideas on this subject amount to a new conception of collective and individual 'consumer sovereignty'. And typically they were accompanied by specific institutional proposals designed to ensure that households would not be atomized in the face of large-scale productive enterprises. In this way he anticipated the preoccupations of socialist economists in the era of perestroika, and outlined broad cultural grounds for rejecting the

9. Raymond Williams, *Towards 2000*, pp. 172–3. Political reflections of crucial significance will also be found in *Problems in Materialism and Culture*; note particularly, in this context, the essay on the work of the East German dissident Rudolf Bahro, 'Beyond Actually Existing Socialism'.

onesidedness of production-centred socialisms, whether of the market or plan variety.[10]

While Williams is most widely known for his distinctive stress on the politics of cultural practice, it is worth noting that he was particularly concerned with the efficacy and adequacy of party and state organization – and especially with whether such organizations were capable of promoting the democracy of the 'long revolution'. In his view the rise of the labour movement had qualified but not challenged, still less transformed, the oligarchic structure of the British State.

The necessity for the labour movement to nourish its own democratic functioning as well as to promote a democratic reform of education or communications is a theme that may be detected at many points in Williams's work. The institutions of the labour movement are major cultural embodiments of collective memory and intelligence, but this does not mean that they are adequate to the tasks before them. In his survey of 'The British Left' in the mid sixties Williams pointed out that the very structure of the Labour Party, dominated as it was by undemocratic block votes, locked the socialist Left into a coalition dominated by the politics of short-term corporate interest and Fabian gradualism. 'The fact that the Labour Party is a coalition has led to an evident poverty in theory; any attempt to go beyond quite general definitions leads at once to strains on this complicated alliance.' Even the most positive social reforms promoted by Labour were infused by a spirit of 'moral paternalism' while in foreign policy Labour governments were 'corrupted by . . . the Cold War', by 'dangerous petty chauvinism' and 'Kiplingesque imperialism'. The structural subordination of the Left within the Labour Party lent a vital role to the Left outside the Party – CND, the Communist Party 'with its guarantee of a measure of militant vigilance' and a more diffuse cultural and political 'New Left'. Already in these early months of 1965 Williams could write in 'The British Left':

> The sound of the young in Britain, so terrifying to all those who have accepted these routines [i.e. 'the grey routines of an alienated society'] is a deep and living sound, and it is significant that when it becomes political it is against the whole structure of society rather than for or against a particular group in parliamentary politics.

Despite his profound criticisms of Labourism and the Labour Party Williams saw the class loyalties it attracted as potentially open to a trans-

10. See for example Diane Elson, 'Socializing the Market', *New Left Review* 172 (1988). For Williams's critique of the passivity of capitalist consumerism see *The Long Revolution*, pp. 286–8; a theme taken up again at several points in *Towards 2000*.

formation beyond its given structure and ideology. He welcomed the emergence of a more radical Left within the Labour Party in the late seventies and early eighties because it sought to change rather than simply capture the existing apparatus. He was to become a sponsoring editor of *New Socialist*, a journal set up by the National Executive of the Labour Party in 1981 at a moment when the ascendancy of the Right within the Party was momentarily disturbed following the fiasco of the Wilson–Callaghan government of 1974–79. *New Socialist*, edited with flair and conviction by James Curran, published a number of key interventions by Williams which are reprinted here. They include attacks on the callousness of 'nomad capitalism' and its instrument the Thatcher government, saluting the extraordinary tenacity of the mining communities during the coal strike; and in another, assailing the continuing subordination of the Left to Labour's peculiar federal structure. In the debate on whether Labour should offer an anti-Thatcher coalition to the political centre, Williams adopted a position which cut through much of the cant surrounding the subject by pointing out that the Labour Party itself had always been a coalition of some socialists with the Atlanticist and pro-capitalist Labour Right: 'Whether it's the big or the smaller version [of coalition], the advocates of either have in effect abandoned the struggle to transform belief and opinion.' In Williams's view commitment either to a coalition with the centre or to a continuing coalition with the Labour front bench meant rallying round a programme that was known to be desperately weak and incoherent, and forswearing the vital work of renewing and extending socialist politics. In an interview with Terry Eagleton in July 1987, to be found in Section 7, Williams warned the Left of the compromising implications of the Labourist coalition. He argued that the experience of the 1987 Election pointed to the beginnings of a realignment of the centre with the Labour front bench. While he insisted that 'such a realignment of the centre just isn't the Left's business' he believed that if it led to electoral reform it could open the way to 'some federation of socialist, Green and radical nationalist forces'. Williams believed that the 'wholesale conversion' of Labour into a socialist party was an illusory objective which too often led the Left to silence itself. But he knew that any new socialist formation would need to build upon the currents of working-class and community resistance that had developed inside and outside the labour movement during the Thatcher years.

In contrast to a traditional Labour left politics Williams refused to accept the structure of the UK State as the necessary horizon of socialist action. Strongly committed to linking up with socialists elsewhere in Europe, he looked forward to a socialist challenge to the very principles on which the UK State was constructed. From the mid seventies he became a regular speaker at events organized by Plaid Cymru, testifying both to a radicalization of the Welsh nationalist party and to Williams's deeper questioning of the functioning of the centralized British State.

In 1982 Williams wrote an audacious programmatic statement 'Democracy and Parliament' to be found in Section 7 of this book. Published as a pamphlet by the Socialist Society this text not only indicted the secretive and hierarchical principles of the British apparatus of public administration but also criticized the centralized, oligarchic and discriminatory character of the system of political representation within the United Kingdom. For Williams, an electoral system which accurately and fairly represented the spectrum of political opinion among the electorate was an elementary necessity. Thus proportional representation as well as the break-up of the top-heavy Westminster system were essential complements to socialist advocacy. The pamphlet ends with a comprehensive programme for the democratization of the state, conceived of as a necessary prelude to asserting democratic control over economic and cultural processes.

One of the reasons for what will be Williams's enduring influence as a socialist can be found in interventions like these; in his patient attention to the cultural and political concomitants of a truly democratic society, and his willingness to address the quite practical problems of institutional innovation that this would require. And though Williams's specific reference here was to the need for democratic transformations in British institutions and the British State, the interventions have a wider application and relevance. Thus throughout the English-speaking world political representation is organized on a first-past-the-post, winner-takes-all basis; this necessarily produces strange coalitions, impedes the emergence of radical new political forces and constricts the development of a democratic public debate.

The reader of this collection will soon discover that Williams's political thought was neither static nor free from its own tensions. But the constancy of the central preoccupations is nevertheless striking. Two decades after 'Culture is Ordinary' Williams redefines his relationship to Marxism and to the 'long revolution' in 'You're a Marxist Aren't You?'. He says that he prefers to think of himself as a revolutionary socialist or Communist and historical materialist than as a Marxist. The term 'Marxist' was being adopted because it was felt to be 'more polite than Communist' but it was, he insists, wrong to reduce a whole tradition in which millions had participated to a 'single thinker, however great'. On the other hand Williams had no hesitation in accepting fundamental propositions of historical materialism and in making his own distinctive contributions to them in the form of a body of work he was to term 'cultural materialism'. Historical materialism helps socialists to identify what stands in the way of the growth of liberated human powers: 'Not just an electoral enemy or a traditional enemy, but a hostile and organized social formation . . .' This hostile social formation could only be challenged by the promotion of a popular self-government alien to the Fabian and Stalinist traditions – and this would inevitably have to contest the roots of bourgeois hegemony within the oppressed and exploited:

> I learned the reality of hegemony, I learned the saturating power of the structure of feeling of a given society, as much from my own mind and my own experience as from observing the lives of others. All through our lives, if we make the effort, we uncover layers of this kind of alien formation within ourselves, and deep in ourselves.

Williams does not counterpose here the cultural construction of meanings to the urgent pressures of material survival as they impinge even on the relatively well-off workers of an advanced capitalist society:

> I believe in the necessary economic struggle of the organized working class. I believe that this is still the most creative activity in our society, as I indicated years ago in calling the great working-class institutions great creative achievements, as well as the indispensable first means of political struggle. But . . . I know that there is a profoundly necessary job to do in relation to the processes of the cultural hegemony itself. I believe that the system of meanings and values which a capitalist society has generated has to be defeated in general and in detail by the most sustained kinds of intellectual and educational work. This is a cultural process which I called the 'long revolution' and in calling it the 'long revolution' I meant that it was a genuine struggle which was part of the necessary battles for democracy and of economic victory for the organized working class. People change, it is true, in struggle and by action. Anything as deep as a dominant structure of feeling is only changed by active new experience. But . . . the task of a successful socialist movement will be one of feeling and imagination quite as much as one of fact or organization.

Even before Margaret Thatcher's second election victory, a startling discrepancy was apparent between the gains of a broadly construed Left in academic culture and the inroads of a 'New Right' in popular culture. Williams's own rise to a preeminent position in cultural studies in the sixties and seventies was accompanied in these same decades by a remarkable flourishing of Marxist historiography and of significant Marxist work in philosophy, politics, sociology and the humanities generally. But just as Marxism and socialism became influential within the academy so Thatcherism consolidated its hold first on the Conservative Party and then on national politics. In 'Problems of the Coming Period' Williams points out that the peculiar nature of the British State had given special advantages to Thatcher's Conservative Party despite the fact that it has never had majority support. Moreover the characteristic economic and ideological pressures of Britain in the eighties stemmed from the failures of Labourism in the seventies and the mirage of Thatcherism's 'mobile privatization', with its blinkered and unequal consumer satisfactions purchased at an appalling social cost. Williams's interrogation of easy credit and easy unemployment, of the myriad intricate means for fracturing and individualizing a consciousness that remains socially determined, already contained within it an awareness of different majorities and alternative organizing principles.

Williams was never content simply with reaching conclusions for himself or with securing recognition for them within the academy. The publication of *Keywords* (1976) allowed him both to deepen his argument concerning the cultural construction of meanings and to render his findings more accessible. The history of the terms 'individual', 'socialism', or 'bourgeois' enables Williams to point up problems in these words even – perhaps especially – for those who see no difficulty with them. In 'Mining the Meaning' Williams argues that socialists must elucidate the key words of the miners' conflict, learning from the tremendous collective experience of the men and women who had sustained the strike:

> The point of growth for a reviving socialism is now in all these crisis-ridden communities: not as special cases but as a general case. It is here, in diversity and respect for diversity, that new popular forces are forming and looking for some effective articulation. It will be long and difficult in detail, but in challenging the destructive catchwords of *management, economic* and *law-and-order*, which now cover the real operations of a new and reckless stage of capitalism, the miners have, in seeking to protect their own interests, outlined a new form of the general interest.

In a lecture published in *New Left Review* in 1986 Williams pointed to the real advances made by the Left in education, especially adult education, but also to the adoption of certain self-isolating theoretical procedures and political watchwords. Looking for ways of breaking out of cultural encirclement and subordination Williams was led to ask:

> Should we not look, implacably, at those many formations, their theories and their works, which are based only on their negations and forms of enclosure, against an undifferentiated culture beyond them? Is it only an accident that one form of theory of ideology produced that block diagnosis of Thatcherism which taught despair and political disarmament in a social situation which was

always more diverse, more volatile and more temporary? Or is there never to be an end to petit-bourgeois theorists making long-term adjustments to short-term situations? Or, in the case of several kinds of recent art, can we raise again the question whether showing the exploited as degraded does not simply prolong the lease of the exploiter? . . . . The central problem of actual and possible class relationships, through which new art and theory can be made, has a new and in some way unprecedented complexity . . . in a shared search for emancipation.[11]

Williams leaves us with many questions, some of them uncomfortable and some more broadly construed than a first reading might suppose. He also leaves us with many pointers as to where the answers may lie – in his great works of culture criticism, in his own exemplary sense of responsibility to past and future generations, as demonstrated in many of the essays and interventions in this book.

Robin Blackburn
New Left Review 1988

11. Raymond Williams, 'The Uses of Cultural Theory' *New Left Review* 158 (1986).

1

Defining a Democratic Culture

Culture is Ordinary

1958

The bus stop was outside the cathedral. I had been looking at the Mappa Mundi, with its rivers out of Paradise, and at the chained library, where a party of clergymen had got in easily, but where I had waited an hour and cajoled a verger before I even saw the chains. Now, across the street, a cinema advertised the *Six-Five Special* and a cartoon version of *Gulliver's Travels*. The bus arrived, with a driver and a conductress deeply absorbed in each other. We went out of the city, over the old bridge, and on through the orchards and the green meadows and the fields red under the plough. Ahead were the Black Mountains, and we climbed among them, watching the steep fields end at the grey walls, beyond which the bracken and heather and whin had not yet been driven back. To the east, along the ridge, stood the line of grey Norman castles; to the west, the fortress wall of the mountains. Then, as we still climbed, the rock changed under us. Here, now, was limestone, and the line of the early iron workings along the scarp. The farming valleys, with their scattered white houses, fell away behind. Ahead of us were the narrower valleys: the steel-rolling mill, the gasworks, the grey terraces, the pitheads. The bus stopped, and the driver and conductress got out, still absorbed. They had done this journey so often, and seen all its stages. It is a journey, in fact, that in one form or another we have all made.

I was born and grew up halfway along that bus journey. Where I lived is still a farming valley, though the road through it is being widened and straightened, to carry the heavy lorries to the north. Not far away, my grandfather, and so back through the generations, worked as a farm labourer until he was turned out of his cottage and, in his fifties, became a roadman. His sons went at thirteen or fourteen on to the farms, his daughters into service. My father, his third son, left the farm at fifteen to

3

be a boy porter on the railway, and later became a signalman, working in a box in this valley until he died. I went up the road to the village school, where a curtain divided the two classes – Second to eight or nine, First to fourteen. At eleven I went to the local grammar school, and later to Cambridge.

Culture is ordinary: that is where we must start. To grow up in that country was to see the shape of a culture, and its modes of change. I could stand on the mountains and look north to the farms and the cathedral, or south to the smoke and the flare of the blast furnace making a second sunset. To grow up in that family was to see the shaping of minds: the learning of new skills, the shifting of relationships, the emergence of different language and ideas. My grandfather, a big hard labourer, wept while he spoke, finely and excitedly, at the parish meeting, of being turned out of his cottage. My father, not long before he died, spoke quietly and happily of when he had started a trade-union branch and a Labour Party group in the village, and, without bitterness, of the 'kept men' of the new politics. I speak a different idiom, but I think of these same things.

Culture is ordinary: that is the first fact. Every human society has its own shape, its own purposes, its own meanings. Every human society expresses these, in institutions, and in arts and learning. The making of a society is the finding of common meanings and directions, and its growth is an active debate and amendment under the pressures of experience, contact, and discovery, writing themselves into the land. The growing society is there, yet it is also made and remade in every individual mind. The making of a mind is, first, the slow learning of shapes, purposes, and meanings, so that work, observation and communication are possible. Then, second, but equal in importance, is the testing of these in experience, the making of new observations, comparisons, and meanings. A culture has two aspects: the known meanings and directions, which its members are trained to; the new observations and meanings, which are offered and tested. These are the ordinary processes of human societies and human minds, and we see through them the nature of a culture: that it is always both traditional and creative; that it is both the most ordinary common meanings and the finest individual meanings. We use the word culture in these two senses: to mean a whole way of life – the common meanings; to mean the arts and learning – the special processes of discovery and creative effort. Some writers reserve the word for one or other of these senses; I insist on both, and on the significance of their conjunction. The questions I ask about our culture are questions about our general and common purposes, yet also questions about deep personal meanings. Culture is ordinary, in every society and in every mind.

Now there are two senses of culture – two colours attached to it – that I know about but refuse to learn. The first I discovered at Cambridge, in a teashop. I was not, by the way, oppressed by Cambridge. I was not cast down by old buildings, for I had come from a country with twenty centuries of history written visibly into the earth: I liked walking through a Tudor court, but it did not make me feel raw. I was not amazed by the existence of a place of learning; I had always known the cathedral, and the bookcases I now sit to work at in Oxford are of the same design as those in the chained library. Nor was learning, in my family, some strange eccentricity; I was not, on a scholarship in Cambridge, a new kind of animal up a brand-new ladder. Learning was ordinary; we learned where we could. Always, from those scattered white houses, it had made sense to go out and become a scholar or a poet or a teacher. Yet few of us could be spared from the immediate work; a price had been set on this kind of learning, and it was more, much more, than we could individually pay. Now, when we could pay in common, it was a good, ordinary life.

I was not oppressed by the university, but the teashop, acting as if it were one of the older and more respectable departments, was a different matter. Here was culture, not in any sense I knew, but in a special sense: the outward and emphatically visible sign of a special kind of people, cultivated people. They were not, the great majority of them, particularly learned; they practised few arts; but they had it, and they showed you they had it. They are still there, I suppose, still showing it, though even they must be hearing rude noises from outside, from a few scholars and writers they call – how comforting a label is! – angry young men. As a matter of fact there is no need to be rude. It is simply that if that is culture, we don't want it; we have seen other people living.

But of course it is not culture, and those of my colleagues who, hating the teashop, make culture, on its account, a dirty word, are mistaken. If the people in the teashop go on insisting that culture is their trivial differences of behaviour, their trivial variations of speech habit, we cannot stop them, but we can ignore them. They are not that important, to take culture from where it belongs.

Yet, probably also disliking the teashop, there were writers I read then, who went into the same category in my mind. When I now read a book such as Clive Bell's *Civilisation*, I experience not so much disagreement as stupor. What kind of life can it be, I wonder, to produce this extraordinary fussiness, this extraordinary decision to call certain things culture and then separate them, as with a park wall, from ordinary people and ordinary work? At home we met and made music, listened to it, recited and listened to poems, valued fine language. I have heard better music and better poems since; there is the world to draw on. But

I know, from the most ordinary experience, that the interest is there, the capacity is there. Of course, farther along that bus journey, the old social organization in which these things had their place has been broken. People have been driven and concentrated into new kinds of work, new kinds of relationship; work, by the way, which built the park walls, and the houses inside them, and which is now at last bringing, to the unanimous disgust of the teashop, clean and decent and furnished living to the people themselves. Culture is ordinary: through every change let us hold fast to that.

The other sense, or colour, that I refuse to learn, is very different. Only two English words rhyme with culture, and these, as it happens, are sepulture and vulture. We don't yet call museums or galleries or even universities culture-sepultures, but I hear a lot, lately, about culture-vultures (man must rhyme), and I hear also, in the same North Atlantic argot, of do-gooders and highbrows and superior prigs. Now I don't like the teashop, but I don't like this drinking-hole either. I know there are people who are humourless about the arts and learning, and I know there is a difference between goodness and sanctimony. But the growing implications of this spreading argot – the true cant of a new kind of rogue – I reject absolutely. For, honestly, how can anyone use a word like 'do-gooder' with this new, offbeat complacency? How can anyone wither himself to a state where he must use these new flip words for any attachment to learning or the arts? It is plain that what may have started as a feeling about hypocrisy, or about pretentiousness (in itself a two-edged word), is becoming a guilt-ridden tic at the mention of any serious standards whatever. And the word 'culture' has been heavily compromised by this conditioning: Goering reached for his gun; many reach for their chequebooks; a growing number, now, reach for the latest bit of argot.

'Good' has been drained of much of its meaning, in these circles, by the exclusion of its ethical content and emphasis on a purely technical standard; to do a good job is better than to be a do-gooder. But do we need reminding that any crook can, in his own terms, do a good job? The smooth reassurance of technical efficiency is no substitute for the whole positive human reference. Yet men who once made this reference, men who were or wanted to be writers or scholars, are now, with every appearance of satisfaction, advertising men, publicity boys, names in the strip newspapers. These men were given skills, given attachments, which are now in the service of the most brazen money-grabbing exploitation of the inexperience of ordinary people. And it is these men – this new, dangerous class – who have invented and disseminated the argot, in an attempt to influence ordinary people – who because they do real work have real standards in the fields they know – against real standards in the fields these men knew and have abandoned. The old cheapjack is still there in the market, with the country boys' half-crowns on his reputed packets of gold rings or watches. He thinks of his victims as a slow, ignorant crowd, but they live, and farm, while he coughs behind his portable stall. The new cheapjack is in offices with contemporary *décor*, using scraps of linguistics, psychology and sociology to influence what he thinks of as the mass mind. He too, however, will have to pick up and move on, and meanwhile we are not to be influenced by his argot; we can simply refuse to learn it. Culture is ordinary. An interest in learning or the arts is simple, pleasant and natural. A desire to know what is best, and to do what is good, is the whole positive nature of man. We are not to be scared from these things by noises. There are many versions of what is wrong with our culture. So far I have tried only to clear away the detritus which makes it difficult for us to think seriously about it at all. When I got to Cambridge I encountered two serious influences which have left a very deep impression on my mind. The first was Marxism, the second the teaching of Leavis. Through all subsequent disagreement I retain my respect for both.

The Marxists said many things, but those that mattered were three. First, they said that a culture must be finally interpreted in relation to its underlying system of production. I have argued this theoretically elsewhere – it is a more difficult idea than it looks – but I still accept its emphasis. Everything I had seen, growing up in that border country, had led me towards such an emphasis: a culture is a whole way of life, and the arts are part of a social organization which economic change clearly radically affects. I did not have to be taught dissatisfaction with the existing economic system, but the subsequent questions about our culture were, in these terms, vague. It was said that it was a class-dominated culture, deliberately restricting a common inheritance to a small class, while leaving the masses ignorant. The fact of restriction I accepted – it is still very obvious that only the *deserving* poor get much educational opportunity, and I was in no mood, as I walked about Cambridge, to feel glad that I had been thought deserving; I was no better and no worse than the people I came from. On the other hand, just because of this, I got angry at my friends' talk about the ignorant masses: one kind of Communist has always talked like this, and has got his answer, at Poznan and Budapest, as the imperialists, making the same assumption, were answered in India, in Indo-China, in Africa. There is an English bourgeois culture, with its powerful educational, literary and social institutions, in close contact with the actual centres of power. To say that most working people are excluded from these is self-evident, though the doors, under sustained pressure, are slowly opening. But to go on to say that working people are excluded from English culture is nonsense; they have their own growing institutions, and much of the strictly bourgeois culture they would in any case not want. A great part of the English way of life, and of its arts and learning, is not bourgeois in any discoverable sense. There are institutions, and common meanings, which are in no sense the sole product of the commercial middle class; and there are art and learning, a common English inheritance, produced by many kinds of men, including many who hated the very class and system which now take pride in consuming it. The bourgeoisie has given us much, including a narrow but real system of morality; that is at least better than its court predecessors. The leisure which the bourgeoisie attained has given us much of cultural value. But this is not to say that contemporary culture is bourgeois culture: a mistake that everyone, from Conservatives to Marxists, seems to make. There is a distinct working-class way of life, which I for one value – not only because I was bred in it, for I now, in certain respects, live differently. I think this way of life, with its emphases of neighbourhood, mutual obligation, and common better-ment, as expressed in the great working-class political and industrial institutions, is in fact the best basis for any future English society. As for the arts and learning, they are in a real sense a national inheritance, which is, or should be, available to everyone. So when the Marxists say that we live in a dying culture, and that the masses are ignorant, I have to ask them, as I asked them then, where on earth they have lived. A dying culture, and ignorant masses, are not what I have known and see.

What I had got from the Marxists then, so far, was a relationship between culture and production, and the observation that education was restricted. The other things I rejected, as I rejected also their third point, that since culture and production are related, the advocacy of a different system of production is in some way a cultural directive, indicating not only a way of life but new arts and learning. I did some writing while I was, for eighteen months, a member of the Communist Party, and I found out in trivial ways what other writers, here and in Europe, have found out more gravely: the practical consequences of this kind of theoretical error. In this respect, I saw the future, and it didn't work. The Marxist interpretation of culture can never be accepted while it retains, as it need not retain, this directive element, this insistence that if you honestly want socialism you must write, think, learn in certain prescribed ways. A culture is common meanings, the product of a whole people, and offered individual meanings, the product of a man's whole committed personal and social experience. It is stupid and arrogant to suppose that any of these meanings can in any way be prescribed; they are made by living, made and remade, in ways we cannot know in advance. To try to jump the future, to pretend that in some way you *are* the future, is strictly insane. Prediction is another matter, an offered meaning, but the only thing we can say about culture in an England that has socialized its means of production is that all the channels of expression and communication should be cleared and open, so that the whole actual life, that we cannot know in advance, that we can know only in part even while it is being lived, may be brought to consciousness and meaning.

Leavis has never liked Marxists, which is in one way a pity, for they know more than he does about modern English society, and about its immediate history. He, on the other hand, knows more than any Marxist I have met about the real relations between art and experience. We have all learned from him in this, and we have also learned his version of what is wrong with English culture. The diagnosis is radical, and is rapidly becoming orthodox. There was an old, mainly agricultural England, with a traditional culture of great value. This has been replaced by a modern, organized, industrial state, whose characteristic institutions deliberately cheapen our natural human responses, making art and literature into desperate survivors and witnesses, while a new mechanized vulgarity sweeps into the centres of power. The only defence is in education, which will at least keep certain things alive, and which will also, at least in a minority, develop ways of thinking and feeling which are competent to understand what is happening and to maintain the finest individual values. I need not add how widespread this diagnosis has become, though little enough acknowledgement is still made to Leavis himself. For my own part, I was deeply impressed by it; deeply enough for my ultimate rejection of it to be a personal crisis lasting several years.

For, obviously, it seemed to fit a good deal of my experience. It did not tell me that my father and grandfather were ignorant wage-slaves; it did not tell me that the smart, busy, commercial culture (which I had come to as a stranger, so much so that for years I had violent headaches whenever I passed through London and saw underground advertisements and evening newspapers) was the thing I had to catch up with. I even made a fool of myself, or was made to think so, when after a lecture in which the usual point was made that 'neighbour' now does not mean what it did to Shakespeare, I said – imagine! – that to me it did. (When my father was dying, this year, one man came in and dug his garden; another loaded and delivered a lorry of sleepers for firewood; another came and chopped the sleepers into blocks; another – I don't know who, it was never said – left a sack of potatoes at the back door; a woman came in and took away a basket of washing.) But even this was explicable; I came from a bit of the old society, but my future was Surbiton (it took me years to find Surbiton, and have a good look at it, but it's served a good many as a symbol – without having lived there I couldn't say whether rightly). So there I was, and it all seemed to fit.

Yet not all. Once I got away, and thought about it, it didn't really fit properly. For one thing I knew this: at home we were glad of the Industrial Revolution, and of its consequent social and political changes. True, we lived in a very beautiful farming valley, and the valleys beyond the limestone we could all see were ugly. But there was one gift that was overriding, one gift which at any price we would take, the gift of power that is everything to men who have worked with their hands. It was slow in coming to us, in all its effects, but steam power, the petrol engine, electricity, these and their host of products in commodities and services, we took as quickly as we could get them, and were glad. I have seen all these things being used, and I have seen the things they replaced. I will not listen with patience to any acid listing of them – you know the sneer you can get into plumbing, baby Austins, aspirin, contraceptives, canned food. But I say to these Pharisees: dirty water, an earth bucket, a four-mile walk each way to work, headaches, broken women, hunger and monotony of diet. The working people, in town and country alike, will not listen (and I support them) to any account of our society which supposes that these things are not progress: not just mechanical, external progress either, but a real service of life. Moreover, in the new conditions, there was more real freedom to dispose of our lives, more real personal grasp where it mattered, more real say. Any account of our culture which explicitly or implicitly denies the value of an industrial society is really irrelevant; not in a million years would you make us give up this power.

So then the social basis of the case was unacceptable, but could one, trying to be a writer, a scholar, a teacher, ignore the indictment of the new cultural vulgarity? For the plumbing and the tractors and the medicines could one ignore the strip newspapers, the multiplying cheapjacks, the raucous triviality? As a matter of priorities, yes, if necessary; but was the cheapening of response really a consequence of the cheapening of power? It looks like it, I know, but is this really as much as one can say? I believe the central problem of our society, in the coming half-century, is the use of our new resources to make a good common culture; the means to a good, abundant economy we already understand. I think the good common culture can be made, but before we can be serious about this, we must rid ourselves of a legacy from our most useful critics – a legacy of two false equations, one false analogy, and one false proposition.

The false proposition is easily disposed of. It is a fact that the new power brought ugliness: the coal brought dirt, the factory brought over-crowding, communications brought a mess of wires. But the proposition that ugliness is a price we pay, or refuse to pay, for economic power need no longer be true. New sources of power, new methods of production, improved systems of transport and communication can, quite practically, make England clean and pleasant again, and with much more power, not less. Any new ugliness is the product of stupidity, indifference, or simply incoordination; these things will be easier to deal with than when power was necessarily noisy, dirty, and disfiguring.

The false equations are more difficult. One is the equation between popular education and the new commercial culture: the latter proceeding inevitably from the former. Let the masses in, it is said, and this is what you inevitably get. Now the question is obviously difficult, but I can't accept this equation, for two reasons. The first is a matter of faith: I don't believe that the ordinary people in fact resemble the normal description of the masses, low and trivial in taste and habit. I put it another way: that there are in fact no masses, but only ways of seeing people as masses. With the coming of industrialism, much of the old social organization broke down and it became a matter of difficult personal experience that we were constantly seeing people we did not know, and it was tempting to mass them, as 'the others', in our minds. Again, people were physically massed, in the industrial towns, and a new class structure (the names of our social classes, and the word 'class' itself in this sense, date only from the Industrial Revolution) was practically imposed. The improvement in communications, in particular the development of new forms of multiple transmission of news and entertainment, created unbridgeable divisions between transmitter and audience, which again led to the audience being interpreted as an unknown mass. Masses became a new word for mob: the others, the unknown, the unwashed, the crowd beyond one. As a way of knowing other people, this formula is obviously ridiculous, but, in the new conditions, it seemed an effective formula – the only one possible. Certainly it was the formula that was used by those whose money gave them access to the new communication techniques; the lowness of taste and habit, which human beings assign very easily to other human beings, was assumed, as a bridge. The new culture was built on this formula, and if I reject the formula, if I insist that this lowness is not inherent in ordinary people, you can brush my insistence aside, but I shall go on holding to it. A different formula, I know from experience, gets a radically different response.

My second reason is historical: I deny, and can prove my denial, that popular education and commercial culture are cause and effect. I have shown elsewhere that the myth of 1870 – the Education Act which is said to have produced, as its children grew up, a new cheap and nasty press – is indeed myth. There was more than enough literacy, long before 1870, to support a cheap press, and in fact there were cheap and really bad newspapers selling in great quantities before the 1870 Act was heard of. The bad new commercial culture came out of the social chaos of industrialism, and out of the success, in this chaos, of the 'masses' formula, not out of popular education. Northcliffe did few worse things than start this myth, for while the connection between bad culture and the social chaos of industrialism is significant, the connection between it and popular education is vicious. The Northcliffe Revolution, by the way, was a radical change in the financial structure of the press, basing it on a new kind of revenue – the new mass advertising of the 1890s – rather than the making of a cheap popular press, in which he had been widely and successfully preceded. But I tire of making these points. Everyone prefers to believe Northcliffe. Yet does nobody, even a Royal Commission, read the most ordinarily accessible newspaper history? When people do read the history, the false equation between popular education and commercial culture will disappear for ever. Popular education came out of the other camp, and has had quite opposite effects.

The second false equation is this: that the observable badness of so much widely distributed popular culture is a true guide to the state of mind and feeling, the essential quality of living of its consumers. Too many good men have said this for me to treat it lightly, but I still, on evidence, can't accept it. It is easy to assemble, from print and cinema and television, a terrifying and fantastic congress of cheap feelings and moronic arguments. It is easy to go on from this and assume this deeply degrading version of the actual lives of our contemporaries. Yet do we find this confirmed, when we meet people? This is where 'masses' comes in again, of course: the people *we* meet aren't vulgar, but God, think of Bootle and Surbiton and Aston! I haven't lived in any of those places; have you? But a few weeks ago I was in a house with a commercial traveller, a lorry driver, a bricklayer, a shopgirl, a fitter, a signalman, a nylon operative, a domestic help (perhaps, dear, she is your very own treasure). I hate describing people like this, for in fact they were my family and family friends. Now they read, they watch, this work we are talking about; some of them quite critically, others with a good deal of pleasure. Very well, I read different things, watch different entertainments, and I am quite sure why they are better. But could I sit down in that house and make this equation we are offered? Not, you understand, that shame was stopping me; I've learned, thank you, how to behave. But talking to my family, to my friends, talking, as we were, about our own lives, about people, about feelings, could I in fact find this lack of quality we are discussing? I'll be honest – I looked; my training has done that for me. I can only say that I found as much natural fineness of feeling, as much quick discrimination, as much clear grasp of ideas within the range of experience as I have found anywhere. I don't altogether understand this, though I am not really surprised. Clearly there is something in the psychology of print and image that none of us has yet quite grasped. For the equation looks sensible, yet when you test it, in experience – and there's nowhere else you can test it – it's wrong. I can understand the protection of critical and intelligent reading: my father, for instance, a satisfied reader of the *Daily Herald*, got simply from reading the company reports a clear idea, based on names, of the rapid development of combine and interlocking ownership in British industry, which I had had made easy for me in two or three academic essays; and he had gone on to set these facts against the opinions in a number of articles in the paper on industrial ownership. That I understand; that is simply intelligence, however partly trained. But there is still this other surprising fact: that people whose quality of personal living is high are apparently satisfied by a low quality of printed feeling and opinion. Many of them still live, it is true, in a surprisingly enclosed personal world, much more so than mine, and some of their personal observations are the finer for it. Perhaps this is enough to explain it, but in any case, I submit, we need a new equation, to fit the observable facts.

Now the false analogy, that we must also reject. This is known, in discussions of culture, as a 'kind of Gresham's Law'. Just as bad money will drive out good, so bad culture will drive out good, and this, it is said, has in fact been happening. If you can't see, straight away, the defect of the analogy, your answer, equally effective, will have to be historical. For in fact, of course, it has not been happening. There is more, much more bad culture about; it is easier, now, to distribute it, and there is more leisure to receive it. But test this in any field you like, and see if this has been accompanied by a shrinking consumption of things we can all agree to be good. The editions of good literature are very much larger than they were; the listeners to good music are much more numerous than they were; the number of people who look at good visual art is larger than it has ever been. If bad newspapers drive out good newspapers, by a kind of Gresham's Law, why is it that, allowing for the rise in population, *The Times* sells nearly three times as many copies as in the days of its virtual monopoly of the press, in 1850? It is the law I am questioning, not the seriousness of the facts as a whole. Instead of a kind of Gresham's Law, keeping people awake at nights with the now orthodox putropian nightmare, let us put it another way, to fit the actual facts: we live in an expanding culture, and all the elements in this culture are themselves expanding. If we start from this, we can then ask real questions: about relative rates of expansion; about the social and economic problems raised by these; about the social and economic answers. I am working now on a book to follow my *Culture and Society*, trying to interpret, historically and theoretically, the nature and conditions of an expanding culture of our kind. I could not have begun this work if I had not learned from the Marxists and from Leavis; I cannot complete it unless I radically amend some of the ideas which they and others have left us.

I give myself three wishes, one for each of the swans I have just been watching on the lake. I ask for things that are part of the ethos of our working-class movement. I ask that we may be strong and human enough to realize them. And I ask, naturally, in my own fields of interest.

I wish, first, that we should recognize that education is ordinary: that it is, before everything else, the process of giving to the ordinary members of society its full common meanings, and the skills that will enable them to amend these meanings, in the light of their personal and common experience. If we start from that, we can get rid of the remaining restrictions, and make the necessary changes. I do not mean only money restrictions, though these, of course, are ridiculous and must go. I mean also restrictions in the mind: the insistence, for example, that there is a hard maximum number – a fraction of the population as a whole – capable of really profiting by a university education, or a grammar school education, or by any full course of liberal studies. We are told that this is not a question of what we might personally prefer, but of the hard cold facts of human intelligence, as shown by biology and psychology. But let us be frank about this: are biology and psychology different in the USA and USSR (each committed to expansion, and not to any class rigidities), where much larger numbers, much larger fractions, pass through comparable stages of education? Or were the English merely behind in the queue for intelligence? I believe, myself, that our educational system, with its golden fractions, is too like our social system – a top layer of leaders, a middle layer of supervisors, a large bottom layer of operatives – to be coincidence. I cannot accept that education is a training for jobs, or for making useful citizens (that is, fitting into this system). It is a society's confirmation of its common meanings, and of the human skills for their amendment. Jobs follow from this confirmation: the purpose, and then the working skill. We are moving into an economy where we shall need many more highly trained specialists. For this precise reason, I ask for a common education that will give our society its cohesion, and prevent it disintegrating into a series of specialist departments, the nation become a firm.

But I do not mean only the reorganization of entry into particular kinds of education, though I welcome and watch the experiments in this. I mean also the rethinking of content, which is even more important. I have the honour to work for an organization through which, quite practically, working men amended the English university curriculum. It is now as it was then: the defect is not what is in, but what is out. It will be a test of our cultural seriousness whether we can, in the coming generation, redesign our syllabuses to a point of full human relevance and control. I should like to see a group working on this, and offering its conclusions. For we need not fear change; oldness may or may not be relevant. I come from an old place; if a man tells me that his family came over with the Normans, I say 'Yes, how interesting; and are you liking it here?' Oldness is relative, and many 'immemorial' English traditions were invented, just like that, in the nineteenth century. What that vital century did for its own needs, we can do for ours; we can make, in our turn, a true twentieth-century syllabus. And by this I do not mean simply more technology; I mean a full liberal education for everyone in our society, and then full specialist training to earn our living in terms of what we want to make of our lives. Our specialisms will be finer if they have grown from a common culture, rather than being a distinction from it. And we must at all costs avoid the polarization of our culture, of which there are growing signs. High literacy is expanding, in direct relation to exceptional educational opportunities, and the gap between this and common literacy may widen, to the great damage of both, and with great consequent tension. We must emphasize not the ladder but the common highway, for every man's ignorance diminishes me, and every man's skill is a common gain of breath.

My second wish is complementary: for more and more active public provision for the arts and for adult learning. We now spend £20,000,000 annually on all our libraries, museums, galleries, orchestras, on the Arts Council, and on all forms of adult education. At the same time we spend £365,000,000 annually on advertising. When these figures are reversed, we can claim some sense of proportion and value. And until they are reversed, let there be no sermons from the Establishment about materialism: this is their way of life, let them look at it. (But there is no shame in them: for years, with their own children away at school, they have lectured working-class mothers on the virtues of family life; this is a similar case.)

I ask for increased provision on three conditions. It is not to be a disguised way of keeping up consumption, but a thing done for its own sake. A minister in the last Labour government said that we didn't want any geniuses in the film industry; he wanted, presumably, just to keep the turnstiles clicking. The short answer to this is that we don't want any Wardour Street thinkers in the leadership of the Labour Party. We want leaders of a society, not repair-workers on this kind of cultural economy.

The second condition is that while we must obviously preserve and extend the great national institutions, we must do something to reverse the concentration of this part of our culture. We should welcome, encourage and foster the tendencies to regional recreation that are showing themselves; for culture is ordinary, you should not have to go to London to find it.

The third condition is controversial. We should not seek to extend a ready-made culture to the benighted masses. We should accept, frankly, that if we extend our culture we shall change it: some that is offered will be rejected, other parts will be radically criticized. And this is as it should be, for our arts, now, are in no condition to go down to eternity unchallenged. There is much fine work; there is also shoddy work, and work based on values that will find no acceptance if they ever come out into the full light of England. To take our arts to new audiences is to be quite certain that in many respects those arts will be changed. I, for one, do not fear this. I would not expect the working people of England to support works which, after proper and patient preparation, they could not accept. The real growth will be slow and uneven, but state provision, frankly, should be a growth in this direction, and not a means of diverting public money to the preservation of a fixed and finished partial culture. At the same time, if we understand cultural growth, we shall know that it is a continual offering for common acceptance; that we should not, therefore, try to determine in advance what should be offered, but clear the channels and let all the offerings be made, taking care to give the difficult full space, the original full time, so that it is a real growth, and not just a wider confirmation of old rules.

Now, of course, we shall hear the old cry that things shouldn't be supported at a loss. Once again, this is a nation, not a firm. Parliament itself runs at a loss, because we need it, and if it would be better at a greater loss, I and others would willingly pay. But why, says Sir George Mammon, should *I* support a lot of doubtful artists? Why, says Mrs Mink, should I pay good money to educate, at *my* expense, a lot of irresponsible and ungrateful state scholars? The answer, dear sir, dear madam, is that *you* don't. On your own – learn your size – you could do practically nothing. We are talking about a method of common payment, for common services; we too shall be paying.

My third wish is in a related field: the field now dominated by the institutions of 'mass culture'. Often, it is the people at the head of these institutions who complain of running things at a loss. But the great popular newspapers, as newspapers, run at a loss. The independent television companies are planned to run at a loss. I don't mean temporary subsidies, but the whole basis of financing such institutions. The newspapers run at a heavy loss, which they make up with money from advertising – that is to say a particular use of part of the product of our common industry. To run at a loss, and then cover yourself with this kind of income, is of the essence of this kind of cultural institution, and this is entirely characteristic of our kind of capitalist society. The whole powerful array of mass cultural institutions has one keystone: money from advertising. Let them stop being complacent about other cultural institutions which run at a smaller loss, and meet it out of another part of the common product.

But what is it then that I wish? To pull out this keystone? No, not just like that. I point out merely that the organization of our present mass culture is so closely involved with the organization of capitalist society that the future of one cannot be considered except in terms of the future of the other. I think much of contemporary advertising is necessary only in terms of the kind of economy we now have: a stimulation of consumption in the direction of particular products and firms, often by irrelevant devices, rather than real advertising, which is an ordinary form of public notice. In a socialist economy, which I and others want, the whole of this pseudo-advertising would be irrelevant. But then what? My wish is that we may solve the problems that would then arise, where necessary things like newspapers would be running at something like their real loss, without either pricing them out of ordinary means, or exposing them to the dangers of control and standardization (for we want a more free and more varied press, not one less so). It is going to be very difficult, but I do not believe we are so uninventive as to be left showing each other a pair of grim alternatives: either the continuance of this crazy peddling, in which news and opinion are inextricably involved with the shouts of the market, bringing in their train the new slavery and prostitution of the selling of personalities; or else a dull, monolithic, controlled system, in which news and opinion are in the gift of a ruling party. We should be thinking, now, about ways of paying for our common services which will guarantee proper freedom to those who actually provide the service, while protecting them and us against a domineering minority whether political or financial. I think there are ways, if we really believe in democracy.

But that is the final question: how many of us really believe in it? The capitalists don't; they are consolidating a power which can survive parliamentary changes. Many Labour planners don't; they interpret it as a society run by experts for an abstraction called the public interest. The people in the teashop don't; they are quite sure it is not going to be nice. And the others, the new dissenters? Nothing has done more to sour the democratic idea, among its natural supporters, and to drive them back into an angry self-exile, than the plain, overwhelming cultural issues: the apparent division of our culture into, on the one hand, a remote and self-gracious sophistication, on the other hand, a doped mass. So who then believes in democracy? The answer is really quite simple: the millions in England who still haven't got it, where they work and feel. There, as always, is the transforming energy, and the business of the socialist intellectual is what it always was: to attack the clamps on that energy – in industrial relations, public administration, education, for a start; and to work in his own field on ways in which that energy, as released, can be concentrated and fertile. The technical means are difficult enough, but the biggest difficulty is in accepting, deep in our minds, the values on which they depend: that the ordinary people should govern; that culture and education are ordinary; that there are no masses to save, to capture, or to direct, but rather this crowded people in the course of an extraordinarily rapid and confusing expansion of their lives. A writer's job is with individual meanings, and with making these meanings common. I find these meanings in the expansion, there along the journey where the necessary changes are writing themselves into the land, and where the language changes but the voice is the same.

Communications and Community

1961

In recent years there has been a very lively movement of radical protest against certain faults in communication in our society, certain abuses of communications and certain fairly evident distortions in our culture. These have been widely discussed and quite widely documented and I don't particularly wish to refer to them again. Because I have the impression that this movement of protest has now reached a very solid wall. After the first excitement that anything at all was happening, that anyone was even bothering to protest, after the exhilaration of the first skirmishes, we are now coming nearer to reality, and realizing that if this protest means anything it has to take account of the wall.

Even to examine the wall is a matter of some interest. Its stones essentially are power. It is impossible to discuss communication or culture in our society without in the end coming to discussing power. There is the power of established institutions, and there is increasingly the power of money, which is imposing certain patterns of communication that are very powerful in the society as a whole. In a sense the wall is so sure of itself that it can regard with some amusement the antics of those of us who are skirmishing in front of it.

The chairman was kind enough to say that my friend Richard Hoggart and some other people including myself are significant figures in English culture, but we know quite well that this really does not mean a thing, that the significant figures in English culture are Mr Roy Thomson, Mr Cecil King and Mr Norman Collins,[1] and that they will

1. In 1961, respectively: Chairman of the Thomson Organization (interests: the *Sunday Times*, several Scottish and provincial daily newspapers, a magazine chain and a 55 per cent shareholding in Scottish Television); Chairman of Mirror Group Newspapers Ltd (interests: three national daily newspapers, a dominant share of the UK magazine market and a 30 per cent shareholding in Associated Television); Deputy Chairman of the Associated Television Corporation and Director of both ATV Network Ltd and Independent Television News. [Ed.]

have much more effect on English culture in the foreseeable future than we will have. To get up under the wall, to realize its height, is to be reminded quite sharply of your own size and where you are, and what you have left to do.

But now it is not only this curious wall, the stones of power. Because holding them together is a very curious thing, a curious English atmosphere which is against theory. I have been very struck by this recently: what a built-in fear of theory there is in the modern English mind – a fear which is all the more dangerous because people are quite complacent about it and rather glad to have it, a fear of theory which is rationalized by the great English love of the practical and the concrete. Now my experience of this English addiction to the concrete is that for the most part they are stuck in it. For at a certain point, in considering questions of this kind, you have to move beyond the kind of random sketchy comment, the incidental observation and criticism, which so far this movement of cultural criticism has been. You have to move beyond it to some kind of theoretical understanding, both to see what is happening, to interpret what is happening, and quite certainly to have any sense of direction for the future.

I do feel that for a generation or so a number of people have settled down quite happily to being critics of what they call mass culture. This is a sort of occupation almost, a position which in one way they might even be sorry to see ended. Suppose there were no *Daily Mirror*, no ITV about which their kind of witty random comment could be made. Theirs is a position which is all too easily reached and held, and I think of this attitude and these people as the mortar between the stones of power, because while they stick to this attitude nothing is going to be shifted. Incidental criticism, random comment, will not shift any of the difficulties in front of us. We need, absolutely, to approach a theory of communication, and to have some idea of how communication relates to community, how it relates to society, what kind of communication systems we now have, what they tell us about our society, and what we can see as reasonable directions for the future. And we can only do this by theory. We can only do it to some extent by abstraction, one of those other curious things which the modern English mind has decided to exclude – abstraction, a thing which you only have to pronounce to suggest that it is bad. I feel very committed to the detail of what is happening, the detail of experience. But experience includes thought, and thought includes abstraction, and abstraction is in fact one of the glories of the human mind. Without it, the concrete, the immediate detail, on which you can make sharp observation, remains for ever a close-up scene which you cannot really interpret and which you cannot really change.

The point we have reached is one where we have to go into theory, we have to go into abstraction. We can be glad that the other work has been done. We hope it will go on being done, and that people will go on making the kind of incidental criticism which has been popular. But if we are serious we must now move beyond that. And I think we are very ill equipped to do it. Because to understand communication is indeed something very difficult. We are brought up with certain ideas about communication which on the whole I think mislead us. We think of it as an activity which takes place after the important things have happened. Communication is, so to say, the news after the event, the passing on of things after something important has occurred. Communication is secondary, just as people think of art as secondary, as a marginal activity, because first there is real life and then there is art. First there is reality and then there is communication about reality. But this is so wholly misleading that unless we can get it right at that level we shall get nothing else right. What we have to try to see, first, is that deeply involved in our own minds and in the shape of our society are certain communication patterns, only some of which we are conscious of. These communication patterns are not something inevitable; they are man-made, subject to change, and subject all the time to criticism. Moreover they have to be relearned by every new generation.

I am very impressed by the recent work of some neurologists on communication at this fundamental level. They have shown us that it is even necessary for us to learn to see: that until we have certain rules of interpretation, built into our brains, what we think of as the ordinary activity of seeing, just opening our eyes and there is the world, cannot occur. The eye is not a camera, or if it is a camera, it is a camera the results of which have to be developed. That development is by a human brain which of course has evolved over uncountable generations, but which at the same time is built up in our growth as children and towards maturity, by sets of rules from our society, from the relationships we are actually in. These rules to a large extent go on determining what we see and what we can describe.

It is at that fundamental level that we have to begin any study of communication. People assume all too easily that they are born into a ready-made world, and with normal relations to it, and that anything they say about it is subject to complete personal choice, that above all it is the individual who communicates. Now it is perfectly true that some of the most valuable communication in the world is the result of exceptional individuals. But we have all learned ways of thinking about this which stop us seeing the problem clearly. For in fact all of us, as individuals, grow up within a society, within the rules of a society, and these rules cut very deep, and include certain ways of seeing the world, certain ways of talking about the world. All the time people are being born into a society, shown what to see, shown how to talk about it. But then – and this also is fundamental – we are able, as we develop, to compare one rule with another, to compare the result of one thing seen with another. We are capable of independent criticism. We are also – and this is one of the most difficult but most interesting things – capable of new seeing. We can learn to see things in new ways, to describe them in new ways, and to communicate this to others. We could not begin this process unless we had first been given a very large part of our mental equipment by the training of our society. But that vital last bit, when we can as individuals go over the thing again, try to see the world in new ways, to talk about it in new ways, that part of learning and communication is equally important.

Every society has communication systems, and these can be of a kind which at first we don't think of as communication systems at all. One very good example is of some prominent feature in the place where we live. Think how much of our sense of where we live can be expressed in some prominent building, some hill, some feature, natural or man-made. This we feel somehow expresses the meaning of what it is to live in that place, and around that building, around that feature, we very often feel ourselves to belong. Some of the deepest emotions human beings can have are emotions about such a place, which in a way has been their community, their society. Yet the hill is saying nothing. The building of course was specially created: it was put there, often, to express the community's sense of itself, some value it held in common. Because it lasts it goes on expressing that value, and when new people see it, they can get the same value back from it as its builders put in. Or sometimes they get a new value, and see it in different ways. But there the things are, built right into the structure of what it feels like to belong to a group, to belong to a community, to belong to a society.

After these of course there are the more formal communication systems: the language of the group, and all the institutions – religious institutions, institutions of information, sometimes of command, institutions of persuasion, institutions of entertainment, institutions of art – all communication systems which in much the same way – you can see this very clearly in simple societies – are right at the centre of what it feels to be a member of that society. The relations between people in the society are often seen most easily by looking at the institutions of communication – how the people regard each other, what things they think important, what things they choose to stress, what things they choose to omit.

And so, from the beginning, we cannot really think of communication as secondary. We cannot think of it as marginal; or as something that happens after reality has occurred. Because it is through the communication systems that the reality of ourselves, the reality of our society, forms and is interpreted. This is why, now, someone who writes about communication becomes, in a sense without ever intending to have become, a social critic. He starts by writing about the use of the language, or about the press, or the cinema, or the modern popular novel, or the theatre, or television. And you find as you listen, that he is not talking about secondary activities at all. He is talking about society, he is looking at society in a different way, and he may be discovering things about the society which could simply not be seen in the older kinds of political and economic description. I don't want to diminish the importance of political and economic description, but it can leave out too much. How people speak to each other, what conventions they have as to what is important and what is not, how they express these in institutions by which they keep in touch: these things are central. They are central to individuals, and central to the society. Of course in a complicated society like ours, it is very easy to lose sight of this, and to discuss the press, or television, or broadcasting, as an isolated thing. This was the reason for my initial criticism, that so much of this work has been random and scattered and sketchy. Because, in the end, we are looking at the communication systems not just to make points against them, but to see in a new way what sort of relationships we have in this complicated society, which way these relationships are going, what is their possible future.

To describe what I think some of these patterns are, in our own society, I should like to introduce and describe certain terms which I think will help us. There are certain basically different ways of organizing communication, and it may be helpful if I can describe these and get them down to certain particular terms which I can refer back to. It seems to me that there are broadly four kinds of ways of organizing communications in a society, and these are – I will say something about each of them – the authoritarian, the paternal, the commercial and the democratic.

The authoritarian way is perhaps the simplest to describe. In an authoritarian system it is assumed that a ruling group – inevitably a minority – is in control of the society, and that it will use every channel open to it to remain in control of the society to get people to behave and think in ways appropriate to that system. It will see that all the institutions of communication are within its control. It will exclude ideas which might disturb that system. It will react very strongly against any attempt by individuals or groups to set up communication systems of their own. The essence of the authoritarian system of communication is that kind of monopoly – not the only kind of monopoly, but that kind – a monopoly of control, but also a monopoly of what is passed through the control: one way of seeing the world, one set of values.

Most societies have passed through this authoritarian phase; some societies are still in it. It often makes for a very tidy culture; it is an easy one to describe because the very emphasis on one way of thinking and feeling makes it comparatively easy to distinguish. It often even – and I say this as a profound opponent of such systems – gains a certain strength by this very concentration. Fundamentally it is an evil system because it denies certain facts about human beings and the way human beings live. It is based always, in the end, on the arrogant assumption that the truth is known; that it has only to be communicated to others; that threats to that truth are so dangerous, criticisms of that truth so dangerous, that it is in the interest of everybody that they should be eliminated. Almost every authoritarian system justifies itself on those grounds. Not only 'we are the few, you are the many, we will decide what you can read', but 'we are the few, we know what is good for the society as a whole, and so we will protect the society against what is bad.' We have certain survivals of this in our own society, but not many. Still, if you look around the world you can see many systems, including many very powerful systems, which are basically authoritarian in this way.

Now quite like the authoritarian system in many ways is the next kind, which I call the paternal. The paternal system is the authoritarian system with a conscience. The difference really is in the attitude of the ruling group to the majority. In an authoritarian system, whatever may be said, the ruling group regards the majority of people in the society as its subjects. In a paternal system the ruling group regard the majority as backward, as having many of the characteristics of children, as being deprived, as being in many ways unfortunate and ill-equipped. But it has, or claims to have, a basically benevolent attitude towards them, and it always looks forward, though invariably at a rather slow pace, to the disappearance of its own superiority. It has many virtues, this paternal system. It is invariably a responsible system, and the people administering it are usually very conscious of ideas like duty, and responsibility, and, indeed, public service. Just because they are so conscious of these things, just because very often they give up their lives to them, they are furious when anybody says theirs is not an ideal system. Because they have worked it all out, that there are these backward people whom they must carefully bring along. And if one of the backward people gets up and says 'I'm ready', a wise but firm parental tone is adopted: 'No, not yet; read that a little later, or in our edition, or you are going through a phase, but of course later you will come round to our way of thinking, we are all a bit lusty when we are young', or something like that.

I will give you an example of the paternal system; it might be easier than general description. I think the BBC as first set up was one of the best paternal systems, with all its strengths and weaknesses, that you could find. If you go further back it is very deep in the whole British patrician tradition: that they did regard the rest of the world, including the majority of their own fellow countrymen, as deprived. They were guilty about this deprivation, which an authoritarian system would not be, but they were quite clear what the others were going to grow up to be. They were quite clear that the others must grow up to be like them. And this, which after all is a thing fought out in every family as well as in every society, imposes peculiar stresses on the paternal system. The paternalists are more exposed, more vulnerable than authoritarians, who after all have an essentially rigid view of the world, and are always much harder towards people. The authoritarians say 'since we know best, you must listen', not 'wait a little and then you will understand, try this first and then that, then come back and ask us what you ought to read next.' If I gravitate towards the weaknesses of paternalism it is almost against the will of my mind, because I do want to emphasize again its strengths. It does produce devotion, it does produce a lot of hard work, and it does often lead people towards certain definite advances. Still, inevitably, at a certain stage, there is the sort of crisis within it that I have been trying to describe.

Now quite different from these two, the authoritarian and the paternal, is the commercial. This is the one we need most deeply to understand, because on the whole this is where we now are. If I had been born two hundred years ago I know I should have been a supporter of the commercial system against both the other two. Because what the commercial system says is: why should any group of people have the right to decide what others can read, what others can see or think? It does not matter whether their intentions are simply to maintain their power, or to offer some kind of benevolent guidance towards the sort of future they themselves want. Why should a minority have that sort of power? Let the people as a whole be free. Instead of monopoly, let us have the market. Let a man write what he wants, and let anybody who wants to go and buy it. Let a man speak as he can, and let people choose whether they go to listen. Let the thing be open. Let it be free in that sense. Let us get away from this idea of a minority controlling the whole system.

The whole history of communications in Britain until this century was essentially the fight of commercial interests of this kind, or rather of interests using commercial means, to end authoritarian and paternal systems. The history of the press in this country is a history of a long fight against every kind of state control. From, in the earliest period, the Crown's monopoly of printing, through the imposition of taxes on paper and advertisements, through bribery, corruption, suppression, prosecution: that is the history of the British press. It only really broke free about a hundred years ago, in 1855, when the last of the taxes went. It was people who said: 'The market is a better system than any kind of authoritarian or paternal system; the market in the end is the best guide', who in fact broke through, who built up our institutions and our ways of thinking about communication.

Whenever I take part in a discussion of communications, nowadays, I feel myself on a kind of time machine, hearing arguments which would have been just as articulate – perhaps more articulate – in about 1780. People learned these rules very thoroughly: that state control is a bad thing; that we should let the market decide. Scratch any Englishman on this subject, and that is what he will say. Why then do I not make this the climax of my account? Why do I not say the system has reached perfection? Well, it would be a feat of abstraction indeed to reach that conclusion, and then have to look around at the examples. But what is it in the thing itself, in this way of organizing, that makes it in the end a bad system, the bad system we now have? It is a bad system in this way, that although it establishes the freedom to publish and the freedom to read, as against control by authoritarian or paternal systems, in the end it imposes a new control. Because it is bound by the law of the market, it is not now what is allowed to be said, but what can profitably be said.

This is the point we have reached in this century, when under the system of an open market in communications we have seen an actual shrinking of independent organs of communication and a diminution in the number of hands which control communications. We have seen in fact a concentration of power over communications, and we have not yet seen the end of this, even though it has begun to alarm people. There is the wall all right, because even when people have seen this concentration they do not know what to say. Because sitting happily along the top of the wall are the people I referred to earlier who say, 'After all, the only way to have a decent communication system is by the free play of the market; you don't want to go back, do you, to those authoritarian and paternal days?' And until there is an answer to that, we are going to get nowhere.

There is no general answer as yet, even now when the thing has become ludicrous, when a very few people control the majority of our newspapers, when a very few people control our broadcasting and television, and when the probability is that they will get even fewer. Already you could get the people who really decide, not only what will be in our newspapers and magazines, but what kind of newspapers and magazines will survive, you could get them not only into this hall, but into the front row of it. And, when that is the case in the communications system of a nation of fifty million people, can we be so sure about the superiority of the system as it was originally argued? It sounded a good system, a free system, as against the paternal and the authoritarian, but now, by different methods, something very like the same result has been produced. Because we are now after all in the practical situation that a newspaper bought by more than a million people can be closed overnight and that its readers and writers will never so much as be asked. It is one of the very saddest things that this idea of the market, in its early stages in many ways so attractive, with all its slogans of individualism, enterprise and freedom, should have reached this crisis, a crisis which is not just something in the press, but is spreading over all our cultural institutions.

Now in Britain, I think it is fair to say we have relics of an authoritarian system, we have one very good example of a paternal system, and we have as our main trend, and the thing which is winning all right, a commercial system. The relics of authoritarianism were on view at the Old Bailey last autumn;[2] they are on view in the Lord Chamberlain's office – but there is something undeniably fusty about them, there is something unquestionably antique; we know that these are the family heirlooms, we do not feel that they are a 1961 model. This does not mean that they will just go. Things don't happen like that in Britain. But you could not honestly pick up those examples and say: there you are, Britain has an authoritarian system of communications. Those things are there, they should not be forgotten, but they are scattered, uncharacteristic, and in many ways diminishing.

The paternal system? Well, just look at the BBC again. I cherish a photograph of an adult tutorial in Balliol in 1908, in which a young man in a straw hat, who is the tutor, is standing on the lawn, while on a bench below him – I am sorry that this reproduces the geography of this lecture – while on a bench below him sit three rather well-dressed working men, not as well-dressed as he, but on the bench, pencil in hand, looking up. I often remember this picture when I walk around Balliol watching adult groups now, knowing first the complete impossibility of telling the tutors from the students, except perhaps by the opposite criterion, and knowing also what would happen in the average adult education class, if physically or spiritually that relationship were attempted or lasted for

---

2. A reference to the unsuccessful Crown prosecution, brought under the Obscene Publications Act of 1959, against Penguin Books for publishing a complete text of D.H. Lawrence's novel, *Lady Chatterley's Lover*. The trial took place at the Old Bailey, London, 20 October–2 November 1960. Williams was one of a number of authors, critics and public figures to appear as a witness for the defence. [Ed.]

long. Yet the BBC has been so clearly like that – a man of great strength in Reith who felt that with this powerful new system, the virtue and character of Britain were in his keeping. So we got very high ideals of public service, very high ideals of morality, very high ideals of the English Sunday: in general a tone which is quite unmistakeable, the tone as it has recently been unkindly described by the commercial television people as that of the golden boys, the patricians, who will educate and enlighten the British people, but on their own terms.

Now the point I want to make is that the BBC has been a great and, in spite of everything, fortunate exception to the normal process of cultural development in modern Britain. It was an exception because people thought of it as important for national defence and security, and once you touch those things exceptions can be made. But it was right against the ordinary trend in all our other institutions over the last hundred years. It was an island; and who would have thought ten years ago that it was an island that the sea would ever come up over, or that would even be threatened with erosion? People felt: well, that's Britain. It has its disadvantages but there it is, this solid public institution with a public service policy. They had forgotten how rapid change is, because in fact when commercial television was proposed, when it was actively campaigned for, it went through as if British paternalism had died with the old idea of the Empire. Perhaps this was not a tragedy. At least it showed us where we really were. It showed us that paternalism had been discovered in this fatal weakness, the fatal weakness that it knew what was best for people. For this was how commercial television was argued; this is how it is now invariably defended: 'Let the people have what they want', 'Why should any group decide for them', 'Why should *they* decide for us?' And so a deadlock came about, in thinking anyway, between people who were critical of paternal systems, certainly of authoritarian ones, and so saw the strength of some of the arguments of the commercial system, yet who nevertheless saw all too clearly what the commercial system itself would lead to. This deadlock has stayed.

Now this is where I want to introduce my fourth category. We have not yet seen in the world a democratic system of communications, but unless we can conceive it, unless we can begin to think about it in detail, the present situation will continue; the good elements in paternalism will in any case disappear; the bad elements in commercialism are quite certain to continue to flourish. Papers will go on being closed down. The effective control of what people see and hear and read will continue to be in very few hands. New spheres will be invaded – I think the one to watch now is books, because books are getting to a stage, reached by newspapers about fifty years ago, when they are being read by a majority of the population for the first time, and so there is money in them, particularly with the development of the paperback. It is no surprise, to anyone who knows the history of the newspaper press, to see the things now happening in publishing – amalgamations, takeovers, concentration of control, the entry of a new kind of capital, which previously would not have been interested in books at all, and indeed it is not interested in books now, because that is not why you invest. All these things, so far from being temporary incidents, the odd disasters which we hope will not happen again, are so deep a trend in this society that nothing can stop them, nothing but a better conception and a better system. And you see I am not sure that the paternal one is better, and in any case I think the time has long passed in Britain when you could get a paternal conception through; the pressures from everywhere are too strong for it to hold. We have to look then, for a new system; a democratic system.

Now in a democratic system of communication, what is the first essential? Surely that communication is something that belongs to the whole society, that it is something which depends, if it is to be healthy, on maximum participation by the individuals in the society. Since communication is the record of human growth, it has to be very varied. It has to disperse itself into many different and independent systems, all of which, however, have to be secure enough to maintain themselves. It has to get rid of the idea that communication is the business of a minority talking to, instructing, leading on, the majority. It has, finally, to get rid of the false ideology of communications as we have received it: the ideology of people who are interested in communications only as a way of controlling people, or of making money out of them.

For it is a terrifying thought that most of the real work on communication is now being done by advertisers, to discover more effective ways of selling the products of whoever hires them. It is just as bad that almost all our terms for talking about communication come from America, where you have among some good sociology a very largely debased and hired sociology. There nothing is an effect or an impression, it is always an impact. People even are not people, they are mass audiences, they are socio-economic groups, they are targets. And the aggression within those terms, the aggression within 'impact', the aggression within 'target', is the expression of people who want to control. But the basis of a democratic system is that ordinary people should have control in their own hands, that they should not be targets for anybody.

Now I think that what we have to do is to discover a system which is certainly the opposite of commercialism, but which is certainly also quite the opposite of state control. Socialism, which ought to have the answers to this, is so sadly lacking because it is associated in people's minds, in this field, with centralization and with censorship. And this is not only the result of hostile propaganda; it is also fact. We have to think of ways which would truly disperse the control of communications, and truly open the channels of participation. My own view is that we shall have to stop thinking in terms of national systems. We shall certainly have to stop thinking in terms of one ideal national system. Instead, can we apply this simple test: are the means of expression, in any particular case, of such a kind that they can be owned by the people who use them? Some means of expression are. If you save up long enough as a writer you can own a typewriter; if you save up long enough as a painter, or go without your food, you can get your brushes, you can beg your canvas. For many individual workers, many individual artists, the means can be individually owned, and where this is so I think it is a public duty to see that any further necessary means are available – local authorities building studios to let to painters, or exhibitions and festivals of all kinds, in which for example the adult education movement could do much more, to let artists bring their work directly to people without the intervention of commercialism. But apply that criterion – can the means be individually owned? – and you immediately realize that over most of the field there are means which the people using them could never individually or even collectively own: a newspaper, a broadcasting station, a television station, even really a theatre or a film production studio, or a network of cinemas. These can never be directly owned by the people who are going to use them. At least, I don't see how. Where they can be, all right. But where they cannot be, we have to try for this new system, in which the means of communication would be owned by the society in trust for the actual producers. So that instead of setting up a large central organization, around public ownership, it would be a matter of public policy to encourage the formation of independent groups of all kinds, to whom the publicly owned means would be licensed. I mean companies of actors, to whom a publicly owned theatre could be let for a period of years. I mean broadcasting stations, possibly with local trusts, which would be leased to companies of professional producers. I mean newspapers, which I think in the end will have to be publicly owned, in some form, by different kinds of organization, but which could then be licensed to working groups of journalists who would have guaranteed control over the paper's policy. Or film studios which could be leased, on long term, to independent groups of film makers. In all these ways, a general policy of decentralization, within public ownership where necessary, and with the decision about what is to be produced resting firmly in the hands of the people who in any case have to produce it. Because talk to anyone now, in any of our communication systems; ask them why does this come out in this form, and they will say: 'Don't ask me, old man, I said just that before it came out.' The people within the system are extremely conscious of the fact that between them and what they want to do is something, something which they know they are subject to, something which is the very opposite of any kind of freedom.

I know all the difficulties there are going to be in this new kind of conception, but I am quite clear about this: that there is no chance of a return to a paternal system, that the commercial system is manifestly not working for good, and yet cannot be reformed while it sticks, as it must, to its principle: that what can be said is what can be profitably said. And so, however difficult it may be, I think we have to go on to try to put flesh on the bones of this new conception, to try to work out the details of a democratic communications system. I don't honestly expect it to happen for some considerable time. People have been kind enough to say that some of us have made a breakthrough, a break through that wall. I am not the only one to say, but my own impression is simply as yet of barked knuckles. And I want to say this: when I look around and see where the resistance is coming from, I see it not only from the people who have a lot to lose – the active speculators – but also from many of the people who have everything to gain, yet who have learned certain dogmas about communication who apply them mechanically, who somehow will not face the true situation we are in and hope that it will all somehow come magically right. I know I used to make people miserable in the fifties by saying the press was going to diminish, that great papers would be closed down. When the *News Chronicle* was closed down, and when this sudden series of closures started, I had this profoundly mixed feeling: sorrow at seeing what was happening, yet this sense of relief that the thing was coming into the open, and that what had been quite evident for a long time, the thing that was going to happen, the thing that it is quite evident now is going to continue to happen, was out clearly enough for people to see it and to think about it. Suddenly, there in front of us, is the wall: quite clear at last. I think myself it is time we started taking it down. We can make something much better, if we have the courage to try.

The Idea of a Common Culture

1968

We begin to think where we live, and it is really not surprising that, in this time and place, I should have been trying to think about culture, as a particular experience which I share with many others, and which is in that sense the preoccupation of a generation. Culture was the way in which the process of education, the experience of literature, and – for someone moving out of a working-class family to a higher education – inequality, came through. What other people, in different situations, might experience more directly as economic or political inequality, was naturally experienced, from my own route, as primarily an inequality of culture: an inequality which was also, in an obvious sense, an uncommunity. This is, I think, still the most important way to follow the argument about culture, because everywhere, but very specifically in England, culture is one way in which class, the fact of major divisions between men, shows itself.

I think, however, that it took me a long time (looking back, it seems an absurdly long time) to understand that there were different meanings within the idea of culture itself, to which one was responding simultaneously but which clearly had to be distinguished. For a long time it seemed to me that the problem of culture was primarily a problem of the relationship between writer and audience – the problem of connecting in writing – and I find that the first way in which I tried to discuss culture was within this context, determined by ideas of the relation of writer and audience which would now seem to me to be limited. The terms I used, then, were 'community of sensibility', 'community of process': the idea of a connection between a writer and his audience which in a sense preceded the act of writing itself, out of which the act of writing grew, and within which the response to that act continued. These terms do not seem to me, now, a particularly satisfactory way of speaking about culture; they had to be developed, inevitably, into thinking about a whole particular society, and into thinking about culture as the most immediately available way of thinking about society itself.

The personal aspect of this development should not be over-emphasized; but it is, nevertheless, a fact that the movement between classes, between life situations and life styles, which has characterized what little extension of higher education has gone on, has focused attention on questions which seem centred in the idea of culture, and are in themselves a way of fusing all those other aspects of living which one believes to be the general experience. It is true that one would probably have thought much more directly about social, political and economic barriers and failures, if it had not happened that a particular English tradition of social thinking contained a vital strand which was really a debate about the nature of culture itself. What was involved in that debate was complicated, including people and attitudes from many different social and political traditions; but the idea of culture had been, from the early nineteenth century – from the generation after the Industrial Revolution – an attempt to focus questions about the quality of life available in a particular community, as a way of putting questions to the simple material progress, or the simple social confidence, of the dominant kind of society. In the debate about the bearings of the idea of culture on the nature of general·community, much of an essentially English kind of social thinking had been done; to any student of literature, this was going to be, inevitably, his first major contact with the process of thinking about contemporary society and its problems – this tradition would be nearest to hand.

Among immediate contemporaries, one was very aware of three writers who represented emphases in this debate about culture: Eliot, Leavis and (one shouldn't call him a contemporary, although he felt like one) Marx. One saw Eliot taking a conservative position, fearing that the extension of a different kind of society and education, perhaps also of urban and industrial living, certainly, too, of democracy, would inevitably dilute and destroy the meaning of culture. One saw Leavis, committing himself to no such systematic case, but undeniably laying the same kind of emphasis on the values of a received minority culture, which it was the business of the student of literature to defend, before there was any question of extension. There was not, here, the same settled opposition to the idea of extending a cultural tradition that one had found in Eliot; but there was a radical scepticism about its possibility, and a certainty that something else came first. And then there was Marx, actually at first the Marxists, insisting that culture is inseparable from the nature of our general living, that in a society divided into classes culture would have an inevitable class content and class bearing, and that, in the historical development of a society, a culture will necessarily change as relations between men and classes change.

This complex of ideas was available for a whole range of questions, which could be concentrated into what is now called the debate about culture. It seemed to me, looking at these questions, that one had to put a certain emphasis which really was different from any of these three approaches. It was impossible for me to accept Eliot's position, both because it seemed essentially to ratify a society which was overridingly objectionable on other grounds, in its intolerable social and economic inequalities, and also because the attempt to preserve a class society in the control of traditional institutions was in any case unrealistic, in a world in which a transformation of that traditional culture by advanced capitalism was going on. What Eliot was demanding was, at a simple level, inconceivable. Leavis's approach was more immediately attractive, in that it offered an emphasis on the primacy of literature which one was very ready to put; it called on one to do a certain job (incidentally of reading, not of writing), and it had a radical tinge which supported a critical interest and engagement in the problems of contemporary civilization. But it seemed to me, ultimately, that when this case was generalized, its emphasis on a minority culture was subject to the same objections as that of Eliot. Indeed, if one found Eliot sourer, it was really only because he had been, in the final analysis, more consistent: because he had faced, and accepted, the implications of what he was saying. The Leavis position seemed to me to lead directly to such a social position, but there was a certain understandable hesitancy about taking the last step: it was said that such a social position was not necessary, and a virtue was made about it not being necessary, but it seemed to me that the cultural position inevitably implied it, and this has been confirmed, as we have watched, as the years have gone by. As for Marx, one accepted the emphases on history, on change, on the inevitably close relationships between class and culture, but the way this came through was, at another level, unacceptable. There was, in this position, a polarization and abstraction of economic life on the one hand and culture on the other, which did not seem to me to correspond to the social experience of culture as others had lived it, and as one was trying to live it oneself.

It was, then, as a way of exploring an alternative emphasis, of discovering a standpoint within this complex territory, that one tried to speak of a common culture, or (the phrase now seems to me different) of a culture in common. Related to this stress was the assertion that culture is ordinary: that there is not a special class, or group of men, who are involved in the creation of meanings and values, either in a general sense or in specific art and belief. Such creation could not be reserved to a minority, however gifted, and was not, even in practice, so reserved: the meanings of a particular form of life of a people, at a particular time, seemed to come from the whole of their common experience, and from its complicated general articulation. And if this is indeed so, that meanings and values are widely, not sectionally, created (and the example that one used in the first instance was that of language, which is no individual's creation, although certain individuals extend and deepen its possibilities), then one had to talk about the general fact of a community of culture, and to assert the need for a common culture as a critique of what was imposed, what was done to that general condition in the structure of particular societies. In talking of a common culture, then, one was saying first that culture was the way of life of a people, as well as the vital and indispensable contributions of specially gifted and identifiable persons, and one was using the idea of the *common* element of the culture – its community – as a way of criticizing that divided and fragmented culture we actually have.

If it is at all true that the creation of meanings is an activity which engages all men, then one is bound to be shocked by any society which, in its most explicit culture, either suppresses the meanings and values of whole groups, or which fails to extend to these groups the possibility of articulating and communicating those meanings. This, precisely, was what one wanted to assert about contemporary Britain, even at a point where we were being assured, in the usual kind of happy retrospect, that most of the social problems had been resolved. It was, on the contrary, perfectly clear that the majority of people, while living *as* people, creating their own values, were both shut out by the nature of the educational system from access to the full range of meanings of their predecessors in that place, and excluded by the whole structure of communications – the character of its material ownership, its limiting social assumptions – from any adequate participation in the process of changing and developing meanings which was in any case going on. One was therefore both affirming a general truth, which I would hold to be independent of any particular historical stage, that there is, in that sense, community of culture; and criticizing a particular society because it limited, and in many ways actively prevented, that community's self-realization.

It is here that a critique which began as cultural extends itself to what is properly social and political criticism. It is as well to make this clear, because I do not think that there is any possibility of a common culture as I mean it, coming about simply by an act of extension of the minority values of a specific group – probably, in any such case, a ruling group – to other people. It would not be a common culture (though it might be possible to call it a culture in common) if some existing segment of

experience, articulated in a particular way, were simply extended –
taught – to others, so that they then had it as a common possession. For
it follows, from the original emphasis, that the culture of a people can
only be what all its members are engaged in creating in the act of living:
that a common culture is not the general extension of what a minority
mean and believe, but the creation of a condition in which the people as
a whole participate in the articulation of meanings and values, and in the
consequent decisions between this meaning and that, this value and that.
This would involve, in any real world, the removal of all the material
obstacles to just this form of participation: this was the ground for the
later interest in the institutions of communication, which, dominated by
capital or state power, set up the idea of the few communicating to the
many, disregarding the contributions of those who are seen not as
communicators but merely as communicable to. In the same way, it
would mean changing the educational system from its dominant pattern
of sorting people, from so early an age, into 'educated' people and
others, or in other words transmitters and receivers, to a view of the
interlocking processes of determining meanings and values as involving
contribution and reception by everyone.

When one had criticized the institutions of communication and the
methods of divisive education, one saw, quite clearly, that these rested
on what was indeed a solid social structure of private property in just
these means of exchange; one saw, too, that this kind of private
property, which prevents the full access of the people as a whole to its
governing institutions, rules also in the direction of the energy of the
community, principally in the forms of control over work. Private
property in the means of labour had resulted in a situation in which the
energies of a majority of men were being directed, under severe and
normally irresistible pressure, to ends decided by a minority; if this were
so, in so central a part of our lives, it was bound to affect the processes
by which meanings and values could be created and exchanged.

In speaking of a common culture, then, one was speaking critically of
what could be summarized as a class society; but one was also speaking
positively of an idea of society which seemed at least to sound different
from some contemporary definitions of socialism. I had no doubt, at any
stage, that the means of changing this kind of society would be socialist
means, or that the institutions which would lead into a different society
would be socialist institutions. But because of what one was meaning, in
the first place, about the nature of society and community in general, the
first question which one put to the idea of a different society was in
terms of its capacity for participation in just this central process of a
people living together. I defined this in a phrase which has since been
widely used, in some places I don't much like, but which still seems to

me important: the idea of an *educated and participating democracy*. Participating, for the reasons which we have said; educated, because it must be the case that the whole tradition of what has been thought and valued, a tradition which has been abstracted as a minority possession, is in fact a common human inheritance without which any man's participation would be crippled and disadvantaged. In this meaning of education, a man would not see himself simply as continuing a particular tradition, educated into a particular way of thought, as so much of education is viewed at present; the point, simply, is that one would not be fully qualified to participate in this active process unless the education which provides its immediate means – developed speaking, writing, and reading – and which allows access to the terms of the argument so far, were made commonly available. So a common culture is an educated and participating democracy, and the idea of a socialist democracy is based, very firmly, on those values. The argument about culture can never pass in a simple way to an argument about politics; but when a political case is made, in these terms, it tries always to base itself on the originating values.

It is this emphasis, on a mutual determination of values and meanings, that I think one has to remember in considering one possible meaning of a common culture. There is some danger in conceiving of a common culture as a situation in which all people mean the same thing, value the same thing, or, in that usual abstraction of culture, have an equal possession of so much cultural property. It is possible to understand the demand for a common culture in any of these ways, but not, I think, seriously, if one has followed the course of the argument. That kind of view of a common culture is perhaps better described by the phrase 'a culture in common', but the argument is in any case unreal. In any society towards which we are likely to move, there will, first of all, be such considerable complexity that nobody will in that sense 'possess cultural property' in the same way; people, inevitably, will have different aspects of the culture, will choose that rather than this, concentrate on this and neglect that. When this is an act of choice, it is completely desirable; when it is an act of someone else's choice as to what is made available and what is neglected, then of course one objects. But it is not only that the society will be complex: that people will not and cannot share it in an even and uniform way. It is also that the idea of a common culture is in no sense the idea of a simply consenting, and certainly not of a merely conforming, society. One returns, once more, to the original emphasis of a common determination of meanings by all the people, acting sometimes as individuals, sometimes as groups, in a process which has no particular end, and which can never be supposed at any time to have finally realized itself, to have become complete. In this common

process, the only absolute will be the keeping of the channels and institutions of communication clear, so that all may contribute, and be
helped to contribute. If that is so, then the fantasy that some critics have
had, that a common culture would be a uniform and conformist culture,
or the fear that some friends have expressed, that a common culture
would be notoriously difficult to attain because it is impossible to find
any large number of people in general agreement, do not seem to hold.
In speaking of a common culture, one is asking, precisely, for that free,
contributive and common *process* of participation in the creation of
meanings and values, as I have tried to define it.

2
State, Administration and the Arts

The Arts Council

1979

The Arts Council has been having a rough ride. Like most other British institutions it is under severe financial pressure; its government grant has been increased in line with, or a little above, general inflation, but there is reliable evidence that inflation in the arts institutions is much higher than the general rate. Then it has had a run of bad publicity about some of the minor events it has indirectly supported; a hasty reader of parts of the press could almost be forgiven for concluding that it subsidizes very little but performance-art sweeping of leaves or butting of walls, or else obscene or subversive pseudo-artists. In just this period, its major grants to several opera and ballet companies and to orchestras were masked from casual notice by a publicity campaign by commercial sponsors, who contributed very much less money but were able to have productions blazoned as 'in association with Imperial Tobacco Limited' and so on. When the Council insisted that its own grants should be proportionately acknowledged, it was told, by this pressure group, that it was the Council's business to provide public money for the arts, while the commercial companies could give or not as they chose. To have accepted this argument would have been to acquiesce, first, in some deliberately misleading prestige advertising; secondly, in the impression of the Council as a promoter of only bizarre eccentricities, while major activities were being substantially funded by others; and, thirdly, in the powerful tendency, in both political parties, to hold or in real terms reduce public funding of the arts and to rely on commercial sponsorship, encouraged by new tax concessions, to develop the arts as prestige amenities.

This has been the rough ground on the Right. But there has been ground just as rough on the Left. While the philistine press gives an impression of the Council as a wanton subsidizer of sub-artistic layabouts, the radical press continues to insist that it is the citadel of bureaucratic establishment art. Meanwhile, there has been sustained criticism of the undemocratic and irresponsible composition of the Council and its panels, and proposals, including a detailed plan by the Labour Party, for its comprehensive reform. Riding this rough ground, looking nervously to right and to left, the Council is, of course, in danger of succumbing to that classical English political trope: that if you are being criticized from both sides you must by definition be occupying some virtuous centre. This would be a quite false conclusion. Under the observable difficulties, and against clear misrepresentations and some evident lies, the Council has been working carefully and responsibly but within structural difficulties of a more basic kind which it is still very reluctant to acknowledge.

I want to analyse some of these difficulties from my very recent experience of the Council's work. In December 1978 I completed three years' membership of the Council. Appointed by Hugh Jenkins, to whom I explained my objections to the Council's constitution and who shared my wish to see it reformed, I concluded within six months that substantial internal reform was impossible and then twice, at critical moments, offered my resignation. I decided to serve my term, finally, so that I could contribute to the necessary public discussion with some detailed knowledge of the problems. During my membership I argued for and eventually got a special conference of the Council to discuss broad questions of its composition and policy. One result of this conference is an internal inquiry into organization which is now in progress. But this, while useful, cannot address the central problems. The ride, in fact, has to become even rougher. Throughout my membership of the Council I was treated with a very general courtesy and helpfulness, and it is indeed a pleasant, relaxed and in its own terms efficient body on which to serve. But that, given the difficulties of the matter, is one of its problems.

An Intermediate Body?

In the broad perspective of a theory of institutions, the Arts Council is an important and relatively original attempt to create a kind of intermediate body which distributes public money without being under the direct control of a governmental organization. The whole question of such intermediate bodies is now being widely discussed. In the case of the arts, and within anything at all like the present social order, the principle can be strongly supported on the grounds, first, that it is impossible for the arts to be adequately supported by the ordinary operations of the market or by occasional private patronage (as the banks and industrial companies would soon discover and indeed know already; their prestige advertising support is only practicable at all on the basis of substantial long-term public funding); and, secondly, that while public finance, from the general revenue, is essential, it is undesirable that any governmental body, subject to changes of political emphasis, should have direct control over artistic policies and practices. We have only to compare the intermediate principle with either of its probable alternatives – a consortium of commercial sponsors, or a government arts department – to see how desirable it is that it should be realistically attempted. A commercial consortium would necessarily subordinate its policies to its own interests, however generally conceived, sustaining certain metropolitan institutions, certain activities in its commercially relevant areas, and certain amenities. It could not undertake the comprehensive regional provision, the deliberate extension of access, and the broad mix of established and experimental arts which the public interest requires. On the other hand, a government department, from such comparative evidence as we have, would be likely, even if it stopped short of direct political interference, to be radically insensitive to the highly varied, often untidy and at times unpredictable practice of so many kinds of art. An intermediate body, responsibly and accountably disposing of public money and including in itself people with direct current knowledge of the arts and their administration, is a much more attractive proposition. But is the Arts Council not such a body? In the broadest terms of principle it is so, but between the principle and its adequate realization there are several major problems, which I will discuss in an ascending order of difficulty.

The first problem is the constitutional definition of 'intermediacy'. Typically it is now ordinarily discussed in metaphors, of which the most popular is 'the arm's length principle'. But this is an unfortunate image: with whatever unintentional accuracy, it describes one weak version of intermediacy. For it is customary for the body to direct its arm, and all that is gained by an arm's length is a certain notion of removal of directly traceable control. When I said, at the special conference, that what was happening looked to me more like wrist's length, I was thought to be merely insulting, but the argument cannot be continued in metaphors. The substantial point is this. Under its existing constitution, the Arts Council is wholly appointed by government ministers and its budget is annually determined, on no fixed public principles, by the same ministers. Within these fundamental constraints it is given a kind of independence; it is even, to a fault, protected from detailed parliamentary questioning. It then requires an effort of will to describe such a body as intermediate in any genuine sense. It is in the pocket of ministers and a department of state, and its marginal independence has as many disadvantages as advantages. It is worth looking more closely at how this actually works.

Administered Consensus by Cooption

The true social process of such bodies as the Arts Council is one of administered consensus by cooption. The first decisive appointment is that of the chairman. Here, indeed, there can be some untidiness in the process, when succeeding governments are of different parties. While I was a member there were two chairmen: one a Conservative nominee, one a Labour nominee. Their terms could not, without some fuss, be precisely adjusted to governmental periods, but in each case not only was the broadly political character of the appointment clear, the observable character of the Council was subtly but significantly changed. This is important in itself, but it becomes much more important when the real processes of appointment to membership of the Council are scrutinized. I say 'scrutinized' when in fact one can only guess; the details are shrouded in the usual mellow dusk. But it seems that there is con-sultation between ministers and civil servants in the Department of Education and Science and the chairman and senior officers of the Council. Names then emerge, on no discernible representative basis. There is then a complication which facilitates cooption. Members serve normally for three years, with a given number retiring each year. New members thus enter a Council of which the majority has established or got used to a certain style of work. But this process of continuity and flow is then cut across by a specific internal procedure. When I said at the special conference that there were quite evidently two classes of member, of which one class passed through on a three-year term while another remained on the Council for longer periods, I was at first patiently and then impatiently corrected. Yet it is the simple truth. If a member is appointed to be chairman of one of the panels for specific arts – of which more later – he can and does serve beyond the ordinary three-year term. And how is he appointed chairman of a panel? It is the mellow dusk again. The chairman or secretary-general announces to the Council that X has kindly agreed to take on this onerous task; the Council relaxes, visibly pleased. I watched this on a few occasions. There was one case when a chairman of a panel resigned from the Council; a successor had to be found. I kept expecting the matter to be raised in Council, but the next I heard of it was from an acquaintance who seemed to be negotiating the scope of his task as the new chairman with the relevant departmental officer. He subsequently became chairman of the panel and a new member of the Council. In another case, an existing member became chairman of an important panel by a process of private consultation between the chairman of the Council and its officers. Given the fact that chairmen of panels can serve longer terms than ordinary members, this is of course a clear case of administered consensus by cooption.

The same process establishes itself at the level of style. New members are made to feel welcome in rather specific ways. 'You've arrived when you sit at this table', I was told, genially, when I first turned up for the preparatory lunch. Not, as it happened, sufficiently arrived to be asked to be a member of a panel, which all but two of us at the meeting were, but this did not concern me since, on the specific understanding I had reached with the minister, I was present to observe and to attempt reform, and in any case to resist the most polite offers of cooption when they eventually came. But this sense of arrival is intended to have its effect. It is not really a matter of privilege in the ordinary sense. Members serve unpaid, though they can get a refund of ordinary expenses. There are free tickets to events sponsored by the Council, but many who use these put in very long hours of unpaid work. The important atmosphere is political. Under the first chairman there were, naturally, a number of contentious issues, but none of these was ever put to a vote. Even under the second chairman I remember only one formal vote. The mood of bewildered benevolence which the weight of complex business already induces is, so to say, funded as a mood of the consensus of goodwill. On one particularly controversial decision, I asked to have my dissent recorded. The present vice-chairman said subsequently that he was astonished by this request, which seemed to him to break the whole spirit of the Council. Who would be interested in such a record of dissent? But within consensus procedures, and the rarity of voting, this is one of the few means of challenge short of actual resignation, and selective resignation only establishes consensus more thoroughly.

The procedure extends through the dependent bodies. Thus panels for each of the major arts are nominated by a process of consultation, typically between the chairman of panel who has arrived in the way already described and the officer of the department concerned. Lists of names are reported to the Council, and I once succeeded, with some persistence, in getting a quite different name added. But the general procedure is, of course, the same mode of consensual cooption.

Yet it goes deeper than this, for the panels are only advisory and the crucial funding decisions are taken by finance committees for each major art. These committees are appointed by the usual processes of selective consultation. Their minutes, with those of the panels, arrive with a great weight of other papers at the monthly three-hour Council meeting. Some matters are referred to the Council for decision, but the complexity and timing of such decisions often make these references relatively formal (some, of course, are thoroughly discussed), while in any case it would be impossible for all those decisions, taken by internally and unevenly selected bodies, to be properly examined. The mood of bewildered consensus is thus powerfully reinforced.

The role of the officers of the Council then requires examination. They are, in the majority, skilled and experienced people. They know much more about most of the business than most of the Council, especially the three-year passers-by. They sit, at first indistinguishably, around the Council table with the lay members. In practice I would say policies are determined by these officers and the panel chairmen, in consultation where necessary with the Council chairman and the Council's senior officers. The distinguishable lay Council, and even more the lay panels, come through as interested occasional parties, though the consensual mood encourages them to see themselves, and the usual public perspective allows them to be generally seen, as a fully responsible intermediate public body.

Some of these difficulties would be encountered in any busy and complex organization. Some can be removed by the internal reforms now being inquired into. It is extraordinary, for example, that two interested members of the Council first learned, virtually by accident, of a major proposal of policy by one of the panels, several months after members of the panel thought it had been forwarded to the Council for full discussion. But whatever local reforms of this kind may be made – and even they will not be easy – it is clear that the procedures of the Council flow from quite fundamental assumptions which are practically embodied in its mode of appointment and constitution. What begins, from a department of state, as a process of selective and administered consensus, cannot become at any of its lower levels an open and democratic public body and procedure.

Definitions of 'The Arts'

A further characteristic of an adequate intermediate body is that it should have a clearly defined and effective area of responsibility. This is not now the case with the Arts Council. In its first formulation, under the 1946 charter, it came directly under the Treasury and was concerned with 'the fine arts exclusively'. This notoriously difficult category was taken in practice to include theatre, opera, ballet, concert music, painting and sculpture. Under the 1967 charter the category became the generalized 'the arts' and, in certain ways, literature, film, photography, 'performance art' and 'community arts' were taken on board; the Council was also moved (1964) to come under the Department of Education and Science.

The later definition is more in line with real needs, but the former, for all its evidently residual character, in a way just because of it, had more consistency. Socially, the original arts were the cultural interests of an older upper-middle and middle class: a limited governmental initiative – a financial rather than a cultural or educational intervention – would help to sustain them and to make them more widely accessible. But the cultural situation was already rapidly changing. Radio was already the primary distributor of concert music and of drama; television, if unevenly, was to become the major distributive channel of all arts, in terms of numbers. Moreover, once the shift to a cultural and educational rather than financial policy had been made, quite different social relations were in question; not just increased access to a relatively enclosed and continuing culture, but a complex and interacting set of new and old arts, new and old media and institutions, new and older audiences. Throughout, meanwhile, there had been the relative exclusion of literature: not because it was clearly outside the 'fine arts' – there had been no period since 1620 when it could be even plausibly argued that the theatre contained more serious art than printed books – but because public provision, at the level of access, was already provided at the level of free libraries. However, once it had happened that the greater part of the Council's money went to sustaining primary producers, and only after that to sustaining and developing means of distribution, this exclusion became in principle untenable, though in terms of relative sums allotted it has continued to this day.

The whole complex of changing social and cultural relations has produced major problems for any kind of Arts Council. The development of socially as well as formally experimental art (the fringe drama companies presenting plays in more public places than theatres; public performance art and the area of locally based community arts) led to problems in assessment which the talisman of 'standards' (itself difficult enough in a restricted 'fine arts' category) could not resolve. Yet strict assessment of the quality of these uses of public money was still obviously necessary. The Council found itself caught between residual notions of quality (the continuing professional 'fine arts'), new notions of quality (movement beyond academic and establishment art) and new social and cultural notions of the inevitable relation between quality and situation: the specific relations of works of art to their audiences, which were relevant not only to problems in non-theatre drama companies and community arts but, by a crucial twist, to the educational aims embodied in the new charter and the new responsibility to an educational rather than a financial government department. And if these problems of assessment were not already difficult enough, the Council found itself given responsibility for 'the arts' in a period in which the broadcasting organizations and a significant number of publishers (especially in paperback) were becoming major providers.

It is not the Arts Council that has failed to resolve this developing complexity and the consequent muddle, though its consensual tone has led to repeated attempts to accept the muddle, to take it as something that has to be lived with. The central failing is at a more public level and specifically at the level of government organization. Institutions and problems relating to the arts, though of course often relating inextricably to other matters also, are distributed across the responsibilities of government departments in what looks like the work of a sorcerer's apprentice. No consistent cultural policy, even at the simplest level of the provision of public money, is, for example, possible without some minimal correlation of the work of the Arts Council and of the broadcasting organizations. Yet broadcasting, from its original context of security in the early 1920s, comes under the Home Office. The press and publishing come under the Department of Industry. The very complicated relations with local authorities, themselves now statutory and often significant providers of artistic events, lead back to the Department of the Environment. To track down every detail of responsibility is to enter a world which looks, repeatedly, like deliberate muddle.

Yet it is not mainly this. It is the incompetent political and administrative reflection of both confused and contested definitions of culture and the arts. The clear need for a Ministry of Arts and Communications, to make possible coherent and connected policies in these inevitably overlapping and interacting areas, is still stubbornly resisted. And indeed I would join in resisting it if the principle of genuine intermediate bodies were not a central part of any such reorganization. As things are, however, and under what is likely to be a permanent financial pressure, the intermediate bodies, and especially the Arts Council, the BBC and the IBA, have to work in ways which confer the impression of independent public responsibility but which prevent or limit any clear and coherent exercise of it. One example will illustrate the general problem. The Arts Council finds repeated difficulties in getting its subsidized metropolitan companies to tour: there are some real and some manufactured financial and physical difficulties. There is one kind of duty to sustain their high quality; there is another kind of duty to make the best work generally accessible. But within the limited remit and the complexity of relevant ministries, is it not possible to move to resolve this problem through some agreed relation between metropolitan and major provincial subsidized companies and a regular amount of broadcasting of their work? Each mode runs back to dependence on public money, and there is both expensive duplication and overlapping and, more seriously, a long list of wasted opportunities. The muddle might continue, in a complacent English way, if it were not for the cash limits at every point in these complex activities, which have the effect of steadily reducing real independence and, because there is no one place where they can be discussed and reviewed, of preventing collaborative resolutions.

The British State and its Ruling Class

It would be naive to discuss the principles and problems of intermediate bodies without paying some attention to the character of the British State and its ruling class. Indeed, it can be argued that intermediate bodies of the kind we have known were made possible by this character. The British State has been able to delegate some of its official functions to a whole complex of semi-official or nominally independent bodies because it has been able to rely on an unusually compact and organic ruling class. Thus it can give Lord X or Lady Y both public money and apparent freedom of decision in some confidence, subject to normal procedures of report and accounting, that they will act as if they were indeed state officials. The British State gets a surprisingly large amount of its public work, from the House of Lords to the governors of the BBC, from royal commissions to consumers' councils, and from committees of inquiry to the Arts Council, done by these processes of out-work and administered cooption. When I described these processes at the special conference and applied them to the Arts Council I was told, hilariously, by the present vice-chairman, that I did not understand 'participatory democracy' (a phrase, by the way, which I seem to have invented, in 1961, to describe something very different) and that it was by this process that we achieved 'the essence of democracy', which was – no need to guess – 'consensus'. And then, of course, this is the reality behind the state's attachment to these processes and to the procedures which control them, such as administered consensus by cooption.

Of course there has been some tension between this conception and newer conceptions of a wider representation and open public selection of representatives. Some appointments and cooptions are made and studiously cited to give an impression that the process is not as narrow as it still, in majority practice, remains. But we have now to face the fact that the principle of an intermediate body, sometimes described as if it were a British democratic innovation, is administered by this essentially different principle of a relatively informal but reliable and consensual ruling class. We have to test the mix in each specific case. The University Grants Committee, distributing public money between universities, is drawn on the representative principle from people in universities – and thus looks like an authentic intermediate body – but the representatives are in fact chosen by the Department of Education and Science, in the familiar practice of administratively controlled intermediacy. The Arts Council is not even a mixed case. It is politically and administratively appointed, and its members are not drawn from arts practice and administration but from that vaguer category of 'persons of experience and goodwill' which is the state's euphemism for its informal ruling class.

Alternatives

Various ways of reforming the Arts Council have been published and discussed. The central principle of most of them is democratization: a wider, more open, more accountable representation. And of course this principle should be widely supported. But it is not primarily a matter of drawing up constitutions and embodying them in party programmes. What is necessary before that, or at least before any attempt to implement them, is a very much wider and necessarily complex discussion. We might list four issues which have as yet been quite insufficiently examined.

(i) Central and Local Organization

The question of relations between some central organization, with general responsibility for supporting the arts, and the many kinds of national, regional and local organization, involved in the same area, is now especially urgent and difficult. There are already problems if there is general devolution to Scotland and Wales, although the Scottish and Welsh Arts Councils, operating with considerable independence within a centrally determined share of the British budget, have been particularly successful. They have shared some of the faults of the central Council, especially in their mode of appointment, but they have gained much from their ability to focus on a physically closer and more specific culture and in this sense have much to teach the English central and regional authorities. The really difficult problems are more evident in England, although they would also soon become apparent in devolved Scottish and Welsh organizations. The most immediate problem is that the local authorities are already substantially but very unevenly involved in arts support and direct provision, and it has been suggested, notably by Redcliffe-Maud, that there should be a steady transfer of responsibility to the local authorities as main supporters and providers. The difficulties of this solution lie mainly in the present unevenness of interest and understanding. They are directly reflected in the very diverse character of the present regional arts associations, some few of which are already in a position to take over full responsibility for the funded arts in their regions, while others, and still the majority, are nowhere near this readiness. It can be argued that they will never be ready until they are given the responsibility, but there are two substantial problems.

First, the existing Arts Associations combine, in their constitution, the mode of selective cooption practised at the centre, and direct local authority representation. And this is often the worst of both worlds. There is usually no clear and even partly defensible intermediate organ- ization to set against the claims of the directly elected and all-purpose representative local authorities. The point about all-purpose repre- sentation deserves a note, because it is a continually recurring problem in current elected structures. The councillor or official who becomes a member of a regional arts association has virtually never been elected or nominated to represent any publicly discussed or even announced policy on the arts. As in so much else, the elected councillor is an all-purpose representative, without either the fact or the duty of specific repre- sentation of public views on the matter being decided. This endlessly displaced and deflected mode of public representation, this virtually unargued and untraceable translation of a general occasional vote into an apparent authority to decide highly specific issues is, of course, a central problem of current forms of representative democracy in many fields. But it is especially visible and important in matters of arts policy, where it has certainly been my experience, in one case after another, that the projection of private preferences or temporary political prejudices has been common. It is a fact that the present Arts Council, for all its faults, has stepped in on several occasions to restrain or modify authori- tarian interventions in policy. Any simple transfer of powers to local authorities on their present all-purpose basis would run serious risks of this kind, and would in any case, while achieving some of the merits of decentralization, be an explicit abandonment of the intermediate prin- ciple. What needs to be done, with as much urgency regionally as centrally, is to discuss and resolve the question of genuinely intermediate local arts authorities.

Then, secondly, there is the broader cultural question. The view has often been taken that the Arts Council should challenge local authorities to make more adequate provision in their areas by restricting centrally provided funds to matched proportions. It is a tempting policy, but it could result in certain areas being steadily run down in arts provision, and even if this might be eventually reversed by local protest, the breaks in continuity would be very serious for many institutions. Anyone who seriously believes in the virtues of decentralization, as I do, must take its whole process seriously. Under the present dominant centralization of general national revenue, a policy of devolving cultural responsibility could be in practice a way of radically reducing public funding of the arts in a significant number of regions, under the quite false title of greater regional democracy. We should remember that just such a reduction of public expenditure on the arts is already the programme of the political Right, and that this might be their most expedient means.

What is needed, therefore, is open and sustained public discussion of the forms of regional arts administration, to include the principle of intermediacy and to try to ensure certain necessary minimum standards and some crucially necessary procedures of continuity.

(ii) Metropolitan and Provincial

These problems are accentuated by the facts of the historical development of British culture. Central among these is the cultural domination of the metropolis, with an unusually centralized press and publishing, and with a concentration of virtually all the most prestigious and expensive national companies. This is already a most serious problem, for the costs of these metropolitan companies have risen so fast (to say nothing of the continuing pressure to add to their number) that it is easy to foresee, at any annual estimates meeting under the present arrangements, an early need to choose between closing some of them or virtually running down all other regional and local operations. Already at a financial and administrative level this is difficult enough, but it is also an acute form of a general British cultural problem. The existing forms of highly organized public support for the arts are already overwhelmingly metropolitan in character, and these are backed up by arguments on tourism (financially very relevant, given the very high proportion of foreign visitors in London theatre audiences) and by the amenity preferences of the commercial consortia. No scheme of regional devolution can evade these problems. No shunting operation – regional arts to the local authorities; metropolitan arts to a government body – ought for a moment to be tolerated. For the metropolitan institutions have, of course, been nationally financed, and must be kept for national use.

This indicates the second area of necessary public discussion. It is improbable, in my view, that it can be satisfactorily negotiated without broadening from discussion of the Arts Council to general discussion of the whole cultural organization, including, specifically, the broadcasting authorities, with their own forms of regional and local development.

And this would require, beyond mere consultation, some new coherence of responsibility at the level of central government. Within the existing fragmentation of responsibilities, the situation will not merely drift on or muddle through; it will, perhaps quite quickly, break down altogether.

(iii) Cultural Policies

The social relations of British culture have been changing so fast, together with changes in media and in forms of art, that neither the residual model of government patronage of the fine arts, nor the succeeding model of funded extension of the received arts, is now adequate. It is then, of course, true that there will be intense controversy about new models of cultural policy to replace them. This is already clear from the public arguments of the last twenty years. At the special conference Richard Hoggart, who does not share all my views about the Arts Council and about ways of reorganizing it, correctly identified one area of choice: between a Council constituted to represent the existing (second) model, with any necessary improvements in that direction; and a Council in which the now essentially alternative conceptions of cultural policy could be theoretically and practically argued out and developed. The first type of Council would be consensual, the second essentially disputative. He did not go on to declare his own preference: there are obviously practical arguments both ways. But if I am right about the nature of the current problems, and about their origins in real changes of circumstance and demand, the case for the second type of Council makes itself. There must be some specific and continuing national body in which the merits of alternative general policies, and at the same time the practicalities of the detailed and complex choices which flow from them, can be properly argued through and decided. Such a Council would necessarily be open to public attendance and report, and to parliamentary questioning, preferably by a specific select committee. Until we get such a Council, some form of national standing conference, open to all the organizations concerned, is urgently required.

(iv) Organization

It is almost too easy, given the manifest and deep-rooted faults of the present Arts Council and its dangerous openness to charges of being unrepresentative, undemocratic and irresponsible, to devise alternative organizations. But any adequate new system would, first, be necessarily very complex and, secondly, need to draw on the important experience of arts funding and administration which the present Council has accumulated. For all the faults of its general style, this body of detail is extremely impressive, and any responsible alternative would have to take it into serious account.

My own view of the elements of an alternative organization is as follows. We should not start from the central body and work downwards; we should start, instead, from forms of organization appropriate for different particular arts, and for different particular regions. Panels for specific arts should be, from the beginning, quite differently constituted, on an openly representative principle. In many of the arts, already, there are producers' organizations, and it would be an immediate improvement, for example, if the Literature Panel, instead of being selected from a central office, were elected by members of the Society of Authors and the Writers' Guild. This would be possible in most arts, and in those where it is not yet possible new organizations could be expected to develop. Such panels would elect their own chairmen and secretaries, and would have Arts Council officers directly responsible to them. Regional organizations could never be so simple, since they would have to include public representatives, indeed in majority, as well as artists. This is the problem, already discussed, of the genuine regional or local intermediate body. At least a proportion of the public representatives ought, in my view, to be directly elected to such a body, to represent various public views on arts policy. These organizations would also elect their own chairmen and secretaries, and have regional professionals directly responsible to them. There then remains a need for a central body, for the necessary and difficult job of allocating and distributing the general fund, and as a court of appeal in certain matters of policy and assessment. But this should not be an imposed or appointed central body. It would indeed be best composed of the chairmen and secretaries of the various arts and regional organizations, in turn electing its own chairman and secretary, and with its own professional staff. Determination of annual funding, from central government, should be made subject to some continuing principle, expressed as a percentage of general revenue (as in the similar case of broadcasting). Public reporting, accounting and auditing would be made to a Ministry of Arts and Communications and, as already described, to Parliament, which should be encouraged to hold public hearings on general and detailed policies. Within arts panels, it should be added, the normal procedures of declaration of interest, and of withdrawal or exclusion when direct interests are involved, should be firmly applied.

Conclusion

'Isn't that syndicalism?', asked the present Chairman, a former Labour minister, when I outlined these ideas. In fact it is not, and could not be. The proposals are conceived as applicable within the existing social order, without necessary changes in the ownership of means of production, and may indeed, if only for that reason, be impracticable: making a reality of democratic management is very difficult in this kind of centralized and minority-controlled society, and its proposals are, understandably, very fiercely resisted. Not syndicalism, then, but a degree of self-management, of diversity and openness of representation, and of vigorous public argument. If we have to go further, we shall go further. But after its recent rough ride, its virtually insoluble financial problems, and its in many ways undeserved loss of public reputation and confidence, the Arts Council ought to be nervous, and the rest of us, while these problems remain unresolved, should be not only uneasy but serious, active and innovative.

3
Solidarity and Commitment

Why Do I Demonstrate?

1968

On Easter Monday I was in Trafalgar Square: a policeman was counting us as we marched in, moving his lips rapidly in silent figures and then looking down and scribbling the number in his notebook. He seems to have got in the end to 22,000. This was the tenth successive Easter Monday I've been on that demonstration – a demonstration with one continuing theme, against British nuclear weapons, though over the years there have been other themes too, and this year it's been directed especially against the war in Vietnam. In the late 1950s that kind of demonstration was still rare or occasional. Today, in a score of countries, the protest march has become a regular part of political activity. In the past in Britain, as at Peterloo and in the marches of the Chartists, there was a style of demonstration that predated liberal democracy: the march of men without votes representing that majority who were excluded from political decision, and a march through the streets with banners because this was still the quickest and most visible means of communication. Today the means of communication are much more developed. Technically, through broadcasting and television and through low-priced newspapers and books, the communication of opinion is much more widely available, and, in most of the countries where people are now demonstrating, most, though not all, of those marching have the vote and other civil liberties. So it's at first sight surprising to people working within orthodox views of society that this political method should have so dramatically re-entered political life in modern societies, and that it should be especially active in some of the most modern societies in the world. I want to try to explain this, but from the point of view of a participant, not an observer. I think this is crucial, for there's a rich field of study, for any student of communications, in reactions to these marches from what we can call professional observers.

Only a few years ago, the CND Easter March was an occasion for little reports in the bright style of the school-leaving essay, on the Easter ritual, the annual turnout of the naive. I haven't seen any of those this year, though when there's a space to fill they can always be brought out again. What's more common now is the sensational headline about mobs and violence, with 'insights' into the ideology and organization of the new demonstrators. Particular men are built into sinister figures, or are interviewed with that characteristically friendly, open-handed malice. Networks of conspiracy and instigation are dramatically exposed in the manner of the prime minister discovering 'a tightly knit group of politically motivated men'.

This is, of course, only the scum on the front pages of the richer newspapers, but the kind of description it offers, the kind of explanation it attempts, seems to me very similar to many more sober reactions of the kind I hear, for example, at Cambridge. People come and ask me – with a remnant of respect for that kind of eccentricity which has been habitual in the old universities, but with a visibly harder undertone – why I, a writer and a university teacher, should get mixed up with what is now usually called 'that sort of thing'. When I tell them that my wife, in an orderly demonstration against UDI in Rhodesia, was knocked down behind a Cambridge lecture room by a group of young men supporting the Smith regime, they say: 'That's what you must expect if you go on demonstrations. Why not stick to official politics' – the due and proper processes of debate, argument and election?

As a matter of plain truth, most of the people I know who go on demonstrations also spend more time than these others on conventional political processes. They write, organize, canvass, and stand for elections. Certainly, speaking for myself, I've done most of these things repeatedly. This winter, for example, for a long period I put aside one of my own books to edit the *May Day Manifesto*, which involved the intellectual collaboration of men in many disciplines from ten British universities, and which offers a closely argued and contemporary socialist view of the British and international crisis. All that, by the terms of the ordinary reaction to the recent demonstrations, is what one ought to be doing – reasoning, describing, persuading. And yet somehow when it comes to it, it isn't.

For the last ten years – indeed during just the period of the revival of demonstrations – there's been a very active renewal of socialist thought in many countries and in Britain as clearly as anywhere. It's a different socialism, in many ways, from some of the forms which preceded it. It isn't, as yet, a system, but it has certain identifying emphases and positions, which are very close to, and sometimes identical with, the mood and purpose of the demonstrations. Anybody who participates in these movements knows of this link and these interactions, between theory and practice, between idea and mood. Anybody who takes the trouble to talk to a regular participant with some readiness to listen, rather than simply to ask the usual questions about long hair and violence, can in fact discover this. Yet even people who are normally well-informed go on saying: to the demonstrators, that what they need is some theory, some serious political position; to the theoreticians, that it is all very well, but rather remote and abstract.

Some part of this must be put down to ignorance, some part again to certain real difficulties, for of course there is no single line among the demonstrators, as anyone who was in Trafalgar Square – or in Belgrave Square, as I was, during the trouble outside the German Embassy – can very quickly see. And in the same way, there's no single theoretical line. There are varying emphases, including some bitter controversy, and in important ways the ideas are still being developed. Nevertheless, it is to that general view of the world, a developed view of the present nature of imperialism, of state-supported capitalism and of managed politics, that most of the demonstrations are now practically related, whether on Vietnam and Rhodesia and Greece, on the struggle of the American negroes, on the wage freeze and the attacks on the social services, on the effects of the communication system, as in the demonstrations against the Springer press in Germany. After a certain point, to go on saying that the demonstrators have no serious political ends, or that we're still waiting to see in cold print the detailed arguments that lie behind the slogans, is to incur the very pointed suspicion of bad faith.

Bad faith, I believe, is just what it is – a very characteristic kind of liberal bad faith. I think sometimes that the real right wing in this country, the more active Conservative politicians, know perfectly well what this movement is about, and are simply against it. But the right wing in Britain is itself in any active sense a minority. I'm more interested in the reactions elsewhere – in the body of opinion which still takes itself as liberal. It's been confused by propaganda, which has raised prejudices against demonstrators and against students. But this couldn't happen if it weren't for the confusion that we're all now living in, when a major political tradition, a tradition which taught most of us to think, is under pressure and in crisis, beginning to break up, and when its habits of thought, its descriptions, its categories, no longer enable us to see and respond to what is happening in the very rapidly changing world.

These ten years of British demonstrations began against nuclear tests, and did something to make the public opinion which led to the test ban treaty. They were soon, though, mainly concerned with the bomb itself, and especially with what was called the British independent nuclear deterrent. It's a profound irony, which can explain some of the bitterness of the marches, that when we took part in electoral politics, supporting Labour in 1964, one of the lines between the parties was just this issue; yet it's the party that won, the party that asked for our support, that now forms the government which has at its disposal, in the Polaris submarines, just what we supposed we were working against. It's like the experience of our American colleagues, who saw the last presidential election as involving, in part, a choice between the politics of Johnson and Goldwater on Vietnam. They saw Johnson elected but got Goldwater's policies.

In the early years when the demonstrations started, the bomb in itself was an issue, but behind it there was a political shock-wave – first felt, as always, among the young – from the combined effects of Hungary and Suez: a bitter reaction against imperialism and that lying invasion of Egypt, but also a bitter reaction against established Communism of the kind associated with Stalin, and persisting, though in less terrible forms, under his successors. That combination of responses against the bomb, against imperialism and against an authoritarian Communism was significant and vital, but it's proved very hard to understand for people whose minds are fixed in old moulds. Yet all over Western Europe now, in Japan and the United States, and coming through in different ways in some East European countries, is this active New Left which is at once libertarian and democratic, and also militantly socialist and against capitalism and imperialism.

The history of the sixties has brought certain rapid developments, bringing in the new formative factor of the liberation of the Third World, often by revolutionary means. As the Cold War broke into actual fighting in just these countries, there's been a necessary hardening of socialist involvement, as in the solidarity with the NLF in Vietnam. The layers of this history and of these active responses are still sometimes separate, sometimes awkwardly angular, even contradictory, but the process of development and clarification is now advancing quite rapidly.

The question can still be put: why demonstrate? Here there's another, and crucial, factor: the quality of response, not simply to these major international issues, but to the experience of living in advanced capitalist societies with parliamentary democratic form. This in the end may be the most critical factor of all, for it determines not only some of the important issues but the consequent strategy and tactics. 'This is a democracy' runs the routine answer to demonstrators, with the obvious implication that there's no need to demonstrate. Yet parliamentary democracy has become increasingly formal under the pressures of consensus. It is in some obvious cases corrupt, in that the relation between an elected programme and actual policies can, as now in Britain, be so contradictory as to pass the boundaries of explanation by circumstance and begin to look like a confidence trick. Moreover, the theory of representative democracy, with all its strengths and limitations, is being itself surpassed in practice by the pressures of modern organized capitalism to channel decisions to many non-elected bodies. And a key role in this replacement of representative democracy is being played by the modern communications system, which is not, and does not pretend to be, democratic at all, except in purely negative ways. When the German students, after the shooting of Rudi Dutschke, demonstrated against a press monopoly, they were taking into the streets, and for their own good reasons, what had been for many years a central part of New Left theory: that in any large and complicated society, the communications system in newspapers, broadcasting and television is a major political institution – in its supply of necessary information, in its capacity to select, emphasize or exclude, and in its power to influence and campaign.

But this institution, most notably in the press yet also to varying degrees in television, is in no sense representative or subject to electoral control, and is, in fact, permanently up for auction to rich men, to the new communications combines, who then claim by simple purchase this immense political power. It just isn't possible, then, to see parliament and its electoral process as having the right to consume and direct all political activity for its own purposes. For parliament has itself conceded many decisive areas of power, in economic planning and in communications, to wholly undemocratic institutions which it is in no way prepared to fight. The measure of the failure of social democratic parties in Western Europe is that by compromising on just those issues, they've excluded themselves from any serious consideration as the means to democracy and socialism. It is in the gap left by that failure that the new movements are being formed.

Demonstration, then, though only one means, is a necessary response to a society of that kind, which builds official opinion on established lines, and which has reduced previous political channels to instruments or diversions. To go out and speak in one's own terms, directly, has become a central political need, and it is, of course, a challenge which the system in the end knows it must take seriously. But need the demonstrations be violent? We must make some distinctions. The last really violent demonstration I went on was across the Rhine in 1945, with what was then called the British Liberation Army. In a world full of actual violence, as in Vietnam, or in the shootings of radical leaders such as Martin Luther King and Rudi Dutschke, it's difficult to use the same word about what are mainly scuffles in the streets. I think we have to remember that violence can be present in an established order where all is superficially calm, just because the reserves of sheer power are effective.

I don't think men who disturb such an order can be honestly charged with beginning violence. But is our society like that? In more ways perhaps than we're prepared to admit. But what I've mainly noticed in recent demonstrations is the frustration of more rational political procedures, breaking out into the streets in an excited militancy and being responded to stupidly. We can measure the degree by the discipline of the British police relative to those of other countries. Even here the situation is under extreme strain, with provocation by a small minority of demonstrators, but also because of the incomprehension of many authorities, who see keeping the peace as keeping their peace, and keeping law and order as keeping their law and order, against the challenge they call, so significantly, 'unofficial'.

It is necessary to say soberly and quietly that the decay and corruption of the political system, and the intolerable violence now actually directed against the poor of the world, will go on being fought by all effective means; and that unless the demonstrations grow into a new and open political movement, that fight will be ugly. Under a strain like this, it's time, not simply for those of us who are demonstrators, who want a new democratic politics, but for the society itself, a society more and more openly based on money and power, to change and be changed.

'You're a Marxist, Aren't You?'

1975

'You're a Marxist, aren't you?' This question would be difficult but not too difficult to answer, if only it ever got asked. But what happens instead of a question is, in my experience, something rather different. There is a kind of flat labelling with this term 'Marxist', which became increasingly common during the 1960s and is now a matter of course. I find, looking into my own experience, that I get described as a Marxist here and there in all sorts of contexts and with all sorts of implications. I looked myself up once in the *Anatomy of Britain* and found myself described as 'the Marxist Professor of Communications' and I thought: 'well, I'm not a professor, I don't teach communications; I don't know whether the first term of the description would be more or less accurate than the others.' Then again, I mix a good deal in what is known in the orthodox press as the extreme Left, which is now composed of many different and in some senses competing organizations. There one very common tactic of argument is to say that somebody is 'not a Marxist', in much the flat way that is used from the other side. Or there is the formulation which has become very familiar (almost as familiar as that famous one from between the wars, 'it is no accident that ...'): the flat announcement that 'this position has nothing in common with Marxism'. Inside the militant socialist organizations, the revolutionary socialist organizations, you hear this kind of argument all the time. People say it to each other about positions which, from the outside, get the one flat label 'Marxist'.

Now it used to be that the political position and the intellectual outlook which I broadly hold were called, with much the same flatness, 'Communist'. One would be referred to as a Communist whether or not one actually carried the party card of membership in the Communist Party or in one of the rival Communist organizations. There was a spectrum which was described as Communist. But that seems to have been replaced by 'Marxist' as this rather flat general term. I suppose the change is, in its most serious part, a recognition of the fact that the world Communist and socialist movement has become ever more deeply divided, that there are rival centres of Communist and Marxist orthodoxy, of which the opposition between the Soviet Union and the People's Republic of China is only the most obvious, and that it is then recognized that it is possible to hold many different and indeed alternative positions on the revolutionary socialist Left. But also I think it is a matter of academic accommodation. In the last ten or fifteen years some knowledge of the Marxist position has got into the universities, and it is then felt, perhaps from both sides, that Marxist is a more polite term than Communist, which might take us back to the days of the Cold War. Yet I often wish, in the description of some particular position, that one were still called a Communist or a revolutionary socialist rather than flatly a Marxist, with all the difficulties that particular description seems to me to entail. I want to discuss some of these difficulties, but must first indicate some reasons for this preference.

For I am bound to say that when I look at the development of socialist thought, when I look at the dependence of many of the most creative periods in socialist thought on the whole experience of the working class, and on democratic and national liberation movements, moreover when I look at the whole temper of that thought and action, and indeed, the temper of the best of what I know as Marxism, it seems to me wrong, in some ways fundamentally wrong, to have a whole tradition, or a whole emphasis within the tradition, reduced to being named after the work of a single thinker, however great. I want to make it clear, when I say this, that Marx is for me, as for many others, incomparably the greatest thinker in the socialist tradition; that his work seems to me still, in many of its parts, very much alive; and that in that sense no honour could be too great for him. Nevertheless, to specialize a militant tradition in which, literally, millions of men have participated, or an intellectual tradition in which thousands of men have participated, to a single name, has an emphasis contrary to what I think should be its real spirit. Moreover, the transition from Marx to Marxism is itself a matter of very complicated history and we have always to remember Marx's own observation that he was not a Marxist.

Now this false specialization – this reduction of a modern mass movement to a single name, as if it were one of the old friends of academic or religious or intellectual schools – is very important. But it is nowhere so important as the issues to which it points, the controversies which it contains and disguises. We all have to try to make our position clear, in relation to those issues and within those controversies, and I also felt the need for some time to try to make my own position clear in respect of this particular kind of description. Back in 1959, in London, we had a founding meeting of the *New Left Review*. It was then a review edited by a different group of people from those who now edit it, although I see an essential continuity between that original foundation and its present work. But that meeting in 1959 was not only the matter of founding a review. Many people felt that some new political direction was needed and that in such a review a new political direction was being found. In the very particular circumstances of the late 1950s we were all trying to define this position. I spoke at the meeting and the definition I offered was that the two major traditions of socialism seemed to me to have broken down. This had become most apparent in the period since the end of the war in 1945, and was now inescapable. This fact that they had broken down imposed a new kind of challenge to socialist activists and thinkers, and in this sense it was reasonable to talk about the need for a new Left. The term 'New Left', with particularizing capital letters, had not then been invented. Nor was it invented, at first, by those to whom it has since been applied. It drifted in. There is of course a certain modishness if a group announces itself as the New Left. There are periods when everything is described as 'new' in an almost obligatory way. The decade which is most conspicuous in this respect is the 1890s. The notion of self-announcement as 'new' or as 'modern' seems to me always very doubtful. But that there was need for a new direction, a quite new direction, I did not and do not doubt.

Now the two traditions which had broken down, I went on to define in this way. On the one hand, Stalinism. On the other hand, that inevitability of gradualism which you can call, in shorthand, Fabianism. Neither Stalinism nor Fabianism, which in the 1930s had seemed the two main competitors in the socialist political tradition, any longer offered us either an acceptable intellectual system or a viable mode of political action. So some quite new direction had to be found. The reason for feeling that Stalinism had broken down is perhaps the most obvious. It was a very great shock for a whole generation of socialists to live through from the 1930s to the 1950s with the steady accumulation of overwhelming evidence of all that had gone wrong with the Russian Revolution. But even more it was the sense that this had gone wrong not only because of historical accidents and historical circumstances but that there was something within the degeneration itself whch related to a political system and a political theory and not just to a man. Indeed it was a sign that Stalinism was not ended in the society which had generated it, that it was reduced in their kind of discussion to something called 'the cult of the individual', or in certain other explanations to the machinations of a particular evil personality. For me at least, and I think for many others, there was a real if not inevitable progression from a mainline version of the dictatorship of the proletariat through the control of the vanguard party to the Stalinist regime which in its ultimate development was an outrage to everything that the socialist tradition and indeed the best of the Bolshevik tradition had stood for. So it was not merely a case of leaving a sinking ship at a time of great stress. Indeed, many people had hung on through the periods of stress – had hung on to what they called 'a belief in the Soviet Union' – because the issue had posed itself in that way, that they should hang on, come what may, when the going was tough. This, after all, had been a real part of the history of the socialist and labour movements. But there was now a recognition that there was something more general than this. A particular kind of politics had played itself out, with a certain completeness. In a different situation it might have been limited, it might have gone differently, but still there was something in that kind of politics which one had to recognize had reached an effective dead end.

But then, as we saw this, we saw equally clearly that the apparently alternative tradition – that of Fabianism, the British Labour Party, the modern social democratic parties – indeed the whole tradition summed up as the inevitability of gradualism, was equally at an end. It had been a very acceptable tradition to people who had been living in the political democracies, who were well aware of the difficulties of starting a violent revolution and of the chances of exceptional hardship and indeed of repression if a revolution made in such circumstances was to be maintained. It was attractive also because it seemed to have a ready base in institutions which were already available. In parliament, in public argument, by public education, little by little, gradually, but with a certain inbuilt inevitable tendency, a capitalist society would be steadily pushed back and replaced by a socialist society. Few people had really doubted the inevitability of that kind of gradualism. Why then did we feel that it had ended?

Well, first, there was the history of the 1945–51 Labour government. Even more there was the reaction in the 1950s inside the labour movement to that experience. It was clear that certain major social reforms had been carried through in the early years of that postwar Labour government, largely the inherited commitments of the Party. It was also clear that overshadowing and finally continuing these was the period of rearmament, the increasing involvement with the political economy of the United States, the movement towards NATO, the whole postwar military and political establishment in which the Labour government had taken an enthusiastic and leading part, and against which the protests of parts of the labour movement had been quite unavailing. It was this double movement – a limited reform within a more powerful and opposite kind of development – which made me feel that to talk about the inevitability of gradualism was stupid and in the end vicious. It radically underestimated the historical process. Gradual changes might indeed be brought about by legislation and even more by changes in public opinion, changes in education and so on. But what this kind of politics really assumed was that there was not an enemy, there was only something out of date. Indeed this was a very popular interpretation: that the political, economic and social arrangements of England were simply hopelessly out of date and needed to be, as the word came through in the sixties, 'modernized'. As Orwell had put it: England was a decent family with the wrong members in charge; if you got rid of these wrong members you got rid of the old outdated institutions, and then gradually and inevitably you established a better form of society. It was all there as material to be worked on, waiting to be worked on, with a certain historical inevitability about it. But this was a radical underestimate of any real situation. Not only were there direct enemies who would defeat and absorb us: by violence, by fraud or by purchase (and the mode of purchase was widely used). Even more there was a sense in which the very changes themselves seemed the creation not of the society that had been foreseen but of a curious hybrid which might be a more dangerous because more durable form of the society which it had set out to change. It was not only, that is to say, that the gradualism was not inevitable, that it was not moving step by steady step towards a socialist society. It was that the very forms of the gradualism seemed to be ways of incorporating the movement which had set out to create a socialist society; indeed forms of conscious preservation of an unaltered, or only marginally altered, capitalist society. And this is where the reaction inside the labour movement in the fifties had seemed, to people like myself, decisive. We began to get alternative definitions of 'socialism' which did not envisage the transformation of the basic economic and political institutions of society. Socialism meant something rather different, we were told. It meant more kindly, more equal and more caring social relationships. What had been called capitalism was now called 'private enterprise', 'free enterprise', 'the private sector'. Most Labour spokesmen went along with this rhetoric of a 'free world'. But this was then the outlook and the programme of a fairly decent but also fairly modest Liberal Party. It had abandoned the analysis that the basic ownership of the means of production, distribution and exchange determined the character of the society or at least set limits to the possibilities of its social relationships. As such, in my view, it had abandoned the possibility of understanding or changing the modern world. And so, rightly or wrongly, people in my position felt that on the one hand Stalinism as a political mode had ended, and now Fabianism as a political mode had ended. There was no possibility simply of moving from one to the other, or even of thinking one was spending one's life usefully engaged in a debate between them. On the contrary, there had to be some different base for the socialist movement and a socialist interpretation of the world.

Now it was at this point, of course, that all the contradictions of the British labour movement itself, indeed of Western social democracy itself, became apparent. Well before the postwar period, the contradictory tendencies within the British labour movement and the Labour Party, had been articulated many times. It was interesting that the 1950s ended with a debate on the retention of Clause Four of the Labour Party Constitution – the socialist commitment – which on the one hand retained it liberally, representing in that sense a survival of the verbal tradition, but on the other hand, in practice, settled down to a programme conceived on quite other grounds, that of making capitalism more efficient and in sharing its profits building a more socially responsible society. Much earlier than that, indeed from the beginning if you read the history, there had been such dispute about basic principles. What I used to hear as a boy working in the labour movement in the thirties was that the British labour movement owed more to Methodism and what I knew I did not like, so I was quite prepared to believe that this was said as an explanation of the inadequacies of the Labour Party. But it always seemed, when I looked again, that it was said as a form of self-congratulation and the more I thought about it the less I saw that they had to be pleased about. Here was a nation of which two thirds were working-class people, and it was still unpleasantly ruled by a stupid and vicious capitalist ruling class, with residual aristocratic pretensions. What was true was that the Labour Party owed a great deal to the method of self-organization of the British working people, of which some aspects of nonconformist organization were simply a part. And in this sense, as a movement, it was primarily practical. It was the self-organization of very hard pressed people to maintain their lives, to better their conditions, and eventually as the eyes were lifted, to transform their society.

The neglect of Marx could have been understood. The positive and complacent exclusion was a very much more serious matter, for it was a deliberate exclusion of theory: not so much of this theory as of any theory; and the real reason for this was that in practice the Labour leadership shared the ruling-class view of the world. They did not need theory; they had their world and there were only practical arguments about their place in it. But the specific and challenging theory which they excluded was Marxism. Now here we have to recognize that what Marx meant, what Marxism is, are properly the subject of intense controversy. In the last ten years, especially in Western Europe and North America, there has been an extraordinary revival of serious study of Marx. This has not been simply popular exposition but is the most searching and at the same time the most scholarly kind of enquiry that has taken place since before the First World War. The benefits of this in the long run are going to be very considerable. But in the position in which we have been since the war, when we have tried to identify the work of Marx and the Marxist tradition, in order, for example, to understand that contrast between Marx and methodism in the sources of the British Labour Party, there has been a competition of emphasis, a competition of selections of what Marx meant, what Marxism really is, and this has certainly not meant that there is brevity and clarity in the demonstration or in the argument. There is, of course, still substantial common ground. And in relation to this common ground, I find no difficulty in affiliating myself with this movement as a whole. The fundamental approach of historical materialism, as Marx defined it, seems to me to be profoundly true. Men make their own history within certain limits that are set by the conditions of their social development, conditions which are themselves profoundly affected by the state of their economic relations which are in turn related to a particular stage of the mode of production. But at every point in a summary like that there is in practice detailed and important dispute about what exactly is meant and implied. Nevertheless, if you hold that general position you arrive at an important general view of history, and especially of the development of capitalist society. You find a perspective on the relations between capitalist and industrial society, and on the relations between capitalism and imperialism. You find, moreover, that you have to believe that the attainment of a socialist society means the transformation of society, the movement from one whole social order to another.

Next, and decisively, you find you have to believe – and in this, from my whole experience, I was well prepared – that this transformation of society has an enemy. Not just an electoral enemy or a traditional enemy, but a hostile and organized social formation which is actively trying to defeat and destroy you. Now this recognition of an enemy is something that the inevitability of gradualism had not allowed for, unless we are to suppose – and such complacent fantasies have occasionally occurred – that its policy of cunning permeation was a way of dissolving an enemy without him noticing. But the real question about an enemy was always this. Was this the kind of enemy who could be defeated by the normal processes of civil society; that is to say by the processes of political democracy, parliamentary democracy, trade union action, social organization and so on? Or was this an enemy who had to be defeated by power, and in the last instance, if necessary, by actual violent defeat? If we look at the history it is clear that within the Marxist movement itself, and within the socialist movement much more generally, this has been one of the most fertile causes for dispute, division, splits and hostilities between different parts of the movement. And this is not, as it might seem, simply a question about strategy and tactics. At a certain point it necessarily goes back to some of the original formulations about the nature of the society, the nature of capitalism, the nature of the transition to imperialism, all of which can be interpreted in this or that way, to indicate that a particular contemporary strategy is correct. It is said that no solution which fails to include the violent capture of state power is either reasonable or honest. Or it is said that any solution which does so include the violent capture of state power is unacceptable because it is undemocratic. These are the positions around which so much of the debate has often rather abstractly moved. Abstractly because the debate often flourishes with particular intensity when neither possibility seems much in view.

Now as I think through the basic positions of historical materialism, the basic definition of capitalist society and its evolution, and then the need to supersede it, to go beyond capitalist society, so that a socialist society, as apart from isolated measures of a socialist tendency, demands the destruction of capitalist society, as I think through these three propositions and try to define myself in relation to them, I have no real hesitation. These are all positions from which I now see the world and in terms of which I try to order my life and my activity. Someone may say: 'it is where you stand on the third point, about the means of transformation, that really defines whether you are Marxist or not, whether you are Communist on the one hand or democratic socialist, social democrat, on the other.' Well, is it really so? This is where I search my experience as much as the theory. I grew up in a working-class family, with a father who fought in the First World War, in an atmosphere in which militant trade unionism and a hatred of war, that amounted almost to conscious pacifism, were almost equally intermixed. When I look back I can see that this was the history of much of the Left in the thirties, that we were at once militant about the transformation of society and pacifist about war. But we were not allowed to live with those contradictions. By 1944 I, who had called myself a pacifist in 1938, was in Normandy. I remember a day when there was a counter-attack by an SS tank regiment and it did seem to me even then, even in that sort of circumstance, that a particular point in my life had in a way clarified and in another way been clarified for me. I found it important that they were the SS and not just German soldiers, still less the Ukrainian and other miscellaneous conscripts from the Hitler Empire who were usually put in front to absorb our attack. That these were the

SS had very great significance. It gave a meaning of the kind I already knew, by report, from the Spanish War. Since that time I have never been able to say that the use of military power to defend a revolution is something that I am against. On the contrary I believe that a revolution which is not prepared to defend itself by military power is meaningless. But this, it can be said, is evading the question. Do you agree with *making* a revolution by military power? Yet here again, having seen the violence with which, when it matters, a repressive system is maintained, I can find no principle by which I could possibly exclude this. When I look at the history of the Chinese, the Cuban and the Vietnamese revolutions, I feel a basic solidarity not merely with their aims but with their methods and with the ways in which they came to power. If I found myself in Britain in any comparable social and political situation, I know where my loyalties would lie.

But of course we don't only find ourselves in situations, we also make situations. If we are to be serious about this question we have to relate our understanding of the society and the nature of our activities to the situation that we want to create, and in which we can act. And I am then very close to the development of the late sixties and the early seventies in North America and in Europe, where with the clarity of a new generation, so many people moved to direct action and beyond the first meanings of direct action to certain kinds of chosen confrontations with state power. I find it very difficult to say that this is wrong in some absolute sense. I see hypocrisy in the facile and orthodox condemnation of 'violence' in states which have either established or maintained themselves by violence and which use it with barely a second thought against so many of the peoples of the world. And yet I do not believe that in societies with functioning political democracies, in societies with very complicated kinds of social organization, these are the only or even the main forms of revolutionary activity. I believe the politics of confrontation is an inevitable response, within a particular balance of forces, to the authoritarianism of the characteristic modern state. And yet, commonly, it is not revolutionary activity. Indeed in some of its extreme forms it is quite clearly in a different tradition. It is in the tradition of one kind of anarchism or of terrorism, and at definite points, as it develops in that direction, I have to part company with it, because I think that it misunderstands the nature of the existing social struggle.

When the New Left was developing in many parts of the world, and particularly as it developed in North America, this kind of politics was often taken as the feature which most identified it: the politics of direct action. But here I think a very necessary distinction needs to be made. In North America the policy of direct action by students and others, like the policy of work in the community, was linked with a theoretical tendency which has also been widely identified with the New Left but which from the beginning I never shared and which, in my experience, very few other members of the British New Left shared. This theoretical position was that the potential of the industrial working class for changing society had, in western capitalist societies at least, been exhausted; indeed it may never, some said, have existed at all. And since this was so, other means of transforming the capitalist state had to be looked for – other 'agencies', to use the term that became popular in the sixties, other 'constituencies', other modes of social change. But as I said, I have never believed this. I believe that in Britain since the war the fundamental resistance to capitalist state power, whether the agency of that power is a Conservative or a Labour government has been from the industrial working class. As I wrote some years ago, there would be very little resistance to contemporary capitalist society if it were not for industrial militancy, in all its forms of pressure and of course in strikes whether official or unofficial. Indeed, it was always true of the British New Left, as it was not of the North American New Left, that the industrial working class and its activities remained central. I am sure that this is now even more true. Nevertheless, there is a combination of that kind of belief in the activity of the industrial working class with the methods of parliamentary pressure and of working towards a parliamentary majority, and this, I think, is not the position of the New Left, but more the position of the left wing of social democracy or the left of the Labour Party. And it is at this point that distinctions become necessary – although to the notions of Marxism.

What we thought we saw emerging in the 1960s was a new form of corporate state; and the emphasis on culture, which was often taken as identifying our position, was an emphasis, at least in my own case, on the process of social and cultural incorporation, according to which it is something more than simply property or power which maintains the structures of capitalist society. Indeed, in seeking to define this, it was possible to look again at certain important parts of the Marxist tradition, notably the work of Gramsci with his emphasis on hegemony. We could then say that the essential dominance of a particular class in society is maintained not only, although if necessary, by power, and not only, although always, by property. It is maintained also and inevitably by a lived culture: that saturation of habit, of experience, of outlook, from a very early age and continually renewed at so many stages of life, under definite pressures and within definite limits, so that what people come to think and feel is in large measure a reproduction of the deeply based social order which they may even in some respects think they oppose and indeed actually oppose. And if this is so, then again the tradition of

Stalinism and the tradition of Fabianism are equally irrelevant. Simply to capture state power and set about changing that hegemony by authoritarian redirection and manipulation involves either unacceptable repression or is in any case a radical underestimate of the real process of human change that has to occur. And Fabianism, with its administrative measures, its institutional reconstructions, does not even seem aware of this problem at all, or if it is, regards it as a problem of the 'low level of consciousness' of what it calls the 'uneducated' or, like Stalinism, the 'masses'. But this is the most crucial underestimate of the enemy. Can I put it in this way? I learned the experience of incorporation, I learned the reality of hegemony, I learned the saturating power of the structures of feeling of a given society, as much from my own mind and my own experience as from observing the lives of others. All through our lives, if we make the effort, we uncover layers of this kind of alien formation in ourselves, and deep in ourselves. So then the recognition of it is a recognition of large elements in *our own* experience, which have to be – shall we say it? – defeated. But to defeat something like that in yourself, in your families, in your neighbours, in your friends, to defeat it involves something very different, it seems to me, from most traditional political strategies.

So, I arrived at a position which at that stage seemed to me very different from Marxism, or at least from what most people said was Marxism, including many orthodox Marxists. And as I developed this position people said that I was not a Marxist. It doesn't really matter, as I said at the beginning, which label is adopted. But in understanding cultural hegemony and in seeing it as the crucial dimension of the kind of society which has been emerging since the war under advanced capitalism, I felt the break both from mainline Marxism and even more from the traditions of social democracy, liberalism and Fabianism, which had been my immediate inheritance.

So if I am asked finally to define my own position, I would say this. I believe in the necessary economic struggle of the organized working class. I believe that this is still the most creative activity in our society, as I indicated years ago in calling the great working-class institutions creative cultural achievements, as well as the indispensable first means of political struggle. I believe that it is not necessary to abandon a parliamentary perspective as a matter of principle, but as a matter of practice I am quite sure that we have to begin to look beyond it. For reasons that I described in *The Long Revolution* and again in *The May Day Manifesto* I think that no foreseeable parliamentary majority will inaugurate socialism unless there is a quite different kind of political activity supporting it, activity which is quite outside the scope or the perspective of the British Labour Party or of any other likely candidate for that kind of office. Such activity involves the most active elements of community politics, local campaigning, specialized interest campaigning: all the things that were the real achievements of the politics of the sixties and that are still notably active. But finally, for it is the sphere in which I am most closely involved, I know that there is a profoundly necessary job to do in relation to the processes of the cultural hegemony itself. I believe that the system of meanings and values which a capitalist society has generated has to be defeated in general and in detail by the most sustained kinds of intellectual and educational work. This is a cultural process which I called 'the long revolution' and in calling it 'the long revolution' I meant that it was a genuine struggle which was part of the necessary battles of democracy and of economic victory for the organized working class. People change, it is true, in struggle and by action. Anything as deep as a dominant structure of feeling is only changed by active new experience. But this does not mean that change can be remitted to action otherwise conceived. On the contrary the task of a successful socialist movement will be one of feeling and imagination quite as much as one of fact and organization. Not imagination or feeling in their weak senses – 'imagining the future' (which is a waste of time) or 'the emotional side of things'. On the contrary, we have to learn and to teach each other the connections between a political and economic formation, a cultural and educational formation, and, perhaps hardest of all, the formations of feeling and relationship which are our immediate resources in any struggle. Contemporary Marxism, extending its scope to this wider area, learning again the real meanings of totality, is, then, a movement to which I find myself belonging and to which I am glad to belong.

The Writer: Commitment and Alignment

1980

Some people, when they see an idea, think the first thing to do is to argue about it. But while this passes the time and has the advantage of keeping them warm it has little else to recommend it. If there is one thing we should have learned from the Marxist tradition it is that ideas are always representations of things people are actually doing or feel themselves prevented from doing. So that the first way to look at the idea of commitment is not as at some general notion about which we can at once argue, citing this or that historical case, but rather to see why the notion of commitment was developed and against what alternative ideas it was directed.

In fact the matters at issue have been discussed in many terms. Commitment became the normal term, in our own time, because of the famous intervention by Jean-Paul Sartre at the end of the war when he wrote:

> If literature is not everything it is worth nothing. This is what I mean by 'commitment'. It wilts if it is reduced to innocence or to songs. If a written sentence does not reverberate at every level of man and society then it makes no sense. What is the literature of an epoch, but the epoch appropriated by its literature?[1]

It was in this sense that a long-standing argument was concentrated around the notion of commitment. But immediately with a certain difficulty. First that Sartre, quite wrongly in my view, said that this should only apply to prose, that poetry was something else. But it is very difficult to argue this case for one kind of writing in ways that make it clear

---

1. Jean-Paul Sartre, *Between Existentialism and Marxism*, London 1974, pp. 13–14.

why you should exclude the same demands on another kind of writing. The distinction between prose and poetry that Sartre tried to make confused the argument from the beginning. Second, and much more seriously, the unstated background of Sartre's intervention was a very specific historical and political context. It was within the climate of the Resistance. It was moreover at a time of real possibilities of significant movement, in France as in other parts of Western Europe, towards a new kind of democracy. The engagement of intellectuals of all kinds, and especially writers, in those great collective movements which had come from anti-fascist war and resistance, had an immediate, concentrated and urgent social resonance. On the other hand in England, by the time the idea had taken its usual inordinate time to cross the Channel (because that must be one of the longest cultural journeys in existence by comparison with the physical distance) it fell into the most difficult times.

Then it sounded like, and of course correctly sounded like, a well-known position in the 1930s. The positions of the British left writers in the thirties, although they were not normally assembled around the term 'commitment', were directed towards the same essential idea. But in the late forties and early fifties it was another time. It was the beginning of the Cold War. There were then three kinds of backlash against the idea.

First, and we should not forget this, there was a backlash against the cause to which those writers had been committed. This was the time when we had to look at the other face of that generation of the thirties. It is true that many of the best had died in Spain or in the general European war. But we had also the beginning of that extraordinary and terrible period in which one writer after another from the thirties renounced what he had then believed in, and explained in what was meant to be a charming and pathetic – anyway an apologetic – manner how he had been taken in or fooled or something of that kind. There were some writers who didn't move in this way but their views tended to be less publicized. By the early fifties you could line up a whole series of writers who said 'Yes, of course, I was like that in my foolish youth, but now I know better.' And from that it was no distance at all to saying that writers should keep out of that kind of political and especially left-political thing. That was the first reason why the argument got off to a very bad start after the war.

Second, there was one very severe problem that ought to be intellectually distinguished from this but of course was not. For there were phases, including the Stalin phase, in the Soviet Union, when the notion of commitment could easily be related to the practice of an authority above the writer which was telling him what to write and how to write. 'We know what you mean by commitment. You don't want to be a real writer, you want yourself and others to be party hacks.' And the fact that some – too many – real historical instances could be quoted to support this made clarity very difficult to sustain. Yet at its best this was always a dispute *inside* the socialist movement. There is still no better statement on this whole matter than that of Brecht, a Communist writer, in the 1930s, replying to an article by the Hungarian Marxist then in Moscow, Georg Lukács. Brecht said of that whole tendency:

> They are, to put it bluntly, enemies of production. Production makes them uncomfortable. You never know where you are with production; production is unforeseeable. You never know what is going to come out. And they themselves don't want to produce. They want to play the apparatchik and exercise control over other people. Every one of their criticisms contains a threat.[2]

So there was a principled position, inside the socialist movement, which could enable a totally committed writer like Brecht to make the necessary distinction between a commitment to production linked to a cause, and on the other hand a subservience to some version of desirable production arbitrarily decided by a party and its ideologists. This remains a crucial distinction, but it was very difficult to sustain it in the period of cold war and that mood of confession of errors which was weakening the confidence of a whole generation of writers. In practice the two very different ideas – of commitment and of subservience – were pushed together and seemed to support each other.

Third, there was a certain backlash among those few left writers who kept their heads through this difficult period. And it was an intensely difficult period, because it was so complex. There was an understandable wariness of what can quite properly be called opportunism. This, then as now, was not the reality of commitment but a careerist version of it. Commitment still meant, at its best, taking social reality, historical reality, the development of social and historical reality, as the centres of attention, and then finding some of the hundreds of ways in which all those processes can be written. On the other hand, at its worst, it could be a superficial kind of writing which took care to include the political references that went with the cry of the moment. If we want an authority on this we have in one of his grumpier moods no less an authority than Engels, who said:

> It became more and more the habit, particularly of the inferior sorts of *literati*, to make up for the want of cleverness in their productions by political

2. Quoted in Walter Benjamin, 'Talking to Brecht', *NLR* 77, January–February 1973.

allusions which were sure to attract attention. Poetry, novels, reviews, the drama, every literary production teemed with what was called 'tendency'.[3]

This was only a few years after Marx had referred to work like that of Eugene Sue as 'the most wretched offal of socialist literature.'[4] And Engels, in an even grumpier mood, thirty years later, talked about 'a worthless fellow who, due to lack of talent, has gone to extremes with tendentious junk to show his convictions, but it is really in order to gain an audience.'[5] Now I don't quote these remarks because we should believe everything Marx or Engels said. In fact, in the later mood, Engels was moving, as in his literary tastes he often did, towards a slightly grumpy bourgeois position rather than necessarily towards a Marxist one. But it is very important, if we are to have honesty on the Left, that we should be quite clear that there is a kind of opportunism which can usurp the idea of commitment, by catching the political cry of the moment whether or not it has any significant reference to the central experience or the integrity of the writing. This is the false commitment of the inserted political reference. It is not what Sartre or anyone else who has taken the idea seriously can mean by commitment.

Anyway this third backlash, this wariness, developed, and in the middle of it one further fact was discovered, one which was memorably expressed by the German Marxist Adorno. He made the point that if you propose commitment you have to recognize that it is what he called 'politically polyvalent'.[6] That is to say, if you ask writers to commit themselves, you can have no certainty at all that they are going to commit themselves to any particular cause. It would have been easier if it had been true that writers of significance could never commit themselves to fascism, or to the most archaic kinds of conservatism, or to the softer kinds of liberalism. But indeed if the idea of commitment is there but undefined, as in the rhetoric it often is, such writers indeed come out, take a position about social reality, engage with political struggle. Indeed this is happening from the right all the time. Then if that is so, at whatever level it is done, in actual writing or in some more general capacity, there can of course be no guarantee that commitment is intrinsically progressive, as some people had assumed. On its own, that is to say, the usual idea of commitment is bound to be polyvalent. We used to have arguments at the end of the thirties about whether a good writer

3. Friedrich Engels, *New York Daily Tribune*, 28 October 1851.

4. Karl Marx, 'The Holy Family', in Lee Baxandall and Stefan Marawski, eds, *Marx and Engels on Literature and Art*, St Louis 1973, p. 121.

5. Friedrich Engels, Letter to Eduard Bernstein, 17 August 1881, Baxandall and Marawski, p. 125.

6. Theodor Adorno, 'Commitment', *NLR* 87/88. September–December 1974.

could be a fascist. It seemed to us then that there was something wrong if that could be so, and some people found themselves in quite extra-ordinary positions, saying either 'yes, he is a fascist but then he is not a very good writer', or 'he may be a good writer but of course he is politically naive'. It is better to recognize social reality, which in our own time as in others has produced good and even great reactionary writers, as well as all the others whom we may prefer, for different reasons, to honour and remember.

Those were bad, confused times. Yet it can happen that the bad times teach us as much as the good times. When there is intellectual confusion, when you undergo a great deal of political rhetoric, when you have all sorts of recriminations and divisions inside your own movement, there is still a chance to learn from within such developments. In the case of a general idea there is a chance to learn what is significant in it and what on the other hand is insignificant or meretricious. And that I think, although people are still nervous of it, is what has been happening in more recent thinking.

There has been a change from the sixties onwards after the end of that confused and frightened period. Actually 'commitment' is still not the word most commonly used because, given that history, there is still a lot of nervousness about it. What we have come to understand, I think, is that commitment was not, for the most part, a positive proposition. It was mainly a response to another position which had become very general and which it wanted to challenge. This was the position that the artist, by definition, must be a free individual; that to be an artist is to be a free individual. Of course there is a version of commitment which can include that, because if you are a free individual you can choose to commit yourself. This was really what Sartre was saying. But to others such commitment was a cancellation of freedom. How can you commit yourself to anything except the practice of your own heart? Is the artist then not necessarily the very type of the free individual?

Now this is an important general case. And one of the advantages of looking at it within Marxist thought is this: that we can see when the idea of the artist as a free individual arose, and this in turn throws important light on the history of the practice of writing and of its always difficult social relations. For the idea of the artist as the type of the free individual in fact arose in the late eighteenth and early nineteenth centuries; that is to say in the period of two very important changes. On the one hand there was the emergence of a new libertarianism in literature, primarily in the Romantic movement. On the other hand the conditions of writing and publishing were changing in unprecedented ways, which on the one hand gave a new professional independence to successful writers, and on the other hand marginalized certain sectors of writing to such an extent that the possibility of feeling related to and wanted by society – either as a whole or by any part of it – had for that kind of writer been in effect excluded.

Now we should not reduce this development to any one of these three factors. All three are crucial in the developing notion of the free artist. The free artist of the Romantic movement was arguing for a kind of freedom which identified itself, in many cases, with the most general human liberation. He was arguing against the tyranny of Church and State, indeed against any authority which tried to dictate to the artist what he should think or write. He was also arguing against the tyranny of artistic rules. There is a standard Romantic complaint against what they defined and opposed as classicist imitation: rules of how to write well; rules of what to write about; rules of how any particular subject should be handled; rules which had been taken to a point, at least theoretically, as definitive, so that the test of good writing was the extent to which you showed the qualities of this known craft, with all its rules and its skills. The new claim that a writer must be free to break the rules, must be free to innovate, free to create works as the experience required, whether or not this corresponded with preexisting notions: that was the important claim of the Romantic movement, and it was accompanied by a conscious revolt against any authorities which would try to seize or suppress or discriminate against new writing of such kinds.

On the other hand the literary market which was then becoming more organized had a very curious double-edged effect. If you were a certain kind of novelist, from about the 1830s, you could become a successful professional man in a way that very few writers had been before. And although this was obviously most true for the most successful, still, given the extraordinary expansion of magazine publications, the cheapening of books and the huge growth of the newspaper and periodical press, the opportunities for a very large number of writers were much wider than those in any preceding period. But of course this was a freedom to go out and compete in that market. So that what came through at this level was the professional ideology of the independent artist, who was defining freedom in this very special sense, that he must be free to compete in the market. In effect he was then taking the market as a definition of his social province, his real social relations. And since society was represented by the market, there could be no question of any other significant social commitments. This is a classic bourgeois definition of freedom.

On the other hand, in other areas of writing, and notably in poetry, the economic situation of writers was moving quite the other way. Certain kinds of writing were marginalized, for the market was replacing earlier systems of patronage, and in the market such writing as poetry was at best a marginal product, at worst quite unwanted. So alongside the newly successful literary professional, claiming his professional freedom but claiming it so that he could enter the market (which would tell him what society wanted) was the unwanted writer, who was soon mythicized as the starving genius. There were indeed some of these; and the starving would-be genius, there were some of them too. But at its worst it became a model of what a serious writer ought to be. You can still find people who think it is something which proves you are a real writer. It was a myth which seemed all the more attractive in this market society in which the leading writers were becoming more and more professionally established solid citizens.

Now we can see what a very complex idea this proposition that the artist must be free is. In one sense who would wish to dissent from it? Who would suppose that we are likely to get better writing if some appointed authority is at the writer's elbow, looking over his shoulder, advising him what to do? It isn't that writers don't benefit from advice; it's that there is an almost insoluble problem of getting the right advice and the right writer together: it is always more likely that you will get the wrong writer with the wrong advice. What we have really to understand is the set of ideas that were being fused in this notion of free independence, which we have really to take apart again if we are to understand the real situation. For the acceptance of the market as the guarantee of freedom is of course largely illusory. Although it is true that, at the point of success, the independent professional writer can operate very freely in the market, becoming himself a seller with a certain real independence, the average writer, and in these conditions these were the great majority, was dependent on the market in ways which were at least as severe and sometimes more severe than the earlier dependence of writers on patrons.

Patronage itself had passed through several stages, only some of which were deeply restrictive. In the very earliest forms patronage was an obligation. In feudal society, for example, it was the obligation of a household of a certain dignity to support and to give hospitality, to sustain the livelihood, of artists, poets, painters, musicians. Later there was a different type of patronage, in which courts, households and similar authorities hired writers and artists for specific commissions. In the course of that hiring every complaint came up that was subsequently heard in the market, but in the most favourable conditions there was a certain diversity; that if you ran into trouble with this patron you could take the work to another, as indeed in the early capitalist market. It was not a comfortable situation, it was not a good situation, but it does not necessarily compare unfavourably with the market. There is also another phase of patronage, which didn't depend on monetary exchange at all but was simply the offering of social support, social protection, and where necessary early encouragement. It often happened, of course, that support and protection were only offered to certain kinds of writing, from the notion that this was a good kind of writing to have done. But this was always potentially a different calculation – let us leave aside whether it was a better calculation – from what became for the market the single criterion, of whether this writing would *sell.* As the market developed this became and is becoming the only criterion. Indeed we are passing through now the biggest change in the writing and publishing market since the early nineteenth century. The criterion of desirability is the promise to sell, and, increasingly now, to sell fast, so that there are no expensive warehousing costs and other accounting considerations. This development set up, within the very conditions which appeared to guarantee freedom to the successful, constraints of a new kind, which however could not be recognized as obstacles to freedom because this was the very competitive area which most writers had sought. A bourgeois writer could not say 'it is the market which is restricting my freedom', because for him the market was his freedom. Yet it has always been clear that the market guides writers, restricts them, pushes them this way and that. It can be a very simple or a very complex process. It is extraordinarily difficult for any of us, as writers, to be honest about it.

The situation now, for example, at a very organized late stage of the market, is often this: that you want to write a particular work which happens to be of an inconvenient length, that length being your best estimate of what handling that material would be. You talk to a publisher or an editor about it, and he often says: 'Well, it's a pity about that length. But we've got an idea for a book in one of our series. Surely you can do that meanwhile.' And suppose this is, with luck, something which you thought someday you might write, but which you wouldn't have written just then, by the time you have decided to do it – and many people do – it has become what *you* want. Indeed unless you are absolutely ruthless with yourself, ruthless in your examination of your motives and especially your more complex adaptations, these pressured decisions come to take on the plausibility of your natural wishes, of your free development as a writer. And of course people say: 'Why should you be a primadonna?' 'Why shouldn't you write what people want?' Indeed the familiar phrases of commitment come back in the rhetoric of the sharply commercial editor: 'Don't you want to write what people are interested in?' 'What's the point of writing for yourself and a few friends?' So the market comes to seem a definition of social duty, even though publishers usually know a good deal less than writers about what people will like to read, as distinct from what they *have* liked. They are at least as often wrong as they are right, but in any case the notion of what people want which has passed through the market comes back as a strange kind of freedom. Yet many writers are afraid that if they say 'the market is not really free', then they deny the accessible basis of their own freedom. So what they talk about instead, in relation to freedom, is not of where they are. They talk about other situations, where the constraints are different: where there is state support of writers, for example, but of course not the state's support of all literature, indeed the refusal to publish certain kinds of book, and that is totalitarian. So indeed it often is. We have all to recognize the faults and deformities – sometimes the crimes – of such systems. Most of them are limited by the fact that public support operates only as *state* support; that will have to be changed, by new and more open kinds of procedure. Yet in any case we have also to look at freedom, and at its enemies, where we ourselves are.

Now I said at the beginning that it is a mistake, when you see an idea, to go straight into an argument about it. The trouble with most arguments about commitment is that they confuse two pairings. Either they confuse the notion of the artist having his own autonomy, which commitment is held to undermine, with the notion of being ordered by some central authority to do something. Or they confuse both with the idea of professional independence, which has been the historical situation of fortunate writers in our own kind of society. And at that point we have to attempt a further disentangling. I put into the title of this lecture not only the word 'commitment', but also the word 'alignment'. Of course in one weak sense 'alignment' is just another word for 'commitment'. But there is another sense of alignment, which I take very seriously and from which, I think, any serious contemporary argument about commitment must begin.

   Marxism, more clearly than any other kind of thinking, has shown us that we are in fact aligned long before we realize that we are aligned. For we are born into a social situation, into social relationships, into a family, all of which have formed what we can later abstract as ourselves as individuals. Much of this formation occurs before we can be conscious of any individuality. Indeed the consciousness of individuality is often the consciousness of all those elements of our formation, yet this can never be complete. The alignments are so deep. They are our normal ways of living in the world, our normal ways of seeing the world. Of course we may become intellectually aware that they are not normal in the sense that they are universal. We come to recognize that other people live differently, were born into different social relationships, see the world differently. Yet still, at certain deep levels – and this matters very much in writing – our own actual alignment is so inseparable from the constitution of our own individuality that to separate them is quite artificial. And then for a writer there is something even more specific: that he is born into a language; that his very medium is something which he will have learned as if it were natural, although of course he eventually knows that there are other very different languages. But still it is the medium in which he will work, the medium which he shares with his own people, and which has entered into his own constitution long before he begins to write. To be aligned to and by that language, with some of its deep qualities, is inevitable if he is to write at all. So, born into a social situation with all its specific perspectives, and into a language, the writer begins by being aligned.

Yet alignment goes deeper again, into the actual and available forms of writing. When I hear people talk about literature, describing what so-and-so did with that form – how did he handle the short novel? – I often think we should reverse the question and ask, how did the short novel handle him. Because anyone who has carefully observed his own practice of writing eventually finds that there is a point where, although he is holding the pen or tapping the typewriter, what is being written, while not separate from him, is not only him either, and of course this other force is literary form. Very few if any of us could write at all if certain forms were not available. And then we may be lucky, we may find forms which happen to correspond to our experience. But take the case of the nineteenth-century working-class writers, who wanted to write about their working lives. The most popular form was the novel, but though they had marvellous material that could go into the novel very few of them managed to write good or even any novels. Instead they wrote marvellous autobiographies. Why? Because the form coming down through the religious tradition was of the witness confessing the story of his life, or there was the defence speech at the trial when a man tells the judge who he is and what he has done, or of course other kinds of speech. These oral forms were more accessible, forms centred on 'I', on the single person. The novel with its quite different narrative forms was virtually impenetrable to working-class writers for three or four generations, and there are still many problems in using the received forms for what is, in the end, very different material. Indeed the forms of working-class consciousness are bound to be different from the literary forms of another class, and it is a long struggle to find new and adequate forms.

Now these are alignments of a deep type, and really I think the most serious case for commitment is that we should commit ourselves far enough to social reality to be conscious of this level of sociality. It means becoming conscious of our own real alignments. This may lead to us confirming them, in some situations. Or it can often lead to changing or shifting or amending them, a more painful process than it sounds. Some of the most publicized cases of 'commitment' are when people shift in this way from one set of beliefs and assumptions to another, and this can involve a quite radical shift in real practice. In fact even when we confirm our deepest alignments, but now very consciously and deliberately, something strange has happened and we feel quite differently committed. Because really to have understood the social pressures on our own thinking, or when we come to that wonderful although at first terrible realization that what we are thinking is what a lot of other people have thought, that what we are seeing is what a lot of other people have seen, that is an extraordinary experience. We can make this point negatively against all those people who appeal to the freedom of the individual artist within their own isolated terms. It is one of the most surprising things about most of them that they say, 'I only write as a free individual, I only write what I want to write', but in fact what they write is, in majority, already written and what everybody already knows. That of course is an illusion of freedom. But beyond it, under pressure, there is a very high kind of freedom. This is when you are free to choose, or to choose to try to alter, that which is really pressuring you, in your whole social formation, in your understanding of the possibilities of writing.

To be committed to that is nothing whatever to do with submission to anybody. It is the discovery of those social relationships which are in any case there. It is what I think Sartre meant by reverberation, resonance: that active consciousness of those social relationships which include ourselves and our practices. It is never likely to be a convenient discovery, in our kind of world. It permits very little in the way of being immediately signed up for somebody else's market or somebody else's policy. But when it really happens, in the many different ways that are possible, its sound is usually unmistakeable: the sound of that voice which, in speaking as itself, is speaking, necessarily, for more than itself. Whether we find such voices or not, it is worth committing ourselves to the attempt.

Art: Freedom as Duty

1978

We can think of the question of freedom and duty in art as a problem of balance – so much freedom against so much duty – a perpetual dialogue on the relations between these two apparently opposite qualities. I would not want to dispute the usefulness of that kind of argument; in many specific situations it is necessary. But I would like to say first, not merely in a paradoxical mood, that, in an important sense the first duty of the artist is to be free and that the first duty of social provision in the arts is to ensure freedom. It is necessary to say this because in very different conditions that freedom is now under very considerable threat. Typically the kind of threat that is cited is that characteristic of societies other than our own. Thus in the capitalist West we are very aware, rightly and necessarily aware, of threats to the freedom of the artist from authoritarian political systems: administrative measures and censorship, and various kinds of legal and political control. I believe as strongly as anyone that we must denounce those kinds of interference and show solidarity with all those who suffer from such interference.

But, just because I feel so strongly, I am aware also of the limitations on freedom in a quite different kind of society, such as our own, where the problems are those of commercial viability. There is, of course, a not inconsiderable area of difficulties of a more political and legal kind, but I am thinking of the commercial constraints primarily, where you can say that at times freedom in our kind of society amounts to the freedom to say anything you wish, provided you can say it profitably. That is to say, there is no problem about saying anything or writing anything except in the sense of finding normal distribution, normal working conditions. There is a deep correlation with profit, and this does impose constraints of a certain kind. In neither of those situations, neither that of authoritarian, political pressure nor that of commercial pressure, does an artist want to hear from one kind of person about duty, because duty is often simply the name for the exertion of that pressure: the duty to serve the state or serve the cause, the duty to entertain the public, or to write something that they want to read, which usually means something that fits somebody's marketing prediction about what others want to read. Against all these restraints on the artist's freedom we have to be very firm.

The philosophical defence of the freedom of the artist can be made in terms of his rights as an individual, or of his rights as an artist. I don't want to dispute either of these defences although they are not the way in which I would primarily put things myself. I think that the need for freedom in the arts is, above all, a *social* need. I think that the very process of writing is so crucial to the full development of our social life that we do, in an important sense, need every voice. The extreme complexity of any historical and social process being lived out in a particular place at a particular time, the extreme complexity of the interaction of individual lives with all those general conditions, means that you can never at any time say that you have enough voices or that you have representative voices, or that anybody can say in advance what are the important things either to be said or to be written about. This need for many voices is a condition of the cultural health of any complex society, and so the creation of conditions for the freedom of the artist is in that sense the duty of society, not for the sake of any individual artist and not in terms of some abstract argument about rights, but simply because society needs all the articulated experience and all the specific creation it can get.

That is why, among other reasons, I refuse to join in a way of talking about cultural production in our kind of society which I find very widespread and particularly, perhaps, in university, professional, literary, and cultural circles. I mean that way of talking in which it can be said that down every back street somebody is writing a novel, in every kitchen or on every suburban Sunday somebody is painting a picture, a sense really that the world is being overrun by writers and painters and artists of every kind, with a strong tone of condescension towards these pullulating amateurs which easily communicates itself as a professional tone. Now I've seen a good deal of this work myself as an adult education tutor, and what I am not intending to say is that all of it is work which can immediately command respect or interest from others. I'm not advancing the mute inglorious Milton hypothesis, but stating that this very widespread kind of production does correspond much more nearly to the way in which I think the processes of writing and the desire to create have to be seen. It is because of this correspondence that I want always to talk of this multifarious production at least neutrally, because after all it isn't possible to say in advance down which of those back streets a novel of great interest to others will be written. There is no guarantee – indeed, the case is often quite opposite – that the significant work is going to come from the recognized centres or in the recognized modes or under various otherwise authenticated or fashionable auspices. I believe that it is even necessary perhaps for many people to try and to fail if some are to succeed – the hypothesis which someone once put that to get one painter you need a thousand people painting and that there is no real way of knowing in advance, or even knowing for certain very early, which one that is going to be.

So, since there is in any case no need for any reasonable person to feel threatened by this great activity of production, we ought to accept it – both on general grounds and because I think it does tell us something about the character of our own society now that certain resources and skills and energies are beginning to be more widely released, a condition of society which after all is likely in that respect to become even more favourable. Then, on the other hand, it has also to be said that in these same conditions there is a quite unprecedented consumption or use of works of art of all kinds. The case I always think of, since it is very sobering to think of it, is that of drama in our own time. Through most of human history, since there has been drama, it has typically been occasional – at great festivals or at some particular time of the year. For certain metropolitan minorities it became, rather late in post-mediaeval times, something that was fairly regularly offered and which a small number of people would take in, and that kind of regular audience expanded down into our own century. But suddenly, in the twentieth century in the cinema, and then through radio and television, it was not only that the audience for any particular production could be millions, and more people might see a Shakespeare play on television on one night than had ever seen that play before. It was much more that, in a quite regular way and with a quite extraordinary intensity and variety, very much more was offered and regularly used. It's difficult to make exact calculations, but there are many people in our kinds of societies who watch ten or twelve hours' drama a week, sometimes three or four hours a night, which is quite easy to do. This would mean that they would often watch more in a month than even quite dedicated theatre-goers would previously have watched in a lifetime, and that this extraordinary intake of very considerable amounts of drama of all sorts, from classic plays to crime series and situation comedy, is now itself regularized. It is not regarded as something exceptional. It is not separated out as a 'cultural' activity. It has become a quite normal part of life, and it is relevant to observe that for many people it must be in one of the top few categories of all their activities. Most people in our society certainly spend more time watching drama than they spend, for example, eating, and the situation of a society in which there has arisen this apparently quite basic central need for this kind of art, with all its variations of level and seriousness, requires a quite different consideration of the place of art in society. And this is to say nothing of that kind of production which is often distinguished from drama, though it uses many of the same methods – the presentation of what is called news, which many people have come to consider it their duty to watch. This deliberate, regular exposure, not really to bare summaries of the facts or reports of events of immediate concern, but to directly filmed, sometimes dramatized, reports – dramatized in the sense of selecting and editing – is in some ways part of the same dimension. Within this context the older problem of the relatively isolated individual artist and a rather distant society which may propose certain duties to him has been transformed.

Thus, when I come to consider what freedom is in detail for any particular artist, I am trying to think its conditions through in our own kind of society and beyond the terms of the received and still important debate, which includes so many of the great positions on freedom and duty. I am very conscious of the fact that freedom is always a social product, and I think that the kind of freedom which opposes itself, on principle and from the beginning, to society, is simply a failure of conception. Many discussions of this kind presume a fully-formed individual as a kind of starting point, who can then, so to say, decide whether to be influenced by society or to resist its influence, to be pushed in this way or that. Now of course we all become, or hope to become, fully-formed individuals, and we do have real choices – to allow ourselves to be pushed this way or that or to resist that kind of push. Nothing I'm saying diminishes the importance of that kind of mature choice. Indeed I wish it was more widely exercised. But I can't think of freedom except in terms of its specific social production. I mean that before I can know myself to be free in any situation to do this kind of work or to refuse to do that kind of work, I have to recognize the whole location of anything that can be called 'the personality which is choosing'. We are born into the specific relationships of a family, of a society, of a historical phase, well before any questions of conscious choice and any realization of the possibility of freedom can arise. And this must not be seen merely negatively. I think of it typically in terms of formation and alignment, and I think that every artist who reflects on his experience and development becomes deeply aware of the extent to which these factors of formation and alignment in his own very specific history have been decisive to a sense of what he is and what he is then free to do. To put the emphasis in this way is to indicate also that the relationships with others, or more abstractly with society, are already part of the original formation and alignment; it is not just a question of those which can be later isolated.

Now I'd like to go on to discuss this more specifically in the case of writing, because here, as it happens, the matter of formation and alignment is very specific and, I think, illuminating. First, and very obviously for a writer, he is born into a language. We can all think of exceptional cases in which a writer has later adopted another language as his basic material, but the normal situation is that a writer has grown into a language before he discovers that it is this precise thing which he has grown into that is the medium from which he must try to make his particular art. This should not be seen as a constraint only; for most writers the resources of their own language are their indispensable resources, and to most writers the richness of their native language is a constant stimulus. Yet it cannot only be described in these positive ways, because a specific language is always, also, in some important sense a set of limits, of constraints, of directions this way rather than that, and most writers discover these in the course of their practice, even if they are not consciously or generally aware of them. The matter can be put even more generally than this, for it is not only a matter of the writer's relations with his native language; it is a matter of any writer's relation with language as what is usually called a medium.

Here, in an important sense, a writer is not free, and knows in the course of his practice that he is not free. There is this very common but very extraordinary way of thinking about writers and literature as if it were a matter of having ideas. Certainly I think writers are encouraged to talk in this way, and readers inevitably get into the habit of talking about works in this way. But if you look at the recorded experience of many very different kinds of writers, you will find that having an idea is one thing, and writing, sometimes all too painfully, is quite another. I mean that between the conception as it moves in the mind – whether it is the creation of a character, the outline of an idea, the perception of a place, the sense of an action – between such conceptions and their quite material realization in the words, there is a very complex process which most writers spend their lives trying to understand, and perhaps never fully understand. It is a material process. The familiar contrast between the material activities (which are thought to have something to do simply with industrial work or business) and what are called imaginative activities (which are thought to go on simply in the head or in the soul) is quite misleading, because although it is true that the source of most imaginative writing – as, indeed of most arts – is of course in an important way a matter of mental process, the actual activity of almost all arts is a very material process indeed. It is more obviously so in certain arts like painting and sculpture. In certain arts it is a matter of mastering certain notational systems which eventually have a corresponding material result. In the case of language it is that experience of finding within what is often a quite resistant medium (indeed, what is not a medium at all – that misrepresents it), finding rather within what is a quite resistant stored area of language the possibilities of saying something quite specific which is not necessarily realized, however free the writer may be, until that process has been gone through.

Let us think of one interesting case which many writers have spoken about, particularly novelists. It can be said that a novelist starts out with a character, an idea for a character. Sometimes this is a character based on some person or combination of persons or aspect of the person that the writer has directly known or observed. What is then said is that the writer starts realizing this character in his early chapters and then finds, after a certain time – I have seen fifty or sixty pages as a quite common specification – that the character takes over, the character takes charge, he starts creating his own life. Now it is all very well to say things like that at literary lunches – it impresses with the mystery of the process. But what is being described, however inadequately, is undoubtedly a quite common experience, that at a certain point it is not just the original conception: something else has happened. Some of this can be explained in very simple ways by mentioning the results of further reflection: putting the character in a new situation so that he develops; bringing him in relation to another character so that some new aspect has necessarily to be created. But that clearly does not cover the whole case, since I think many writers have correctly observed a moment of surprise when the creation seems to be going in a way which they had not fully intended. And while this can, in some instances, be diagnosed as failure, in other cases it is something different in that what happens at that stage comes to be seen as more important, as having more substance in it.

It is important to try to find a reasonable way of talking about that process which is in itself only an instance of something much more general. It is, I think, the result of the writing process itself. You might say that ideas are free precisely because they don't have to be specified and wrought, but that writing, written characters, written ideas, written actions, are not at all in the same sense free, because they are engaged in their very process with something which is much more than the operation of the free mind, of the free imagination on unresistant material. There is an engagement now with the resources of a specific language. There is the process of contact with what is at once an enabling and a resistant resource.

And what, then, is freedom? Or what is duty? Certainly freedom, in that important general sense in which we usually take it, is essential for the continuation of that process, unrestricted by arbitrary interferences. Indeed, one of the greatest pressures on writers at just those points where they are engaged with this process (which they are bound to feel in local terms relatively mysterious) is that they are subject to an internal temptation which can become overwhelming when it is supported by pressure from outside. I mean the temptation at those difficult points of working in a language to fall into the habit which Orwell described so well when he talked of many political speeches as simply arranging gummed strips of words which other people had put into order, gumming these strips together until you had something of sufficient length, the words falling into familiar patterns which appear to make sense of a kind. In much important writing it is the hesitation at that point, when the words can come all too easily – when the words are, so to say, ready-made – it is that hesitation which is the crucial condition: a hesitation from which they may never in the worst cases emerge, and from which I suppose no writer ever completely emerges, but a hesitation which is of great consequence to significant production in writing because at that moment something new is happening in the language itself. So, to be free to prolong that moment, instead of being directed into what a cause or a marketing director has already decided is the solution, is indeed essential. Or to put it another way: to hold yourself at that point as a writer, to recognize the need to hold yourself at that point as a duty and, indeed, more than that, to hold yourself with some hope of moving beyond it – that is the only kind of duty that I think writers ought in the first instance to recognize. What I want most to say is that these situations which are often cast into a rhetoric of 'leave me alone, I'm an artist' can really be referred to something much more fundamental in the general social process. It is crucial that as many people as possible both understand this process in others and try to develop these conditions as they are relevant for themselves, because in those encounters something of general social use is capable of happening, whatever the value of any particular product at a particular time. This is why the claim for the freedom of the artist is necessarily a claim for quite new kinds of freedom, an acknowledgement of the need for freedom for everyone in society. This sense connects with the deepest notions of an educated and self-managing democracy as the best cultural and political model, distinct from the received models with which other ideas of art have been so commonly associated.

Instead of taking up rhetorical positions on one side or another of the freedom versus duty argument, or even at what is always thought that virtuous point in the dead middle of the argument, we should be trying to understand in much more detail what is really involved in the concept of formation, the formation of the capacity to be free. We should be

trying to understand alignments not just as conscious choice or commitment or bias, although these things happen at certain important stages of
life, but also in terms of those things which are, so to say, in-built, which
are the ground of our real connections with our own people and our
own time.

I am not of course saying that we have to take any of the terms of a
formation or an alignment as given. I'm saying only that they go much
deeper in every individual creator than the usual discussion of freedom
ever acknowledges. It is like the argument about originality – I think it
was Empson who said that to be 1 per cent original is difficult enough
but that to be 5 per cent original was to be into the category of genius.
Obviously this can't be quantified, but I think figures like that give one
some sense of what the freedom to create in one's own way really
involves. We carry necessarily – not as a limitation, or only as a limitation – a great body of formed experience, directed attention. We have
available to us certain channels of energy which, at certain points, turn
out to be blocked channels, and at those points all the resources of
ourselves and our societies have to be gathered if there is to be any hope
of clearing them. And that clearing, of course, is always a duty. We have
to think that the most significant freedoms may therefore be discovered
in the consciousness of our true conditions, including conditions which
necessarily set certain limits on us. Not the arbitrary limits, which we
must always refuse, but that placing in a people, in a language, and in a
time, which is not a denial of freedom but, properly used, the means of
its realization.

4

Resources of Class and Community

Welsh Culture

1975

When we hear the word 'culture', some of us reach for our fancy dress.
Real life is home, family and a job; wages and prices; politics and crisis.
Culture, then, is for high days and holidays: not an ordinary gear but an
overdrive. So if you say 'Welsh culture' what do you think of? Of *bara
brith* and the *Eisteddfod*? Of choirs and Cardiff Arms Park? Of love
spoons and *englynion*? Of the national costume and the rampant red
dragon? All these things are here, if at different levels and in different
ways. But over and above them is another culture. Not the alien Saxon,
who belongs, in truth, with the fancy dress. Not even, in any simple way,
the alien or at least different English. Taking culture in its full sense you
would be speaking of something quite different: of a way of life determined by the National Coal Board, the British Steel Corporation, the
Milk Marketing Board, the Co-op and Marks and Spencers, the BBC,
the Labour Party, the EEC, NATO. But that's not Welsh culture.
Maybe, maybe not. It's how and where most people in Wales are living,
and in relation to which most meanings and values are in practice found.
Depopulation, unemployment, exploitation, poverty: if these are not
part of Welsh culture we are denying large parts of our social experience. And if we have shared these things with others, that sharpens the
question. Where is it now, this Wales? Where is the real identity, the real
culture?

It's worth walking with this question around the Folk Museum at St
Fagans. It's a lovely place. Along the paths and under the trees are the
re-erected farmhouses and cottages of the periods and regions of Wales.
Inside the houses are the old furniture, the old utensils, the old tools.
You can touch the handle of a shovel and, closing your eyes, feel a life
connecting with you: the lives of men and women whose genes we still
carry; the labour now dissolved into what may seem a natural landscape

of high field and culvert and lane. And beyond these the tannery and the weaving factory, the chapel and the tollhouse and the cockpit. It is all there, you say, the real Wales. And then you look up at the big house on the mound, in whose park this image, so precisely material, has been rebuilt, reconstructed. It is not that it cancels the decency or the dignity of the farms and the cottages, but it is there all the time, as another part of the culture.

The castles of Wales, most of them the monuments of an invading and occupying political system: are they too part of Welsh culture, to be set down indifferently in the tourist literature? Maybe, again. Anything old enough will do, it can seem at times. Even the steam locomotives, once they stopped running, became a cultural attraction. It's very hard to hold this in balance. The feeling for the past is more than a fancy, but it's how past and present relate that tells in a culture. You go out of the park, your mind still filled with the peace of those farmhouse interiors – of course an unreal peace; there is never any dirt on the tools or on the floors; the attendants have prepared for us a clean homecoming – and there you are, suddenly, in the car park, among the Cortinas and the Allegros, and then the traffic lights and the road signs.

The Welsh Folk Museum: a lovely place. But what happens to a people when it calls itself, even temporarily, a folk? That hard German sound is softened and distanced in English, and it is in the softening and distancing that you select your memories. For it's significant, isn't it, where that Folk Museum stops. Just before, precisely before, the Industrial Revolution. You look among all those places and instruments of work, and you remember, up the road, industrial South Wales: coal and steel and their derivatives; the thickly populated valleys, the terraces, the slagheaps; the place of life and work of the majority of the Welsh.

I had a fancy once, looking across from the oldest of the farmhouses. Give the present generation of industrial bureaucrats their head, stop fighting them, and the Folk Museum could be remarkably expanded. A nostalgic colliery cage would rise beyond the tannery. An out-of-date ironworks would share a stream with the weaving. A depressed and ravaged country, passing quickly through the status of a marginal region, would find its cultural reincarnation in the lovingly preserved material relics of an open-air museum.

It isn't only, when you think of it, the industry. I remember a young bureaucrat, just back from California, describing rural mid-Wales as a 'wilderness area', for the outdoor relief of the English cities. He never understood why I was so unsocially angry. In the North American continent there are still real wildernesses: untouched and some of it untouchable country. And here was he, with the concept in his flight bag, looking on a map at rural Wales: at fields and hills soaked with labour, at the living places of farming families, and not even seeing them, seeing only a site for his wilderness. He had a friend, an economist, who used to prove to me, once a week, that the sheep, by nature, is an uneconomic animal, and that all this marginal farming, with returns on capital that would cause instant suicide in the Barbican, must be simply written off. 'And the people with the sheep?' I ventured to ask. 'Of course, in that capacity', he replied without hesitation.

If you forget the past and think about the future for a minute, you can see this whole model: the uneconomic collieries, the out-of-date heavy industry, the marginal farms. Save a few bright spots – Port Talbot, Milford Haven – where the terms measure up to those planning standards, and what have you got? Poor old Wales. And how will the Welsh live, those at least who haven't followed their fathers down the Black Rock to England? 'The region', they said 'has obvious tourist and leisure potential'. And that, I suppose, is where the culture comes in again: as a resort and a festival, both meticulously and distinctively Welsh.

But this is the problem: the real problem of cultural identity. I wish I could see it in one of its popular forms: in a kind of emphasis on Welshness against an alien and invading culture; in a consequent emphasis on culture as tradition, and on tradition as preservation. I can feel, very easily, the strength of that position. Here is a language spoken and written since the sixth century, still a native language for a significant minority, and to want to keep it, to insist on keeping it, is then as natural as breathing. With the language goes a literature, and with the literature a history, and with the history a culture.

It is a real enough model, as far as it goes. The language wasn't only driven back by the Industrial Revolution and its movements of people. It was also driven back by conscious repression, by penalty and contempt, and in a late phase by deliberate policy in the schools. You can still see, as carefully preserved as the old tools, the little boards, the 'Welsh Nots', which children caught speaking their mother tongue had to hang round their necks, for shame. It is bound to be wrong to forget or forgive that. It is bound to be right to use and to teach a language still living, after all the attacks on it.

But does the rest follow: the history, the culture? Only part of it, in fact. It is easy to speak of a proud independent people. The rhetoric warms the heart. But you can be proud without being independent; you often have to be. In the older epochs of conquest, and in the modern epoch of industrial capitalism, there hasn't been that much choice. The self-respect, the aspirations, were always real and always difficult. But you don't live for centuries under the power of others and remain the same people. It is this, always, that is so hard to admit, for it can be made to sound like betrayal. And so a genuine identity, a real tradition, a natural self-respect, can be made to stand on their own, as if nothing else had ever happened.

I was late learning this. At school I was never taught any English history. First it was Welsh history, with brave princes and heroes amassing gold and cattle: the English or Saxons (the terms interchangeable) usually slain ('slain' for a child; keep 'killed' for later); slain in great numbers, though there were always, I remember, some young beauties left, for the contracting of noble alliances. That at elementary school; indeed elementary enough. And I went straight on, as it happened, by the form of the School Certificate syllabus, to British Empire and Commonwealth history; more slaying and amassing, though now called the spread of civilization. This left me not only with some understandable confusions about the identity of the enemy, to say nothing of the identity of our own side. It left me also without much clue to this very odd world I started noticing outside school. There was a gap, that is to say: a gap in the Welsh history for the four centuries after the Acts of Union; a gap in the English history, or was it also Welsh, which had brought the tramroad and the railway through our valley, and which was there visible every night, above Brynarw, when they cleared the blast furnace at Blaenavon and the glow hung in the sky. All the complications, all the real difficulties, are there in those gaps, and it is these that not only I, but most of us, find so hard to grasp, to decipher, to connect, as we try to make sense of what is called Welsh Culture.

Where there are real gaps there is not only inquiry; there is also the making of myths. Trying, under pressure, to define our identity, we have invented and tolerated many illusions. That we are physically distinct, for example: a specific race; the last of the old Britons, hanging on in the west. But the physical mix of the people of Wales is essentially that of the whole island, though in different areas, including the different regions of wales, the proportions in the mix vary. Another form of the illusion is that we are the Celts, whoever they may be. The tall fair-haired warriors who charged the Roman legions, naked except for their ornaments of gold. That doesn't fit very well with the dominant physical image, to say nothing of the rest of the cultural match. Or then the Celtic temperament, in either of its versions. Natural radicals, dissidents, nonconformists, rebels? It depends which period you take. Think of Catholic, royalist Wales, as late as the Civil War. Are these the same people as the radical nonconformists and later the socialists and militants of the nineteenth and twentieth centuries. It was not the race that changed; it was the history.

Or the other incarnation: the dark brooding and magical imagination; the nation of poets and scholars; or in the cut-down English version: the people with that endless gift of the gab. These too are history: Welsh literature with its very marked and very distinct classicist and romantic tendencies, manifesting quite different qualities; Welsh talk, with its range from a fluent, dynamic enlivening articulation to an overbearing, repetitive windiness. Facing ourselves as we are, we know all these possibilities. What comes out, on balance, is indeed distinct and distinctive, but it contains elements too complex, too infolded, to be defined by the simple traditional images. Who has not heard, for example, of the fluent, quicksilver Celt, making rings round the slow dumb English? The energy of the talk is indeed not in doubt, but we have to listen more carefully to what it is really saying. It is often a lively exuberance. It is just as often an unmitigated flow to prevent other things being said. And what those other things are we hear more often among ourselves, an extraordinary sadness, which is indeed not surprising, and at the edges, lately, an implacable bitterness, even a soured cynicism, which can jerk into life – this is what makes it hard to hear – as a fantastic comic edge, or a wild self-deprecation, as a form of pride: a wall of words, anyway, so that we do not have to look, steadily and soberly, at all that has happened to us.

What is it that has happened? It is nothing surprising. It is in general very well known. To the extent that we are a people, we have been defeated, colonized, penetrated, incorporated. Never finally, of course. The living resilience, in many forms, has always been there. But its forms are distinct. They do not normally include, for example, the fighting hatred of some of the Irish. There is a drawing back to some of our own resources. There is a very skilful kind of accommodation, finding a few ways to be recognized as different, which we then actively cultivate, while not noticing, beyond them, the profound resignation. These are some of the signs of a post-colonial culture, conscious all the time of its own real strengths and potentials, longing only to be itself, to become its own world but with so much, too much, on its back to be able, consistently, to face its real future. It has happened in many places.

Real independence is a time of new and active creation: people sure enough of themselves to discard their baggage; knowing the past as past, as a shaping history, but with a new confident sense of the present and the future, where the decisive meanings and values will be made. But at an earlier stage, wanting that but not yet able to get it, there is another spirit: a fixation on the past, part real, part mythicized, because the past, in either form, is one thing they can't take away from us, that might even interest them, get a nod of recognition.

Each of these tendencies is now active in Wales. The complexity is that they are so difficult to separate, because they live, often, in the same bodies, the same minds. There is the proud and dignified withdrawal to Fortress Wales: the old times, the old culture; the still living enclave.

There is the moving out from the enclave; the new work, the new teaching, the sense and in places the reality of a modern Welsh culture. But there is also the accommodation, in its different forms. There is the costume past, as a tourist attraction: things never distinctly Welsh, the tall hats and the dressers, presented as local pieties, things invented in the bad scholarship or the romantic fancies of the late eighteenth and nineteenth centuries – versions of bardism and druidism.

And more harmful than either is an evident tendency to play to our weaknesses, for commercial entertainment. If the Welsh, as the English sometimes say, are dark, deceitful, voluble and lustful Puritans, find a scene, find a character, play it on English television; admit and exaggerate your weaknesses before they have time to point them out. Or play the larger-than-life exile, your local colour deepening with every mile to Paddington or across the Severn Bridge and up the M4. Be what they expect you to be, and be it more. Tell the joke against yourself before they do, like Jewish humour in an anti-Semitic time. Show the distinctive bits and pieces they've already cast you for. It's easier and more successful than living with the whole of yourself. It's not me exactly, or you exactly, but by God it's Welsh, and by God it will slay the English.

A last word about these English. They are much more various than the myths allow. Anything really of our life can find alliance there, as well as the evident antipathy and patronage. A friend from the north of England said to me recently that the Welsh and the Scots were lucky to have these available national self-definitions, to help them find their way out of the dominance of English ruling-class minority culture. In the north, he said, we who are English are in the same sense denied; what the world knows as English is not our life and feelings; and yet we don't, like the Welsh or the Scots, have this simple thing, this national difference, to pit against it. Then you might get through, quicker, to the real differences, the real conflicts, I said. No, he said, to get the energy to do that you need the model. I still don't agree, altogether, but it is how we might look at it.

People have to, in the end, direct their own lives, control their own places, live by their own feelings. When this is denied them, in any degree, distortions, compensations, myths, fancy dress can spread and become epidemic. But to define what has denied them, so as to see it and change it: that is something different and difficult; you need all the help you can get, and the doubtful help is the problem. As Welsh culture changes, and as on the whole it gets stronger, it is this living complexity which we must come, are perhaps coming, to understand, to possess, and to work with.

The Social Significance of 1926

1977

I came down this morning from a village above Abergavenny: travelling the quite short distance to this centre of the mining valleys, and travelling also, in memories, the connections and the distance between one kind of country and another. In 1926, in that village, my father was one of three signalmen in the old Great Western Railway box. He was an ardent participant in the General Strike; so was one of the other two signalmen, and the stationmaster, who was subsequently victimized; so too were the platelayers. One of the signalmen was not. In the discussions and arguments that took place during those critical days, among a small group of men in a very specific social situation, some of the most important themes of the general social significance of 1926 became apparent. They were often recalled, in later years. I heard them throughout my childhood, and I went through them again, consciously, with my father, when I was preparing to write the General Strike sequence in *Border Country*. In a way it can seem marginal to rehearse them here, in places where the direct causes, the central actions and the long consequences of the strike are so close and evident. But while joining in paying homage to that central action, I see a need to consider the complex social action, and the complex problems of consciousness, which occurred, precisely, at a relative distance and in a more mixed situation. These seem to me to raise issues which have become more rather than less important in the subsequent history of British industry and the subsequent development of the working class.

Consider first that specific situation. These men at that country station were industrial workers, trade unionists, in a small group within a primarily rural and agricultural economy. All of them, like my father, still had close connections with that agricultural life. One of them ran a smallholding in addition to his job on the railway. Most of them had relatives in farm work. All of them had gardens and pigs or bees or ponies which were an important part of their work and income. At the same time, by the very fact of the railway, with the trains passing through, from the cities, from the factories, from the ports, from the collieries, and by the fact of the telephone and the telegraph, which was especially important for the signalmen, who through it had a community with other signalmen over a wide social network, talking beyond their work with men they might never actually meet but whom they knew very well through voice and opinion and story, they were part of a modern industrial working class. It is a special case, of course, but a significant one in the context of the General Strike, which is still too loosely assimilated to strikes of a different kind, with which it of course has connections but from which, in crucial ways, it has extensions – extensions that raise quite central problems of consciousness.

Think only, to begin with, of our traditional virtue of solidarity. This begins – and how could we expect it to be otherwise? – in very local, even physical ways. It is the ethic of a group which has already been decisively established, often it is true by the initial action of others – the capitalist employers who have offered work and who have drawn men, as to these valleys, to take it – but then, in shared immediate working experience, in the developing experience of a local community, in growing ties of family and kinship, a group which has the potential of solidarity already physically present within it. This is not to underestimate the long struggle that then must occur: the organizing, the raising of consciousness, the hard experience of recovering from disappointments or betrayals, the equally hard learning of collective disciplines, as when action against blacklegs is sometimes required, that especially difficult action, against members of the known group. And then there is variation, obviously, between places and kinds of work, written everywhere in the history of trade unionism: the relative ease or difficulty of organizing and of sustaining organization. Along these lines, with a necessary unevenness and variation, the labour movement builds itself. One of the decisive extensions is, to unionization of one whole industry, across wide physical distances. Both the miners, relatively concentrated, and the railwaymen, relatively dispersed, had achieved this extension, and of course it was crucial. But there is then the problem of another kind of extension: from the workplace, from the industry, to the class.

Now of course, theoretically, this had been achieved again and again. It is the history of socialism as distinct from (though always connected with) the history of industrial unionism. But nobody close to that history, at any point, can fail to recognize the difficulty of that particular extension of organization and consciousness: an extension which indeed when it is complete – and it is still not complete – must transform the whole social order and allow existing social relationships. It is hard enough to sustain organization and consciousness when they are directly centred on an immediate and local material interest: the stuggle to improve conditions and wages, within a systematically or blatantly exploiting work place, or, as in 1926, not to improve or even maintain but to fight against actual worsening. And then think what is being attempted when other men, in another situation, perhaps just emerging, bruised and depleted, from some struggle of their own, or perhaps in some temporary lull, are asked, urged, to act in solidarity, now in a different sense: not by place or work or by physical connection, but in essence by an idea, an idea that may even contradict their immediate and local material interest: an idea of the class, of the solidarity of the class, and of this, often – as notably in 1926 – in contradiction of the idea of a larger loyalty to which we have all been trained: to what is called the nation, the national interest, and expressing this the significant formalities of contract and of law.

What remains of decisive importance from the events of 1926 is the achievement of that consciousness. It is still a tangled story; all I can offer you is this immediate and local experience, with a sense of its wider significance. The theory of the General Strike was already important in certain socialist tendencies. There had been successes and failures in its practical application, in different countries. There had been the difficult history, in Britain, of the attempts at conscious alliances between major unions, the miners and the railwaymen prominent among them. But always, when it comes to the point, in an action of this kind, which is at the far end of the scale from some bureaucratic or representative collective action, individual men and groups of men have to cross a line in their minds. All history and all theory may be there, but real men, under difficulty have to struggle to make their own effective choices.

Now of course, there in that country station, there were real connections – of neighbourhood, of kinship, of trade – with the mining valleys. It was not a struggle from a blank, though another social reality – the small farms, the mixed rural villages – was of course physically much closer. 'To help the miners'; 'to stand by the miners': these were there from the beginning, in most conscious men, as effective impulses. And then working in the same direction, there was loyalty to their own union and to the general trade union movement: the instruction to join – what? The National Stoppage. It is an extraordinary phrase: deliberately limited and negative, but of course, even at that, a challenge sufficient to bring out all the power and anger of the state and the ruling class. And as it turned out, as we all now know, these had made their preparations more effectively than our own people. From patriotic ideology to the OMS, they were ready. Also, as it happened, they were more in touch with modern social communications. Our side relied on print, and even in that were under grave difficulties with distribution on a national scale; the local strike papers were always more significant. The ruling class had the wireless, and this was indeed a portent. By now we all know these and other reasons for the eventual defeat.

But what has also to be registered is the element of victory: nothing to be idealized, for it is important to draw lessons from the general defeat, but certain advances, certain clarifications, which as a matter of fact are still resonant in consciousness, as this anniversary, which is much more than formal, reminds us. At the level of national history, big-time politics, the General Strike is written off as anything from a disaster to a mistake: a consequent moderation and reformism is ideologically deduced from it. But the part of the history that most needs emphasis, and that was actually very evident in that country station and in thousands of other places up and down the country, was the growth of consciousness during the action itself. What began with relative formality, within a representative dimension, became, in its experience, the confidence, the vigour, the practical self-reliance, of which there is so much local evidence; and this was not just the spirit of a fight: it was the steady and remarkable self-realization of the capacity of a class, in its own sufficient social relations and in its potentially positive social and economic power. The detailed discussion, on the railways, about priority traffic and exception traffic, was an experience of decision-making of a quite new kind: not just instrumental, within an imposed system, but from the bottom up, as a way of deciding what came first in the society, what mattered in it, what needs and values we live by and want to live by. Certainly, in that station, the positive confidence grew, slowly, during those days, though of course in a small station, and with their other rural work always there for them, there were limits to what they could do, and there were marginal alternatives, which had much to do with their sense of confident independence. There, as elsewhere, when the stoppage was called off, the response was one of amazement and then of bitterness. The support had been growing not declining. The mood was very positive. And then the extraordinary and wretched business of the railway company's counter-action, its demand for signatures to an impossible document, its selective victimization, and through this the confusion of the misleading telegrams from union headquarters: all this raised the level of the action. Nationally, as you know, there were more men out on the day after the action was called off than during it. This, indeed, was the high point, and the national failure was a failure to go on from that: the very opposite lesson from that which we are usually asked to draw.

But there are also other lessons. In the half-century since 1926 the physical locations, the types of community and the social distribution of the British working class have changed very significantly. In 1926 the mining villages were modern communities; our village, even with the railway through it, an older type. Today we have to deal with a social and physical distribution in which mixed communities, not centred on single industries, are much more characteristic. The special struggle for class consciousness has now to be waged on this more open, more socially neutral ground. I still find it impossible, whenever I come to the mining valleys, to understand, at first, why there is not yet socialism in Britain: the need and the spirit have been evidenced so often, in these hard, proud places. But then I remember all the other places, so hard to understand from this more singular experience, although the actual development of industrial South Wales in the intervening half century has been in that other direction, with a complex intersection with the older type of community. In the local studies of 1926, which are now so usefully being extended, we need to look for the differentials between different types of community: differentials in action and support for the strike, which are quite marked but which should not be exaggerated. For the significance of 1926, in so short a time, is still the rise and extension of consciousness, during those days, to an effective national and class presence; differentials also, though these are less heroic and more distasteful studies, in recruitment against the strike, in the OMS and in other ways. The legendary figure of 1926, on the ruling-class side, is the undergraduate driving the train, the middle-class housewife shifting supplies. They were there, of course, but also – and differentially, in different parts of the country and in different types of community – there were working men, wage-earners, indeterminate class figures, whom the ruling class hired; but that is only one way of putting it, for there were also volunteers. In our village, the signalman who opposed the strike had his own place to go to: his smallholding. In the cities and towns it was and is different, and money is money, as we start by knowing. But it is also more than that. During the General Strike itself, and in the long months after it, when the miners held out, it mattered, in our village, that we had a physical and communal and not an abstract connection: at a distance, it is true, but one that did not cancel the sense of neighbourhood, a district, perhaps a country. The collection and transport of food, from where it was available to where it was needed, followed the strike along some of the same paths of social connection. It was not so everywhere. Then, as now, the hungry can be simultaneously recognized and neglected, at an effective social distance.

These differentials are crucial, because they connect 1926 and 1976, in old ways and in new. A child of five, as I was then, can gain from a father who had experienced that complex struggle for consciousness – a spirit and a perspective that have lasted, often under pressure, in the radically different places, where I have since lived and worked. But part of the perspective is the sense of complexity and difficulty, in the differential social and industrial and communal history and geography which was then and is now, increasingly, our world. My brief and inadequate contribution to this historic anniversary is offered as a reminder that necessarily alongside the central, concentrated and heroic actions are the smaller, the marginal, the mixed, the diffused scenes in which the effective struggle for a new consciousness also occurs.

The Importance of Community

1977

Late evening, and the television humming in the corner. A programme, not by a Welshman, on last year's National Eisteddfod. Between listening and drowsing, the balance was tipped when I heard one phrase which I thought first was a misreading of the script. He said at the end of that account of the Eisteddfod – which was very sympathetic, sentimental, selective – he said suddenly: 'Here we have a nation trying to become a people.' I suppose verbal analytic training is an inevitable part of the kind of literary education I had. I thought 'Well, he's reversed the terms, an understandable error.' He wasn't reading from autocue, he was simply reading from a script. But a *nation* trying to become a *people*! It must have been written as a *people* trying to become a *nation*. But then I thought, if you counterpose either term you see that each is problematic. This is not the most difficult problem in the terms with which we now try to do our political thinking. But 'nation' and 'people', just to start with, indicate the problems – problems of history, problems of perspective – which are right inside the very terms that are necessary methods of exchange in the most urgent political issues.

A *nation* once was unproblematic, with its strong connections with the fact of birth, the fact that a nation was a group of people who shared a *native* land. This meaning was overridden but never destroyed, by the development of the *nation-state*, in which what really matters is not common birth or the sharing of native land, but a specific independent kind of political organization. A *people* on the other hand, was always slightly problematic: a mutual term to indicate a group which then at a certain point went through a very significant development in which there were people and there were others within the same place who were not people or who were not *the* people. There was a very significant use in radical politics in the eighteenth and nineteenth centuries in which you set *the people* against what? – against the system, against the ruling class, against *them*. That use, a very specifying use, a very uniting use, disappeared, I suppose, or became much more difficult when you got to the era of electoral politics and found that all parties were claiming this appellation of the people. It lost that earlier social specification.

In orthodox modern political thought, these earlier terms – *nation* and *people* – have often been replaced by the simple abstract term *society*. Its uses are familiar, yet it, too, is not as simple as it may look. If you look through an eighteenth-century writer, for example, and see how he uses the word 'society', you'll find that in one paragraph he will mean what we would now have to express as 'company' or simply 'being with other people' – society as our active relations with others, being in society as distinct from being alone or being withdrawn. He will in the next paragraph be likely to use 'society' to mean what I suppose we now generally take it to mean – the systematic set of political and general arrangements by which a given people live: society as a social *system*. And this simultaneous use of the same term for quite different meanings has a piece of history in it which may be crucially relevant in the attempt to think nationalist politics in our generation. The term 'society' began with a very strong stress on direct relations with other people, specifically physical relationships of contiguity, contact, relating. It was a word that was consciously opposed to the word 'state' – 'state' with all its implications of the power structure, the display centre of decision and authority. This had been the contribution of a developing middle class: to find or try to find a term which was alternative to *state*, which should nevertheless express something which was not a private construction but a public one. The attempt to counterpose *society* to *the state*, to insist that there was a whole area of lived relationships which was other than that centre of power and display: this was a very crucial phase. But then in its turn 'society' moved towards that meaning which it had originally opposed. In the course of the nineteenth century, and now again today, we are trying to find terms which represent an emphasis of certain kinds of direct and directly responsible relationships, as against a centre of power and display.

Now the word which touches the nerve, the word which has had to carry most of the freight of this very difficult sense of direct and responsible relationships – this word is 'community'. I want to talk about some of the meanings of community at the point where I think they are becoming extremely problematic and yet when the issues inside the term have never been more important. Community is unusual among the terms of political vocabulary in being, I think, the one term which has never been used in a negative sense. People never, from any political position, want to say that they are against community or against the community. You can have very sophisticated individualist arguments about the proper sphere of society, but the community, by contrast, is always right. I think on the one hand we should be glad that this is so, on the other hand we should be suspicious. A term which is agreed among so many people, a term which everybody likes, a notion which everybody is in favour of – if this reflected reality then we'd be living in a world very different from this one. So what is the problem inside the term, what is it that allows people to at once respond very positively to it and yet mean such very different things by it? Here I have to go back over some of the phases of my own understanding of this word and try to relate it to some direct aspects of social experience.

I happened to grow up in a very small rural community right on the Welsh-English border. I didn't realize until many years later that many of the ideas that I had absorbed in that particular situation, and had later expressed, were in a sense common property throughout a very wide area of Welsh social thought. And the difficulty, if you lived on that border, of knowing who you were in terms of any *larger* grouping, certainly prevented me from seeing in the first stage that this had a relation to Welsh social thought. It was pointed out to me by some Welsh commentators that this was so; it was much more often and more rudely pointed out by English commentators, who described my first definitions of community in terms which showed that in one sense they knew where they came from. One called it 'chapel rhetoric', with that particular single image of the Welsh. Someone more recently called it 'radical eisteddfodism'. That would be a very curious notion actually: a festival at once strongly cultural and distinctly professionally competitive. But I'll let that pass.

That original experience was in a way so special and in other ways so marginal. What it meant for me was, first, the experience of a relatively stable community, which had acquired a certain specific identity in opposition to certain external forces mainly on the land issue, and then which practised – and I felt the great importance of this – within that kind of scattered rural society, certain habits which, I came to recognize when I moved away from it, could certainly not be taken for granted. If I could give an example of this. When I went to Cambridge I heard a lecture by Professor L.C. Knights on the meaning of the word 'neighbour' in Shakespeare. He said that the word 'neighbour' in Shakespeare indicated something that *no* twentieth-century person can understand, because it signified a whole series of obligations and recognitions over and above the mere fact of physical proximity. And F.R. Leavis was leaning against the wall and nodding vigorously (it was the time when this was *the* going position in Cambridge) and everybody was saying: Yes, in the twentieth century nobody understands the meaning of 'neighbour'. Well, then I got up, straight from Pandy, so to say, and said I knew perfectly well what 'neighbour', in that full sense, means. That got hissed – it was a remark so against the common sense that here was something in literature which was not now socially available: the notion of that kind of recognition of certain kinds of mutual responsibility. Now this was not to idealize my own place. I do not mean that people – and above all perhaps to this audience I do not need to explain – I do not mean that people all liked each other. I do not mean that people didn't play dirty tricks on each other sometimes. I do not mean that people didn't have disputes. I mean that there was nevertheless a level of social obligation which was conferred by the fact of seeming to live in the same place and in that sense to have a common identity. And from this sense there were acts of kindness beyond calculation, forms of mutual recognition even when they were wild misinterpretations of the world outside. My father had to go to the local pub to stop them taking up a collection for me when I won a scholarship to Cambridge. He had to explain to them that having won a scholarship I had enough money to go. People assumed that going to a strange place like that ... I mean the one thing they could identify about Cambridge was that you'd need a lot of money up there. And so a collection was taken up, to try to look after me.

This was entirely within that sense of neighbour, of community. But it was still – as I soon realized when I moved out – so marginal a case, there were so few places like that I subsequently went to, that I had to learn to see a whole range of other possible meanings. And it did come to seem to me that a very different kind of community was actually physically quite close to where I'd grown up, but which I'd not known so well. A community that didn't depend at all on this sense of relative stability, relative custom, but a community that had been hammered out in very fierce conflict, the kind of community that was the eventual positive creation of struggles within the industrialization of South Wales. The connections between these very different kinds of community – rural and industrial – have still not been sufficiently explored: how much of one went into the other, the very complex interlocks inside those struggles, the very complex conflicts inside them, in the earlier stages, between the older tradition and the new. I think probably we are still in the early phase of understanding this.

For there is, of course, a habit of mutual obligation which easily becomes the ground on which exploitation is possible. If you have the sense that you have this kind of native duty to others it can expose you very cruelly within a system of the conscious exploitation of labour. And it is for a long time a very powerful appeal, one that is still repeatedly used in politics, that you have this kind of almost absolute obligation to 'the community', that the assertion of interest against it is merely selfish. Yet what happened in South Wales, as strongly as anywhere in the world, still seems to me an immense achievement. Out of some of the most bitter and brutal struggles came the intense sense of a community of a different kind: the notion of a much more collective community than any I'd been used to, which cast its institutions in collective forms and which did propose to change society radically but to change it in a very particular direction; to attempt to establish from these received and new notions of mutuality and brotherhood, a total society which was possible, one which seemed, if you read the earlier arguments, only just around the corner. You only really had to go to London and pronounce them, it sometimes seemed, and it would happen.

I am reminded in that sense that Robert Owen's proclamation of cooperation, a century and a half before, had also come out of Wales. Owen had that same sense that once it was announced it would be seen as so obviously just, so obviously a higher kind of living, that he even took it as a plan to the prime minister and was very surprised when they said 'Well, I don't think that we can do that quite now.' We have all had this sense of shock, that this is not a message which is instantly received. But that association between a specific understanding of community in terms of the extending obligations of neighbourhood, very much attached to a place, moving on through the sense of a community under stress, under attack, through conflict, finding its community and its collective institutions and attempting to move on from that to a political movement which should be the establishment of higher relations of this kind and which would be the total relations of a society: that association, for all its difficulties, has been a most significant part of the history of Wales. But the difficult thing within it, and it had been the difficulty with the earlier term of society, is that because it had begun as local and affirmative, assuming an unproblematic extension from its own local and community experience to a much more general movement, it was always insufficiently aware of the quite systematic obstacles which stood in the way. If you think back, for example, to that change of meaning in the word 'society', it can seem a loss. It was indeed in one sense a grave loss, that 'society' lost its sense of immediate direct relation to others and became the general abstract term for a whole social-political system. It is undoubtedly a loss, and yet that abstraction was a crucial way of understanding the nature of a quite new historical phase which was presenting problems which could not be negotiated, let alone understood, if the sense of something quite systematic and distant, something which was not in that sense accessible in any direct local mode, was established. This I think was the experience that we're repeating with our attempts to extend new meanings of community towards a whole movement, and it is particularly a problem that is mixed up with our very specific assertion, which is one of national community. Because what the abstraction of society represented, given the losses, was the perception that there were now fundamental and systematic historical changes, above all in the mode of production but carrying with them virtually every other kind of institutional change. Something had happened which put certain of the basic elements of our social life beyond the reach both of direct experience and of simple affirmation, affirmation followed by extension. In came, necessarily, the politics of negation, the politics of differentiation, the politics of abstract analysis. And these, whether we liked them or not, were now necessary even to understand what was happening.

The thing that always seems to me significant is that almost contemporary with this new abstract meaning of the word 'society' was the quite necessary invention of statistics as a mode of understanding our actual social environment. Everybody knows the limitations of statistics, they are too well-known to be argued, but there was a moment in that historical development when it would have been mere ignorance and we would have lived like people in the dark, without the statistics. As indeed we still would if we hadn't that kind of necessary access to things that are indeed our common life but which are not accessible by means of direct observation and experience. Certain things which are now profoundly systematic, which happen in complex ways over very large areas, and which we had to understand in ways that, by comparison with the simple affirmatives extended from experience through community to the making of new societies, seem and indeed often are distant and dehumanized: the apparent opposites of community. The system of ownership, for example, in the modern economy, which cannot be observed, which has to be consciously discovered. New characteristic social relations which have, in a sense, to be discovered, not only by factual enquiry but by very complex interpretation, discovering all kinds of new systems and modes. And these things which are the determining tendencies in modern history can be put into conflict with those other affirmative notions which, whether they come from older kinds of rural communities or from militant working-class communities, are always more closely tied to experience. And around them still centres the notion of community, contrasted now with what? Often I found, as this argument continued, contrasted with 'real politics' or 'practical politics'. That is to say, people would point out that to attempt to build a modern society in terms of the values of rather simple communities was simple idealist nonsense. A modern community – a word they still sometimes appropriate because they know what a positive charge it carries – simply could not be built in the model of these simpler earlier ways of life. And of course that is right. Then again there were people who said that the idea of community is always in its affirmations and in its pieties weakening, because it is less capable of perceiving an enemy, it is less capable of identifying what is truly hostile to it. It contains within it complacencies which really do lack the practice of politics in a modern world at once as extensive and as hard as this one. These are the objections being made in this phase of the revival of community and nationalist thinking. I think they have to be taken at their full and proper weight. They have to be superseded rather than pushed aside as simply the talk of our opponents. Because it must be the case that the projection of simple communities, even on the smaller scale of a new national independence, is a projection of reductions rather than of expansions, a projection of simplifications rather than of the kind of complex liberation which genuine community and new national politics could be.

It is evident also that the hostile and opposing elements to this new kind of politics are very strong, are very identifiable there and that they are not only in some distant power centre. This was my saddest discovery: when I found that in myself – and of course by this time I had been away and through a very different experience – in myself that most crucial form of imperialism had happened. That is to say, where parts of your mind are taken over by a system of ideas, a system of feelings, which really do emanate from the power centre. Right back in your own mind, and right back inside the oppressed and deprived community, there are reproduced elements of the thinking and the feeling of that dominating centre. These become the destructive complexities inside what had once seemed a simple affirmative mood. Nor can we simply react by saying that the values of community, which are strong and affirmative, are superior to those values of the power centres and the identification of power centres, the identification of destructive actual relationships, actual forms of ownership, actual ideas and feelings which are oppressing us. Where we have now got, it seems to me, within the politics of change in the centres of the metropolitan counties, is that we have learned all too harshly and bitterly the truth of this latest phase, the phase of negation, the phase of knowing that you have to go beyond the simple community, the phase of the quick identification of enemies, the phase also of very conscious and prolonged political abstraction. If we merely counterpose to that the forms of a simpler kind of politics, I very much doubt if we shall engage in the central struggle. On the other hand, if that negative politics is the only politics then it is the final victory of a mode of thought which seems to me the ultimate product of capitalist society. Whatever its political label it is a mode of thought which really has made relations between men into relations between things or relations between concepts. And yet to re-establish the notion of politics as relationships between men, to re-establish the ideas of community politics, would mean superseding, going beyond, that kind of politics rather than merely in turn negating it.

Now this is what interests me so much about the present political situation, that reaching the end of that kind of politics which I'm sure we are, reaching also the end of that kind of radical politics, we are finding certain signs of the possibility of going beyond, carrying the kind of affirmatives of community through those negotiations into a different kind of politics. And those signs, here and now, are very specifically national. I live in Cambridge among young radical students who would not recognize many of the analyses that are made about the condition of a dependent or deprived nation within Britain or any of the other deprived nations and regions of Europe. Yet they start from very similar but less negotiable feelings: feelings of social distance, of alienation, of political frustration and powerlessness. But the steps that they can then take, they find extremely difficult. It seems to me that what is happening – and this is what gave me a very strong sense of retracing a journey and finding that I'd come back to the same place but that place had changed – is the possibility in nationalist politics of making new affirmatives through necessarily confronting all the forms of negation, not simply to identify these as enemies but to see them as the whole complex of forces that at first sight we are against but that are parts of what has meanwhile happened to a whole human historical phase which in fact also includes us.

The moment when we move from a *merely retrospective* nationalist politics to a *truly prospective* politics, we begin that affirmative thinking which some of the most developed and intelligent left politics in certain other centres of Europe has truly lost. For however sophisticated, however militant that politics may be, it has lost something at its heart which is recognized again and again by those who are inside it: the sense of what any of this liberation is for, the sense of what the struggle would be able to attain, the sense of what that human life would be, other than merely Utopian rhetoric, which is the object of all the preoccupied conflict and struggle and argument. That sense has been so truly lost in so many of those areas, especially through the complications of the modern history of socialism, that what is now being contributed, I think still very incompletely, but what is being contributed and almost alone is being contributed from the new nationalist movements, is a reconnection inside the struggle, including the negations, but also the sense of an objective which has the possibility of affirmation. And if I read the nerves of my contemporaries rightly, I realize how exhausted those nerves are after the extraordinarily confused and frustrating politics of the last thirty years. The new moment of affirmation is to me the quite crucial ingredient and at present it is coming from the periphery. It is the renewal of a crucial ingredient without which politics will be only the capitalist interplay of interests, and that would be the end of politics in any sense which would have been understandable by me when I first started looking at political life.

And so the movement curiously is from an initial naivety, which I remember very well not understanding – as I still sometimes can't understand – how it could be that people should not want to live in real community. I mean, is it not so clearly a much better way to live? What on earth is stopping us? And still I went back a year ago to the fiftieth anniversary of the General Strike at the National Union of Mine-workers' conference at Pontypridd. As people talked about it it seemed incredible that there had not been socialism in Britain for fifty years. What on earth was stopping us? I found out; we have all found out. But in the course of finding out, what has been learned is in so many ways so negative that the renewal of effort back in those metropolitan centres is a matter of fibre, is a matter of emotional strength quite as much as it's a matter of intellectual ability or organizing capacity. That then is the thing which I see as the importance of the renewal of national politics, and especially here in Wales. It would be absurdly flattering to say that it has done more yet than feel at the edges of what this new kind of affirmative and liberating politics could be, but it almost alone is attempting it.

Mining the Meaning: Key Words in the Miners' Strike

1985

In the cutting of coal there is noise and dust and unwanted stone. Similarly, in the coal strike, there are central issues of great importance to the society, but around them, and often obscuring them, the noise and dust and stone of confused, short-term or malignant argument. A large majority of miners have done their duty to their union in a collective endurance of extraordinary human quality. It is now the duty of socialists, not only to continue to support them, in all circumstances, but to clarify and campaign on the central issues on which, over the coming decades, the future of this society will be decided. These issues can be defined in four keywords of the strike: *management*; *economic*; *community*; and *law-and-order*. I will discuss each in turn as a way in to the general issues.

'The Right to Manage'

The strike began in response to a unilateral decision by 'the management' to close certain pits. Here, beyond the more immediate arguments about previous agreements and procedures, and also beyond important matters of political context and style, there is an issue which should be at the centre of the whole socialist project. This is the claim of workers to control not only the wages and conditions, but also the very nature of their work. The human substance of this claim is absolute. To deny it, or even to qualify it, is to subordinate a whole class of men and women to the will of others. It is to be expected that capitalists will deny it. Their world is built on the power of capital to subordinate actual majorities of workers to conditions of managed employment. They meet every challenge to this power with anger and contempt. Socialists, on the other hand, have attempted, over several generations and under immense practical difficulties, to move towards a society in which the human substance of the claim could begin to be recognized or could finally be realized. In the mainstream of our own labour movement, a particular path was chosen. The major industries and services would be nationalized, so that instead of embodying a capitalist interest, in private profit, they would embody a national or a public interest. It seemed a reasonable path to follow, as an alternative to the old irresponsible capitalism.

But this coal strike, more clearly than any other single event, has shown us where this path can lead, and how far this can be from the original human claim. The key to understanding this is in that slippery word *management*. For it is a fact about the development of all modern industry that there has been serious and at times deliberate confusion between this term 'management' and the older terms 'master' and 'employer'.

Along the path of nationalization, a board representing the public interest and a technical management supervising production and distribution were the ideal elements of the new structure. The claim of workers to control their own production was set aside, under the presumed priorities of a wider national interest and the most efficient possible production. These presumed priorities remain important, but it is essential to see what has happened as they deny or qualify the wider human claim. First, the Coal Board, instead of representing the most general public interest, has become, in practice, a corporate employer, with political and financial relations only to the state. Second, the distinction between a public board and a technical management has been blurred to the point where 'management' – that supposedly professional operation – has become a simple cover word for the will and calculation of a *de facto* employer.

The confusion is especially serious because there is of course, virtually everywhere, a need for genuine management. Research, organization and planning are crucial in any complex operation. What is false in the currently imposed meanings of *management* is the reduction of these necessary processes to elements of the corporate plan of an employer looking only, on his own terms, to his version of profitable operation. What 'management' says is offered as a set of unchallengeable technical decisions, when the actual management – now very clearly the old master or employer – again and again arrives at these within a determining context of short-term political and commercial calculations.

Thus when the miners challenged that unilateral 'right to manage', and large bodies of opinion were mobilized to defeat their presumption, a key issue in the whole modern organization of work became clear. In the immediate decisions they had not been offered even consultation, but if they had been, it would have been short of what is necessary. The claim for which they have fought is the claim of any worker to be involved, from the beginning, in the long-term direction of the industry to which a whole lifetime is being given. Genuine management is a continuous and complex process of information and negotiation which goes on until some general and always renegotiable agreement is reached.

The supposed 'right of management' to ignore, abort or override this difficult process is false to the core. It is in fact doubletalk for the categorical and arbitrary right of an *employer*. In challenging that arrogance and confusion, in an especially crude phase of its assertion, the miners have been fighting for a principle which is of profound importance to every employed worker, over a range from hospitals and universities to offices and factories. For this now is the general interest: that people working hard at their jobs should not be exposed to these arbitrary operations of capital and the state, disguised as 'the right to manage'. In a period of very powerful multinational capital, moving its millions under various flags of convenience, and in a period also of rapid and often arbitrary takeover and merger by financial groups of all kinds, virtually everyone is exposed or will be exposed to what the miners have suffered.

Our protection, hitherto, has been in our unions and in the idea of a public sector. Each kind of protection has been attacked, in the conditions of this strike, at a key point. It will be unforgiveable, whatever the fate of the immediate action, if we fail to build and extend a consciousness and a movement to defend and advance this central condition of democracy: that our labour remains ours, and that it is not at the arbitrary disposal of others.

What is 'Economic'?

But face the facts, says another kind of qualifying voice. If your labour is not economic, have you any right to live by it? It is, of course, a real question. But not in the terms in which it has been put against this strike: terms which are true noise and dust. Thus it is clear, at a first level, that *economic*, like *management*, is by no means necessarily an informed, professional, neutral judgement. Work on the direct trading accounts of actual pits has produced quite different and even alternative definitions of which are 'economic'. Work on the general accounting procedures of the Coal Board has cast serious professional doubt on their clarity and relevance. Any of this work can be challenged, in the same way as the ruling official calculations, which cannot be intellectually protected by some general 'right to manage'.

Yet, however that argument may go – and it is precisely this which should be the substance of genuine management and negotiation – there is another level at which *economic*, as a keyword, must be examined. It is characteristic of all capitalist economics, and even of some socialist economists who have been drawn into local arguments on those terms, that particular commercial operations are isolated from the economy as a whole. As a technical move this is understandable. Particular operations and investments require specific examination. But any and all of these results have then to be returned to the whole economy of which they are part, and beyond that to the society which it is the purpose of the economy to support.

Coal is in this respect both a very strong and a very special case. It is a deep economic resource of this island, and any reasonable economic calculation of its mining has to include not only current trading calculations, but long-term and interrelating calculations of general energy policy. Thus the concentration of production into the most currently profitable pits, and the closing of all those which on one kind of calculation are not now profitable, is even as an isolated economic process questionable while it fails to include economic calculations about the effects on long-term reserves.

But the full case is very much wider than that. What has actually happened is that isolated accounting has usurped the functions of any general economics. It is not only, as the miners' union has argued, that the costs of defeating the strike and of financing redundancy are greater than the costs of sustaining the existing industry. It is also, and more generally, that there is a vast amount of social capital and continuing social investment in the old coalfields which, under the 'right to manage', it is proposed to make obsolete. Houses, schools, hospitals, and roads in these areas compose a huge economic investment which dwarfs the trading calculations of any particular industry. It is here, at the most fundamental level, that the miners have begun to define the real issues and problems of a socialist economy, and to expose the long-term destructive character of a capitalist economy. It is on this, in much wider areas, that the policies of a reviving labour movement must build.

Defending Real Community

The miners' strike is being represented as the last kick of an old order. Properly understood, it is one of the first steps towards a new order.

This is especially the case in the emphasis they have put on protecting their *communities*. Here is another keyword, which needs to be understood.

What the miners, like most of us, mean by their communities is the places where they have lived and want to go on living, where generations not only of economic but of social effort and human care have been invested, and which new generations will inherit. Without that kind of strong whole attachment, there can be no meaningful community.

However, there is another use of *community*, to mean not these actual places and people but an abstract aggregate with an arbitrary general interest. Any wider community – a people or a nation – has to include, if it is to be real, all its actual and diverse communities. To destroy actual communities in the name of 'community' or 'the public' is then evil as well as false.

Yet this is the implacable logic of the social order which is now so strongly coming through: the logic of a new nomad capitalism, which exploits actual places and people and then (as it suits it) moves on. Indeed, the spokesmen of this new nomad capitalism have come less and less to resemble actual human beings, and more and more to look and talk like plastic nomads: offering their titles to cash at a great distance from any settled working and productive activity, and expecting to be told, wherever they go, under whatever flag of convenience, that they will do nicely. Back in the shadow of their operations, from the inner cities to the abandoned mining villages, real men and women know that they are facing an alien order of paper and money, which seems all-powerful. It is to the lasting honour of the miners, and the women, and the old people, and all the others in the defiant communities, that they have stood up against it, and challenged its power.

Yet any challenge that can really defeat it has to be much wider. Coal was a good first case, because of its general and lasting importance. But the broader campaign will have to enter more difficult areas. The basic question of the relations between an economy and a society will have to be thoroughly reworked. For what lies ahead of us, within that alien order, is a long series of decisions in which one industry after another will declare more and more people redundant. The private talk of these alien forces – some of it submissively copied into the media – is a prolonged statistical crowing about increases in productivity and profit through getting rid of more workers. At the end of their road, it will be not only particular communities but whole societies – and what was Britain, but what they now call the Yookay, is an early candidate – that will be declared uneconomic and redundant.

We need not worry about the plastic nomads who hold our own nominal nationality. They will move on, or draw their heavily protected profits from elsewhere. The rest of us, here and needing to stay here, will have to find an alternative economic order if we are to continue to have any real society; and without that real society there can never in any case be any kind of socialism.

Some nominal adherence to socialism will not meet this challenge. The practicalities are immensely difficult, which is why we should be starting serious work on them. Socialists have always recognized the inherent inequalities of a class society. But we have often overlooked the similarly inherent inequalities of the earth itself, and of our own pieces of land. The strike has taught us again to think of coal as a native resource, and it is that kind of thinking – a practical and specific audit of the means of our livelihood, in resources and in skills – which will enable us to challenge the current ruling definitions of wealth and profit.

For, in fact, beyond all the alien categories, there is wealth only in people and in their lands and seas. Uses of this wealth which discard and abandon people are so profoundly contradictory that they become a social disaster, on a par with the physical disasters which follow from reckless exploitation of the lands and the seas. An economic policy which would begin from real people in real places, and which would be designed to sustain their continuing life, requires a big shift in our thinking, but a shift which in their arguments about pits and communities – their refusal to separate economics from a people and a society – the miners have begun to indicate.

The Idea of 'Order'

It is in this context that we should examine the final keyword: *law-and-order*. I take this as a single word, as it is currently used, for example in opposition to picketing. For it is the arbitrary combination of what should be two quite different words and concepts that is the key to its contemporary ideological effects. All societies need laws, and all complex societies both make and remake them. The real problem is *order*. Listening to some ministers, it is easy to pick up their real sense of *order*, which is command: obedience to lawful authority; indeed, when combined with the 'right to manage', obedience to all authority. It is clear, in context, that this is the miners' most substantial offence. Yet the idea of *order* is much more important than this. Laws are necessarily the instruments of a particular social order. None can survive without them. But then what is at issue, in any conflict about particular law, is the underlying definition of the desired social order. Thus there are now laws specifically designed to limit the powers of trade unions, or of assemblies of workers, to intervene in what is otherwise a free market in labour, necessarily dominated by capital. To challenge that order is to challenge those laws.

It is, therefore, of vital importance to socialists, who are regularly attacked for supporting disorder, to reply in something better than a negative way. For what is at issue, in the struggles about the rights of management, about alternative economic policies, and about the conditions of communities, is in a profound way a matter of *order*: not of command or authority but of a way of life chosen by a substantial majority of its citizens. Instead of being defensive about disorder, socialists should take every opportunity to show what is now really happening: the dislocation of our habitual social order and the destruction of specific communities, in a combined political and economic offensive.

For the miners and their families in the most threatened coalfields this is already quite clear. What they are directly defending is indeed a way of life, part of a particular social order which from developments elsewhere is now being cruelly overborne. Yet there are then extending lessons for socialists. It is already apparent, from divisions and differences between various coalfields and indeed from the way the strike then happened, by area decisions rather than national ballot, that the material inequalities which are literally inscribed in the earth have profound effects on the possibility of any wide and agreed social order.

The most profitable coalfields, and the pits with the easiest seams, can see quite different futures for their own immediate communities. The theoretical ability of a national union, or a national movement or party, to compose these differences into a single policy, a single alternative order, is sharply limited by these very practical differences of circumstances. This is why, from the beginning, a socialist policy has to rest on quite different bases from capitalist policy and any of its minor modifications.

Capitalist policy, which is still one of buying in the cheapest market and selling in the dearest, has in recent decades been profoundly subversive of what is still the most freely chosen social order of our people: that is, existence as an independent and self-sustaining nation. The continued legitimacy of appeals to either *law* or *order* rests primarily in this identity. Thus when supposedly public corporations, in steel or electricity or now coal, openly subordinate the interests of this true national to their own immediate market calculations – hauling coal, for example, across the seven seas to undercut, reduce or close down any supposedly national industry – a profound social crisis has begun.

At its centre is that version of *economic* or *uneconomic* which in practice, whenever convenient, overrides all other social considerations. But if it goes on doing this, what is left for any appeal to our supposed social order and its laws? Indeed what is left as *economic*? The few remaining industries and services, capable of withstanding any international competition in production under any conditions of labour? But there is no way in which, on those international capitalist criteria, a viable social order, without enforced redundancy, could in the long term be maintained.

The present government's policy – if it deserves so serious a name – is to let this rundown happen, indeed to hurry it along, in the belief that all the redundant people and discarded communities can continue to be politically marginalized or, if they act on their own behalf to be controlled by centralized communications (the political argument, as in this strike, taking place not in Parliament but on radio and television) and by new forms of policing.

In two major respects, then, the miners have taken us to a point of decision. By any criterion of future policy for this island, their coal and their skills are a central resource. They are not some arguable market sector but a key to our sustainable economic life. But it is in the second respect, in pushing the argument through to the question of the survival of all our communities, that they have gone beyond their convincing general economic position to the social issue on which the future of this society, and with it of its labour movement and of any project for socialism, will be decided. The point of growth for a reviving socialism is now in all these crisis-ridden communities: not as special cases but as a general case. It is here, in diversity and in respect for diversity, that new popular forces are forming and looking for some effective political articulation. It will be long and difficult in detail, but in challenging the destructive catchwords of *management, economic* and *law-and-order*, which now cover the real operations of a new and reckless stage of capitalism, the miners have, in seeking to protect their own interests, outlined a new form of the general interest.

As the strike ends, there will be many other things to discuss and argue about: tactics, timing and doubtless personalities. But it is of greatest possible importance to move very quickly and sharply beyond these, to the decisive general issues which have now been so clearly disclosed.

5
Beyond Labourism

The British Left

1965

Any analysis of the state of the Left in Britain must begin with an analysis of the nature of the Labour Party. For here is a mass party, based on an essentially undivided trade union movement. For at least the last twenty years it has been always a potential government, and in good times for the Left it is capable of governing alone. From its foundation it has been a coalition of left organizations, and the essential political battles of the Left have been fought out within it. The Independent Labour Party offered an alternative political organization until its merger with the Labour Party in the early 1930s: one more strand was then added to the coalition. The Communist Party, since the early 1920s, has worked as a militant wing of the labour movement: often involved in local struggles against the Labour Party, often influential in particular trade unions, but never looking likely to become a mass party. A Labour government, with the maintenance of a militant Communist minority, has in practice been its normal political aim.

The strengths and weaknesses of this domination of the Left by a mass party capable in the short term of winning decisive parliamentary power are then the essential terms of any realistic analysis. The weaknesses are easy to see. The fact that the Labour Party is a coalition has led to an evident poverty in theory: any attempt to go beyond quite general definitions leads at once to strains on this complicated alliance. The prospect of parliamentary power, within the existing political system, leads regularly to a muting of necessary arguments, and the needs of the Party, in parliamentary and electoral terms, are given a quite frequent priority over political principle. The prospect of power, in this constitutional way, leads to a strengthening of those already large elements in the Party who broadly accept the existing political and economic system and who, apart from substituting themselves for

131

Conservatives as ministers, wish to make only comparatively minor reforms. When these lines of opportunism or liberalism become very pronounced, there is a scatter of breakaway movements, and the very structure of the Labour Party is widely seen as the principal weakness of the British Left. Among intellectuals of the Left this kind of movement is particularly common. But the strengths of this peculiar organization are quite steadily underestimated. At several times and for different reasons in the last thirty years it has indeed seemed likely that the Party would disintegrate: that its contradictions and tensions were too deep for it to last. The Right, in and outside the Labour Party, have proposed a detachment from the class identification with the trade unions, and from the formal commitment to socialism. The Left, in and outside the Labour Party, have proposed a detachment of militants from this unprincipled and amorphous and often compromised organization, and the building of a principled socialist party. It needs emphasis that from these successive and different crises the main strength of the Labour Party has emerged relatively unscathed. The inability, as yet, of the Right to shatter this organized strength is, in fact, deeply encouraging. Certain deep strengths are here, as well as the obvious weaknesses. The similar inability of the Left to detach any significant body of the working class from its Labour allegiance is a fact about British society as a whole. In one sense this allegiance is an obstacle to militant socialism, but in another sense it keeps open the possibility of putting socialism on the political agenda without civil conflict or violence. There is a balance here of strengths and weaknesses, which is our real political context.

The existence and endurance of the Labour Party has tended to confine the arguments about socialism to parliamentary terms. These are evidently insufficient, but even so there have been many false statements about this matter of voting strengths and it is worth correcting them. The most common is the assertion that the relative postwar affluence of the working class has led to a weakening of the Labour Party. The Conservative victories in 1951, 1955 and 1959 have been widely interpreted in this way. The effects of relatively full employment and higher real wages are indeed complicated, but in this matter of voting strengths it is indisputably true that the Labour Party has been stronger in the postwar period of relative affluence than it ever was in the prewar periods of mass unemployment and poverty. Its victory in 1945 was gained with 12 million votes. Before the war its vote had never been higher than $8\frac{1}{2}$ million. The situation after 1945 is said to be one of voting decline due to 'affluence', but the figures are: 1950, over 13 million; 1951, nearly 14 million; 1955, over 12 million; 1959, still over 12 million; 1964, again over 12 million, which, with a decline in the Conservative vote, was enough to regain power. The relative decline during the 1950s, which cost Labour power, is still within the terms of an absolute and major improvement over the prewar situation. The truth is that as the 1945 Labour government carried out its programme, it gained some working-class support but also united against it a formidable and in the end decisive body of opinion. When it lost power in 1951, it still had, due to the peculiarities of the electoral system, a higher popular vote than the Conservatives. The evident material improvements in Britain during the 1950s gave the Conservatives the relatively narrow advantage in the popular vote on which they governed for thirteen years. In 1964 this advantage was marginally altered, and Labour could again form a government. Additionally, all through this period, Labour has retained a clear majority among men; it is the anti-Labour majority among women which has kept them out. In the large towns and the industrial areas, including, recently, the most prosperous industrial areas, Labour has been exceptionally strong, even under Conservative rule.

The Labour Party remains then, in spite of postwar changes, a mass party and a permanently potential government, based primarily on the most organized sections of the working class. Yet, given this strength, why has it seemed so often an improbable instrument of socialist change? Here we have to turn from the limited arena of parliamentary politics and examine the complicated intellectual and structural traditions of other kinds of social criticism and opposition.

The origins of the British working-class movement, in the years 1780–1835, show a complicated combination of political radicalism and defensive industrial organization. (The period has been well described in Edward Thompson's *The Making of the English Working Class*.) The major challenge of Chartism in the 1840s failed, but produced in the ruling class, in the following decades, a series of reformist attitudes and measures, in the beginning as the explicit cost of avoiding revolution. Within these reforms, a leading section of the previous movement – the artisans and skilled workers – became relatively acclimatized to a capitalist society which was growing in wealth and steadily extending suffrage. When economic depression came again in the 1880s, there was a revival of general trade union organization, but the political consequences of this were confused. The acclimatized trade union leaders saw no need for a new political party. It was from the leaders of the new unions that the demand for a political initiative came. An ambivalence in the trade unions' attitudes to working-class political initiatives was thus already evident. In practical terms the new leaders won, but the ambivalence has continued. Even when, in subsequent decades, the Labour Party had been accepted as the political instrument of the trade unions, there was a clear division of opinion, among trade union leaders, on what this political role should be.

On the one hand, the Labour Party was seen as an instrument for the transformation of capitalist society and its replacement by socialism: an aim to which a number of the unions are, by their written constitutions, committed. On the other hand, by a majority of trade union leaders, the Labour Party has been seen primarily as a representative of working-class interests within the existing system, so that when it governs it need go no further than certain limited kinds of protective and welfare legislation. These opinions have fluctuated according to the nature of industrial conflict. The General Strike of 1926 was a major working-class challenge to the existing political regime, but it is significant that it was defeated, not by any failure in popular support, but by a final willingness to compromise among the trade union leaders. After this defeat the tide ran strongly towards acclimatization, and there was a further development of bureaucracy and centralized control within many of the most important unions. These factors are still apparent, and there is still an important section of the trade union leadership which, while formally supporting the Labour Party, might even welcome the separation of the trade unions from political commitments, leaving them as only negotiating and bargaining bodies. American influence in this direction has been particularly strong.

At the same time, the undemocratic nature of many of the largest trade unions is itself a source of instability. The most striking recent demonstration of this was the succession of Cousins to Deakin (after a brief interregnum) as general-secretary of the Transport and General Workers' Union, with a membership of more than a million. Under Deakin this union had been the principal supporter of the Right leadership. Under Cousins it has been the most important supporter of a whole range of left policies in domestic and international affairs. The fact that a million votes can be swung so completely from one side of the power struggle to another is a clear sign of how far bureaucratization has gone. It shows also, however, how what looks like a powerful and monolithic orthodoxy can be quite seriously, if only temporarily, disturbed.

The internal politics of the Labour Party, in recent years, are best understood as a series of struggles between essentially undemocratic groups. The Party conference is dominated by the trade union bloc votes. The constituency parties normally represent only the militant minorities of party members. The parliamentary Party claims a practical independance of the other bodies when policies conflict, and, by the nature of its involvement with the parliamentary system, is drawn continually into the orthodoxies of contemporary capitalist politics. Out of this complex situation, continually biased towards accommodations with existing political power, the general trend of Labour policy emerges. Thus we have the paradox of a mass party, formally committed to socialism, in practice functioning as the inheritor of the reforming Liberal Party with which the first generations of the working-class movement eventually worked. At the same time, the commitment to socialism, however formal, is often an electoral weakness and is exploited as such by the Right, while the continued loyalty to the Party of the majority of organized workers prevents any significant initiatives from the Left.

This situation is reinforced by the nature of the inherited systems of ideas. Here, again, there is a complicated mixture of strength and weakness. The main ideological element in the British working-class movement is one of moral critique. Again and again, even during the periods of fervent political radicalism, this moral critique has revealed itself as the decisive line. The ideas of brotherhood and cooperation, against selfish individualism, have always been more influential than ideas about political power as such. The developed language of Marxism, with its emphasis on class power, has sometimes qualified but never altered this decisive bearing. Thus it has often seemed that the British working class have been more interested in building their own brotherly and co-operative institutions than in taking overall political power. This has led to many weaknesses, for the obvious theoretical reason that the brotherly and cooperative institutions have been forced to function within an individualist economy, and the margin has often been very narrow indeed. Again and again, it has seemed to Marxists that the British working-class movement is in this sense hopeless: that the option, under pressure, is always for the maintenance of their own institutions rather than for the transformation of the society as a whole. In many circumstances this has indeed been a weakness, but also outside observers have normally overlooked its strengths. For just this factor has been responsible for the maintenance of an essentially undivided mass party which is capable of parliamentary power. Further, as many right-wing ideologists sadly admit, this inward-turning loyalty of the British working class has created a continually surprising endurance and resilience, under the pressure of economic or political defeat.

It would indeed be very difficult to imagine the British working-class movement, or any significant section of it, being captured, even temporarily, by an opportunism from outside itself. When it is betrayed, as so often, it is from within, but it is again surprising how comparatively little these frequent betrayals affect the main body of strength. Nor is it only a matter of the endurance of an organized and undivided movement. It is also a question of the endurance of certain pre-political values, which to a surprising degree survive the political frustrations and betrayals. The right wing of the Labour Party, to say nothing of the Right in the country as a whole, has won an almost continuous succession of victories in the short term, only to find that there is still ranged against it, almost as if the victories had not happened, the same complex of moral pressures and demands. Even here, the weakness of this social character of the British working-class movement is often evident. It can be frequently limited, or even corrupted, by nationalism, as it was so grossly corrupted by imperialism. The fact that the pre-political values have not often become politically significant has commonly been the very cause of the frustrations and defeats. Yet, in the persistence of this self-generating tradition, the option for the future, as well as the organization of the present, is continually there. In one sense, this kind of insularity (of an island, indeed, within an island) has to grow beyond itself, if there is to be socialism in Britain. The process of this transformation is all that matters, politically, in Britain. But it has been significant, recently, how most of the attacks on insularity have come from the Right. There is a very brisk line of right-wing argument designed to detach the British working class from its own social tradit-ions, and it is not only because of the sources of this argument that one sees it as double-edged. The truth is that if the British working-class movement could be detached from its own kind of unemphatic and pre-political self-reliance, the way would be completely open for the triumph of the new capitalism. The campaign to 'modernize' Britain, and to make it less 'insular', is, in its most common forms, a campaign espec-ially directed against the particular strengths of the British working class.

The moral critique of industrial capitalism, which has mainly informed the British working-class movement, has been paralleled throughout by a literary tradition of comparable importance. At the level of local organization, the working-class movement has been nourished by the important tradition of religious nonconformity. Puri-tanism has taught it restraint and the limitation of human demands, and in this sense has been frustrating and weakening. Puritanism has also taught it self-reliance and endurance, and these, correspondingly, have been strengthening. But there has been an important tradition of ideas and feelings which is not puritan, and which in my view lies just as deeply in the moral consciousness. The claims of Cobbett, Ruskin, William Morris – to name three of the most influential writers – were no more puritan than the novels of Dickens. What is asserted in this tra-dition is the claim to life, against the distortion of humanity by the pri-orities and disciplines of industrial capitalism. D.H. Lawrence is best seen as the latest writer in this important tradition. If we actually look at British working-class life, rather than at the stereotypes provided for political analysis and export, we find this, again pre-political, emphasis breaking out again and again. It is often anarchic, in its immediate forms, but in its insistence on satisfaction and excitement it is a moral

challenge of no less weight than that of puritanism. Nobody really knowing British working-class life would suppose that puritan was a whole
description of it. In recent years, with the weight of economic suffering
lifted, this energy, if still crude, has flowered, and is now, factually, the
most important challenge to the routines and orthodoxies of a society
basing itself on the class satisfactions of industrial capitalism. Here, if
still at a pre-political level, the grey routines of an alienated society are
so strongly challenged that more alarm is caused, to the effective ruling
class, by the way people take and use their leisure than by any overt
political challenge. The sound of the young in Britain, so terrifying to all
who have accepted the routines, is a deep and living sound, and it is
significant that where it becomes political it is against the whole structure of the society rather than for or against a particular group in parliamentary politics.

Unfortunately it is just here that the Labour Party is at its weakest. It
tries, from time to time, to get in on this life, but its whole bureaucratic
and official structure is against it. Against it, also, is its inheritance of
two other systems of ideas, which in essence are those of the nineteenth-
century bourgeoisie. Cobbett, Dickens, Ruskin, Morris, Lawrence: all
these in their lifetimes fought utilitarianism, and all except Ruskin
fought the kind of moral paternalism which was the other main line of
reform. What they claimed, positively, was man's absolute priority as a
creative and independent being. From this creativity and independence
came cooperation and a good society. From the setting of other priorities – political duty, economic discipline, the postponement and fragmentation of satisfaction – came the essential denials of life which bred
competition and inhumanity. But just these priorities – duty, discipline,
the division not only of labour but of life – were being enforced by
industrial capitalism. The utilitarian criterion of efficiency was often
progressive, against the early anarchies of industrial capitalism, but in its
later stages it reduced all social questions to this bleak and limited
dimension. Its reduction of life to a simple process of reciprocal production and consumption made it the perfect ideology of developed
industrialism. Moral paternalism was the only qualification. All the
human needs which the system of production and consumption could
not satisfy were relegated to a special area: art and suffering, education
and pleasure – these by-products or by-processes of the system were to
be dealt with by charity, by the administration of experts, to the degree
that could be afforded within the absolute priorities of the economic
system. People should have nothing for its own sake, and nothing as
themselves. All the satisfactions outside the straight economic system
would be administered by a charitable minority to the 'deserving poor'.

Utilitarianism survives in Britain in its crudest forms. Moral paternalism has become more sophisticated, and has even been built into the organs of state: education and the social services are administered in essentially its spirit. Between them, these kinds of thinking have dominated the modern Labour Party. On the older moral critique of industrial capitalism there was superimposed this other and alternative ideology. The principal agents of this were the Fabians, who really saw life in this way. And here is another complication. When the minority of English Marxists challenged the Fabians, as the makers of Labour ideology, their weaknesses were of a complementary kind. They too, whether in betrayal or uncritical acceptance of the main Marxist tradition, taught the priority of the economic system, and its inevitable control of other human activities and demands. Instinctively they were often against the Fabian spirit, but they worked in the same way: regarding the people as the material of power, and offering their revolutionary cadres as an alternative to the expert cadres of the Fabians. Between them, they confirmed the Labour Party in a tradition of economic priorities and rigid centralized direction. At every level this was a direct denial of the mainstream of the moral tradition of the British working-class movement, with its emphases on local democracy, participation, and the setting of human above economic standards. Thus the moral tradition not only failed to develop into a fully political maturity, but found its main political instrument dominated by the very ideologies it most bitterly opposed. The subsequent confusion, often expressed as a cynical withdrawal from politics, has been very great.

Thus when we look at the contemporary Left in Britain, we find many paradoxes, from many sources. The Labour Party as led by Wilson is, in the short term, an effective government, and is the most likely agency of the deeply necessary changes in British economic policy. As such it is, for any short-term programme, the only choice for the Left. But it is not only that its international policy is profoundly and dangerously obscure: in itself a sufficiently serious limitation when it is remembered that the last Labour government, with its useful domestic programme, was finally corrupted by the pressures of international politics and the Cold War. It is also that the spirit likely to dominate it is that of a reforming middle class, accepting the main purposes and organization of contemporary society, but concerned to make just this society more efficient. The deeper causes of 'inefficiency' are then inaccessible to it, and its conceptions of modernization are a mere blinking towards the future, with little real human content. It proposes not to alter social relations but to rationalize them, and at the first choice between economic orthodoxy and human need, as in the case of the pensioners, chooses orthodoxy as if this were need. Similarly, it offers to rationalize military aircraft production, or the command structure of the alliance, but hardly attempts to alter, or even discuss, the foreign policy which these serve. Even, it displays a dangerous petty-chauvinism, as in talk of the tradition of the navy in dealing with 'brush-fires' – an extraordinary description, by a Left government, of policies towards the revolutions of the Third World. The tired phrases of Kiplingesque imperialism, such as 'East of Suez', come from the same lips which seem to know no word for the future but 'modernization'. In these respects, a Labour government will not only fail to satisfy the deeper human demands of contemporary politics, but can even operate directly against them. And if the Labour Party were only this, it would be necessary to oppose it.

Yet much of the real strength of Labour is drawn from quite different human sources, and, further, the loyalty to it is of a kind to make certain that any real advances will come from developments within the movement, which cannot be captured from outside. Thus, as the Labour government runs into the seemingly inevitable contradiction between its official structure and ideology and the mainstream of the British working-class movement, the next decisive stage in our growth may well have been reached.

It is for this reason that two movements outside the Labour Party are now important, quite apart from the Communist Party with its guarantee of a measure of militant vigilance. The Campaign for Nuclear Disarmament has been, in recent years, the main bearer of the long moral tradition in British politics, and its relation to the official Labour Party has always been controversial. Because of its nature, it will not either support or oppose a Labour government; it will support or oppose actual policies. Since it is not part of the formal coalition of the Left, it is in a position to take initiatives which the existing structure of the Labour Party often prevents. In view of the continuing importance of the issue of nuclear politics, CND is of critical importance. It is, in fact, now deeply confused by the familiar conflict of loyalties on the Left, since so many of its members are active Labour supporters. But, equally, many are not, and nothing is more certain than that CND, or the grouping represented by it, will continue its challenge, at the level of argument and at the level of demonstrations, where it should be remembered that it is the only recent movement in British politics to have brought active political dissent into the streets.

The other relevant movement is the New Left. This is not, in spite of the intentions of some of its originators, an organizational political grouping. Its partial attempt to become one broke on the usual rock of majority loyalties and the centralizing pattern of British politics. But this, in my view, was never its real importance or function. What it can do, and what in present circumstances it alone can do, is to challenge the governing ideology of the labour movement, and in particular its attachment to utilitarianism and paternalism. The New Left is a group of writers and political thinkers, essentially based on the tradition of the moral critique of industrial capitalism which has been so important in the British working-class movement. From this position it is able to attack the Fabian ideology which captured the official Labour Party, and also to take part in the general attack on dogmatism within the Marxist tradition. There are already signs that it has in important ways influenced some Labour Party thinking, though it would be wrong to overestimate this degree of success. It must also be emphasized that the New Left has still a great deal to do in clarifying and developing its own positions. It has succeeded in defining the cultural crisis which is perhaps the most specific feature of advanced capitalism, and thus opening up a new political perspective. It has also emphasized the new international context of socialism, with the development of alternative paths in Communist societies and with the evident variations of socialism in the Third World. What it has not been able to do is to show, convincingly, the necessary consequences of ideological change on the structure of the British Left. Here, as we have seen, the issues are so complicated that prediction is virtually impossible. But perhaps we can say, in conclusion, that the mounting internal and external pressures on the present structure of British society make it likely that the changes will have to be lived rather than only debated. The critical period began in October, with Labour's narrow victory, which was nevertheless sufficient to break the set of the last thirteen years. An extraordinary instability of politics, reflecting the deep and postponed tensions of the society itself, seems now ahead of us. In this situation, the development of the British Left is again open and active.

Ideas and the Labour Movement

1981

Bad governments damage many things – they can even damage the intelligence of their opponents. A government may be so bad that it seems necessary only to remove it; anything else would be an improvement. This is good rhetoric but bad intelligence. Even under closed tyranny, opponents must think very hard about how to overthrow a regime and how to prevent it coming back. In more open situations, the processes are different but the problem is similar: how to convert the negative forces a bad government generates into positive forces that lead not only to its removal, but to a change in the circumstances in which it was instituted or could once again be instituted. Equally, no new government can do much with the assembly of negative forces generated by a previous bad government: the central activity by which a new government stands or falls is the very difficult process of converting enough of these negations into positive ones for practical construction.

Classical points – yet in practice they are often forgotten or excitedly overridden. In modern electoral politics the pressures to do so are very strong. There is not only an official government; there is also an official opposition. The underlying theory is alternation by general election. As the negative forces assemble, sustained thinking about new circumstances and new policies is cut short by the appearance of a ready-made alternative. 'This lot are no good, we'd better try the other lot', says a more-or-less resigned, half-cynical public opinion. But the party machines are more active: 'Cheer up, the Tories are coming'; 'Get Thatcher out, get Labour back'. On the screens, hoardings and car-stickers the slogans multiply, and the underlying message is always the same: 'Trust *Us*, Rely on *Us*'. Not them, us.

Within an electoral system, political parties are obliged to campaign at this level. But there is increasing evidence that if they define themselves only in these terms, they will become obsolete. Positive electoral support for the major parties has been declining for a generation; settled patterns based on principle, interest or custom have been radically disturbed and confused. Though the simple situation of a party 'representing' an established body of people survives as a basis for membership and organization, the electoral contest is decided beyond it, in shifting and unattached majority opinion. Such conditions, while very unfavourable for the conversion of frustration and opposition into positive construction, are ideal for the simple substitution of one party for another in government. But the underlying circumstances persist, and the negative processes will begin yet again. Many people now see this. Even party leaderships see it, after a few years in government and as the next election approaches. They are the main beneficiaries of the existing politics and exert great pressure to keep the ruling definitions intact: not them, *us*. What in government is a demand for loyalty – 'you put us in, now support us' – is expressed in opposition as the persuasive 'don't rock the boat; unite to get this lot out'.

Strong and ultimately necessary feelings of solidarity and comradeship are vigorously recruited in these mutually misleading directions. Propaganda has election and office as its horizon; political intelligence includes these, but is necessarily concerned with much wider forces. Everybody knows this, some of the time, but bad government either makes us forget it or persuades us to impatiently admit it, so that we can get on to the simpler and more emotionally satisfying business of telling each other about the damage and the prospects. Either way, the forces that eventually will be decisive are evaded or pushed into the background. Moreover, this is done with the appearance of virtue. 'Action not words' (though it is mainly words) appears urgent and practical, though on the record it is neither. It is a systematic habit that needs to be changed. The labour movement can change it. That is why the movement is important. But this importance depends almost entirely on it being a *movement*, rather than just a set of institutions adapted to 'playing their part' in the existing social order.

Our founders knew what they were doing when they called their actions a movement, but today the word is often just repeated out of habit. It is the same when we talk of the industrial and the political wings of the movement or of industrial action. The latter meant acting in work-places to change social conditions, alongside political action through Parliament and councils. But the term is now usually a euphemism for any kind of strike or work-to-rule, whether it is seen as connecting to the aims of a movement or not. At the same time the movement's political institutions are uneasy about any kind of action to change social conditions which is not regulated by them. As these reduced definitions operate, the idea of a movement is weakened and is substituted by the idea of orthodox institutions playing their part in political alternation or in bargaining within existing terms – even by people who still on festive occasions talk emotionally about 'the movement'. Yet the movement had to change, in part as a result of its own success in building itself to the point where its institutions had to be taken seriously as major organized social forces. This major historical success which has improved the conditions of working people led obviously, in some minds, to the idea of stabilizing the institutions, under the partly changed social order, and then to the idea that the movement existed mainly to maintain the strength of those institutions.

This idea underlies the still-common notion that the Labour Party has one secure and built-in characteristic: merely by its name and existence it represents all working people and their families. This parallels the notion that since, in another but not clearly defined capacity, the trade unions represent all working people and their families, the common interests of the party and the unions are self-evident. These notions are retained, in this customary theory, even when repeated electoral evidence shows that many working people do not accept that the Labour Party represents them and vote against it, and when the repeated experience of Labour governments shows that common interests and policies between the unions and the party-in-government are far from self-evident – indeed are usually at best matters for difficult negotiation, at worst an area of open conflict.

Ironically these problems are the result of weakening the idea of a *movement* and strengthening the idea of *institutions* adapted to the existing social order. The party, it is said, must govern, but governing is not always the process of representing what people actually want done, and the whole idea of 'representation' quickly becomes abstract. Often it means no more than the customary presumption that the name guarantees the identity of interest. Meanwhile the unions, representing their members in more immediate and localized ways, put the whole question of common interest and its representation at issue, not only as against policies evolved by government but – to the degree that they are reduced to sectoral bargaining units – as against coherent definitions of what the general interest is or could be.

Any social order is very difficult to build, and some of these problems would persist in the complexities of any real society whatever definitions had been adopted. But this should not be exaggerated to the coarse rhetoric, which we hear now too often, in which 'having to live in the real world' is offered as the excuse for anything and everything. This classic definition of 'realism' has been the motto of exploiters, manipulators, exponents of *Realpolitik* and turncoats through all the centuries of history which the labour movement set out to change. What is just as bad is that 'realism' – in practice a codeword for adapting to existing circumstances – often pushes away actual realism – facing deep underlying historical and material changes and thinking them through rather than reacting ad hoc in existing and familiar terms – as mere intellectual or academic speculation.

This brings us to the heart of a central problem of the modern labour movement. There are historical reasons why it has been quite common to distrust or to show open contempt for 'intellectuals'. Tories also distrust intellectuals and academics as disturbing and impractical people who succeed only in upsetting perfectly satisfactory arrangements by insisting on analysis, historical comparison, projections and warnings. What comes naturally from the conservative interest – to keep things as they are, to insist that in general all arrangements are the result of mature experience (including the experience of other attempted arrangements having failed) or to pretend that things are still basically as they have been even when they have visibly changed – is, or ought to be, very surprising when it comes from inside the labour movement. In fact, some of these feelings come from a comparably conservative habit of mind. You do not spend generations and whole working lives building institutions without becoming attached to them as such, and proposals for radical change are then easily seen as mere disloyalty and troublemaking. Even people in the labour movement now talk of 'subversives' and 'left-wing elements', words which used to be only the vocabulary of the ruling class.

But there are other, more serious reasons. Most intellectuals, even now after changes in education, either come from or soon identify with the ruling or privileged classes – the successors of all those writers, thinkers and publicists who told working people that their conditions and wages were the inevitable result of basic economic laws. Indeed, that is often still what they say. Moreover, in lifestyle, in speech and in habits, many of them were visibly strange and even alien, not even as sporting as lords or as practical as employers. Their one identifiable activity seems to be using words or statistics to confuse or screw you. But this view was always held, even though, from the beginning of the labour movement, there has been constant cooperation between working-class organizations and historians, scientists, social theorists and economists. Such people were always a minority in their own professional groups, but what they both taught and learned in active cooperation with the movement was a necessary part of its growth. Moreover, it was a formerly recognized part of the business of the movement to build educational and cultural organizations, as necessary elements of the aspirations of working people. From adult classes to theatre groups, and from labour colleges to newspapers, magazines and bookclubs, these parts of the movement were seen as integral to its success. Some survive, some new ones have been added. But it is fair to say that, in proportion to the resources of a now much more powerful movement, there has been since 1945 a quite extraordinary neglect of such enterprises. We now need to be very frank with each other about the reasons for this.

The first reason, or excuse, is that the expanded public educational and cultural systems have made them unnecessary. Previously, it is said, intelligent and enquiring working men and women had no real chance to fulfil their potential. Now (here comes a deep breath and a few prudent remarks about the continuing need for improvement) they have this chance, and specifically labour educational and cultural organizations are marginal. But it is not true that everyone now has his or her chance; education is still deeply distorted by the effects of class and privilege, not only in its selection of those who can take full advantage of it, but just as fundamentally in the kind of education which is then offered. A good, bright learner today still has a quick route to the habits of mind, the prejudices and rationalizations, the selective interpretations and the balance of certain kinds of knowledge with certain kinds of ignorance, which form so much of current education. Indeed, and I speak from the inside, from my own real world, in this sense the labour movement does not distrust intellectuals and educators nearly enough. In historical terms, the working class is still new to the idea of education. Either it is seen as success to learn what you are being taught (which even at primary levels may or may not be true and at advanced levels is rather unlikely to be true). Or, in reaction to this (as working families see their sons and daughters moving away from them, not only in what they know but in what they believe and do) there is reinforced the old distrust as voiced by the plebs' slogan 'Do you suffer from class consciousness? Come to Oxford and be cured.' Except that, for real reasons, it is often the other way round: some of our present worst enemies are working-class boys who have made it and demand not only privilege but a hierarchy because they themselves have shown that if you are good enough, you get your just reward – and if you are not good enough you are getting all that you are entitled to.

Thus, alongside improved public education, the labour movement needs institutions of two kinds. First, it needs places of serious research, learning and teaching based on its own values and aspirations. It is a delusion to suppose that the existing social order will provide these. Second, it needs professional groups of men and women committed to the movement, who will develop their knowledge and disciplines in autonomous ways but also have genuine contacts with the political and industrial organizations of the wider movement. It is a major development of the last fifteen years that such professional groups have been developing among socialist economists, historians, doctors, lawyers, architects, philosophers, writers, cultural analysts and so on. A current attempt by these groups to collaborate in a new society of socialists could in new ways do for the movement today what the Fabian Society and the smaller Marxist organizations did for the movement of the past. It will be very interesting to see how this open and unsectarian intellectual initiative is received; there is bound to be advantage in further developing socialist professional groupings, but the real test is whether the highly developed forms of knowledge and inquiry which such groupings contain can flow freely to and from the wider movement. But the problem is very much broader: if it assumed that, by definition, the movement represents actual, stable majorities of working people, and that further electoral and organizing progress depends only on overcoming old fears and prejudices, then the educational and cultural organizations of the movement are simply there to 'bring the message' or spread the truth. This still does apply, and both Party and unions have done too little – the Party especially.

Yet this touches the second reason or excuse. It is still widely believed that even progressive intellectuals and cultural workers are not really interested in the movement's fundamental character and aims; indeed, at times the movement suspects that it is a soft touch for all sorts of groups simply wanting to do their own thing. The hard-won resources of the movement, it is then said, must be used for primary and practical purposes; as for the propaganda, the existing organizations can do that for themselves, if necessary with skilled communicators like advertising agencies and television personalities. This is so bad a misreading of the situation that it is difficult to discuss it with any patience. The fact is that 'the message' – in its assumed simple forms – has been distributed again and again, and an increasing number of people are not only not listening to it, they are actively irritated by it and see it as just one more line of politicians' or union bosses' talk. If the only response to this mood is to repeat the message louder, or employ even more advertising agencies and build new personalities and images, then further defeats are inevitable.

The movement's institutions were shaped in a pre-modern culture, but cannot then be changed by anything so simple as modernization. Cultural changes over the last thirty years have been profound, and are of a kind that cannot be engaged with by traditional political and industrial organizations alone, or by occasionally hiring the market research, opinion polling and advertising techniques of late capitalist society.

Through the movement's struggles, the working class has made major gains towards its traditional objectives, but within a capitalist state and economy and within a capitalist *culture*. At the core of unprecedented levels of distribution of information, opinion and persuasion is a set of pervasive capitalist values based in large-scale state and capitalist corporations. Thus a complex society, divided by class, by region, by gender and by ethnic origin, is massed as 'public opinion', with internal sectors designated as areas of a market. Like goods and services, political opinions and definitions of politics are sold, and people are defined as 'consumers' – a word which comes as readily to the lips of Labour ministers as to the capitalists and marketeers who first defined people in this passive and subordinate way. A version of people as primarily possessing and consuming individuals has been so widely propagated that most political argument feels obliged to start from it, and the electoral contest is often a process of competitive bids. Given the generations of deprivation in the working class, and the recurring phases of new deprivation, it is not surprising that this version has been locked into so many minds and determines so many votes.

At the same time there is incessant propagation of certain selected people as leaders and celebrities. Indeed, much of the human interest excluded by this version of people as possessors and consumers is, at the level of the distributed culture, expressed by the attention given to the lives of these selected people: the royal family, entertainers, sportsmen, criminals and politicians. The induced gaze is always upward, though edges of spite and gossip operate as controls on the natural resentment of a regularly cricked neck. We are invited to possess and consume at appropriate levels, as delivered by this or that set of leaders and celebrities; the ordinary enjoyment of some possessing and consuming locks us – or is intended to lock us – into this deep sense of the nature of society.

Yet all this operates within a world of people in their own real places, organizations and families. The passing show can often ignore these, but if anything occurs in the real world which contradicts or threatens the glossy, orthodox world, the same powers and techniques of distribution are at once turned against the interruption with a ferocity that indicates something of the falsity of the general blandness of the glossy world. Workers on strike, 'unofficial' or 'extremist' leaders or spokesmen, are portrayed to others and themselves as the demons and wreckers in this possessing, consuming and stargazing homeland. Of course it does not always work in the same way for everybody. But the movement has radically underestimated the deep damage that has been done to older kinds of popular and working-class consciousness, on which it continues to rely in what are now its minority organizations, and which in certain situations it can still mobilize and revive.

We all talk about distortion by the media, but if the movement as a whole had been serious about it, how could we possibly have let the last Labour newspapers disappear or get sold out? In the twenties and thirties, many working-class families took the *Daily Herald* as an act of commitment, and still took it after its ownership and character had changed. It is a bitter history that this paper became first the Cudlipp *Sun* and now the Murdoch *Sun.* Yet at no point has the modern movement, with all its resources, offered or helped to offer a real alternative. The *Mirror* dazzles and fades. *The Guardian* has a different vocabulary. The labour movement looks on, confident that because of its name and inheritance it still at root represents, even owns, its own people. It has in fact been a rake's progress through a dwindling inheritance, and the rakishness has been high-level metropolitan politics, around Westminster and Downing Street.

Or, to look at it another way: in the early days of bringing the message, the pioneers did not have to encounter minds already filled to overflowing and often to boredom with political opinionation and economic doubletalk. Today the level of information and opinion, of a kind, is higher than ever and the movement joins in, at what seems the only available level. But there is at best only a temporary advantage. The information and opinions are reasonable, provided the deep assumptions are taken for granted. To give radically new kinds of information, to shift not opinions but beliefs, is from the beginning a different kind of activity. And this is why the movement now needs not only political and industrial wings, but on a scale not yet contemplated new kinds of educational and cultural organizations.

The possibilities are good. Since 1945 there has been a remarkable expansion of the sons and daughters of the movement who have gone on into intellectual and cultural work. In every field, from theory to theatre, there is now a more active Left culture than there has ever been. Some of its work is strange to the older movement; some of it has suffered by its very isolation and become brackish and involuted. But this energy is crucial to the whole movement and can become popular, challenging the capitalist culture on its own ground, if the rest of the movement now sees its importance. It will conflict at certain points with some of the routines and pieties of the inherited movement, but it deserves a genuine test of its commitment, not least because it will then learn and grow. In the last few years there have been signs that this is beginning to happen. The appalling press of the winter of 1979 shocked many influential trade unionists. Changes in the party are bringing in many more enquiring and open-minded people, and political education officers are again becoming active in some constituencies. Links and initiatives are being widely attempted, beyond both the orthodox and the metropolitan culture.

These are hopeful beginnings, but still only beginnings. The real tasks are very large indeed.

My final example embodies my whole argument. The present levels of unemployment – the terrible damage inflicted by this exceptionally bad government – have led to vigorous responses from the traditional movement: party and union demonstrations, the People's March. These build a popular opposition, and must of course continue. But then comes the critical point where, in the past, we have failed and failed again. The negative forces against Thatcherism build up strongly. But are they then merely channelled into alternation? To judge from most speeches, you would think so. 'Get a Labour government and get back to full employment.' Of course a Labour government would make an important difference. But it is not only that people remember the already high levels of unemployment under the last Labour government; it is that there are real and difficult questions about whether any government, in the present deep crisis of the world capitalist order, and in the especially exposed condition of the British economy, could within one parliament restore anything like full employment. Why then say so? Because it assists the passage to alternation, at the next general election? And because, in any case, the Labour Party has some genuine plans for reviving British industry? These reasons have an orthodox plausibility, but they are not the reasons of a genuine movement.

The plans for revival depend on very difficult measures of restructuring and on controls and redirection of investment. Their success, against already formidable capitalist opposition, will depend very largely on a high degree of popular support, and above all understanding. Such understanding, which includes the admission of all the unpalatable facts about the long-run crisis of the economy and of the fundamentally weak prospects in the old capitalist countries for full industrial employment of the old kinds, is not to be gained by the slogans of alternation or by propaganda based on dramatizing the currently negative facts. The real forces will in any case come through, when actual policies are attempted. Should not a real movement face them from the beginning, institute the widest possible processes of genuine information and discussion, specify and cost the real options, admit and above all share the very hard choices, which go far beyond any alternation of governments or leaderships?

I do not underestimate what is already being done within the Party and the unions. But the processes will have to go far beyond Party and union activists. The negative forces, which may or may not bring electoral victory, will become positive as part of a process of widespread, active and intellectually rigorous education and discussion, or not at all. The most sophisticated alternative strategies will not succeed without this wide degree of popular understanding and support. And its building involves a new and extended kind of politics: not replacing the older forms, though it will change them, but taking seriously, on a large scale, the realities of the modern politics of information, education and culture.

False, half-false or merely hopeful promises will be seen through eventually, perhaps seen through before there is even a chance to implement the genuine promises. It is not a risk we can take within the now mounting dangers. And we do not have to take it. We have the resources of a potential movement of a new kind: working to change the ways in which we see the world as part of the long, hard process – still a long revolution – of actually changing it.

An Alternative Politics

1981

This challenge must be accepted, for at least two reasons.[1] First, because the Labour Party is now subject to change, though to what extent and in what direction is still uncertain. Second, because those of us who are committed to the labour movement, yet who are critics of what has been accurately called Labourism, have an obligation to engage with practical policy, at the levels at which this is ordinarily determined, even when we also insist on discussing those problems of theory and assumption which these processes typically evade.

It is of course perfectly possible that there will not, again, be a monopoly Labour government. The coalition with Liberalism and with right-wing social democracy, which has been a fact of life for socialists inside the Labour Party, may become an even more formal constraint. Significantly the chances largely depend on the variables of negative voting. If we cannot believe that enough people will vote against Thatcherism there is no point in any projection. Yet the probability of the continuation of much merely negative, anti-government voting, and of this as decisive, is itself a critical factor in the evolution of those political forces which, in a sense arbitrarily, benefit from it. The depth of the real crisis can be in effect ignored by identifying it with an existing government, until it seems that the mere fact of an alternative government is itself a solution. Yet since memories of identification of the crisis with a Labour government are still quite fresh, negative voting may produce quite new forms of confusion.

However, the only reponse that is then possible for British socialists is

---

1. This essay was written as a response to the following question: If a Labour government were to be elected, and taking into account all that we know about past performance, what would you want such a government to do? [Ed.]

a serious attempt to build positive forces and programmes for real change. The current position of what is called the leadership – 'don't rock the boat, let's unite to get Thatcher out' – is not only an opportunist negativism; it is also complacent in its assumption that it is bound to be the beneficiary, and that if it is it will know what to do (except to go on being the leadership). On the other hand, a serious alternative is not only a matter of programmes; it is above all a matter of building (for they will not be inherited from that sequence of negations) reasonably adequate social and political forces for positive change.

In an earlier essay[2] I tried to describe the programmes and initiatives which are necessary before any serious left policy is possible or is attempted in government. I agreed with current proposals and campaigns to democratize the Labour Party and to reorganize the independent Left, but I mainly emphasized a major effort in research and education, on a scale which has not been attempted for at least two generations. The present essay follows from that perspective and emphasis, and is mainly concerned with what could be done, in government, to extend and sustain that effort.

This is deliberately different from listing certain major political and economic policies. Of course these are crucial, but some of the best of them – the nuclear disarmament of Britain; the control of banks, insurance companies and pension funds for productive investment; exchange and import controls for the recovery of British industry – are typically presented as if they could be carried through on the basis of a parliamentary majority. This, even on the Left, is the Labourist perspective which is at the heart of the problem. For to carry through any of these policies, which would radically change economic and political power in this country and change also its formal alliances and its now enmeshed relations with international capital, would require a degree of sustained popular understanding and support which is of a quite different order from an inherited and in part negative electoral majority.

For the Left has not only been deceived by Labour governments. It has often been defeated, and can expect to be defeated again, when its policies are at any real distance from serious and organized majority or potential majority opinion. The very powerful forces it is certain to encounter, in any of these initiatives – over a range from national and international institutions and companies, through widely distributed organizations for influencing public opinion, to the confusions, uncertainties and lack of information among its own potential supporters – are not of a kind to be defeated from a parliamentary centre alone. Thus

2. The reference is to the preceding essay in this volume, 'Ideas and the Labour Movement', which was originally published in *New Socialist* 2, November/December 1981. [Ed.]

however urgent any of these policies might be, in its own terms, the struggle for it will inevitably take place in much wider terms, and with all the forces in play. The 'alternative strategy', that is to say, is no more than an intellectual exercise unless it carries with it, and indeed as its priority, an alternative politics.

We can assume, for present purposes, that a Labour government, with left policies, has some four years of parliamentary majority. The first question is then whether what happens is (a) steady implementation of its programme or (b) a very early transition to what is called, significantly, 'crisis-management' or (c) some mixture, in critically variable proportions, of (a) and (b).

It is very striking that (b) almost always happens, and that it determines the mixture in the eventual (c). In fact this is only to say that in any country, but especially in one so exposed and involved in a wider arena as Britain, the reality gap between a manifesto and a government is to some extent inevitably wide. Vietnam, Rhodesia and Ulster had at least as much to do with the reality of the Labour governments from 1964 to 1970 as any programmes and policies it had itself foreseen or instituted. It is this regular experience which underlies the right-wing opportunism, or even open cynicism about any planned public policy, which is now endemic among most politicians with actual experience of governing. Most of them go on presenting policies as if this were not so, but this means very little and in any case has the effect, beyond them, of sapping public belief in planned and rational policies. The current contempt for 'politicians', however deserved, is a major obstacle to all traditional socialist construction.

At the same time those who have come to view government as crisis-management, with themselves as its self-evident candidates, have in one way bridged the reality gap, by the practical cancellation of any hope of planned and radical change. This world-weary adaptation behind a screen of public relations is, however, more than a historical-occupational feature of contemporary political leaders. It is also, among better or more deserving people, a readily available response to an actual and prolonged complexity of crisis. To speak differently and positively, with actual commitment to change, is morally refreshing but is still on its own no alternative. It is not only that the reality gap is repeatedly ignored or denied, for what sound like good idealist reasons. It is also that the reality gap cannot, by definition, be bridged by *proposals*, however internally coherent or convincing these may be. For the reality of what is called, with a certain heroic air, crisis-management, is that the crises are simple exposures to existing real relations, as distinct from the presumed and limited relations within which most programmes are formulated, and moreover that what is called management is never a merely neutral process of local response and negotiation, but is a practical disclosure of existing real forces and interests. Against such real pressures, not only public-relations manifestos but on their own even genuine and coherent programmes stand little chance of success. For these become, to the extent that they are serious, the crises that others move in to manage, with all available real forces.

We can take examples from three major policies already mentioned, all of which I strongly support. The nuclear disarmament of Britain would involve, at any of its stages, confrontation with the embedded forces of the military-political alliance (both NATO as such and the political and economic relations which underlie it). The redirection of the financial institutions to British-based productive investment would encounter not only their massive immediate interests in their own profits, and not only their retaliatory capacity in government finance and the international monetary system, but also, unless other things were changed, the incorporated interests of those who now invest or save in them. Exchange and import controls would encounter not only the powerful interests of existing trading and monetary relations, and not only the direct interests of the powerful transnational companies, but also, in their effects on consumption, and certainly on prices and availability, the existing habits of a majority of our own people.

None of these points is an argument against the policies. Each of them, however, is an argument that should determine their actual politics. Beyond a parliamentary majority for a manifesto, which promised them, and again beyond a party made accountable to such a manifesto – the two powerful campaigns which now command most energy, and by which the success or failure of the Left is ordinarily measured – the crucial requirement is a genuine popular majority or potential majority for the quite extraordinary struggles that would in fact, in any of these cases, ensue. Such a majority cannot be taken for granted in the fact of an electoral majority, since this typically includes negative and alternative voting of a less specific kind, and is in any case a vote for a bundle of policies which cannot by the act of general election be discriminated. Indeed many of the positive votes, here as so often before, would be for more employment, lower prices, less taxation and the usual ideal mix. None of these aspirations would have sufficient specific weight to sustain successful struggles on the scale that must be expected. Yet we are still asking, and for at least one more parliament reasonably, what can be done, if this is so, within the existing party and parliamentary structures.

The defining centre of any successful left politics is the radical extension of genuine popular controls. This will have to take many forms. Some of these depend on institutional changes, which a government and parliament can effect. Some again are legislative changes, with direct parliamentary availability. Some, finally, are broader cultural changes, which can be radically encouraged by a left Party, both before and after its election to government.

The underlying purpose of all these changes is to build popular majorities from within but also going beyond the organized working class – for both local and general struggles. It is an attempted break beyond the politics of the most benevolent or determined representative administration. It is both a practical necessity if the representative administration is to have any chance of success in its most serious conflicts with existing real forces, and is in itself the only acceptable direction, in societies like our own, of socialist change.

Consider first, then, some institutional changes. It is part of the weakness of Labourism, as we have known it, and also a main reason for a certain deep-rooted unpopularity, that it has nationalized important sectors of the economy, and proposes to nationalize more, without significantly altering either the internal class and work relations of such industries and services, or their external relations with the general economy and society. It should then be an early priority of a Labour government to direct each nationalized industry and service to prepare and present proposals, based on the views of all those working in it, which will at least democratize and at best socialize what are already, nominally, publicly owned and controlled institutions.

This would be only one side of the necessary reform. Alteration of existing financial directives to the productive institutions, and of existing financial limits on the service institutions, comes within more normal definitions of policy. But this needs to be supplemented, and made more rational, by new coordinating arrangements of a horizontal kind, at first alongside the existing vertical arrangements with different ministries. National planning councils, in both the productive and service sectors, could be instituted by direct and independent election from the bodies concerned. It is a particular vice of the modern state, with its important 'public' sectors, that on top of the process of parliamentary election there is a system of monopolist appointment to the control of public bodies, which is in fact intended to ensure verticalism, concentration of power and dependence.

It is clear that the requirements of public finance and investment necessarily involve responsibility to an elected government. But there would be substantial advantage in alternative and parallel forms of public responsibility, of a less monopolist and dependent kind. A process of coordination based on election from the various public bodies would give an alternative presence and voice in the determination of public policies. Such councils could, for example, have direct access to

Parliament, alongside their relations with ministries. Further reforms could be made in the network of what are now called consumers' advisory bodies, now typically appointed and recruited by obscure and indirect procedures. Direct election to such bodies, either generally or from constituencies of actual users, could begin to make a reality of public responsibility, in phase with the increased reality of public ownership in the reformed constitutions of the providers.

Such changes would probably in fact improve efficiency, since there have been radical failures of coordination in the public sector, most clearly in energy policy, and since feedback from users is now notoriously impeded by bureaucracy and divided responsibility. But the main purpose of the reforms would be political. There is no real prospect of socialist advance, along the necessary paths of public ownership, unless the deep unpopularity of many of the nationalized institutions is admitted as something more than reactionary prejudice. There are already quite enough enemies in the affected capitalist order, and it is crucial to shift majority opinion about existing and further public ownership by real measures of democratization and direct public accountability. That would then be the political base from which further public ownership could proceed.

Such changes would take time to work out, but for that reason should be initiated very early in a parliament. There would be severe competition for priorities, most evidently from the general crisis of employment and finance. But the crucial choice between a socialist programme and what would quite quickly become an adaptation to crisis-management would occur almost at once, at this overtly political level. Exchange controls and some forms of import control need not encounter significant public opposition, in their early stages, and these would in any case have to be priorities. But every indicator of the probable shape of the economy at the time of an incoming Labour government shows desperately narrow margins for any policy of regeneration. The Labour Party, right and left, seems still to believe that it could simply cancel Tory restrictions and resume a relatively indiscriminate expansion. It would quickly discover otherwise, and would soon be forced back to negative policies, after the first rush, and especially to negative kinds of wage controls.

It is within this context that the institution of public controls over the use of public money accumulated for specific purposes – in insurance, pension funds and bank savings – has to be politically directed. The forms of control would vary, and would doubtless begin with legislative requirements of minimum levels of publicly authorized investment in Britain. Yet since it will be necessary to go beyond this, in the especially sensitive area of insurance and pension funds, it is crucial that the policy should be designed from the beginning to defeat the inevitable and powerful propaganda against what will be called a state grab. Here as elsewhere (for example in taxation and especially national insurance policies) it is politically vital that the destination as well as the source of the funds should be both visible and a matter of sustained public discussion. The acquisition of such funds by an indiscriminate and secretive Treasury, or by some ministerially appointed board, would generate formidable and perhaps decisive opposition. This is why all procurement for public investment must be accompanied, stage by stage, by the development of visible and publicly approved investment plans. This political requirement is even more important than the evident economic requirement.

There are some precedents on which to build, such as the National Enterprise Board in its original conception. But the whole planning process will have to be taken very much more seriously. Singular planning, either from ministries or from a ministerially appointed enterprise board, should be steadily replaced by more complex and more open economic planning procedures. For it is a residual delusion, which the deep crisis of the economy would in practice quickly dispel, that the flow of public money to existing British industrial structures, or to these marginally modified, would be generally regenerative. Different principles have now to be introduced at a very early stage, and because they will involve many radical shifts in the shape of the economy they are from the beginning a political problem.

Nobody can delineate all these shifts in advance. Opposition parties and groups can make opportunist proposals, in which 'Investment' is merely investment in anything and everything. The most rigorous enquiry into genuine priorities will have to be undertaken, within what is now a quite desperate contraction. Because any such decisions will have radical social effects (no less so because it is obvious that the absence of decisions or the handing-over to international market forces will have effects even more disturbing) the problem of public planning will have to be made political in new ways. The attempt to develop a national plan will have to be resumed, and as more than an assembly of ad hoc or existing market decisions. There is some realistic preparatory work for this in the industrial and sectoral working parties of NEDC, which need to be vigorously revived. But what is most needed is the introduction of some new principles.

Any national plan must eventually rest with the elected government, but the stages of its development should not be monopolistic and internal, as typically in inherited socialist ideas. At an early stage, a Labour government should appoint and fund at least two qualified planning groups, each of which should have access to all available public and industrial information. Each should have the responsibility of reporting, stage by stage, both to parliament and more generally. The point of having at least two qualified organizations is that it makes the processes of rational choice at once more visible and more practicable. Public hearings on what would be likely to be alternative sets and mixes of priorities would be a process of building actual majority choices and support, and parallel public hearings on actual investment resources – bringing the financial institutions to the bar of opinion – would have the important political effect of the construction, stage by stage, of a genuine public interest.

We would of course have to learn by doing, and the difficulties are obvious and formidable. But it is my judgment that the time has passed, in this society, when a majority can be found for any sustained delegation of major controls over our work and our resources to any monopolist bureaucracy backed by a temporarily elected government. Ministries can have major short-term effects, but at certain levels they can now be effectively frustrated by a range of autonomous social actions, from strikes and protest movements to the equally widespread forms of non-cooperation and evasion: often necessary but also almost all negative. As these build up, in their diverse forms, they assemble the eventually decisive negative voting. Thus the planning process will either be open and public, and in those senses pluralist, or it will not occur at all, except in short-run programmes. Moreover, as it weakens, it will be swamped, as always before, by capitalist power and its highly experienced market forces.

I would add, in parenthesis, my own sense of the very general priorities which would have to govern such a plan. It is in my view crucial to alter the indiscriminate emphasis on exports. It is clear that there are important and sustainable export areas, in high technology and some other advantageous sectors. But the priority, in my view, should be that of import substitution, in any area in which the marginal differentials are not too unreasonable. This includes, incidentally, food, where the current prejudice against European-type agriculture on so much of the Left is, even in the medium-term, absurd. Given actual developments in the world market, it is not going to be possible to re-establish the old simplicities of manufactured exports and imported cheap food, and a Labour government could waste many of our real resources in attempting to re-establish that residual Imperial pattern. (This governs, incidentally, my attitude to the EEC. A national plan, of the kind described, would, if it came to it, have to take priority over EEC membership, but there are some indications that one kind of national plan, especially in its relations to the world monetary system and to the transnational companies, would at its best and strongest be coordinated with the other

European economies, and while there is any chance of this the institutional connections could be retained.)

The political character of initiatives in international policy hardly needs emphasis, but it is obvious that any radical initiative – and at the top of the list is nuclear disarmament – is quite extraordinarily sensitive and politically vulnerable. Here also I attach great importance to an extended policy of European cooperation. The policy of a nuclear-weapons-free Europe, East and West, has a much more sustainable political base than any simple unilateralism, though unilateral refusal of new developments in the arms race is important as one way of initiating and indeed enforcing more general negotiations. Any such refusal should be accompanied by proposals for a disarmament conference conducted directly between European powers. The delegation of European disarmament negotiations to the USA and USSR should be firmly challenged and resisted.

At the same time much could be done, within Britain, to open up the defence debate. A Labour government could at once authorize serving members of the armed forces to give their views, directly to parliament and public, on the very complex and technical options now being internally argued. At the same time members of the armed forces could be given the trade-union and democratic rights already available elsewhere in Europe, and laws forbidding direct discussion between servicemen and civilians repealed. Any government which appears to threaten national security on the basis of one among many manifesto statements will become so weak, politically, that it will either not survive or will soon fall back into the existing lines. A vigorously promoted public discussion on the realities of national security is then the only sustainable political course for any radical initiatives.

The common thread in these arguments is the positive institution of a more active and better informed democratic process. In this, beyond the particular areas of policy mentioned, there is much formal and informal work for a Labour government to do. A Freedom of Information Act is an early priority. Virtually all other processes depend on it. Major investment in the new electronic communications systems is, in my view, another priority, since many of the kinds of public discussion described could best be carried out through these technologies, with their incomparable advantages of speed, interaction, and availability and recall of information. Most of these technologies are now being developed for marketing or for marginal entertainment, though their potential for public information, discussion and decision has already been demonstrated in pilot projects which have not yet attracted the necessary public funding.

Within the older communications technologies, and especially in broadcasting, there should be new policies of non-commercial decentralization, with professional companies leasing publicly owned resources and being responsible to elected regional and local boards. The same transition to elected boards should be made in such bodies as the Arts Council. In education the present system of appointed governing bodies, at all levels, should be scrapped, and replaced by bodies elected from the relevant communities and immediate users. At the same time, as was argued in my earlier essay, the labour movement, with all necessary support from a Labour government, should develop as a matter of urgency alternative institutions of research, education and more general publicity.

Further areas for early action, in a wider field, include the development of new national policies for Scotland and Wales, related to extended English regional autonomies. Within these different areas the same popular processes and institutions must be given priority. One crucial example would be the transfer of day-to-day administration of council housing to elected tenants' associations.

These are only indications of a general direction of policy. It is reasonable to object that to carry them all through would take more than four years. But my argument has been that the generation of active democracy is the central policy on which all more specific socialist programmes will stand or fall. What should frighten all of us is the prospect of a Labour government, in part elected on a negative vote, trying in centralized and bureaucratic ways to effect radical shifts of power, and then, in all probability not only failing but appearing to discredit the whole socialist enterprise, thus opening the way, as the British crisis continues to deepen, to an authoritarian Right which would make the present Thatcher government seem liberal by comparison.

The old options for moderate and centrist policies seem to me, for both economic and social reasons, to have disappeared or to be fast disappearing in this now failing capitalist country. This may mean that the next Labour government, if we even get that far, would be, in the medium term, a last chance. Many necessary policies are now being proposed and indeed, on paper, adopted. The struggle inside the Party is bringing some of its own decision-making processes into the open. But the issues will have to be fought in a very much larger arena, and since this is so the struggle is not only for the Party but for the people: for an informed, mobilized and determined majority which can alone make real changes.

Problems of the Coming Period

1983

The title I was given for this talk was 'Problems of the Coming Period'![1]
When this was set, some six weeks ago, the coming period that was in
mind was the twenty years or so up to and through the millennium; that
term which we still have to use, millennium, for the Western Christian
date of 2000, but which also has its ironic echoes of the coming good
time, the transformation. It happens that the period up to the year 2000
is by any reckoning, whatever numerical system you employ, one of the
major periods of crisis in all human history. So the perspective of that
period seems an important thing to discuss.

Since then, however, the coming period has been redefined as the
next four weeks, until the general election. There's a sense in which one
could be tempted to drop all that long-term thinking about the period
up to 2000, and just talk about the next four weeks. That I think would
be wrong, if only because some of the things that will be happening in
the next four weeks, and certainly the situation that may then emerge,
require us to think of a scale of problems and challenges which, for all
the efforts of a number of people in this and other countries, the Left
has not really met. In other words, while we can recognize, respect, and
even where we can't respect, discount the kind of opportunism and
short-term argument that becomes the daily fare of a general election
campaign, we have all the time to be looking through and past it at the
underlying problems. The most central of these is this: How can it be,
and who at any period could have predicted, that the most open right-
wing government for half a century in Britain, coming after the
supposed liberal and social-democratic consensus of the postwar years;

1. The text of a talk given to the Socialist Society, London, 11 May 1983. A general
election had been called for 9 June. [Ed.]

a government, directly responsible for massive de-industrialization of the British economy and for massive unemployment; engaged in an absurd military adventure twelve months ago; virulent in cold war attitudes; rigid and resistant to all initiatives towards disarmament and the problems of nuclear weapons; how can such a government outstrip, as it has done so far, not merely the challenges of the Left (we have been accustomed to being in a minority), but all those apparently solid formations of British society – what we thought we had most to analyse: the liberal, social-democratic and right-wing Labour consensus? How can it outstrip both?

It is so unreasonable that much of the time one thinks, and not just as a pleasant kind of fantasy, that it cannot be objectively true. We can imagine that at some point, in what has after all been a very volatile and changing situation, there will again be some massive and unforeseen shift of opinion which will make this apparent possibility the real impossibility which one hopes it is. Yet I think we're quite deluding ourselves if we suppose that using our received ideas, our received kinds of analysis, we can intellectually or politically anticipate that kind of shift. Nobody can rule it out, but there is still the sheer scale of the shift required. One would have been reckoned deranged rather than merely mistaken (and we sometimes tend on the Left to call people deranged where we only mean mistaken) if in 1960, 1968, or 1974 we had said, look, in 1983, there will be this kind of situation. It would not have seemed possible. And therefore there is a very acute problem for analysis, and this I think can only be met if we start by putting the British situation into a much wider context. Both wider geographically and wider in the sense of the temporal perspective, than we have, again in spite of many efforts, so far succeeded in doing. Because we have to try to understand how this consciousness, which is not only hostile to us, but which appears to be profoundly destructive of the very people who uphold it, has been generated.

So I see the coming period as a question not only of the next four weeks but of the next twenty years or so. And what we have to say has to make as much sense on 10 June as on 9 June, when I think we may be in need of sense. It isn't necessary for me to say much specifically about the immediate issues that will crystallize in this election campaign. Anyone likely to be at this meeting could say those things as well as or better than I. The current agenda, the current issues, are set. What I want to say is that the key to understanding the general situation is the extraordinary gap between a specifically generated British consciousness and the real situation of this now very diverse British people and society in the world. This distance is the cause, or one of the causes, of the extraordinary failures to recognize the situation and to respond to it, which is most characteristic of current majority political opinion. I put it that way, as a distance or gap, with the intention of being relatively optimistic. If it is a gap it is something which might be bridged. If it is a confused misrecognition, it is something that might eventually be recognized.

I'm dissenting therefore from the kinds of analyses which some of my friends have been making (and which I see the strength of) in which it is argued that Thatcher has somehow encapsulated something which was endemic in the society: a peculiarly hard, authoritarian, anti-intellectual, racist consciousness, which was latent and which Thatcher has now materialized. Good people are arguing this, and the evidence for that kind of crystallization is in a sense there. But we have to remind ourselves that supposing Thatcher wins, at the existing level, or with some addition or some deduction, in four weeks time, this cannot allow us to conclude that the majority of the British people can be defined as Thatcherite in consciousness. I mean this is simply a matter of elementary analysis. If that happens, even if it happens as a worse version of the present situation, it will still be the case that it is only our extraordinary electoral system which permits the continuation of that kind of absolute power. On the very worst showing, less than half of British voters approve the Thatcherite policies in the terms asked, which is whether they will vote for a Conservative government. And from that figure, somewhere in the middle forties, you have to deduct another figure. It's difficult to put it in exact quantity, but it would be well over 30 per cent, it might be higher, which would vote Conservative if the Conservative Party were led by Prior, Pym, Gilmour, Heath or whoever.

In other words, there is a core Conservative vote which is temporarily commanded in the Conservative Party by Thatcher and her friends. So the too quick identification of certain very dangerous tendencies in the society, becoming a majority or even a dominant tendency, could actually disarm us from thinking about what the situation and its possibilities are. Its existence at the level of 10 or 15 per cent, whatever it may really be, is very serious, and it is also very serious that it is growing. But we have to place it within a situation, as I was describing a few minutes ago, of misrecognition and confusion which, if we could understand it, might provide a base for the directions in which a whole new kind of socialist argument has to be developed. Whereas if we think that this sector of opinion, which is often spoken about in the metaphors of virus or epidemic – pathological metaphors anyway – is the sign of a whole culture becoming Thatcherite, then really only an extreme defensive response is possible: of battening down the hatches, as some would say, of preparing for a very rough time, of concentrating on the maintenance of our own organizations and so on.

But it seems to me that is not at all the situation. On the contrary, although that danger is there, there is at least an equal danger from acquiescence by the Left in an interpretation which, as it were, would blame the majority of the British people for not accepting a socialist analysis. Again the shift from that to a kind of blame or contempt for the majority is a latency which can always be exploited. Negative feelings, which socialists in bad times are particularly prone to, could take the place of the kind of analysis, and therefore the kind of activity, which a different reading of the situation would support. What I'm saying is that there is this confusion and misrecognition because of the very specific situation of a nation, if it can still be called that, which has in all serious senses lost its confident social identity and its confident sense of its present and future; and which is, therefore, (this being the paradox) all the more vulnerable to an artificial and even false, in any case a very narrow, version of what it is.

Let's dwell on that point for a moment. It is not because the British people are excessively nationalist and self-confident that you got the absurd jingoism of the Falklands episode. It is because the real national self-identification and self-confidence that once existed have gone, that a certain artificial, frenetic, from-the-top, imagery of a nation can be injected. The most serious comment I heard on the Falklands War was from a German friend of mine, an old student, who said, 'We talked about this for a long while and we wondered what would be the difference in the mood in England if they were fighting us.' This seems to me absolutely the correct response. For if it had been a real war, and we had been fighting Germany, or fighting the Soviet Union, the difference of mood would have been extraordinary. The kind of spectacular consumerist militarism which that episode was – with all the guns going off eight thousand miles away, thus with war reduced, for all but the unfortunate people who were sent there, to television screens, rhetoric, flags and so on – simply cannot be identified with other versions of nationalism, let alone of national identity. It is in absence and distance that this kind of artificial and superficial image of the nation can be generated and temporarily adopted.

In the same way, consider the sense which is now so worrying, that many unemployed people, including some of the long-term unemployed, when at least some of the causes of unemployment are wholly open to rational explanation and change, identify with the interpretation of a certain inevitability which has been one of the main propaganda lines of the Thatcher government. That it is all inevitable, that it is a world depression and so on. But in one way this is a true recognition of the powerlessness of most of us, both within a national capitalist system and even more within an international capitalist system. This powerlessness gets translated into a sense of inevitability before forces which are respected if only because they are there to confirm inevitability, producing their cold logic: money. This is what the ruling class has so often done. But what of the resilience that has often been there, that was often there in the thirties, in an equally bad situation, among I think more active groups than now? What of the real beliefs (as distinct from propaganda beliefs) that there are accessible alternatives, and the sense of those alternatives gathering around a meaningful political movement? There is a difficult relationship between these two quite alternative interpretations of a situation which is often personally desperate, in some cases tragic, and which is going to be prolonged for so many years into the future. This again gives a sense of inevitability, and of a certain radical dislocation, of people not able to connect with movements which they really believe could change the world and their situation.

In other words, what I'm arguing is that many of the negative signs which ought to be alarming – that kind of jingoism; that kind of acquiescence; a quite new kind of submissiveness to the deliberate reduction, in some cases destruction, of people's lives, of whole communities – these should be seen as factors which arise from the dislocation, rather than the alternative reading, as the evidence of some essence of the people which Thatcher has in some way managed to distil. At least if one reads it that way – this is my argument – then one may begin to connect with those factors which are capable of identification and connection if we can learn to speak in new ways.

Perhaps I needn't remind you of the major factors within which the situation of this small and increasingly marginal society is being determined. They are more than anything what the ordinary education and self-image of the British people allows. This is a weak, second-grade capitalist economy; for many years a conscious junior partner in a military alliance; for a generation now, having little chance of serious independent initiatives, except through change on a scale which, in a way because of that old perspective, it has been unwilling to contemplate. But this sense of the real wider condition is subject to a very curious recognition and misrecognition. Let us then look at what the major factors are, within which this still apparently independent and autonomous society is being determined.

It is, first, in a very precarious position because of its historical preponderance of external trade; exposed to the extraordinary disturbances and dislocations of an instituted global economy in which it was originally one of the principal players, and of which, in certain sectors it is still an important component; but in which, as an economy, it is now a very weak and exposed member, especially vulnerable to what happens elsewhere. It is in the same sense unusually exposed by the very residue of its history, as the leftover colonies, the old political commitments and connections continually demonstrate; exposed in this case to the extraordinary turbulence of political upheavals in the imperialist and post-imperialist world. There is a series of conflicts for which nothing in the British perspective has prepared people to understand or participate. There is the sheer complexity of action and reaction in that transition from an imperialist world – or a confident, strong, and, except internally, unchallenged world order – which began in 1919. And if one is estimating the thing long term, who could say that we should expect to be more than half way along that transition from that world of 1914?

And yet, once one puts it that way, the third general consideration within which this exposed society is being determined, and yet cannot recognize its determinations, is that alongside these causes – the chaos of an imposed global economy, subject to extraordinary dangers of dislocation and breakdown, all the time, in a very complex and prolonged political struggle and disturbance – precisely at this time the consequences are appearing not only economically and in the older terms of politics, but with military means – the nuclear weapons systems – which are of a kind to make any ordinary projection of the future, even to the millennium, problematic to put it at its softest. Socialists have often emphasized the long process of struggle, the long process of the emergence of a different world order out of the ruins and contests of the old. But this is now not only being conducted, in all its so-called local fields, with weapons of a destructive power and sophistication which are quite extraordinarily damaging even in local terms, sustained by a conscious arms export from the advanced technological centres, which is truly wicked in its persistence and scale. Over and above this, at certain key points, there is the danger of any of these conflicts involving weapons systems which are literally, and not just metaphorically, capable of the destruction at least of urban civilization, and probably of all or most human and other life on the planet.

Yet the scale of these disturbances, difficult to recognize for any individual, any group of any society, is peculiarly difficult for the British to recognize. For so long they have been succoured upon the ideology of being a leading power, of commanding events, of being economically advanced. You can still hear it in the way ruling-class journalists, politicians and their imitators discuss what they will do about some part of the world when they look at a map. It takes up an extraordinary amount of their time; as if they were still deciding, as once they did, who should come to power and who should not be in power, as if they were still the arbiters of destiny, and yet, within that deluded sense of false grandeur, they are peculiarly the victims, of this shifted position, which they cannot recognize, or which, at best, is only very unevenly recognized.

Now, if you add to these three major determining conditions, a fourth, which is that we are moving into a very deep ecological crisis – of resources and of dangerous technologies; of degrees of shortage and competition within scarcity which will exacerbate all the former kinds of conflict – and moreover that elements of the industrial mode of production itself can now be perceived as inflicting kinds of damage on people and on the physical environment which were not fully recognized when the system was more successful, you have again this curious confusion and misrecognition. It's apparent in discussions of what's called 'de-industrialization': that on the one hand people are regretting the collapse of the traditional British industries, the old heavy industries, engineering and so on; and on the other hand are recognizing that going out with those jobs are some of the most dangerous kinds of work, some of the kinds of work that, precisely because of the early stage of British development in these industries, devastated and damaged so many parts of this land, leaving the appalling problems of the old industrial areas, the inner cities, the dock areas, the places that are now the centres of the most apparent social crisis. In other words, there's a very curious interlock between the sense of loss and of dereliction, and yet the only available response is to reconstitute, perhaps in some hopefully cleaner and lighter form, those precise kinds of work and environment.

It's very curious, historically, that the comparatively few remaining miners of South Wales, and I support them, should be fighting for that desperately dangerous work in that devastated landscape. They are fighting because, in wholly practical terms, if they don't keep that work, whole communities that were arbitrarily crowded into those valleys, are simply left without any means of livelihood at all. It is the same in the docks, in the old shipbuilding areas, and in the inner cities themselves. As the capitalist process has moved on, we're beginning to understand the real ecological crisis, which is much deeper than what's usually considered environmentalism or conservation. Issues like endangered wild species or the preservation of unspoilt countryside are just causes, and the Labour Party has suddenly decided to ban hunting with dogs. Although these mild liberal causes are of no serious consequence to the system, they often mask the true ecological crisis, which is that at this stage of the industrial order, elements of depredation and stress have been recognized whether in success or in failure. Yet, the only response to the failure seems to be the wish to reconstitute it. To reconstitute its terms. Because what alternative after all is recognizable?

Now I'm saying that because these are the real determining conditions, within the true general crisis of a world order, because they are the conditions within which the substance of British life, and especially British political life, is being actually determined, we have to go on to interpret British political life not in the terms in which it offers itself, because that is merely reproducing the misrecognitions and confusions, but in terms of its adequacy to recognize these real kinds of crisis. Let me then put it this way. It is very striking that there is now an unevenness between extremely active and successful movements of a relatively new kind in British society, and a corresponding – if it is that, but in any case coincidental – decline, weakness, at times seeming irrelevance of the more orthodox political movement. I mean that anyone looking at the last twenty-five years in Britain would at once identify as the important radical politics the peace movement, the women's movements, the ecology movement, the movements of anti-imperialism and of solidarity with particular struggles in the Third World, and the alternative culture which is still very resilient. These are where the forms of real activity and direction have been in recent years.

In the sixties we called them all single-issue campaigns. We said peace was a single issue, women a single issue, ecology a single issue. As if somewhere there was the great collection of issues that was everything. And this was partly right, but partly and very significantly wrong. The curious thing is that these movements are growing and that they are not really minority movements. What strikes me as most interesting in the current political situation is that if you take measurements of public opinion on Cruise or Trident missiles, or even on more radical measures of nuclear disarmament, you find significantly more people supporting those initiatives – which are characterized from the ruling political orthodoxy as the extremist fringe – than you find in the older and more familiar forms of left and radical politics. On the most favourable issues they are supported, at times, by rather more than half the people expressing an opinion. In the case of the women's movements (and I use that as a plural because the strongest thing about the women's movements is that they are making so many different emphases), there is little question that they have majority support, and that conscious head-on attempts to resist them, to throw them back, would be defeated by public pressure. If you take the ecology movements, they're very diverse and it's in their weakest, least systematic forms that they're most popular; but nevertheless the levels of public involvement, interest and support are very high in certain cases and never insignificant, over a range from simple things like resistance to some destructive piece of planning, through to real concern about nuclear power and public transport policies and so on.

Now if one undertakes the political arithmetic of adding together the people involved in the peace movement, in the women's movements, in the ecology movements, in the radical and alternative culture (even recognizing that you are often counting the same people twice and three times) the sum is very considerable. You might even say here is a natural in-built majority. Which is why it's been so surprising to open the newspapers and see what the actual distribution of opinion amongst political parties is. There's a dramatic lack of fit between these very active moments and the general political situation. The only advantage I have of being my age is that I can compare the present state of these movements with other periods, in which I've been involved with and watching them, and I don't think any of them have ever been as strong. I don't think any of them have ever previously been as impressive intellectually, or in terms of real distribution in the society. They are not just a clever projection of a few able groups.

But if this is so you have then to explain the lack of fit between this real growth and the decline of what is usually, sometimes oddly, taken as an indication of left political opinions: the intention to vote for the Labour Party. You have to put it that way because one has to recognize that if out of Thatcher's 45 per cent, or whatever it's now reckoned to be, you've deducted 30 odd (which would be Conservative whatever), you also have to say that out of 35 per cent or so for Labour, you have to deduct a substantial number who couldn't, by any stretch of the imagination, be reckoned socialists or even left in any very conscious sense. That residual traditional vote is declining, but it's still significant. It may be an accident, but it's surprising how often one hears in these casual interviews about why somebody's voting, the familiar response, 'We've always been Labour. My father was Labour.'

This kind of political opinion is a matter of inheritance rather than choice of affiliation. So, you've got the lack of fit between these active movements which are not mere minorities (however one might quantitatively assess them) and the weakest political situation the Left has been in since the mid-thirties. This is whether you take the Left in its broad situation or in terms of apparent support for the Labour Party or certain actions of the last Labour government. But what I'm saying is that there is a lack of fit between these new perceptions, these new causes, and the notion of left politics, whether Labour or socialist, as it has become defined and fixed; and this is so even when it has formally absorbed some of the new causes.

Of course it is true, and we must put it to their credit, that the Labour Party have absorbed some of the emphases of the peace movement. They've absorbed some of the emphases of the women's movements. Not many but a few. They've taken some of the milder positions of the ecology movement. They've even, though not very strongly, picked up elements of the alternative culture and of anti-imperialism. But nevertheless, the dominant definition, at the point when you move from what's called the single issue to what's called the grouping, the general political gathering which is a movement capable of changing the society, does not offer that connection. And this is what we have most to try to understand.

Let me try to summarize briefly. First, I would say that we have to distinguish between areas of consciousness which are genuinely open to recognition of real situations (thus allowing some real possibility of choice) and those different real pressures in which people are truly conscious of the determinations on their lives: determinations that are exercised in very short-term and absolutely unmistakeable ways. I interpret the lack of fit in this sense, that there are disciplines of capitalism as a social order which really do – and increasingly in its present phase – exert a control on people based not so much upon positive assent as upon the absence of immediate alternatives.

I think that the immense involvement of a majority of the population in what used to be called debt but is now called credit, which really does, (and anybody who has been in this situation knows it) exert short-term pressures on what you're going to do and think next month, is a new sort of situation. For example, in any decision about going on strike, workers today have to reflect: 'I've got my mortgage to think about. I've got the house payment and so on.' Not only that, but in the current slump the sheer discipline of employment itself, the deliberately chosen weapons of threats to job security, exert an immense and obvious pressure. You really do, when you're subject to pressure of this kind, have to go a very long way if you are to resist it. Or you have to reserve some part of your mind into which a different consciousness can enter. It is no surprise to me that among people who are relatively privileged, in these respects, who are either not so frightened of that kind of debt or not so frightened about employment, or who have some inbuilt protection of situation or qualification (more mobile people and so on); that among them there has been just that larger space in which an alternative consciousness on certain issues could crystallize.

It would be foolish, I think, to describe those issues as middle-class issues and the others as working-class issues. All of them are all-class issues in that sense. Most of them are very general. But the pressures that capitalism can exert, at short range and in the short term, are in certain periods, of which this clearly is one and likely for some years to remain, very hard. In a sense, the same person can have this regretfully or cynically submissive position, learned in debt, in employment, in the everyday social order, and yet in parts of their minds be quite free to respond to what is said about the liberation of women, to what is said about peace, to what is said against nuclear weapons, and so on.

Indeed, in their lives they make such space. But it is a space which has to coexist with the hard short-term determinations. Now the obvious riposte to this line of argument is that in certain situations before, where the pressures have been even more intense, the repression much harder (and if we get into a self pitying mood in the next four weeks, one of the aspirins for it would be a bit of history and a comparison with what people in our situation at different periods have had to face), that in those situations there were different and stronger responses. Why was that so?

Because, I would argue, there is one new and special offer of an effective identity that has been made and very widely accepted. I don't mean British chauvinism; that is strictly for events which are either football matches or made to resemble football matches. It is something that I think is relatively new, and now very powerful and very ambivalent. I can't find an ordinary term for it because it is such a relatively new condition, which is why I have to call it, in one of the ugliest phrases I know, 'mobile privatization'. But I don't know what else to call it. It's something like this: that the identity that is really offered to us is a new kind of freedom in that area of our lives that we have staked out inside these wider determinations and constraints. It is private. It involves, in its immediate definition, a good deal of evident consumption. Much of it is centred on the home itself, the dwelling-place. Much of it, in those terms, enlists many of the most productive, imaginative impulses and activities of people – moreover sanely so, as against the competing demands of orthodox politics. Because what you put in, in effort, in this way, you usually get to live with and have its value.

At the same time it is not a retreating privatization, of a deprived kind, because what it especially confers is an unexampled mobility. You may live in a shell of this kind in which you and your relatives, your lovers, your friends, your children – this small-unit entity is the only really significant social entity. It is not living in a cut-off way, not in a shell that is just stuck. It is a shell which you can take with you, which you can fly with to places that previous generations could never imagine visiting. You can move all the time in the society, choosing the places you're going to. You take the shell with you. You're given this sense that is offered as a primary identity, as your real life. And most people underwrite it as their real life, against which those big things, in whatever colour of politics they appear to come, are interpreted as mere generalities, mere abstractions, as at best rather boring interferences with this real life and at worst destructive interventions in it.

And why I think it's ambivalent is this; because it has given people genuine kinds of freedom of choice and mobility which their ancestors would have given very much for. At the same time the price of that space has never been accounted. The price of that space has been paid in terms of the deterioration of the very conditions which allow it. I mean that it all depends on conditions which people, when this consciousness was formed, thought were permanent. Full employment, easy cheap credit, easy cheap petrol. All the conditions for this kind of life were assumed to be both abundant and permanent. And the consciousness that was formed inside them was hostile, in some cases understandably hostile, to anything from outside that was going to interfere with this freely chosen mobility and consumption.

The Right has selected this social interpretation and identified it (however falsely) with their own economic policies and value system. It is only in certain marginal and superficial ways that the Right has ever really offered this kind of opportunity to people; but they aggressively pander the *idea* of it. The Left has on the whole been talking about something else. Necessarily talking about something else, as the credit gets tighter, as the jobs get scarcer, as educational mobility becomes harder to attain. Still the consciousness is preserved, and yet what is seen as breaking in on it are forces which are identified almost from the beginning as hostile: wrongly identified, misrecognized.

I get the sense now that every time we on the Left talk about the needs of the public services, collective provision, or common need, few people have the nerve to answer us in direct moral contradiction, but many people have this quite different habit of switching it to a part of the mind where it's not going to be either much attended to or answered. And the terrible thing about it is this: that to the extent that this is observed in the behaviour of others, we confirm our impressions of the real intentions of others, until, gradually, (and this is now very noticeable in this society, we're getting a worse and worse opinion of each other) when we observe destructive behaviour of this kind we're very ready in disparaging remarks about other people and their forms of behaviour. We're very willing to be led along those paths of social and cultural analysis which identify foolish, deluded, selfish, greedy, aggressive mass behaviour.

All those things that one has been hearing from the Right, we are now, in certain forms, beginning to hear from the Left. The elements of real behaviour in this situation feed into our sense of what others are like, and then into that very common conclusion that a different way of life would be alright if we all followed it. It would be alright if everybody behaved like that. It would be alright if we all really cared for each other or had a sense of common responsibility. But that kind of positive position, announced on its own, is comparatively weak when confronted with the real pressures in which is still the majority situation, in which, with whatever fear and under whatever pressure, this private and mobile kind of life may still be available to you; even if an increasing number of your neighbours drop off the list and simply become unemployment statistics.

In other words, I think that socialists have now to recognize that the central problem of the coming period is to create an authentic rather than an inherited sense of what a society is and should be. Not a society which is crudely counterposed to conditions of individual security, freedom and achievement, for these are not going to be given up except under force. Not a society which can be counterposed to that active, mobile life, as so often in the old language of the Left. Instead, a sense of society which will really have to come from some different roots. And that's the question I must leave you with: with this thought only, that if you study where socialism has been strongest, whether in the full sense of socialism or in the simpler tally of the Labour vote, you will find that it was in aggregated communities and the most tightly packed areas of cities. So that if the only roots of socialism were that kind of aggregated community, then you would have to accept the analysis that socialism is a diminishing tendency; indeed that it will be phased out. Because if one thing is certain, it is that communities of that kind are going to become exceptional, marginal.

On the other hand is this the full analysis of where and how socialism grew? What strikes me most about those traditionally militant areas is that people were not forced to define themselves along any single dimension. True, they were – as was always said – employees or workers in a common situation. But they were also, and insisted on being, neighbours, interconnected by family. They were inhabitants of a particular place, often with a very strong local consciousness. There were non-contradictory relations between being working class and being socialist, or between being locally patriotic and the family relation meshing with it. These are conditions that arose in those communities from special circumstances which cannot be resuscitated or duplicated.

Yet they may give us an indication of the kind of socialism that we now have to redefine. This is precisely not a socialism that can rely on objective economic positions alone to define a political identity or a political movement. But look at the areas which are now most in crisis: in the definition of what local government is; in the problems of what it is to be in a minority nationality, or in what's called an ethnic group inside British society. These are problems of having to identify not along large national-unit categories, but in actual social relations of a more general kind. Here is where a bonding of a different sort – a bonding which is the basis of a different consciousness from that of mobile privatization – could begin steadily to establish itself, to take over, to be the base of an alternative movement. I'm not saying it's all going to happen in the next twenty years, let alone the next four weeks. I am saying that this is the kind of analysis on which our real effort should be based. Because what now appears massively hopeless is in fact an extremely unstable and uncertain situation of contradictory pressures and mis-recognitions which people will have to find their own way out of. Nobody will lead them out of it. Yet into this search, an input of a quite different kind of socialist ideas and socialist language could be the crucial component.

Socialists and Coalitionists

1984

Since the 1983 general election there has been a marked change of
political mood in Britain: a recovery of morale by Labour; a series of
misfortunes for the Tories. At the same time there has been comparatively little change in the underlying political realities. This contrast
between mood and reality can be misleading and even in some respects
dangerous. The very hard questions posed by the defeat of last June can
be softened or allowed to slip away in the name of necessary resilience
or a merely foolish optimism, each strengthened by the passage of time.
It is for this reason that we have still to take seriously the questions
defined by Eric Hobsbawm, with his usual plainness and lucidity. I
disagree strongly with the answers he suggests or implies, but I find
myself at an even greater distance from those who think they can
dispose of the questions by simple and self-righteous cries against
'coalition', which in this context is often little more than a swearword.

It is true that it has long been the purpose of right-wing and centrist
commentators to get rid of the Labour Party as a significant independent
political force. This is also the explicit intention of the Alliance parties.
Indeed for more than thirty years there has been a sustained attempt to
form a left-of-Tory party or grouping in which the socialist component
would be minimal or altogether excluded. Moreover it should not be
forgotten that elements of this attempt have come from within the
Labour Party including, at times, its leadership. It would be a simple
matter for the whole of the current discussion to be absorbed by this
long and dangerous campaign.

But this would be too easy. The current problem is not so much in the
campaign itself as in the deteriorating political situation to which it is a
response. It is a fact that we have a very dangerous right-wing government elected by only 43 per cent of the electorate. Yet appeals against

its legitimacy, on this ground, cut little ice against its actual monopoly of state power. It is also a fact that on all recent and current evidence there are now three parties or party groupings each capable of gaining at least 20 per cent of the popular vote. Both Labour and the Alliance believe that they can make the other go away and there are some signs, among the ideologists of each party, that they give higher priority to driving out the left-of-Tory rival than to opposing the main enemy. They rationalize this by the belief that the only way to defeat the Tories is to dispose first of the alternative anti-Tory vote. But it is then reasonable to ask how this displaced emphasis will affect real political opinion, when it is Tory support that has really to be reduced. Reasonable also to ask what will happen if, regardless of the energy devoted to such efforts, it turns out that a three- or four-party system has come to stay. This connects with the alarming central fact that the 'Labour vote' had declined to 28 per cent: a low point only reached in any comparable situation during a period when there were, as now, three contending parties. It is tempting to link this obvious correlation between so low a vote and the existence of three parties to the tactic of giving priority to eliminating or reducing the third party. But this is especially dangerous for the Labour Party because it obscures or postpones the question that has really to be answered: what kind of party is it? Is it a broadly socialist party, or is it (as it became during the generations of Liberal decline) the only realistic left-of-Tory coalition?

For we have in fact been living with one kind of coalition politics for many years, inside and – on both wings – outside the Labour Party. The real question raised by Hobsbawm is whether that kind of coalition – the Labour 'broad church' and its friends – can be successfully continued or revived, or whether some new kind of coalition is now necessary, given the rise of a third party grouping. It seems clear that he would be glad to see either, though with a preference for the first. It is here, especially, that the grounds of the whole argument need to be widened. On the hitherto limited electoral terms no useful resolution of the argument seems to me possible.

The true context of any practical politics is always the general social and economic situation, and only secondarily the party dispositions and shares of the popular vote which follow from this. One obvious weakness of recent electoral analysis, as with the analysis which followed Labour's defeat in 1959, is that it treats current distributions of votes as if they were primary data from which the social and economic situation, or at least the main responses to it, can be inferred. There is a related habit of inventing social entities in the form of 'the Labour vote' or 'Labour voters' and so on. It is true that there are some significant numbers of people who vote consistently for this or that party over a long period, and that relative increases or decreases in these numbers are significant. But these groupings taken together are never anywhere near the sum of the electorate. A pattern of multiple shifts this way and that, even at times appearing to cancel each other out in a relatively unchanged general distribution, has been characteristic of British politics since the 1950s and has increased markedly in recent years. These multiple shifts have been in evidence even since the June 1983 election.

Moreover, although speculative reasons for shifts are often advanced, very little is known about their causes. Some appear to be settled shifts in social affiliation; others are almost certainly short-run impulses. In practice, it is impossible to infer from these, or from relative changes in more sustained groupings, either the true social situation or the requirements of political practice. This is especially the case when there are more than two electorally significant parties. It is instructive that the erstwhile 'Liberal vote' and the more recent 'Alliance vote' have been exceptionally 'unstable' in these terms. This is only one of several reasons why we should not begin a political analysis from 'shares' of votes, but from the more important and more objectively discoverable general situation.

Whether Britain is viewed in isolation or, as should be the case, the uncertainties of 'Britain' are seen in the context of a critical and uneven world politics and world economy, the general situation is even more unstable and volatile than any pattern of voting. No realistic policy for, say, the next ten years of the labour movement can be based on simple projections from the present situation or even the present crisis. Britain, in so far as it is still an autonomous economy, is now a weak and exposed sector in a severe and prolonged world crisis. As far as it is still an independent political nation, it is a junior partner in a system of military alliances, and an uncertain partner in the attempts at a Western European community which is itself now in crisis.

Within these very broad determinations, all of which indicate continued and dangerous uncertainty and instability, there can be varying assessments of what will happen within the sphere of British electoral politics. The orthodox view from the left assumes a steady, chronic degeneration of the existing social order: a still failing economy, continued mass unemployment, a greatly reduced welfare state, an extending domination of capitalist values. The orthodox view from the right, though it speaks of recovery and regeneration, transposes these damaging changes into the vital reconstitution of a profitable capitalist economy. This is not to be confined to Britain alone, but to be extended by the worldwide deployment of British capital. Continuing mass unemployment, reduced welfare costs, weakened trade unions and the defeat of socialist ideas and organizations are the deliberate conditions of this reconstitution. So also is the pursuit of an aggressive and heavily armed foreign policy in the struggle for control of key areas of the newly industrializing and dependent poor world.

Another orthodox view from the left goes beyond the usual account of 'Tory mismanagement' and understands current Tory policy as a hard and, in its own terms, rational programme. It then assumes that there must eventually be a gathering of political opposition to its inevitably heavy costs, of a kind that will return the Left to power. This is very much better than the older assumption that there will be sufficient opposition to mere 'mismanagement': ground on which Labour, from its recent record in government, is in no strong position to fight. But it may still not be strong enough, for there is a third possible assumption, different both from the hard Right and from the orthodox Left in either of its versions. What is interpreted from the left as a process of chronic degeneration, and from the right as a process of profitable capitalist reconstitution, is seen from this third perspective as imposing strains on the whole social order which will radically change the terms of British politics. A minority of Marxists believe this will lead eventually to some kind of pre-revolutionary situation in classical terms. But alongside them other Marxists see the danger of a further break to the right, with much harder authoritarian controls to contain the pressures which the capitalist reconstitution must inexorably increase.

This perspective does not often appear directly in current arguments for left coalitions or similar arrangements, but I think it is no coincidence that its kind of response – in effect an updated version of the popular front – is now coming from some eminent Marxists. Nor, in any real historical perspective, should this kind of thinking be dismissed by mere labelling. There are undoubtedly possible circumstances in Britain and in the rest of Western Europe in which the organization of a popular front would indeed be a priority. The historical lessons of the defeat of the Left in Italy in the early 1920s and in Germany in the early 1930s cannot be forgotten, and must indeed still be taken seriously. But any such proposal must be assessed in contemporary terms. The historical memories and the futurist projections have to be related to where we are. It still matters very much which of these assumptions of the nature of the next ten years we adopt, but in any case we have to move on from retrospective accounts of the movements of votes and into this real area of political analysis.

One useful way of testing the arguments about electoral policies and arrangements is to set them in their real or probable political context. Let us suppose, for example, that the 57 per cent of votes against the present Conservative government had not been distorted by an absurd electoral system but had produced a majority of non-Conservative representatives. On what kind of political programme would they have been able to agree? The answer is, I believe, disconcerting to both main sides in the current argument, but at first sight it is most disconcerting of all to those who dismiss the whole discussion with cries against 'coalition'. For it would almost certainly have been possible to form a government with the following main heads of policy: first, deliberate reflation of the economy by extending the public sector borrowing requirement to some figure between the Labour and Alliance proposals; second, cancellation of cuts in the welfare services, education, transport and general infrastructure; and third, refusal – or at least delay – of Cruise missile installation, and introduction of Polaris into general disarmament negotiations. Obviously there would be other areas in which simple agreement would be out of the question – wages policy, trade union legislation, the electoral system itself. But the three areas cited above are of such commanding importance that in practice few people would turn down the chance of realizing them, whatever other disagreements remained. Moreover, such policies would, without question, produce some marked improvements in our present circumstances. They have only to be compared with current Tory policies for that to be evident.

It is from this conclusion, and from seeing the alternative as prolonging current Tory policies while the non-Tory vote remains so divided, that the coalitionists – whether explicit or not – draw their strongest arguments. But of course any such coalition is hypothetical. There are, as Hobsbawm fairly said, substantial objective and subjective obstacles to its practical realization. One of these is the electoral system itself, currently a major difference between the prospective partners. Even where this is modified, as in the 1983 election, by a good deal of tactical voting (which, it should be noted, itself distorts the crude figures of shares of the vote), there is no way of effecting a practical coalition of policies except by negotiations before the election. Yet such bargaining instantly challenges the full national ambitions of the separate parties, and is indignantly rejected.

What then happens is an appeal to balance the political advantages of some new arrangement – positive advantages, as in the three heads of policy; negative advantages, in that at least the Tories would be out – against what can be seen as merely residual and hidebound party positions. Alternatively, these probable gains are seen to outweigh the likelihood that one of the potential partners, Labour or Alliance, can in the next four years so thoroughly defeat or reduce its anti-Tory rival that it will itself gain majority power to execute both the main heads of policy and its other, more particular, commitments. Put this way, the appeal seems very strong.

So what's wrong with it? The answer lies in the politics rather than in the electoral calculations. The main objection follows from the fact that, in the present electoral system, such arrangements have to be made in advance. For even if we could agree that current objections to such arrangements are decisively outweighed by their political advantages, the actual effect would be a relative freezing of current policy positions: not only agreement on the main heads of policy, which in real terms would not be difficult in current circumstances, but agreement also that certain other kinds of policy, while they could of course be independently retained, would be relatively played down so as not to threaten any proposed, plausible agreement. Thus there would at least have to be some loose coalition of policies *before* any practical electoral arrangements were possible.

It can, of course, be argued that this is desirable, as a way of achieving at least the major policies. Or it can be said that this kind of advance agreement is very much more desirable than a post-election coalition resulting from a hung parliament, in which broadly similar policies would probably be agreed – but behind closed doors between the leaderships rather than in the open between full parties. In fact we cannot now say which of the two election results relevant to this argument is more likely next time: a Tory government even on a reduced minority vote, or a hung parliament in which some kind of coalition would inevitably occur. Perhaps one of the best reasons for having this argument in the open now is to force us to think not only about the relatively improbable pre-election agreements but also about the much more probable post-election problems in which Labour would be embroiled if it failed to get its own majority.

Everything, in the end, must come back to the real politics, and here there is a more challenging argument. For we have to ask what real differences there are between these proposals for what can be called the big coalition – Labour and the Alliance in any of its possible forms – and what has to be called the smaller coalition, which is that version of the Labour Party which draws on the same types of argument as the explicit coalitionists – pressing for electoral unity around certain main heads of policy while other differences lie on the table – as a way of maintaining the practical coalition of diverse tendencies which the Labour Party has long been. There is one clear difference between the two kinds of coalition. To the extent that the Labour Party maintains or extends its recently improved democratic structures so that policy decisions are of an openly discussed and contested kind, the implicit coalition of socialists and social democrats within the party will be continuously active, as distinct from manoeuvred coalition agreements between separate leaderships. At the same time we can all imagine circumstances in which the appeal for electoral unity could be made to override this active process, and some of the same arguments as those of the big coalitionists would then be deployed: the need to maximize the vote against the real enemy; the subordination of contentious policy decisions to the unifying imperatives of electoral organization.

One version of these arguments is acceptable – at least initially. All of us who have experienced the defeats of Labour and the Left not just as analysts or observers but where they really hurt, in the lives of our own people, are understandably determined not to be defeated again. In fact, from this determination a new kind of politics can really begin. But there is another version of what are apparently the same arguments which leads us directly back into the old politics of defeat. The distinction between the versions is not primarily in relation to elections: it is in relation to actual policies. For what has to be said very clearly is that if Labour's major policies are broadly the same as those of the Alliance, it would be very foolish indeed not to seek some mutually beneficial electoral arrangements. (There is an obvious practical limit to how many centre or left-centre parties there can be: even two is already too many in the present electoral system.) Of course it is indignantly denied in both camps that there is any such identity. Minor, marginal or dispensable differences are maximized as a condition of becoming the only true contender for the sensible anti-Tory vote. And if this sensible ground is where majority public opinion now is, but two or three parties are contending to represent it, there are only two reasonable tactics: driving out the rivals or coming to an arrangement with them. Hobsbawm assumes such a ground, and while he would doubtless prefer Labour to drive out the Alliance he is realistic enough to face its great difficulties and to contemplate the alternative.

Yet to be reduced to a choice between these two limited tactics would be the most important defeat which the Left could now suffer. The reasons for this are political. They become clear if we look again at the main heads of policy which might now be agreed in some anti-Tory coalition, or which might alternatively be most strongly emphasized in Labour's drive for its own government. None of the policies is in any distinctive sense socialist. Reflation of the economy, in the terms usually proposed, is a continuation of Keynesianism. Restoration of the welfare state is in the broad tradition of the liberal and social-democratic consensus out of which the Labour governments emerged. Limited measures of disarmament are within the broad internationlist and peacemaking consensus of the same tradition at its best. None of these identities proves any of the policies wrong or insufficient. Yet the underlying identity, while it is held at this practical level, indeed makes dividing and splitting votes between parties which broadly adhere to it foolish. What is wrong, from any socialist position, is the definition of such policies as adequate for any sustained recovery or advance. Nor is it enough to add in some of Labour's more distinctive policies, such as opposition to the Common Market, opposition to incomes policies or repeal of anti-union legislation. None of these makes the basic body of policy more realistic or coherent. It is in the main heads of policy themselves that there must be significant and convincing socialist development, if we are to substantiate Labour's claim to be a unique alternative not only to Tory policies but also to the liberal/social-democratic consensus now electorally available in the Alliance.

Some people think that this development can be brought about by a bold announcement of a commitment to socialism. But for many years this has been not the solution but the problem. Nominal socialist commitment has broadly coexisted with actual liberal/social-democratic policies, and this has led to confusion inside the party as well as to justified criticism of it by others as incoherent and unconvincing. What really needs to happen in the next four years is a radical reconstruction of all the main directions of policy in the light of the most open and informed contemporary socialist analysis.

So in the case of the general direction of the economy, it is necessary to move beyond 'one-nation Keynesianism' in each of its component terms. It is clear from the experience of the French socialist government that economies of the size of Britain or France cannot pull away on their own from the main forces of the international capitalist economy. Thus coordinated or integrated policies with other left governments are a condition of any sustained success and need to be carefully discussed and agreed in advance, at least in general outline. One obvious route for this is within the EEC; it could mean changing the residual option for negotiated withdrawal to a policy of forcing the pace for a coordinated socialist reconstruction of a group of European economies and thereby reforming the EEC itself. But the simple Keynesianism also needs to be changed. Centralized management of credit and the money supply, as in simple reflation policies, has to be only a part of a much more developed process of democratic economic planning and control, including hard *selective* policies on investment, prices, taxes and incomes.

This connects with the need to go beyond a simple welfare state. In the current employment and demographic crisis it is impossible to isolate an area of services and benefits recommended only in their own terms (pensions and compensation for early retirement are only the most obvious examples), without reference to the direction and priorities of the general economy. Opportunism in this area has already been heavily paid for politically, and it is essential to rework the principles and costs of the system as part of a general policy on investment, taxation, employment and benefits.

On the third head of policy, in relation to peace and disarmament, it is necessary to transcend the limited holding initiatives which are now being emphasized and rework from the beginning a coherent and sustainable international policy. This must include realistic relations between the requirements of British security and the problems of membership of either a nuclear or a non-nuclear military alliance. It must also include policies for the reconstruction of economic and political relationships with the Third World – a greatly neglected area. It is here especially that general monetary and economic policies beyond Keynesianism interlock as matters of political struggle with policies to change the role of British finance capital in the international economic order.

These are brief examples in relation only to the three main issues previously defined. A whole range of other social policies has to be developed in coherent relationship to them. It is then easy to say that getting even provisional agreement on them by majorities in the Labour Party would be a formidable political task. For it would be particularly important that the policies be developed well beyond the status of conference resolutions into genuinely practical programmes. There would need to be professional detailed and continuously updated work drawing on the research resources and practical experiences of the whole labour movement.

Yet even this would not be enough. The whole point of this new political direction would be the attempt, by informing and educating each other in the hard realities of the contemporary world, to launch the widest possible public process of reconsidering and (where necessary) changing every popular assumption, habit and attitude. Indeed the centre of this new politics would be a campaign to shift the popular ground on which we have in fact been defeated: not to adapt to it or to manoeuvre around it, but to go out and try to transform it. As it happens this would also be the best possible kind of electoral campaign, with the organization of an electoral machine genuinely powered by an expanding socialist awareness and conviction. Otherwise, as so often before, there will be arguments about who is to drive, which maps will be used, even how best to tune the machine. And still there will not be enough bloody petrol.

This kind of politics is, I am sure, the only immediate and practical alternative to the politics of overt or covert coalition. I am not saying that the answers to come out would be the ones known and already advanced by the left of the party. On the contrary, that assumption – still common on the Left – is merely the way to more divisive factionalism. Until the work has really been done and has come to include detailed, convincing answers to the objections already made and acted upon by the right of the party and beyond it, there is no ready-made socialist programme to translate into simple resolutions and majorities.

The long neglect of fundamental research and political education has produced an uneven but unmistakable mixture of half-formed policies and half-convincing protests. Much of the most essential detailed work is being done outside or at the edges of the party – in the peace movement, in the women's movement, in the ecology organizations – and all these bear especially on that politics of the future to which Labour must now redirect itself from the depths of defeat. But there is also promising work inside the party itself as well as great potential within the trade unions and their research departments for work on the central issues of employment and investment – an area in which all convincing policies need to be very specific. Through these various channels and through the Socialist Society, the Fabian Society and constituency political education officers, the necessary work *can* be done. The true intellectual resources of the labour movement have never been so rich and diverse, and the political problem is to bring them to bear in general public debate rather than internal dispute.

The campaign must be much more than 'bringing the message' or even 'winning the intellectual argument' (though that, too, is necessary). In one linked area after another what we really have to discover – and as far as possible agree on – is what that intellectual argument actually is: the fully contemporary intellectual argument for socialism. This is why coalitions must be opposed. Whether it's the big or the smaller version, the advocates of either have in effect abandoned the struggle to transform belief and opinion. In a cold climate, they say, the many but now disparate remnants of decent and sensible opinion must huddle together, pooling their surviving resources against the Tory storm. I can see how easy it is to feel like that or to respond hopefully to a few brave words flung back against the wind. I also know that the kind of campaign for renewal which I have been describing has been proposed before, and has never fully happened. Are these words, too, no more than a cry against the wind?

It is for many of us to answer. If this new kind of politics is too hard for us, if there is too little time or if we already believe that these more radical tactics must fail, there are still answers – indeed now common answers. Ruling the new politics out, or merely paying it lip service without the practical changes which need to go with it, leaves plenty of room for other kinds of political activity: we can sustain the smaller coalition without any real work on policies, or reach out for the larger coalition, adapting ahead of its formal arrangements by trimming or underplaying those innovative socialist policies which are known to be incompatible with it. But we can then draw a clear line, to our mutual advantage, between socialists and coalitionists. We can begin to see where we really are, and what we have to change.

6
The Challenge of the New Social Movements

The Politics of Nuclear Disarmament

1980

Since autumn 1979 there has been a vigorous renewal of campaigning against the nuclear arms race. Its immediate occasion was the NATO decision to deploy Cruise missiles in Western Europe, with further effects from the failure of the United States to ratify the SALT II agreement. But it was then rapidly intensified by the development of a complex international crisis, involving the Iranian Muslim revolution, the Soviet military action in Afghanistan, and heightened tensions in the Middle East and in the Gulf oil states. Yet while these conjunctural reasons are evident, it now seems that the specific campaigns against nuclear weapons have emerged with renewed authority, independence and strength. Residual and new campaigning formations have attracted many new members; successful meetings and demonstrations are again being held; and there has been a significant body of new writing and new analysis. The issues are so fateful that there can be nothing but welcome for this vigorous renewal of attention. Yet it is at just this moment that we have to look very closely again at the politics of nuclear disarmament.

It is not simply that we have been here before; that in the late fifties and early sixties we had a powerful Campaign for Nuclear Disarmament which, for whatever reasons, was contained and dissipated. Indeed the most salutary effect of the renewed campaigning is that the more complacent conclusions about the decline of CND have been decisively challenged by the more substantial dimension of actual strategic and weapons developments, which the merely political conclusion – 'we've had CND' – sealed off in thousands of minds. Anyone who has read the details of these new developments must be shocked by the extent to which 'the bomb', as fact or slogan, has operated in the culture as a static if terrible entity, provoking resignation, cynicism or despair, while the reality has been the unceasing development of new and ever more dangerous systems. Moreover, in left politics especially, 'the bomb' has for the most part been pushed into the margin of more tractable arguments about political strategy and tactics. When we now read, with full attention, the most sober descriptions of the appalling new military systems and strategies, it can seem like a waking after sleep, though it is not really that; it is yet another and perhaps now absolute demand, when we have already given available time and energy to other necessary work.

This is now the central political question. As the nuclear arms race again dominates attention, where is the rest of our politics, or is there indeed any other important kind of politics? Many comrades and friends are now arguing, eloquently, for an absolute priority of specific, autonomous and collaborative campaigning against the nuclear arms race.[1] The shock waves of recent events are pushing many thousands in that direction. But then it is here, at whatever risks of misunderstanding, that we must, as comrades and friends, ask and indeed insist on certain fundamental questions, and begin to suggest some answers.

There is a first and relatively simple set of questions. They can be summarized as: give absolute priority to *which* campaign against the arms race? In Britain, for example, there are at least three campaigns, all gaining support. There is the revived Campaign for Nuclear Disarmament (CND), campaigning broadly but centred on a demand for unilateral British nuclear disarmament, in very much its original terms. Coherently but not exclusively associated with this is the urgent campaign against the siting of Cruise missiles in Britain. Then, second, there is the new and important campaign for European Nuclear Disarmament (END), still needing to resolve its relations with an older unilateralism, but centred on proposals 'to free the entire territory of Europe, from Poland to Portugal, from nuclear weapons, air and submarine bases'.[2] Third, there is the World Disarmament Campaign, centred on the comprehensive proposals of the United Nations Special Session on Disarmament, convened in 1978 and to be renewed in 1982. In the urgency of actual campaigning against powerful opposing forces, the differences of emphasis, some radical, between these campaigns can and at times must be set aside. Yet it is not only that the differences are already being exploited by the political and military establishments. It is that arguments drawn from these differences of emphasis become

1. The most eloquent example of this position is Edward Thompson's 'Notes on Exterminism, the Last Stage of Civilization', *NLR* 121, May–June 1980.
2. END statement of which the present author was a signatory; reprinted in E.P. Thompson and Dan Smith, eds, *Protest and Survive*, London 1980, p. 224.

confused, even in single minds, and that genuine differences of policy and affiliation are overridden by the too simple conclusion that since all are against the arms race, all know how they will work to end it.

This state of mind was memorably and damagingly indicated at the 1980 Labour Party conference, when motions deriving from all three positions were passed, allowing endless opportunities for subsequent confusion and double-talk. Moreover it is significant, as was again evident at the Labour conference, that at just the points where these differences of emphasis need to be discussed there is a regular reversion – of course in its own terms impressive – to simple restatement of the horrors of nuclear war, which are indeed the beginning but cannot function as the conclusion of any of the arguments. Nobody is quicker to agree about these horrors than the defenders and actual executants of the arms race, who then derive their own models of deterrence and swing much public opinion behind them. If a version of absolute priority to the anti-nuclear-weapons campaigns is then practically dependent on simple restatement of the terrible consequences of nuclear war, it is plainly insufficient.

There seem to me to be three broad questions. First, whether the development of nuclear weapons, and of the political and military systems associated with them, has so changed the character of otherwise determined social orders, that what we now confront, as Edward Thompson has powerfully argued, is in effect a new social condition of exterminism. Second, within a different context, there is the question of the current real meanings of the leading terms of the general argument, notably 'deterrence', 'multilateralism' and 'unilateralism'. Third, and now of critical importance (though it depends on our answers to the preceding questions), what is or should be the specifically socialist contribution to activity against the nuclear arms race, whether autonomous or as an element in broader collaborative campaigns?

Nuclear Weapons and the Social Order

'The Bomb' and Technological Determinism

'If "the hand-mill gives you society with the feudal lord; the steam-mill, society with the industrial capitalist", what are we given by those Satanic mills which are now at work, grinding out the means of human exter-mination?'[3] The question is urgent and relevant, but behind it, of course,

3. Ibid., p. 7.

is another question: who 'gave us' the hand-mill, the steam-mill, the missile factories? The intricate relations between a technology and a mode of production, and indeed between a mode of production and a social order, are only rarely of a kind to permit simple analysis of cause and effect. Technological determinism, as indicated in that combined sentence from Marx and Edward Thompson, is, when taken seriously, a form of intellectual closure of the complexities of social process. In its exclusion of human actions, interests and intentions, in favour of a selected and reified image of their causes and results, it systematically postdates history and excludes all other versions of cause. This is serious everywhere, but in the case of nuclear weapons it is especially disabling. Even when, more plausibly, it is in effect a form of shorthand, it steers us away from originating and continuing causes, and promotes (ironically, in the same mode as the ideologies which the weapons systems now support) a sense of helplessness beneath a vast, impersonal and uncontrollable force. For there is then nothing left but the subordinated responses of passivity or protest, cynical resignation or prophecy.[4] That the latter response in each pairing is infinitely better, morally and politically, should go without saying. But that the tone of a campaign can be radically affected by the initial assumption of so absolute and overpowering a system is already evident, mixed incongruously as it also is with the vigorous organization and reaching out to others which follow from different initial bearings.

In the case of nuclear weapons, nothing is more evident than that they were consciously sought and developed, and have continued to be consciously sought and developed. It is true that, as so often in modern technological innovations, much of the basic research had been done for quite other reasons, without foreseeing this particular result. But again as in many other comparable cases, the crucial moment of passage from scientific knowledge to technical invention, and then from technical invention to a systematic technology, depended on conscious selection and investment by an existing social order, for known and foreseen purposes. Thus the atomic bomb was developed within a situation of total war, under the familiar threat that the enemy might also be developing it, by states which were *already* practising the saturation-bombing and fire-bombing of cities and civilian populations. The atomic bomb gave them very much greater destructive power to do the same things more absolutely, more terribly, and (with the new genetic effects of radi-

---

4. The common use of the term 'apocalypse' (cf. *Apocalypse Now?*, Spokesman Pamphlet, London 1980, and Thompson, p. 28), with a curious shift from the sense of 'revelation' to a sense of ultimate destruction, marks this development. For a nuclear war would not be an 'apocalypse'; it would be at once more terrible and more sordid, with no revelation.

ation) more lastingly. Yet while it is true that massacre is not a twentieth-century invention, it has made a radical difference that massacre was first industrialized in the nineteenth-century development of high explosives and the twentieth-century development of the bombing plane; and then, in the late-twentieth-century development of guided missile systems, in effect automated. It is not only, though it is most immediately, a matter of nuclear weapons. Contemporary developments in chemical and bacteriological weapons, also capable of combination with missile technology, belong to the same escalation in the extent and practicality of massacre.

Military technology has often, perhaps always, been a significant factor in the constitution of a social order. It also directly affects the struggles of classes. If the characteristic effective weapon is within the reach or use of peasants and workers there is a different ultimate balance of class forces from those periods in which effective weapons depend on control of major industrial plants or advanced scientific research. What we have really to ask, about the full range of nuclear and related weapons, is what specific *variations* they have introduced into the shifting but always crucial relations between a military technology and a social order. Two types of variation are evident: international and internal.

Nuclear Weapons and the International Order

It was commonly said, when the atomic bomb had just been invented, that there were now only two or three states capable of waging major war. Indeed this perspective, learned with much else from James Burnham, was the basis for Orwell's projection of *1984*, in which three super-states, in shifting alliance and counter-alliance, with absolute repressive and propagandist control of their internal populations, were in a state of effectively permanent war. It is essentially this Orwellian nightmare ('1984' as 'exterminism') which is now being revived. The mere fact of revival does not affect its truth, either way. But it is worth comparing the prophecy with the history. The emergence of super-powers was correctly foreseen. As it happens this was not primarily a function of the atomic bomb or even of the hydrogen bomb, even though these had conferred immediate and in certain situations decisive military advantages. For there were definite stages within the new tech-nology, and the crucial stage, we can now see, was the combination of nuclear weapons with advanced missile technology, from the mid-1950s: a combination, at its continually rising level, which still keeps the United States and the Soviet Union as superpowers in a period in which other states have acquired nuclear weapons but less effective or more

vulnerable means of delivery. All the other projections are more arguable. There has been a very powerful and dangerous grouping of
secondary states in direct alliances with the superpowers. In the dimension of nuclear weapons and related military strategy these alliances
have indeed taken on something of the character of super-states, though
at other levels this development is much less complete and is subject to
other, often major, political interests and processes.

At the same time, the rest of the world, which had been conveniently
incorporated and in effect neglected in the Orwellian perspective, has
been both object and subject in this dominating and dangerous history.
It is ironic that one of the principal (mainly Chinese) arguments against
agreement on the non-proliferation of nuclear weapons has been the
evident danger of superpower hegemonism: an impulse to political
independence which, combined with certain regional rivalries, has in fact
multiplied the nuclear arsenals. In direct military ways, in the search for
bases in the global strategy which accompanied missile-nuclear and
related technology, there has been constant pressure to reduce independent or ex-dependent states to objects in the superpower military
competition. But then while much of this has followed from the imperatives of military technology, and has even been continued, in blind
thrusts, when changes in the technology made it no longer so necessary
in military terms, it is also true and crucial that the central thrust of this
deadly competition has been not primarily military-technological but, in
the broadest sense, political. But this fundamentally political character
of the competition in its turn modifies the directly military competition.
It is necessary for the superpowers not only, as often, to pretend, but in
many cases actually to be concerned with those broader interests which
originate in the rest of the world. Thus political and economic struggles
which a simple military hegemonism would have a priori excluded have
in fact continuously and powerfully occurred, and have included the
substantial if still incomplete liberation of many peoples who are
nowhere near having nuclear-weapons capability. At the same time not
only the superpowers but many secondary states have exported other
forms of armament with a recklessness, often distinct from the terms of
the primary competition, which has led to twenty-five million (and
rising) war deaths in a period in which nuclear weapons had been
supposed to be determining and in which none had been actually used.
Nothing in this argument reduces the central danger of direct nuclear
war between the superpowers and their locked-in nuclear alliances. But,
as we shall see again in analysing the ideology of deterrence, the
apparent technologically determined process has been at most imper-
fectly realized, and in many significant cases has been inoperative,
within the complexities of a necessarily broader world history.

Nuclear Weapons and Internal Controls

The other half of the Orwellian projection has also to be taken seriously. First, in the Cold-War competition for the development of nuclear weapons, then in their continuing technical development, there have been dramatic increases in the levels of surveillance and control, and of espionage and counter-espionage, in capitalist societies like our own. Whether there has been a similar increase in Soviet-controlled societies, and especially in the Soviet Union which before nuclear weapons already had an immense apparatus of this kind, is more arguable. But there can be no denying that, taken as a whole, as not only direct repression and control but as an increasingly powerful propaganda for war preparations, secrecy, xenophobia and distrust, these internal developments have been contemporary with nuclear weapons. Yet there is again a major qualification. Precisely because the central competition is not only military-technological but is also, in the broadest sense, political, it is an underestimation of the dangers to suppose that they relate to nuclear weapons alone. On the contrary, what is now most dangerous in capitalist societies is the powerful attempt, already too widely successful, to achieve a symmetry between the external (military) threat – directly identified as the Soviet Union – and the internal threat to the capitalist social order which is primarily constituted by an indigenous working class and its organizations and claims. We should be in a much better situation than we now are if surveillance and secrecy were directed only against actual and possible Soviet agents, or for national military security. In fact, significantly, there is at least as much use of these controls, now aided by major technological developments of their own, against indigenous working-class and related political organizations. If this threatening symmetry of an external and an internal enemy is ever fully politically achieved, we shall indeed be in extreme danger.

At the same time, while the centralized secrecy-and-security state cannot be reduced, causatively, to nuclear weapons and their systems, there is one particular and vital respect in which the threat to democracy is indeed, in effect, technologically determined. This is not the possession of nuclear weapons as such, but their combination with missile technology. There has been a dramatic shortening of time for effective military decisions. The greatly increased accuracy of recent guidance systems, in the period of microprocessors, and the related shift from counter-city to counter-force strategy, have again reduced this margin.[5] It is then not only that secondary states have ceded their

5. See Michael Pentz's excellent pamphlet *Towards the Final Abyss?*, Bernal Peace Library, London 1980.

powers of ultimate political decision while they remain in nuclear alliances, but that within such a technology this ceding and centralization of powers is, in its own terms, rational. While much might be done in the more normal political areas of approaches to such a crisis, the fact remains that to assent to missile-nuclear technology is to assent to the loss of independence in ultimate decisions and, spreading back from that, to a steady loss of independence and openness in a much wider political area. It is this dangerous reality which now confronts the peoples of Europe, East and West. Combined, as it now is, with the siting of medium-range missiles, controlled from the same foreign centres, in the developing strategy of a 'theatre' (European) or 'limited' nuclear war, it compels, while we still have time, the most far-reaching political struggles.

Deterrence, Multilateralism or Unilateralism?

Deterrence as Strategy and Ideology

Deterrence is both a strategy and an ideology. We should be wrong if we failed to acknowledge some limited validity of deterrence as a strategy. Just because there is no effective general defence against nuclear weapons, or more strictly against nuclear missiles, there is some initial rationality in the argument that if an enemy possesses them, the only policy, short of pacifism, is to acquire and maintain a deterrent capability of the same kind. We have only to look at the international politics of the mid–late 1940s, when the United States but not the Soviet Union possessed atomic weapons, and when proposals for use of this monopoly to destroy the world centre of Communism while there was still time acquired significant support, over a surprising range, to realize that in this as in so much else a monopoly of such terrible power, in any hands, is profoundly dangerous.

It was then argued (as by Burnham in *The Struggle for the World*, 1974) that as soon as two hostile nations possessed atomic weapons nuclear war would follow almost immediately, and predictions of this kind – that possession implied inevitable use – have been made ever since, with a recurring confidence (in fact a recurring despair) unshaken by the passage of several predicted crucial stages. It has not been only military deterrence which has so far falsified these predictions. The whole complex of political struggles, the widespread public revulsion from any *first* use of nuclear weapons, and further those characteristics of nuclear weapons themselves, which in the unpredictable effects of fallout introduced a new qualitative, and, in some respects, qualifying element in calculations of aggression have been powerful and at times even leading factors. Yet also, in its limited direct context, deterrence has not been ineffective. Indeed it is significant that when we place this fact of 'mutually assured destruction' – in itself so insane a basis for any lasting polity – within actual world-political relations since 1945, we find that it was just because deterrence was operative in direct relations between the United States and the Soviet Union that steadily, and very dangerously, it had to be masked as a real strategic concept and replaced, confusingly under the same name, by deterrence as an ideology.

The crucial dividing line, now so vital in the struggle for public acquiescence or support, is, to put it bluntly, between deterrence from direct military attack, which is still widely and understandably supported, and on the other hand the deterrence of Communism per se. Of course in practice the strategy and the ideology are intricately connected, but at the level of public argument they are intolerably and often deliberately confused. If it is evidence of Soviet aggression that an Asian or African country makes a socialist or Communist revolution, then the simplicities of deterrence against a direct military attack are left far behind. The natural and wholly reasonable desire of all peoples to be secure against direct attack, which ought never for a moment to be denied or even questioned by those of us who are against nuclear weapons and the arms race, is systematically exploited for these other and only ever partly disclosed objectives. It is then a necessary element of any effective campaign to so clarify the differences between the strategy and the ideology that it will be possible to isolate all those who can, without hyperbole, be called warmongers. Thus it is only on the powerfully organized right of West European and North American politics that the ideology becomes again a strategy: to destroy Communism everywhere. Yet it has in practice been far too easy for this grouping to enrol natural desires for security and independence into their quite different objectives. Moreover we make it easier for them if we do not ourselves start, genuinely, from these desires, and go on to show their ultimate (if not always immediate) incompatibility with nuclear weapons and the arms race.

We can best do this if we can show that it is indeed from the limited success of deterrence against direct nuclear attack that the most dangerous recent strategies have been developed. It is clear that it has been in periods of significant political and economic change beyond the terms of direct US–USSR relations that intensification of what is still called deterrent nuclear weapons development has occurred. This has been so especially in periods of intensified national liberation struggles, with peaks around Cuba in the early sixties and after Angola in the seventies.

At these points the distinction between strategy and ideology is particularly evident, and it has been evident again, though in confused ways, in the complex of changes in Iran and Afghanistan. Moreover it is clear that *direct* deterrence had been achieved by the mid–late 1950s. We have then to allow something – perhaps much – for the internal improvement and modernization of these systems, at this level and within this strategy. It then becomes clear that the vast development of overkill capacity, now continuing at a rising rate, belongs strictly to the ideology, and has to be firmly referred not to matters of national security but to a both overt and covert world political struggle. Moreover it is within the limited success of direct US–USSR deterrence that the particular and now exceptional danger for Europe has developed. It is from the facts of that standoff that Europe has been nominated as a 'theatre' for another 'scenario', in which it is (on the military evidence, quite irrationally) believed that a limited nuclear war could be fought as a controlled part of the global struggle. Here, decisively, for the peoples of Western Europe – and especially in these years in which the nuclear weapons for just such a war are being actively deployed – the strategy and the ideology can be seen as distinct. From deterrent subjects, which we could still, however unreasonably, imagine ourselves to be, we have become objects in an ideology of deterrence determined by interests wholly beyond us as nations or as peoples, though significantly not beyond our frontiers as the interests of existing ruling classes. Whatever the scenario might be for others, for us as peoples it is from the opening scene the final tragedy. Global deterrence would have achieved a Europe in which there was nobody left to deter or be deterred.

Multilateralism: Codeword for Rearmament?

'Multilateralism', as a concept, is often paired with 'deterrence'. This is the consistent orthodox argument which has so far commanded majority support. We can begin to break the pairing when we have distinguished between deterrence as strategy and as ideology. It is not impossible that from deterrence as military strategy, at a certain phase of its development, staged mutual disarmament might have been negotiated. But within the *ideology* of deterrence, in which vast political forces of an absolute kind are at once and necessarily engaged, there can and will be no disarmament. The long-sustained promise, that from this necessary strength disarmament can be negotiated, has been thoroughly falsified, and it is extraordinary that it can still be so brazenly asserted, as cover for yet one more stage of military escalation. At the same time, however, multilateral disarmament is indeed the only way to security. The World Disarmament Campaign is on very strong ground when it argues not only for this, but for the urgent inclusion of other than nuclear weapons. Nuclear war is indeed the worst possibility, but chemical and bacteriological war are only minimally less appalling. Even what is called conventional war, with the combined use of advanced high explosives and the present capacities of missile technology, could now destroy urban civilization. Thus only multilateral disarmament can be accepted as an adequate objective. At the same time we have to distinguish between multilateralism as a political strategy and multilateralism as an ideology.

To a very large extent, in current debates, 'multilateralism' is in fact a codeword for continued acquiescence in the policy of military alliances and the arms race. In deceptive or self-deceptive ways, the longing for disarmament is ideologically captured as the cover for yet another stage of rearmament. It becomes an essential objective of any campaign to break this false pairing, but again this can only be done if the reasonableness of genuine multilateralism is fully acknowledged. One important way of doing this is to break the multilateralist 'code' at its weakest point which while speaking of 'multilateralism' really entails an exclusive *bilateralism.* It is not, for example, the governments of Europe who will attempt negotiation on the deployment and possible reduction of nuclear missiles within their territories. Within the logic of the alliances, this primary and indeed multilateral responsibility is virtually without protest surrendered and displaced to bilateral negotiations between the United States and the Soviet Union. 'Multilateralism' is then only a code for those processes of polarization and submission to the loss of national independence. It is against this dangerous and habitual obscuration that an impulse to genuine multilateralism has much to contribute. This is the crucial significance of the campaign for European Nuclear Disarmament, both in its own terms, of resuming direct responsibility, and in its genuine compatibility with the World Disarmament Campaign.

Unilateralism Today and Yesterday

This may and in my view should be the way in which the campaign for European nuclear disarmament develops. But it is already evident that the campaign overlaps with both a residual and revived 'unilateralism', and the current meanings of this concept have now again to be carefully examined. 'Unilateralism' must first be distinguished, historically, from pacifism, which has always, and coherently, proposed the unilateral pacific act, including the renunciation of all weapons, as the first move to break the dangerous deadlock of armed confrontation. But 'unilateralism' acquired more specific and more limited meanings in a particular period – the late 1950s – in which certain circumstances were operative. Britain was at that time the only nuclear-weapons state other than the superpowers, so that on the one hand unilateral British renunciation could be argued as the first necessary practical step to prevent the proliferation of nuclear-weapons states and on the other hand as a moral example to all states including the superpowers. Furthermore, there was the desire to get out from under this dangerous superpower rivalry, whether positively as a non-aligned state, or negatively as 'leaving them to get on with it'; in either case on the assumption that Britain could be independent and autonomous. What matters now, within a resurgence which is also in some respects a continuity, is to re-examine circumstances before we simply resume old responses. Thus the argument against proliferation is significantly different in the 1980s as compared with the 1950s, and in any case has now to include attention to the problems of superpower monopoly ('hegemonism') which, quite apart from being insufficiently analysed in that earlier phase, are now major political realities. Deprived of this immediate practical bearing, the argument of moral example has, in my view, no reasonable resting place short of pacifism, which remains, in the multiplying dangers of international violence, one of the most profound and accessible responses to evil in our world and culture.

This unilateralism of a non-pacifist kind, in the 1980s, has either to be coherently political, with all its consequences followed through, or to resign itself to rhetorical evasiveness. It is clear that the loose assembly of diverse political forces around unilateralism, which for a time held but then failed to hold in the late 1950s and early 1960s, cannot now for long be reconstituted on the old terms. What has always been insufficient in its arguments, but now much less forgivably, is any realistic facing of the full significance of such an act by a state like Britain. It is significantly often at this point, when in any political campaign aiming for majority support the most stringent realism is an absolute requirement, that there is a rhetorical loop back to the undoubted evils and dangers of nuclear war and to the abstraction of 'the bomb'. What then must we really face? The central fact is that Britain at every level – military, political, economic and cultural – has been locked into 'the alliance', which is at once a life-or-death military system and a powerful organization of the most developed capitalist states and economies. To take Britain out of that alliance would be a major shift in the balance of forces, and therefore at once a confrontation of the most serious kind. Every kind of counterforce, certainly economic and political, would be at once deployed against it, and there could be no restriction of the resulting struggle to the theoretically separable issue of nuclear weapons. Thus a theoretically restricted campaign, based on an eventual popular refusal of the dangers of nuclear war, would arrive in reality at a stage of general struggle for which it would be quite unprepared.

At the same time the general notion of the unilateral act, now commonly construed as 'renunciation', has in practice to be divided into separable political acts and stages. What most immediately enters the political argument is, first, on a European scale, the decision about medium-range missiles specifically designed for a 'limited' nuclear war on our own territories; and second, in Britain, the decision about the renewal, into a third generation, of the so-called independent nuclear capability, by the purchase of Trident missiles from the United States. Political campaigns around each of these decisions can, but need not, be conducted in terms of old-style unilateralism. It is significant that there already seems to be more political support for the refusal of these stages of escalation than for a general and indiscriminate 'unilateralism'. It is understandable that many who have taken the full measure of the existing dangers of nuclear weapons and nuclear-alliance strategy should advocate absolute positions, which can alone express our full moral sense, and reject or even despise more limited positions as mere political calculation. But since the dangers are indeed so great, there is also a case for saying that we must advance wherever we can, and that campaigns against Cruise and Trident need not, in these critical years, involve, and often be politically limited by, the full unilateralist case. For to refuse the siting of Cruise missiles on our territories, as part of a process of demanding multilateral European negotiations for the removal of all such missiles and the related bomber and submarine bases from the territories of 'Europe from Poland to Portugal', is not, in any ordinary sense, 'unilateralism'. It is the exercise of independence and sovereignty as a stage in a negotiating process for which there is still (just) time. Similarly in the case of the Trident purchase: it can be also a conscious entry into the negotiating process of strategic arms limitation, by refusing the (in fact unilateral) escalation of British-based missile-nuclear systems. Positive campaigns for these specific initiatives can then in practice be very different from the relatively unfocused demand for 'unilateral renunciation', and should be kept rationally distinct.

Of course what remains to be faced, although at a different level from old-style unilateralism, is the full consequence of such positive refusals and initiatives. For these more specific moves would not only challenge existing strategic dispositions and calculations but would also, just as radically, challenge the logic of superpower hegemonism. The consequent political struggles would be on an even wider stage than that of the consequences of old-style British unilateralism. But that the stage would be wider is an opportunity as well as a problem, and it is in this context that we must examine one of the deeper structures of British unilateralism.

Europe, Unilateralism and the Labour Left

It is very noticeable now that there is a congruence, within that spectrum of opinion which we can describe, broadly, as the Labour Left, between economic, political and peace campaigns which are all, in a general sense, unilateralist. Proposals for a siege or near-siege economy, protected by the strongest version of import controls; proposals for the recovery of political sovereignty or actual withdrawal from the EEC; proposals for the unnegotiated unilateral renunciation of nuclear weapons and bases; all have this common style. There are strong arguments within each of the positions, but the decisive common factors seem to be a radical overestimation of Britain's capacity and effect in independent action, and a radical underestimate of the degree of actual penetration of British economy and society by both international capitalism and the military-political alliance which exists to defend it. There can be no question that we have to find ways to contain this penetration and to roll it back, but it is then a matter of very intricate and realistic economic and political argument to find the most effective ways.

The Labour Left position, at its simplest public level, seems to be not only an abstract short-cut through all these actual difficulties, but based in a very deep political structure which characteristically idealizes desirable conditions and forces, while, as a protection against more radical perspectives, reducing real opposing forces to abstract and alien entities. For the question is never what we could legally do, or find some temporary majority for doing. The question is one of broad struggle. And if the question is one of struggle, the political campaign must be a matter of mobilizing real forces on the most favourable possible ground. It would be unfair to say that the passing of resolutions, even within relatively etiolated structures, is a deliberate evasion of this much harder political reality. Properly understood, it can be part of the process of actual mobilization. But what does seem to be an evasion is the simple rhetoric of 'go it alone'.

A characteristic but crucial example, can be given in this context. If we are seriously proposing a collaborative campaign of European nuclear disarmament, is it sensible at the same time to propose simple withdrawal from the EEC? What is necessary and possible, in both cases, is a radical negotiation, and this can only really be undertaken on a European rather than simply a British scale. None of the actual negotiating steps is easy, but I have found in discussion that the dominant mood thus far, on the EEC as on nuclear weapons, is an impatient insistence on the 'swift, decisive unilateral act', after which all the radical consequences, and the radical struggles, for which a maximum of carefully prepared collaboration and alliance would undoubtedly be necessary, would be faced ad hoc.[6] Yet in any of these struggles, and especially in the struggle against the polarized hegemonism of the nuclear alliances, only combined action on a European scale (of course based on what are also nationally conducted and to some extent uneven and differently inflected campaigns) has any realistic chance of success. Thus we must consistently advance *European* rather than British-unilateralist arguments and objectives.

The Socialist Contribution

It is understandable that some comrades should argue that the danger of nuclear war is now so great that we should set aside all other considerations and unite to achieve disarmament and peace. Anyone who does not at times feel like this is indeed underestimating the appalling immediate dangers. Yet some of us at least must go on to say, first, that specifically socialist analyses of the production and reproduction of these dangers are, while undoubtedly incomplete, still centrally relevant; and, second, that we have still to look to specifically socialist analysis and mobilization to generate the linked forces that will in fact be capable of significantly reducing and finally ending these dangers.

This should never be said arrogantly, or within some exclusivist rhetoric. There is an urgent duty on all socialists to join in collaborative campaigns in at least seven general areas: (a) heightening public consciousness of the specific as well as the general dangers of modern missile-nuclear and other weapons systems; (b) exposing the deceptive official campaigns about the possibilities of 'civil defence' against nuclear attacks; (c) organizing public pressure for all possible measures of arms limitation and negotiated disarmament; (d) publishing and explaining the details of current weapons development and rearmament, and, in close relation to these, the complex of actual offers, counter-offers and stages of negotiation in limitation and disarmament negotiations; (e) organizing campaigns to widen the negotiating process, not only between states but within societies, thus including opposition to arbitrary secrecy and security controls; (f) demonstrating the real links between nuclear-energy and nuclear-weapons programmes, including the realities of some consequent proliferation of nuclear weapons (as in the newly formed Anti-Nuclear Campaign); (g) opposing the

---

6. An idealized projection of a Labour government, under 'Left' leadership, which would resolve and execute such policies, may be as misleading now as it was in the early 1960s, when the cause of nuclear disarmament was widely entrusted to just such a projection.

naturalization of arms production and export as part of the economic strategy of the advanced industrial world.

This is already a heavy list, yet on each of these issues there is already significant public campaigning and active socialist involvement. What has then still to be asked, however, is whether there are further specific socialist contributions to be made both within collaborative campaigns and independently. Some answers can be suggested in three areas: (i) relations between the concepts of a 'ruling class' and a 'military-industrial complex', with evident effects on the question of substituting 'exterminism' for existing or possible categories of socialist analysis; (ii) the very difficult question of what is called, in some circles, the 'socialist bomb' or 'the missiles of the international working class'; (iii) the problem of linkages between military and economic crisis.

The Ruling Class and the 'Military-Industrial Complex'

It is obviously correct to identify and to stress the specific complex of arms-production, military, research and state-security interests within contemporary advanced capitalist societies. It is also necessary to identify an analogous but far from identical complex within such socialist states as the Soviet Union and China. Yet it is almost certainly wrong, first, to fuse these different formations as a single entity, and, second, to override more general concepts of a ruling class by the priority of these specific complexes. The problem would have to be analytically separated to recognize its specificity within the two contrasting systems, but there are still some preliminary general points.

It is of the essence of a ruling class that it possesses a monopoly or a predominance of overt or threatening violence. This is not a consequence of nuclear-weapons systems, and indeed it has been mainly in non-nuclear societies that the specific military-state-security formation has acquired absolute or determining power. The realities of more general productive development have created, in more advanced and complex economies, other effective major formations within the ruling class; and the true political process, at this level, is much more a matter of the shifting relations between these formations than of any inevitable dominance. The military-security formation has major advantages, and these are increased in conditions of international conflict. But just because what it produces is at once so deadly and so negative, it can only temporarily achieve that command of resources and policies which would ensure its stable dominance.

It is then true that the present nuclear arms race is producing conditions in which the possibilities of dominance form a rising tendency. Yet the ruling class as a whole still has other interests, both in its own immediate terms and in relation to assuring its continued dominance over the whole life of the society, which must include satisfying increasing non-military economic needs and demands of its people. It has also political interests in its need to present its central objectives in those broader terms which can command a necessary consent or acquiescence. Therefore, no ruling class, and a fortiori no whole social formation, can be reduced to the military-security element. If it is true that the military-security complex, just because of its negativity, moves on its own towards certain ultimate irrationalities in which the whole social order exists to serve and supply it, it is also true that other ruling-class formations, to say nothing of other classes, exert constant and powerful practical pressures of a different kind, which are then the materials of real politics. The observable fluctuations of military spending programmes and of broad political strategies are the indices of these continuing internal and externally affected struggles.

In lieu of more precise analysis of these dangerous internal formations, within the different social orders of the two major systems, we can note certain contradictions. Within capitalist societies, the military and related industries may not, for all their command of research, be a genuine leading sector. Their crude counter-cyclical role, and their privileged rate of profit, can distort the programmes and the interests of the capitalist class as a whole, while their massive levies of public revenue can disrupt investment programmes and produce unintended crisis and socio-economic discontent. The present crisis of ordinary manufacturing industry, with its consequences in major unemployment, is perhaps just such a case, and it is significant that it is often from within the ruling class that campaigns against the 'military-industrial complex' have been mounted. Meanwhile in the centralized socialist systems it is evident that the scale of military expenditure is economically crippling and has virtually no advantages for any productive sector. There the linkage is different, between the bureaucratic formation of the ruling class itself and the necessary support of military and state-security formations. The contradiction between an unproductive high-military economy and the dependence of a political leadership on exceptional monopoly of power and force is indeed very dangerous, but is itself reciprocally affected by external developments within the contradictions of its opponent system. Thus we need not conclude that there is any genuine inevitability in the formation and tendency to dominate of these powerful internal sectors. A full analysis must include a recognition of the 'dysfunctional' aspects of the arms race for both social systems.

'The Socialist Bomb'

The simplest version of the argument that Soviet nuclear-weapons systems are in effect the 'socialist bomb', demanding the support of the international working class, scarcely merits attention. It is an inescapable fact of nuclear weapons, with their indiscriminate destruction of whole populations, that they cannot be class-selective. The real consequence of that kind of argument is an impotent alienation and, ultimately, treason against every particular working class. Yet there are more serious arguments, as for example the position taken by Ernest Mandel in 1970.[7] In place of the essentially abstract propositions of 'international tension' and the 'dangers of war', such arguments begin from the facts of the imperialist world-system, including its ineradicable hostility not only to existing socialist states but to all national liberation struggles which threaten imperialist economic and strategic interests. All socialists who share this analysis of the present world crisis are faced with exceptionally difficult questions when they also, as they must, recognize the extraordinary and quite unprecedented dangers of nuclear war. It is one thing to hold to a strategy of victory against imperialism, but it is quite another to suppose that there can be any victory worth having through the ultimate devastation of a nuclear war.

There are then two possible positions. The first, which is more often drifted into than consciously adopted, involves using the legitimate fear of nuclear war, which after all can in the West be very freely expressed and campaigned on, as a way of objectively weakening the imperialist defence systems, thus tilting the strategic balance. The fact that this is constantly alleged, by the Right, against *every* campaign for nuclear disarmament (and then often with ludicrous misidentifications), ought not to blind us to the fact that it can be, in some cases, objectively and even subjectively true. It would make for intellectual honesty if those who have really adopted this position would say so, elaborating the radical case for a non-pacifist unilateralism. What is wrong with this position (and with any of the tactics and emphases which consciously or unconsciously follow from it) is, however, its uncritical identification of the interests of socialism and of anti-imperialism with the Soviet state. It is necessary, of course, to oppose absolutely all those who wish to destroy or threaten the Soviet state and its allies, or socialist China, or the new revolutionary states. This involves radical opposition to nuclear rearmament, to strategies of global containment, and to the whole complex of imperialist military alliances and arms-export client regimes.

7. 'Peaceful Coexistence and World Revolution', in Robert Blackburn, ed., *Revolution and Class Struggle*, London 1978, pp. 284–93.

Yet this duty of all socialists must be distinguished from naive or false-naive positions in the matter of the central nuclear-weapons confrontation. There are duties of defence of the international working class, but these necessarily include the whole working class, in each of the systems and beyond them, and cannot be discharged by deliberate or as it were accidental projection to the interests of a single state military order.

The second available position is more complex, but more adequate. It begins from the fact that it has been primarily the long pressures of imperialism against the new socialist and national-liberation states that have distorted, often disastrously, the realization of revolutionary socialism and democracy. From such a position it is possible both to recognize and struggle to end the crimes of imperialism and at the same time look full in the face the consequences, within the revolutionary states, new and old, of prolonged militarization and a state of political siege. Nor is this some neutralist position. It is centrally in the interests of socialism itself that these dangerous and objectively anti-socialist conditions should be diminished and finally abolished. Thus initiatives for disarmament must be primarily directed to the *inseparable* processes of weakening the imperialist offensive and strengthening the forces of socialism against those formations which now distort it. This requires, in the matter of proposals, the most scrupulous attention to real popular interests, rather than to any existing state interests. There is then an overwhelming socialist interest in nuclear disarmament, since the missile-nuclear systems objectively strengthen bloc politics, hegemonism and centralized military-security state apparatuses.

This emphasis can be the particular merit of the emerging campaign for European nuclear disarmament. Committed, as it must be, to East–West reciprocity, to the steady enlargement of demilitarized zones through the various layers of weapons systems, and then to the necessary gaining of some real *political* space in Europe, it is the only campaign which is entirely congruent with the long-term interests of all European socialists. It will remain very difficult to keep the emphases right, not only against misrepresentation and opposition, but between ourselves. Real responses will be required from within the Soviet alliance, and these are more likely to come if we make it clear that our disarmament proposals are integral with renewed efforts to advance socialism within our own countries; that they involve significant and difficult breaks with the strategy and ideology of the imperialist and anti-Communist alliance; and, crucially, that the condition of success of any of these struggles is a serious reciprocity, allowing the development of movements of national-popular support, rather than any simple taking of advantage of peace campaigns. It would be a very serious misreading of our campaign by anyone in the East to conclude that it is manipulable in the interests of bloc-politics and military advantage. But then it would be also a serious misdirection of our campaign if it became, at any point, in fact or by default, manipulable.

Necessary Linkages

To support the campaign for European nuclear disarmament does not necessarily mean believing that the central fracture and confrontation is in Europe. The most dangerous nuclear arena is here, but the crucial political struggles and dangers are very much more widespread. Thus the socialist contribution to the politics of nuclear disarmament must be more than simply collaborative, and must include solidarity with Third World struggles against an imperialist economic system which globally reproduces hunger and exploitation. This is no matter of riding the peace campaigns for some partisan objectives. There is now a profound linkage between the most actual and recurrent dangers of war and the specific crises of the imperialist world system. The use of military force and intimidation to maintain systems of power and exploitation – over and above the systems of military-strategic deployment – is still the central threat to peace. If we are to understand and explain this fully, we have to move on from the known and still crucial facts of the international economic order, to the now rapidly emerging facts of the crisis of resources.

It has become an absolute duty for Western socialists to prepare, in good time, the positions from which we can oppose and defeat attempts to secure scarce resources – the case of oil is the most urgent current example – by military interventions, whether direct or indirect. Such interventions will of course attempt to recruit popular opinion by appeals for the protection of our (privileged) 'way of life'. Given the effects of the simultaneous crisis of imposed unemployment and deprivation on the working peoples of the West, no socialist can suppose that these attempts will be easy to defeat. But there is no contradiction between such work and campaigns for nuclear disarmament. Indeed unless such campaigns are developed, in practical and predictive ways, the more isolated peace campaigns could be simply overwhelmed.

Such considerations are also relevant to what is now the major problem of the traditional linkage between opposition to rearmament and opposition to unemployment and social deprivation. There are still real links between essentially wasteful military spending and poverty and deprivation in the rest of the social order. But here, as elsewhere, there is not going to be any simple return to the status quo ante. We may have to face the old problem of a reactionary connection between rearmament and the revival of employment. But beyond this there are new and quite major problems of change, if both peace and decent living standards are to be maintained in the old capitalist world. It is not just a matter of cancelling useless or obscene military expenditure, nor even of redirecting investment to alternative civilian manufacture. The changes will have to involve radical transformations, internally and externally, rather than simple cancellations or reversions. Despite the difficulties of such transformations, they must be central priorities within any agenda of working for peace.

This can appear only to add to our burdens, for which our present strength is still insufficient. But this must be the final point of the present argument. It is, fortunately, still possible to generate movements for peace and for disarmament on the most general human grounds. That these are again growing is a significant gain against the culture and politics of violence. Yet alike for their intellectual adequacy and for extension of their support it is necessary to reach beyond the moving and honourable refusals on which many of them still characteristically depend. To build peace, now more than ever, it is necessary to build more than peace. To refuse nuclear weapons, we have to refuse much more than nuclear weapons. Unless the refusals can be connected with such building, unless protest can be connected with and surpassed by significant practical construction, our strength will remain insufficient. It is then in making hope practical, rather than despair convincing, that we must resume and change and extend our campaigns.

Socialism and Ecology

1982

In recent years some of us have been talking about ecological socialism –
though it's a bit of a mouthful. But in many countries and at a growing
pace there is an attempt to run together two kinds of thinking which are
obviously very important in the contemporary world; yet the attempt to
run them together is by no means simple. There are a number of
questions which we have to look at both in practical contemporary terms
and also in the way in which the different bodies of ideas have
developed.

It's ironic, actually, that the inventor of the concept of ecology was
the German biologist Haeckel, in the 1860s, and that Haeckel had a
significant influence on the socialist movement throughout Europe
around the turn of the century. Indeed Lenin referred to the influence of
Haeckel as at one time having been enormous. But it was not at all the
kind of influence which would now be represented by the concept of
ecology, although that was Haeckel's invention. His work was influential
because it was a materialist account of the natural world and among
other things a physiological account of the soul. This found its place in
the fierce debate about the relation between socialism and religion and
other ethical systems, which was central in the socialist movement of
that period. So that although at that time there was a relation between a
version of ecology and a problem in socialism it is not one of much
contemporary significance.

Yet if we go back beyond the particular name – ecology – and look at
the kinds of issues which it now in a broad way represents, we can find a
very complicated relation earlier in the nineteenth century and particularly from the period of the Industrial Revolution. The relations of
that kind of thinking to socialist thinking have been and remain important, contentious and complicated.

The Industrial Revolution

The Industrial Revolution dramatized the effects of human intervention in the natural world in ways which – although at first the effects were rather scattered, rather specialized – were bound to come within the attention of any serious observer. I say dramatized the effects because it was one of the common errors of that period – and it remains a common error – that substantial interference with the natural environment began only with the *industrial* revolution. Still, quite clearly, when you had the major extractive industries, the developing iron and steel and chemical industries, and then concentration of production in factories with quite new problems of aggregated housing and pollution because people hadn't been used to building towns in that way, there were effects of a quite extraordinary kind which it is still impossible to overemphasize. The world was being physically changed wherever any of these valuable substances could be found in the earth. Understandably there was an extraordinary response, in terms, normally, of natural order which was being disturbed by reckless human intervention. This was said by the most surprising people – not just by rural or literary people at some distance from it. One of the most remarkable accounts is by James Nasmyth, the inventor of the steam hammer who was right there in the centre of the new industrial processes. His account of the iron workings at Coalbrookdale, around 1830, is a classical text of environmental devastation. 'The grass had been parched and killed by the vapours of sulphureous acid thrown out by the chimneys; and every herbaceous object was of a ghastly grey – the emblem of vegetable death in its saddest aspect. Vulcan had driven out Ceres.' The effects were *so* dramatic. And the ordinary terms in which they were described centred on an idea of the 'natural' which had been disturbed, driven out, by this kind of industrial intervention.

Now this kind of thinking, which is still too little known, remains a crucial part of modern social thought. I say too little known because I was very surprised by one passage in an interesting article on the relations between ecology and socialism by the important German writer Hans-Magnus Enzensberger. It was in *New Left Review* 84, in 1974.[1] He tried to make a point against the modern ecological movement by recalling that, especially 'in the English factories and pits', industrialization 'made whole towns and areas of the countryside uninhabitable as long as a hundred and fifty years ago', yet that 'it occurred to no one to draw pessimistic conclusions about the future of industrialization from these

1. Hans-Magnus Enzensberger, 'A Critique of Political Ecology', *NLR* 84, March–April 1974, pp. 3–31.

facts'. It was only, he continued, when the effects reached the districts where the bourgeoisie was living that we had environmentalist arguments.

Now this is simply untrue. From Blake and Southey and Cobbett, in the early decades of industrialization, through to Carlyle, Ruskin, Dickens and William Morris, there were constant observations and arguments of just this kind. I analysed many of them in *Culture and Society*. It remains a curiosity that this whole body of social observation and argument, which arose very early in Britain for the obvious reason that the most spectacular industrialization was taking place here, is often not known at all by educated continental socialists, who can then build a wholly misleading history of the ideas. And after all it was a German observer, Engels, in Manchester in the 1840s, who provided one of the most devastating though by no means the earliest accounts of the dreadful living conditions in the new and explosively expanding industrial towns.

That body of thinking is varied in tendency, from those who rejected industrialization altogether, through those who wanted to mitigate its effects or humanize its conditions, to those others, and they were many, some of them socialists, who wanted to change its social and economic relations, which were seen as causing the greatest damage. Yet there was undoubtedly a very general tendency to see industrialism as the disturbance of a 'natural order'. In the early stages people were too near to a pre-industrial order to make the grosser errors of later periods. It eventually happened that people idealized the pre-industrial order and supposed, for example, that there had been no significant and destructive intervention in the natural environment before industrialism. In fact of course – and this probably goes back to neolithic times – certain methods of farming, over-grazing, destruction of forests, had produced natural physical disasters on an enormous scale. Many of the great deserts were created or enlarged in those periods; and many local climatic alterations. We shall get nowhere in thinking about these problems if we think that it is only the distinctive forms of modern industrial production that represent the problems of living well and sensibly on the earth.

Yet this emphasis, this foreshortening of history, had important intellectual effects. In a large part of the ecological movement as it developed – using that term to describe all such tendencies before the specific adjective was attached – there was an in-built tendency to contrast the damaging industrial order with the undamaging, natural, pre-industrial order.

Now, although there are important differences of degree, and some of the new processes caused more serious damage and destruction than any of the earlier processes, that is a false contrast. And this is particularly important for socialists to realize. For it allows us to distinguish the real history and therefore a possible future from what is otherwise a very weak version of the environmental case, which is that we should revert from industrial society to the pre-industrial order which didn't do this kind of damage. In its false contrast of physical conditions, and its characteristic evasion of social and economic conditions, this weak but popular case altogether misses the point.

I must make it clear that I say this as one who believes that the rural economy has been cheated and marginalized, in many places but quite especially in this country. I was born and bred in a rural economy, and I still find most of my priorities in it. But it is no use talking historically as if there can be that kind of simple contrast or reversion. Much of the worst damage, to people and to the land, happened in the rural economy from the rural economy. For one of the best recorded cases of that kind of damage we can go back to Thomas More and the expansion of the wool trade in the sixteenth century when, as he rightly said, the sheep were eating the men. Grazing sheep can be beautiful, very different from 'sulphureous vapours' though actually in Britain no more natural. It is the whole effect that matters, and that uncontrolled commercial exploitation of land and animals, reckless of its effects on other people, is what has really to be focussed. If you only pick up the physical appearances, you are likely to miss all the central social and economic questions, which is where ecological thinking and social thinking necessarily converge.

Socialism and Production

On the other hand there can be simplification the other way round. As socialism, from around the middle of the nineteenth century, began to distinguish itself from a whole body of associated and overlapping movements, there was a tendency to make a quite different emphasis: to say that the central problem of modern society was poverty, and that the solution to poverty was production, and more production. Although there would be incidental costs of this production, including changing and perhaps to some extent damaging the immediate environment, nevertheless poverty was the worst evil. Poverty had to be cured by more production as well as by the more specific policy of changing social and economic relations. Thus socialists for three or four generations, with only occasional exceptions – and this we still find to be the main tendency within socialism today – made the case that production is an absolute human priority, and that those who object to its effects are simply sentimentalists or worse; moreover that they are people who speak in bad faith, from their own comfort and privilege, about the effects of reducing poverty in the lives of others.

This had an extra effect when it was associated with that central idea of nineteenth-century society, which you can still hear encapsulated in such phrases as 'the conquest of nature', 'the mastery of nature'; attitudes which you can find as far back as Bacon's *The New Atlantis*. Indeed, if you compare More's *Utopia* and *The New Atlantis* you find these two contrasting positions very early in the history of the argument. Modern scientific production was the one necessary way of increasing wealth, decreasing poverty, extending man's dominion over nature. You keep hearing these phrases 'conquest of nature', 'mastery of nature', not only in the dominant bourgeois thought but also all through socialist and Marxist writing in the second half of the nineteenth century. You'll even find them quite centrally in Engels's *Dialectics of Nature*, although at a certain point he suddenly realized what he was saying, what this metaphor of conquest implied. Because of course these attitudes of mastering and conquering had from the beginning been associated not just with mastering the earth, or natural substances, or making water do what you wanted, but with pushing other people around, with going wherever there were things which you wanted, and subjugating and conquering. That's where the metaphors of conquest and mastery came from. They were a classic rationale of imperialism in just that expanding phase. They form the whole internal ethic of an expanding capitalism: to master nature, to conquer it, to shift it around to do what you want with it. Engels went along with that and then suddenly remembered where the metaphor came from and said, quite correctly: we shall never understand this if we fail to remember that we are ourselves part of nature, and that what is involved in this mastery and conquest is going to have its effects on us; we can't just arrive and depart as a foreign conqueror. But even then he shifted back, under the influence of this very strong nineteenth-century triumphalism about nature, and took up the metaphors again. And still today we read these triumphalist arguments about production. They are a bit less confident now, but if you read the typical case for socialism, as it became standard between the wars in the dominant tendency, it is all in terms of mastering nature, setting new human horizons, creating plenty as the answer to poverty.

Now we have to take that case seriously. It is a very important case and there are many hypocrisies, many false positions, to root out if there is to be an honest and serious argument about socialism and ecology in our own time. But under the spell of the notion of conquest and mastery, with its mystique of overcoming all obstacles, of there being nothing too big for men to tackle, socialism in fact lost its own most important emphasis. It did not really look at what was visibly happening in the most developed and civilized societies in the world, at what was happening in England, this wealthy advanced industrial country which was still full of aggregated poverty and unbelievable disorder and squalor. For it is a capitalist response to say that if you produce more, these things will put themselves right. The essential socialist case is that the wealth and the poverty, the order and the disorder, the production and the damage, are all parts of the same process. In any honest account you have to see that they are connected, and that doing more of one kind of thing does not necessarily mean that you'll have less of the other.

That central socialist case was always put; there is not a generation in which somebody has not been seriously putting it. Yet under capitalist and imperialist influence, and especially since 1945 under North American influence, the majority position amongst socialists has been that the answer to poverty, the sufficient and only answer, is to increase production. This is in spite of the fact that a century and a half of dramatically increased production, though it has transformed and in general improved our conditions, has not abolished poverty, and has even created new kinds of poverty, just as certain kinds of development create underdevelopments in other societies. It is that which is now the central question for socialists.

William Morris

The writer who began to unite these diverse traditions, in British social thought, was William Morris. He was at once, especially in his later years, a socialist – indeed a revolutionary socialist – and a man who, from direct practice, from the use of his own hands, from the observation of natural processes, was deeply aware of what work on physical objects really means. He knew that you can produce ugliness quite as easily as you can create beauty. He knew that you can produce the useless or the damaging as easily as the useful. He could see how many kinds of work seemed specifically designed to create ugliness and damage, in their making and in their use. He thought about this not only in general ways but from his own practice as a craftsman. His critique of the abstract idea of production was one of the most decisive interventions in the socialist argument. Instead of the simple capitalist quantum of production, he began asking questions about what kinds of production. In this, in fact, he was following Ruskin, who argued much the same case – who insisted that human production, unless governed by general human standards, rather than by mere profit or convenience, could lead to 'illth' as readily as to 'wealth'. But Ruskin did not have Morris's explicitly socialist affiliations.

Morris said: 'Have nothing in your home which you do not either believe to be beautiful or know to be useful.' It sounds a trite recommendation. But it goes to the centre of the problem, and to take it seriously still today would lead to a pretty extraordinary clear-out. And it's not just in the home. Suppose we said: 'Have nothing in your shops but what you believe to be beautiful or know to be useful.' That is a criterion of production which instead of a simple quantitative reckoning is relating production to human need. Moreover it sees human need as something more than consumption, that incredibly popular idea of our own time, which from the dominance of capitalist marketing and advertising tries to reduce all human need and desire to consumption. It is an extraordinary word, 'consumer'. It is a way of seeing people as though they are either stomachs or furnaces. 'And what sort of effect will this have on the consumer?', politicians ask, the consumer then being a very specialized variety of human being with no brain, no eyes, no senses, but who can gulp. Moreover if you have a notion of production which is to supply that kind of consumption you can only think in quantitative terms. You can never really ask: 'do we have to accept certain losses, certain local damage, because we need this production?' You cannot ask whether we need this or that production because of need or beauty. Production becomes insensibly an end in itself, as in ordinary capitalist thinking, but also within this strain of socialist thinking – weak socialist thinking – in which it is seen as in itself and as such the answer to poverty.

So when Morris brought these questions together, and campaigned over so many issues, he was making the kind of junction of two different traditions which ought to have come earlier, ought to have been better sustained after Morris, and ought to be much clearer and stronger than it is even today. One reason, however, why it was not immediately sustained and followed up after Morris's day, was that he too was a victim of that delusion which I described as being very general earlier in the century. I mean the delusion that before factory production, before industrial and mechanical production, there had been a natural, clean, simple order. For Morris it was located, as for so many nineteenth-century radicals and socialists, in the Middle Ages. Thus a notion that the future, the socialist future, would be some kind of reconstitution of the medieval world, established itself deeply in his thought, although it always worried him. He conceded that if a machine would save us from boring work, so that we could use our time on other things, then we should use it. But the main tendency was always towards the reconstitution of an essentially simple peasant and craftsman order.

Now I don't have to tell you how strong that kind of thinking still is within the ecological movement. It is still seen by many good people as the only way of saving the world. It is seen by others as something which they would themselves prefer to do, dropping out from modern industrial society and taking a different course which gives them more satisfaction. It is even seen – and this is a harder case to sustain although it may be morally stronger – as a possible future for still densely populated countries.

But for everyone else Morris seems easy to dismiss, because in that world he imagined in the twenty-first century, after the socialist revolution of 1952 (which, I don't need to remind you, was a bit off the date), in that world of the twenty-first century you've got a small clean London in which more or less everything happens easily and naturally. If you feel like doing something then you do it, because in any case there's enough. Yet this sufficiency all happens somewhere mysteriously offstage. And back by the river there is only the visual beauty, the sensitivity of friendship and comradeship. There is a pervading sense of leisure and space and peace, where all the human values can be sustained and developed. But that's it. It is a sweet, spacious, clean little world, where the problems of production have not just been questioned, as in that earlier, necessary intervention – 'don't tell me that it is needed for production, tell me production for what and who needs it?' – but now as problems of production, of human sustenance, have been pushed out of sight. Actually Morris was right to observe, towards the end of his life, that he probably thought and imagined in that way because he was himself born rich by inheritance and was always able, as a marvellous craftsman, to earn a good living by doing the kind of satisfying work that other people actually wanted done. Rich people, incidentally, were the only customers who could afford to buy craftsmanship of his quality. He said that all this probably coloured his views.

Well, yes it did. It is an honest admission. It is one of the tangles that we have to sort out. The association of that notion of deliberate simplification, even regression, with the idea of a socialist solution to the ugliness, the squalor and the waste of capitalist society has been very damaging. All it leads to, really, is a number of individual and small group solutions, such as the arts-and-crafts movement, or people like Edward Carpenter and a whole succession of good, plain-living, honest and honourable people who have found this way of coping with and living through the twentieth century, damaging nobody, helping many. But in general they have fostered the notion that somehow this would solve the problem of the whole social order, in effect by cancellation of all the other things that have happened. And if you associate that with a certain kind of socialism, you must expect people to say: 'well look, it's just not on in a twentieth-century world. It's all gone too far, there are too many of us. The problems have to be solved in modern terms or they won't in practice be solved at all.'

That is indeed my own position, for all my respect for Morris and the others. It is from this position that I recognize the importance of the ecological movement in our own period, still making its necessary advances, especially among the most intelligent young, and yet I also see the movement's reluctance to think through its true complex relationship with socialism.

'Non-political' Ecology

Let us first notice that a lot of general ecology is, as they say, 'non-political'. It is a quite common response among many serious people now: that politics is a superficial business, it is just the in and out of competing parties, the old Left–Right seesaw, and is anyway just reconstituting the same damaging and boring old order. We have to strike out, they say, on a different route, and we want nothing to do with what you call politics; we're tackling the social problems at a deeper level. This is a serious position. But it is not an adequate one, if only because, as anyone knows who's knocked around in politics, 'no politics' is also politics, and having no political position is a form of political position, and often a very effective one. What happens in practice is that you get a kind of movement (it is very strong in certain countries, particularly the United States) to find small group solutions or individual solutions, family solutions, in which people can begin living *at once* in a different way. That, I think, is the most sustainable position intellectually.

It is a very different matter when you come to the more general non-political ecological case, in which a group of people, often highly informed, well-qualified to speak of what they are speaking about – the problem of food in relation to growing populations, problems of energy, problems of industrial pollution, problems of nuclear power – issue manifestos and warnings, usually addressed to the leaders of the world, saying that there must be immediate crash programmes, that in the next five years we must reduce energy consumption by x per cent, that we must outlaw certain harmful manufacturing processes, and so on. These are lists of objectives which I'd sign now, and which most of us would sign. But the special character of these pronouncements is revealed when you look at who they are addressed to. Having reached such conclusions, where in fact do you go next? If the pronouncements are directed towards specific public opinion, that is a reasonable procedure, because then people who need to know about the problems, to be concerned about them, are informed and encouraged. But that is not commonly what is done. Characteristically, this non-political approach calls upon generalized public opinion or upon 'the world'. But in the latter case, they are calling upon the leaders of the precise social orders which have created the devastation to reverse their own processes. They are calling upon them to go against the precise interests, the precise social relationships, which have produced their leadership. Moreover, at a certain point, although the actual pronouncements are honest and important, the political position can be worse than merely mistaken, because it creates and supports the notion that the leaders can solve these problems. Of course the leaders can at once say: 'well, we'd love to proceed and have a really serious cutting back on certain kinds of harmful production, but it wouldn't be popular with the electorate. We'd love to do it, but who'd vote for it?' This is at least what the more enlightened ruling-class people say under pressure: it would be unpopular, it would be too difficult to do. Increasingly, meanwhile, the really effective ruling class dismisses the whole case as sentimental nonsense, which simply limits or delays production and national power.

At this point it is not enough to go on issuing these general warnings, which as they multiply (I get weary of the dates, for some of the five-year crash-programmes are now at least twenty years old) focus the problem quite wrongly. I am not mocking the defeated, because everybody on the left is defeated, we've all been defeated. I am not criticizing these pronouncements because they haven't succeeded. I'm just saying we must take a long look at where the movement gets to, when it issues pronouncements to the leaders of the world or to unspecific public opinion. For the facts are, as I read them, that the necessary changes really do involve substantial social and economic dislocations as well as mere changes. There would, in my judgement, be major disturbances in any serious programme for resource saving, resource management and above all in the diminution of radical poverty in the poorest parts of the world. This is not an argument against the programmes, but if it is the case we must say so openly, and see what positive forces can be assembled to support them. And it is here that we come back to the relation with socialism, which I see as crucial.

Socialist Alternatives

Let us look at this first in the developed industrial countries, which by in a sense ignoring the kinds of consideration to which ecology now draws attention, have become rich overall and, whatever inequalities there still are within the societies, have produced kinds of work, standards of living, habitual uses of resources, which clearly people now assume and expect. These can only ever be equitably negotiated out of. They can never be argued out of, they can never be converted out of, they can only be very carefully *negotiated* out of. It is no use simply saying to South Wales miners that all around them is an ecological disaster. They already know. They live in it. They have lived in it for generations. They carry it in their lungs. It happens now that coal might be one of the more desirable energy alternatives, although the costs of that kind of mining can never be forgotten. But you cannot just say to people who have committed their lives and their communities to certain kinds of pro-duction that this has all got to be changed. You can't just say: 'come out of the harmful industries, come out of the dangerous industries, let us do something better.' Everything will have to be done by negotiation, by equitable negotiation, and it will have to be taken steadily along the way. Otherwise you will find, as in all too many environmental cases and planning enquiries in this country – on a new airport, for example, or on some new industrial development in a previously non-industrial region – that there is a middle-class environmental group protesting against the damage and there's a trade-union group supporting the coming of the work. Now for socialists this is a terrible conflict to get into. Because if each group does not really listen to what the other is saying, there will be a sterile conflict which will postpone any real solutions, at a time when it is already a matter for argument whether there is still time for the solutions.

I believe that only socialists can make the necessary junction. Because we are not going to be the people – at least I hope we are not going to be the people – who simply say 'keep this piece clear, keep this threatened species alive, at all costs.' The case of a threatened species is a good general illustration. You can have a kind of animal which is damaging to local cultivation, and then you have the sort of problem that occurs again and again in environmental issues. You will get the eminences of the world flying in and saying: 'you must save this beautiful wild creature'. That it may kill the occasional villager, that it tramples their crops, is unfortunate. But it is a beautiful creature and it must be saved. Such people are the friends of nobody, and to think that they are allies in the ecological movement is an extraordinary delusion. It is like the country-house industrialist or banker in Britain, often an occasional supporter of the environment or what he calls 'our heritage', who makes money all week from the muck and the spoil, and then – because this is the English pattern – he changes his clothes and goes down to the country for the weekend; he is spiritually refreshed by this place, which he's very keen to keep unspoiled, until he can go back, refreshed, back into the making of the smoke and the spoil, which is the precise resource for his escape. If – and I don't think that it is going to happen, because there are too many people coming in from the other side – but if that is the kind of case that environmentalists are going to make, then I hope socialists are against it, because it is the sort of thing with which we can have no truck at all.

On the other hand it is perfectly clear that at a certain level, in the major ecological issues, it is not really a matter of choice. This is the case that socialists can begin to make: that it is not really a matter of choice whether we can go on with certain existing patterns and conditions of production, with all their actual looting of the resources of the earth and with all their damage to life and health. Or even when they are not damaging, there is the certainty that many of the resources at their present levels of use are going to run out. That is the case which any socialist should recognize: the fact of real material limits to the existing mode of production and to the social conditions which it is also producing.

One of the disadvantages of some of the most publicized ecology is that it has been very free in projections about when these various limits and failures will happen. The truth is – and every honest worker in the field knows it – that most of the projections are at best guesses. But they are serious guesses. That the notion of some limits is real, somewhere along the line, is, I suppose, beyond question. And if this is so, then even at the simplest material level the notion of an indefinite expansion of certain kinds of production, but even more of certain kinds of consumption, is going to have to be abandoned. It is interesting to remember that it is only ten years or so since we were having those projections of the two-car family by 1982 and the three-car family by 1988, and heaven knows how many cars there could have been, on one of those extrapolating lines, by the year 2000. We've now learned the answer to that! The idea that the unit electricity consumption of a North American family could become a standard of living for the world – or at least for the industrialized world – can now be clearly seen to be a fantasy. It is this kind of rational assessment, on the best evidence and on the changing evidence, that underlines the fact of material limits, and that should now force our societies to the most important kind of rethinking we have ever had to do.

It is here that genuine socialism can make a contemporary connection with the rational assessments of ecology. We have to build on the socialist argument that productive growth, as such, is not the abolition of poverty. What matters, always, is the way production is organized, the way the products are distributed. It is also, and now crucially, the way in which priorities between *different forms of production* are decided. And it is then the social and economic relations between men and classes, which emerge from such decisions, which determine whether more production will reduce or eliminate poverty or will simply create new kinds of poverty as well as new kinds of damage and destruction.

International Perspectives

In that context the question becomes more than national, although it is a very important component of a redefinition of socialism within countries like our own. It has always been a running argument within the Labour Party, especially since 1945, whether we're going to get equality, and what are usually referred to as 'the things we all want' – schools and hospitals are usually the first to be named – when we've got the economy right, when we've produced enough, enlarged the national cake and so on; or whether equality and the priority of human needs require, as their first and necessary condition, fundamental changes in our social and economic institutions and relationships. I think we now have to see that argument as settled. The usual 'national cake' position, the soft political option, can be seen to rest on a basic fallacy, which the United States has demonstrated to the world – and no society is ever going to be relatively richer in gross indiscriminate production than that one – that by getting to a certain level of production you solve the problems of poverty and inequality. Tell them that in the slums, the inner cities, of rich America! All socialists are then forced to recognize that we have to intervene on quite a different basis. We have to say, as Tawney said sixty years ago, that no society is too poor to afford a right order of life. And no society is so rich that it can afford to dispense with a right order, or hope to get it merely by becoming rich. This is in my view the central socialist position. We can never accept so-called solutions to our social and economic problems which are based on the usual crash programmes of indiscriminate production, *after* which we shall get 'the things we all want'. By the ways in which we produce, and the ways in which we organize production and its priorities – including, most notably, the inherent capitalist priority of *profit* – we create social relations which then determine how we distribute the production and how people actually live.

This is at a national level. But it is even more true at the international level. For we are bound to notice – and the people from the poorest parts of the world do increasingly notice – that the world economy is now organized and dominated by the interests of the patterns of production and consumption of the highly industrialized countries, which are also in a strict sense, through all the different political forms, the imperialist powers. This is shown most dramatically at the moment in the case of oil. But it is true also over a very wide range of necessary metals, of certain strategically important minerals and in certain cases even in food. We can now reasonably say that the central issues of world history over the next twenty or thirty years are going to be the distribution and use of these resources, which are at once necessary for a contemporary pattern of human life but which are also *unequally* necessary in the present distribution of economic power. Already the struggles over the supply and price of oil, and of other commodities, determine not only the functioning of the world economy but the key political relations between states.

This is where the problem of a reformulated and practical socialist economic programme, within old industrial countries like Britain, and the rapidly developing problems of the world economy, can be seen to interlock. Because it is possible to look forward – yet that is quite the wrong phrase, because no one who has taken a true measure of the problem could look forward to it – to see ahead a situation in which the shortage of certain key raw materials and commodities, which are necessary to maintain existing patterns of production and existing high levels of consumption, will create such tensions within societies which have got used to these patterns that they could in majority be prepared to resort to every kind of pressure – not only political and sub-military, but openly military – to assure what they see as the supplies necessary to the maintenance of their order of life. This is already a dangerous current of opinion in the United States. We can all see, as the shortages and costs come through, the danger of this happening. We can see also the possibility of recruiting wide areas of public opinion to cast as enemies the poor countries which have been assigned the role of supplying the raw materials, the oil, the whole range of basic commodities, at prices which are convenient to the functioning, in received terms, of the older industrial economies.

There are other dangers of war, in the rivalry and the arms race of the superpowers and in the filth of the export and import trade in armaments. In fact even there the economic issues are deeply involved in the political and military rivalries. But more generally there is the virtual certainty of a conflict over scarce resources and the prices of scarce resources becoming an attempt to dominate in new ways in the world economy. And this will be initiated by the advanced industrial societies which of course, by the nature of their development, dispose of the technologically developed weapons of war and subjugation, including nuclear weapons, which is where all the issues now come together. So this is one answer when people ask: how are we to argue the case for a sensible use of resources within our kind of society and economy, when this will involve changes – in some cases reductions – in existing patterns of use? How are we going to persuade people to accept this? It goes so much against their own self-interest that as a political programme it doesn't even begin. Well, there are the other ways we've already looked at, in facing the fact that there are material limits to the kinds of production and consumption to which we have specialized ourselves. There is also the case, which is winning significant support, of the development of other kinds of production, notably the renewed interest in agriculture and forestry, in new forms of energy production and of transport, and in various kinds of more locally based, non-exploitative and also renewable and non-obsolescent kinds of work. But it is clear that however strongly this alternative current develops, it will not be sufficient, in any immediate period, to solve the problems of the whole existing economy. And then will come the crisis point, when there is a profound challenge to the existing ways of life. The problem of resources – the pressure point on the whole existing capitalist mode of production – will become the problem of war or peace. This problem will be presented, through all the powerful resources of modern communications, as a problem of hostile foreigners who are exercising a stranglehold over our necessary supplies. Opinion will be mobilized for what will be called 'peacekeeping'; in fact wars and raids and threatening interventions to ensure supplies or to keep down prices.

Thus the continuation of existing patterns of unequal consumption of the earth's resources will lead us inevitably into various kinds of war, of different scales and extent. And then the case for changing our present way of life has to be argued not only in terms of local damage or waste or pollution, but in terms of whether we are to have the possibility of peace and friendly relations, or the near certainty of destructive wars because we are not willing to change the inequalities of the present world economy.

If the issue is put in this way, if we are able to look clearly at what a standard of *life* really is, we ought to be able to reach more people with the argument that a crucial component of any rational definition of a standard of life is the maintenance of peace. Of the many causes of war, this is the one which seems to me likely in the next half-century to be central. Thus the link to wider political agencies, which must be the object of search of all who are now seriously concerned with environmental problems, is in a sense given to us by the nature of the argument. We can properly link the argument about resources, about their equal distribution and their caring renewal, with the argument about the avoidance of war. Ironically, in that, we may even find friends in some of the most innocent supporters of a consumer society, for of course that happy and thoughtless consumption depends on peaceful production, without major interruptions, or without priority being given to rearmament and the militarized state. There could even be an argument for the maintenance of peace which could connect with some of the deepest habits and assumptions of a consumer society, because nobody will want that kind of interruption. Yet it could still happen, by a kind of inertia. The more consumption is abstracted from all the real processes of the world, the more we are likely to find ourselves in these dangerous war and prewar situations. All the attractions of desirable consumption could push us, in contradictory ways, towards war, towards a chauvinism of the old rich countries, towards a slandering of the leaders of movements and peoples of the poor countries who are striving to redress these major and unforgivable inequalities.

For any ecologist this is a special challenge. It is too easy, in the rich industrial north, to say that we have had our industrial revolution, we have had our advanced industrial and urban development, and we have known some of its undesirable effects, and so we are in a position to warn the poor countries against going down that same road. We have indeed to try to share that whole experience of indiscriminate production. But we must do it in a kind of good faith which is in fact rare. It must not become an argument for keeping the poor countries in a state of radical underdevelopment, with their economies in fact shaped to keep supplying the existing rich countries. It must not become an argument against the kind of sensible industrialization which will enable them, in more balanced ways, to use and develop their own resources, and to overcome their often appalling problems of poverty. The case, that is to say, has to be made from a position of genuinely shared experience and from a deep belief in human equality, rather than from the overt or, even more dangerous, covert prejudices of the developed northern societies.

Bringing these issues together, then, we can see that in local, national and international terms there are already kinds of thinking which can become the elements of an ecologically conscious socialism. We can begin to think of a new kind of social analysis in which ecology and economics will become, as they always should be, a single science. We can see the outline of political bearings which can be related to material realities in ways that give us practical hope for a shared future.

Yet none of it is going to be easy. Deep changes of belief will be necessary, not just conveniently, where they are in fact impossible, among the existing power elites and the rich classes of the world, but in all of us who are now practically embedded in this general situation. We are bound to encounter the usual human reluctance to change, and we must accept the fact that the changes will be very considerable and will have to be negotiated rather than imposed. But the case for this new kind of enlightened, materially conscious, international socialism is potentially very strong, and I think we are now in the beginning – the difficult negotiating beginning – of constructing from it a new kind of politics.

Between Country and City

1984

I wrote *The Country and the City* in the late 1960s and early 1970s. Looking at it again, the other day, I was surprised to find how many things had happened, in both country and city, in those few intervening years. It is true that the main tendencies I had identified seemed strongly confirmed. I do not mean only that there has been an intensifying crisis in the cities, and especially in the inner cities, though that record of a mounting pressure on housing and services, of financial emergencies and in some extreme cases of actual riots and burning, is evidently grave. Nor do I mean only that there have been some important changes in the country districts: the further rapid development of agribusiness and high-input arable farming; the rapid relative increase in the importance of the agricultural sector in the national economy, especially since joining the European Community; and the continuing growth of country settlement and rural work of new kinds. But my central case in *The Country and the City* was that these two apparently opposite and separate projections – country and city – were in fact indissolubly linked, within the general and crisis-ridden development of a capitalist economy which had itself produced this division in its modern forms. With the increasing development of a more fully organized agrarian capitalism, ever more closely linked with the general money market, this is clearly even more true now than then.

Yet this was always the underlying social, economic and historical analysis. What I was more immediately concerned with was the set of human responses, in everyday attitudes and activities but also in art and writing and ideas, to these always practical facts and developments. Here again I found much to confirm what I had argued. There was a continuing flood of sentimental and selectively nostalgic versions of country life. Identification of the values of rural society with the very

227

different values of certain dominant and privileged mansions seemed even more strong; indeed these mansions were now often defined, flatly, as 'our heritage'. I say 'mansions' rather than 'country houses' because that ordinary term is part of a very revealing ideological confusion. These places of the landed aristocracy, but now much more of the rich of all kinds, including notably the leaders of City finance and of urban industry, are 'country houses' in necessary relation to their 'town houses' or apartments. The real country houses are those of the people who find their diverse livelihoods *in* the country. The presumptive 'country house' is, by contrast, the formal expression of the double base – in city and country alike – of a class based on linked property, profit and money. A more modest and economically different version of a comparable double base is the 'country cottage' of those who mainly earn their livelihood in salaried employment and professional fees in the cities. There is a wide variation of scale, in both kinds, but it is always necessary to distinguish 'the country' as a place of first livelihood – interlinked, as it always must be, with the most general movements of the economy as a whole – and 'the country' as a place of rest, withdrawal, alternative enjoyment and consumption, for those whose first livelihood is elsewhere.

Yet while that distinction is clear and firm, there is no simple corresponding distinction in attitudes to 'the country' or in the 'country' images that we make and exchange. There are, it is true, some obvious general differences, notably in accounts of rural work, which vary according to how often and on what terms – above all, for whom – it is done. But in the increasing interaction of 'country' and 'city' several interesting changes in more general attitudes seem now to be happening, some of them in complex ways. It is these I will now try to define, at least provisionally, as a contribution to an ever more widely based argument.

The first and most obvious change, which has been developing for many years but is now at a critical stage, relates precisely to the rapid increase in agribusiness, and specifically to the practices of high-input arable farming and new forms of intensive animal and poultry rearing. In a historical perspective these new methods and techniques are evidently the result of the application of industrial methods to traditional farming practices. They are thus a prime case of the interaction of 'country' and 'city' within a single industrial-capitalist economy, just as the closely associated changes in land ownership, agricultural finance and modes of capitalization are elements of the operation of a single money market. It is then not surprising that there should be some familiar but also some unfamiliar kinds of opposition to them. In cities in arable areas, but perhaps even more in country towns and villages, there is intense and often angry opposition to such effects as straw-burning and crop-spray drift, which have markedly increased. In a more general way there is strong organized opposition to conditions of intensive animal and poultry rearing which are seen as cruel.

This overlaps in one direction with intense opposition to most forms of the exploitation and even use of animals, and of course with strong objections to older forms of country sport such as hunting. But it overlaps in another direction with a much more general ecological case. Straw-burning is seen as not only polluting but typically wasteful. Crop-spraying, even when there is no drift, is seen as in at least some instances a characteristic example of profitable production taking priority over both public health and the natural environment as a whole. Selective breeding of some plants and animals is seen as diminishing the necessary genetic range, and this is related to the underlying dependence of these varieties on heavy use of imported fertilizers and feedstuffs, itself necessarily connected, not only in the long but even in the short run, with the facts of finite natural resources, renewable and non-renewable, and their now biased distribution in favour of the old rich economies. Thus there are several new kinds of antagonism between what are no longer simple 'country' and city' positions, but between and across changing versions of both.

This already complex situation is made even more complex by the fact, unlooked-for even a generation ago, that agriculture is now the most successful sector of a generally failing economy. The time is past when a powerful and influential contrast could be made between busy and thriving industrial areas and a depressed and neglected agriculture. Moreover, and greatly to the long-term advantage of the whole society, the proportion of food raised within the country has increased remarkably, and could be still further increased, with important effects on the viability – and in extreme cases the survival chances – of this heavily populated island. It is common to reply to criticism of the new methods and techniques with the facts of this genuine advantage. What is then replayed within agriculture is the old argument, from the nineteenth century onwards, between the advantages of increased production and the full social, human and natural effects of its processes.

But this has been, from the beginning, a much more difficult argument than it is usually made to seem. The producers, in majority, deploy their powerful statistics of supply and demand, and dismiss most objections as sentimental or at best marginal. This is clearly expressed in that ideological term 'by-product', which is an attempt to separate out the often unwanted but usually predictable and even necessary results of a whole productive process, keeping only the favourable outputs as real 'products'. On the other side, many objectors to these processes are indeed only objecting to the inconvenience of any production, if it happens to blow their way. There is a long tradition of *rentier* objection to physical productive processes of all kinds, though its profits are regularly taken and used to finance other styles of life. There is some continuation of these attitudes among many who are not strictly *rentiers* (people living on incomes from invested money and property) but who, finding their own livelihood elsewhere, are intolerant of other people at work, especially in those country areas which they have chosen for withdrawal and rest. While the argument is confined to exchanges between these two large groups – statistical producers and *rentiers*/weekenders – there is plenty of heat but little light. The real arguments are at once more discriminating and more general.

Thus it is not reasonable, in my view, to pick out a few obviously damaging agricultural applications of science and technology and suppose oneself to have proved some general case. Every particular technique and method needs specific assessment. I am myself persuaded that very-high-input arable farming, with its expensive reliance on heavy fertilizer, energy and pesticide applications, and with its necessary relation to varieties selected for these conditions, leading to some consequent neglect of other possible (including new) varieties, is unsustainable in the long term, given probable developments in both world economics and world ecology. I am similarly persuaded that intensive animal and poultry breeding on imported feedstuffs or on the deliberate surpluses of high-input grain production is wrong both in terms of world food needs – where the surpluses of meat, grain and dairy products in the old rich countries coexist with widespread basic starvation in the growing populations of the poor majority of the world – and in terms of any sustainable economy in our own land. But there are shadings to put on even these conclusions, and in other cases there are significant and valuable real gains, especially in scientific agriculture, as from improved grasses and improved breeds of sheep – which I have been watching fairly closely.

Underlying all these problems of intensive production there is an increasing actual pressure of a financial rather than an economic kind. The huge involvement of agriculture in high-interest debt and credit is usually a truer cause of the most frantic attempts to increase production at any environmental cost than the causes more often assigned, of merely cruel or greedy exploitation. This is not to say that there is no cruelty, no greed, but these can be better distinguished when this much more general pressure is defined and traced to its sources in a specific kind of money-market economy. Moreover this is something that could be changed, with the provision of longer-term and lower-interest credits, for more generally agreed kinds and levels of production: reforms which would have to carry with them the acceptance of realistic prices for food, realistic interest on savings, and some dietary changes – especially in sugar, meat and dairy products – if a general and long-term policy were to have a chance of holding.

Why do most of us not now think in these ways? The superficial divisions of country and city – and specifically, now, of 'agriculture' and 'the rest' – push in to prevent us. This latter division, between 'agriculture' and 'the rest', is especially significant and interesting. For what has happened, at one level, is a misleading simple identification of 'the country' with agriculture. This is better than identifying it with 'country houses', but it is still misleading. A rural economy has never been solely an agricultural economy. Indeed it is only as a consequence of the Industrial Revolution that the idea (though never the full practice) of rural economy and society has been limited to agriculture. It is obvious that food production will always be central in any rural economy, as indeed in any stable whole economy. But this does not mean that a more complex and diverse economy and society cannot or should not develop beyond this base. All rural economies and societies of the past have been more than agricultural: they have included, because that was their natural place, a wide diversity of crafts and trades. The unbalanced development of cities and industrial towns, through the periods of centralization of state power, concentration of the money market, and large-scale factory production, drained the rural economy of much of its work and, with that, its relative autonomy.

Yet all these developments are now moving, or are capable of being moved, the other way. There is a powerful demand for the decentralization of state power. There are early opportunities for altering the conditions of the money market, in the now critical circumstances of local government finance and development capital: a range of possible initiatives for more local resource audits, financing and control. Meanwhile there is a firm trend away from factory processes requiring the physical concentration of large numbers of workers, and towards smaller and more specialized workplaces, which with the advantages of new energy and communications technologies can be more diversely sited, including in country areas.

At such a time it is especially necessary to broaden the arguments about rural economy and society from the simple specialization to agriculture. Beyond even the environmental and resource effects of high-input farming is the effect of the reduction of human work on the land, through mechanization and automation, with damaging results not only for rural employment prospects of the traditional kind, but for the cities which are no longer the thriving centres to which displaced workers can go. It is here that the structure of modern capitalist agriculture has complex and even contradictory effects. The revitalizing effects of a profitable agriculture are real, in many areas, but its political base in the whole society is uncertain and even precarious, given the present scale of subsidies and arranged markets. If it is at the same time, as in the arable areas, actually reducing the broader rural economy and society, it will soon find that it has few friends. It could be overwhelmed at any time by a shallow urban consumerism, pushing its way back, however shortsightedly, into a global free market. Hatred for the Common Agricultural Policy is already intense, and its political outcome – reduction or cancellation – could be disastrous for our rural economy. Yet if profitable production and market criteria are the only norms, as in capitalist agriculture itself, there is no principled way of resisting their global extension. The only sustainable objective of a Common Agricultural Policy is – as some French ministers have correctly stated – the maintenance of a viable rural economy *and* society. If capitalist agriculture is concerned only with itself, and not with rural society as a whole, in a necessary and changing balance with urban and metropolitan society, it has little long-term future and virtually no political defences.

This has several effects on our ways of thinking about the future of rural economies. First, it is necessary to oppose the current drive to get rid of what are called 'small inefficient producers'. This drive is powered by an unholy combination of large agrarian capitalists and the urban Left. It is one of the miseries, indeed crimes, of agrarian capitalism, throughout its history, that it has reduced the spread and diversity of landholding and repeatedly made so many of its neighbours redundant. The cruel fact about contemporary redundancy, by comparison with earlier periods in which the cruelties were of a different kind, is that there is now almost literally nowhere to go: not the old Empire; not the new lands; not the expanding factory towns.

Yet in these new conditions the number of farms in Britain has declined from a pre-1914 figure of 400,000 to some 200,000 today. The pressure to reduce this number yet further comes from a whole range of political and economic bodies which disagree about almost everything else. The identification of efficiency is almost wholly in capitalist terms, as return on capital. Real returns on land use need to be quite differently assessed, not only by extension from the immediate operation to the true full costs in the economy as a whole, but also by extension to an accounting of the full social costs, including the costs of maintaining growing numbers of the displaced and unemployed and the usually overlooked costs of the crisis of the cities to which so many of them gravitate.

This is a worldwide phenomenon, much more serious in many other countries than in Britain, but its shape is already discernible here. What is called environmentalism resists pollution and the destruction of habitats by high-input large-scale farming. Ecology, in its usual forms, resists in terms of the unbalanced and often reckless use of non-renewable resources. Agrarian capitalism answers both with its own version of the priorities of profitable production. What is then necessary is a new kind of political ecology, based in but surpassing these earlier cases, which can trace the processes to the economic and social structures which develop and are strengthened by them, and which can reasonably propose alternative kinds of economic and social organization.

Thus efficiency must never be reduced to a monetary criterion, or to a simple criterion by gross commodities. Efficiency is the production of a stable economy, an equitable society and a fertile world. Every local measurement is important but the full accounting has to be in these broad terms. Ironically, in all such real accounting, the maintenance and development of rural economies and rural settlements comes out as a high priority. All those who are really committed to them have a central interest in such wider accounting, and in resisting the kinds of calculation, derived from urbanism and industrialism, which have become specific to capitalist agriculture and especially to money-market agribusiness.

Among its many other uses, this perspective helps us to understand a growing contemporary tendency which still awaits its full analysis. There has been a good deal of scattered comment on the movement of a new kind of people into country areas: not just the retired and the commuters, which is an older phenomenon, but a wide range of active people in a diversity of occupations. Some of this has been disparagingly described as the descent of the dropouts, and there have indeed been many odd encounters between these new arrivals and an older rural population. Yet it seems in reality to be a very mixed phenomenon. Some of course have 'dropped into' forms of farming and smallholding, including some experimental forms. But others are simply taking advantage of independence of location for their particular kinds of work, finding the physical country a major attraction and able, in part, to settle in it because of the relative depopulation caused by earlier phases of industry and agriculture. If we look at this tendency in terms of a whole rural society, rather than of a rural economy limited to agriculture, the judgement seems to alter.

I noted down recently the first occupations of my neighbours within five miles of my house in the Black Mountains. This wasn't a proper statistical survey, just a series of informed impressions. The largest single group of the economically active are of course farmers; most of them sheep-farmers. Just beyond these are the growing number of small contractors: hedge-cutters, tree-fellers, shearers, earth-movers, and (travelling because little grain is grown there) harvesters. Then there are the carriers, of animals and of straw. There are butchers and in one case a sausage-and-pie maker in a new small factory unit. There is the usual range of trades: jobbing builders, electricians, plumbers, plasterers, carpenters. There are the council roadmen. There is a septic tank emptier.Then there are the doctors, the teachers, the school bus drivers, the parson, the police, the publicans, the shopkeepers, the postmen, the garage and petrol station people. All these already show the actual diversity of a working rural society.

But it is the rest of the list that shows the change: weavers and knitters; potters; cabinet-maker; pine-furniture maker; booksellers; book-illustrator; antique-clock restorer; antique dealers; painter and gallery owner; writers; sculptor; restaurateurs; glass engraver; stained-glass maker. The majority of all these are comparatively recent immigrants, but consider how much they are, taken as a whole, restoring a genuine fabric of rural society. There are some problems of integration and settlement, but at least in the pastoral areas, with their natural beauty, there is some real movement towards a more diverse and more balanced society. For look also at the move from the other direction. Several of the sheep-farmers double as pony trekking providers, a rapidly increasing activity. There has been an equally rapid development of farmhouse bed-and-breakfasts, holiday cottage letting and, along quite another line, of farmshops and of growing pick-your-own fruit and vegetables (including potatoes). There is even the beginning of a system of shares in breeding sheep. Some of this is directly related to the attraction of such districts to tourists. Some, again, is part of that pattern of part-time country living which can have depressing effects when many houses and cottages are shut up for the winter. But, taking it all in all, this movement has very interesting implications for the future of a balanced rural society.

It is important to look at some continuities and changes in images of the country in the context of this kind of development. They tell a strange, mixed story. On the one hand there is a continuation of the false or weak pastoral and landscape images, as can be seen in some of the painting and writing and in some pottery. On the other hand the weavers and knitters and furniture-makers are working with the grain of the actual rural economy, and bringing to it qualities of design and, even in reproductions, of workmanship which had been thought to have been exiled to the towns. It is the same with country knowledge and lore. There is a distinct strain of the merely quaint and also of the highly irrational and unhistorical, including the ley-line, medical-magic and supernatural tendencies. In the Black Mountains this seems perverse, since the real history and prehistory are so very much more interesting and surprising. Yet the only real local anger I have seen was against a few isolated cases of cannabis-growing and a more organized camp to celebrate the 'liberty cap' fungi: pitched, as it happened, on a neolithic site.

Yet it would be false to make this odd tendency the dominant element. On the contrary the major element is undoubtedly the recovery, exploration and propagation of kinds of natural knowledge, some strengthened by modern learning and science, which were in part drained out of the surviving rural population in the period of urban and industrial dominance. For every cranky or overstated case, as at times with some of the descriptions of medical herbs, there are twenty cases of genuine practical knowledge, interacting with the best of the surviving rural economy: in the wholefoods, the honeys, the culinary herbs, the fuels, the jams and cordials. As this floods into print and into shops it can be seen as mere fashion, but in general it is a healthy practical recovery of the skills and resources of the land. Moreover it is reaching back into the cities and suburbs, providing a different and better base for urban attitudes to the country.

Necessarily, however, these are marginal uses and forms of production. The commitment to an industrial and then imperial social order has occurred in much more than the head. It is now literally on the ground and in the air, not only in its massive physical and social embodiments but above all in its crowded population, which has for at least a century gone beyond the possibilities of any acceptable model of natural subsistence. Thus there are deep current contradictions. First, between the true necessities of production as such, industrial and agricultural, and the inherited and monetarily imposed patterns of production which obscure but then make others unreasonably deny these absolute necessities. Second, between the country areas as necessary places of production, in either mode, and the inherited and culturally imposed patterns of rural enjoyment, placing access to the 'unspoiled' as primary, in the long dream of a simple Rural England which could export, to the colonies, a large part of its rural working population. There are good ways forward beyond each of these contradictions, but much of the cultural and intellectual argument is still held, confusingly, within them.

I have, for example, watched the problem of access in two very different areas: one eastern arable; one western pastoral. The three fields behind the house in which I was living when I wrote *The Country and the City* have been cleared into one, and the old ponds drained. A council signpost still indicates a footpath that used to run beside a hawthorn hedge but is now across the middle of the large field. If you have the nerve or indifference to walk across growing corn you can still always use it, but country-bred I found I could only walk it in autumn and winter: the respect for crops is still too strong, though I saw clearly enough what had happened. Then in the Black Mountains I admired the arrangements for access to the open tops, with so many miles of attractive hill-walking: the car parks, the picnic sites, the signposts. Yet I have watched, only this summer, a car arrive at the edge of a mountain full of grazing sheep, and three large dogs immediately released and of course chasing and terrifying them. A young farmer neighbour told me that much of his cut winter firewood had been stolen from a stack by his gate, but that he had only lost his temper when the newly made timber gate had also been stolen. There are also more frequent reports of the theft and butchering of sheep and cattle. In the actual country community you can leave anything open around the place, without the least chance of theft or damage by your neighbours.

Again, once or twice a year, a notice is put through our doors that there is to be an overnight car 'rally' by an urban club: no rally but a timed race in the dark along the narrow twisting lanes where all year it is necessary to reverse or manoeuvre if another vehicle is met. There are procedures for objection and complaint, but the cool advice to keep animals off the roads, as if they were dogs on Guy Fawkes Night, is a voice from another world. It is intolerable, I believe, that offences and indifferences of this kind are unnoticed or underplayed within a general position which has its own strong examples: of the destruction of habitats and earthworks, including many that have been listed; of resistance and obstruction on real rights of way; and of organized prejudice against national parks and even some minimal planning regulations.

None of these complex matters can be resolved within the simplifying images of a polarized 'country' and 'city'. I would take the naming of 'wilderness' – a cultural import from the United States – as an example. It is indeed important that some 'wild' places should be kept open and within the forms of natural growth. The acid blanket-peat uplands are those I know best and most value. Yet these, as I have seen them over many years, are enitrely compatible with extensive sheep farming. Some of them would be more inaccessible without it. When I see the amount of hedging and ditching that goes on in our valley I know what would happen if, for their own reasons, the sheep-farmers were not doing or paying for it. There is not much wilderness in this anciently worked island, and most of it is a man-made facsimile of the real thing, but we might find there was too much for most tastes if this kind of tending stopped. When I see the amount of work on urban parks and gardens, publicly paid for as a matter of course, I wonder at the common urban blindness to all this work that actually produces and preserves much of the 'nature' that visitors come to see. If there were not farmers on these uplands, with the hill-sheep subsidy and guaranteed prices, there would have to be paid wardens if much accessible country were to be left.

Indeed I have often thought that some direct part-time payment of that kind would be the fairest kind of settlement on rights of way and important sites.

On the other hand I know that there are sharp and perhaps absolute differences, in these matters, between the pastoral and the arable areas, and especially the arable areas in their current phase of high-input mechanized farming. The linkage between grain surpluses and intensive livestock feeding, in those areas, has to be contrasted with the natural benefits of sensible grassland improvement for pastoral livestock-rearing of a radically different kind. It is a matter, always, for specific judgements, as when I find myself a friend of bracken above a thousand feet and an enemy below that contour. Yet when I once mentioned grassland improvement as an investment priority, to an eminent socialist friend, he looked at me as if he thought I had gone mad.

The deepest problems we have now to understand and resolve are in these real relations of nature and livelihood. I argued in *Towards 2000* that the central change we have to make is in the received and dominant concept of the earth and its life forms as raw material for generalized production. That change means, necessarily, ending large-scale capitalist farming, with its linked processes of high land costs, high interest-bearing capitalization, high-input cash-crop production. But in the equally necessary perspective of what I called in *The Country and the City* an apparently unmediated nature – the living world of rivers and mountains, of trees and flowers and animals and birds – it is important to avoid a crude contrast between 'nature' and 'production', and to seek the practical terms of the idea which should supersede both: the idea of 'livelihood' within, and yet active within, a better understood physical world and all truly necessary physical processes.

Both industrial and agrarian capitalism have overridden this idea of livelihood, putting generalized production and profit above it. Yet the dominant tendencies in socialism have mainly shared the same emphases, altering only the distribution of profit. The most hopeful social and political movement of our time is the very different and now emergent 'green socialism', within which ecology and economics can become, as they should be, a single science and source of values, leading on to a new politics of equitable livelihood. There is still very much to be done, in clarifying and extending this movement and in defining it, practically and specifically, in the many diverse places, requiring diverse solutions and resolutions, where it must take root and grow. But here, at least, is a sense of direction, born in the experiences between city and country and looking to move beyond both to a new social and natural order.

Decentralism and the Politics of Place

1984

Philip Cooke[1]: *In your recent writing the questions of territory, national movements, and so on have figured prominently. Does this mean that for you national movements are essentially progressive forces?*

Raymond Williams: It is important to make a distinction about nationalism in the context of the unitary British state. There are two kinds of nationalism. There is that nationalism which reinforces the idea of the traditional nation-state. This nationalism has been given added impetus under the Thatcher governments as we saw at the time of the Falklands/Malvinas episode. But this kind of nationalism is also shared by the Labour Party, as was so vividly revealed by their support for the British intervention in the South Atlantic. The other kind of nationalism is that which questions the whole basis of the unitary British state. I think that the first kind of nationalism is reactionary and the second is progressive. This argument starts from the analysis that existing nation-states of the size of Britain are both too small and too large for useful politics. They are too small because of the nature of the international economy and the structure of military politics. The average nation-state simply cannot be independent. And if it pretends to be, it has to carry this off through a falsification which seeks to cover up the fact that it is subordinated to the larger thing and driven by wider forces than those which can be internally controlled. This dishonesty leaves the nation-state morally and politically extremely vulnerable.

The argument that the nation-state of Britain is too large derives from the given unevenness of development and the diversity of areas within.

---

1. Philip Cooke is Reader in Town Planning at the University of Wales College of Cardiff; he is a member of the editorial collective of *Radical Wales*. The interview took place in January 1984. [Ed.]

These conditions make it impossible to have policymaking in a general sense dominated by a single centre. Then you ask the question: What are the genuine alternative units capable of developing a politics speaking to the interests of the people rather than the unjustified units of a presumed nation-state? Where there is a national entity such as Wales or Scotland, there is already a measure of self-definition, a real base. But it does not only occur in such places. There may well be another base to be found in large cities such as London and Liverpool. These are refusing to submit their perceived interests to the nation-state interest. This is a pragmatic analysis on my part – there is an objective need for alternative definitions having relevance to definable numbers of people.

Places like London are having their attempts to satisfy real popular needs stopped by the central machine. This of course reproduces the case that has been made in Wales and Scotland for a long time. There are perceived needs, there is the possibility of political majorities which are not to be mocked, we are talking of large numbers of people – yet they are all reduced to the subordinate sense of 'locality'. This is doubly wrong when the nation-state is both subordinating, yet not large enough to manage, its own affairs.

Does this open up the prospect of alliances between the new urban Left and the old depressed industrial regions?

Yes, although clearly it first raises the prospect of competition between the newly depressed cities and the older depressed regions. Yet all these places are suffering. But one thing is clear, they may agree on the causes of their suffering but you can't make much of an alliance out of negatives; the only real basis of alliances is agreement on positive proposals for transcending the negatives. This needs nothing less than the reconstruction of the Left on a new basis. Left policy would no longer be attached to the nation-state itself. Whether the Labour Party can do that given its attachment to the nation-state remains in serious doubt. But electoral defeat has provided the basis for recasting the Left – there is a new political activity in the cities and regions. These are natural units of government which also relate to wider issues.

There are of course, massive problems in Wales and Scotland, where the Labour Party has a mixed record, especially because of its attachment to a centralized nation-state and associated policies. The politics of alliances are very difficult and it would be impossible for the national movements of Wales and Scotland to work with old-style Labourist policies, but not so much so with the new urban Left. The real problem with traditional politics is that where alliances have existed they have been leadership alliances and thus of very limited usefulness. It's basically no good if only the leadership engages in alliance-building; if alliances are to happen they will come from the people rejecting leadership and building a popular base. A problem of the Left is that, often, ideas are good; leadership, even, may be satisfactory, but there is an inadequate popular base.

This seems to me to be one of the problems with the Hobsbawm thesis, which has become rather popular in left intellectual circles of late. I mean the idea that there needs to be some form of agreement between opposition parties to prevent them cutting their own throats and keeping a Thatcher government in virtually permanent office. It is, once again, an alliance of negatives, the priority being to unite against an immediate evil rather than concentrating upon the development of a truly popular programme with mass support from below. Then, a popular front, as it were, might be a feasible proposition. I think territorially based popular mobilization may be a way forward here.

Reading Towards 2000 *one is struck by the extent to which a policy of decentralist socialism is argued for. Can you say something about the development of this conviction in your thinking?*

In the 1960s and 1970s I felt close to the arguments being put forward by nationalists leading up to and during the devolution debate. I even joined the Welsh party for a year or two; however, I found it difficult to discharge my obligations living at a distance from Wales. I felt my thinking on culture and community was more reflected there than in the Labour Party then or now. When I said this I didn't fully realize the complexities of nationalism in Wales, especially its traditional difficulty with adhering to fully socialist principles of common ownership. The support it gets from rural areas is clearly not based on a demand for the common ownership of land, for example. I was told at the time by those inside and outside that I was idealizing it, but many of its ideas remain closer to me than those of the contemporary Labour Party. I think there was just a coming together – a tendency and a movement on the ground developing against centralism. But, of course, it's not just in that context that I've found shared ideas; I find I'll also come across it with one kind of Swede, Yugoslav, or American. I saw socialism differently from the English Fabian or English Marxist intelligentsia – I still get rebukes from them for being too community-conscious and not universal enough. But, of course, English middle-class universality is something of a contradiction in terms!

You've mentioned the significance of Wales for your thinking on the question of decentralism, but Wales is a subject to which you've often returned in your more general analyses. What, for example, has the Welsh experience of capitalism taught you in particular?

Well, really, that's how I learnt it in large part. I was in a border position, close to a formative industrial experience but also seeing what happened to rural Wales. It was a simultaneous transformation producing curious effects. There was a new Wales of the industrial valleys, and the old Wales of emptying rural areas. The relations between them have always been fraught and this uneasiness is reproduced in Welsh political thinking, which is very complex here. But there is now the possibility of getting beyond this division based on competition between the urban and the rural areas of Wales. Both these separated orders are becoming relatively old. There was the question of how to relate the new boisterous South Wales to the old rural Wales, but when you get the particular experience of continuing depression affecting both, there is the possibility of transcending the old divisions. I'm particularly struck by the situation of rural Wales where strange things are occurring – outside financial capital is putting pressure on farmers, the Common Market fragments the farming community along deeper class lines.

There is, of course, a problem here, that of arriving at a point where unity is being stressed through more negatives. Nevertheless this fracturing of the old urban and rural bases is going on and it is powerful outside interest that are responsible equally for the sufferings both of urban and rural societies.

You've stressed the importance of 'bonding' in Politics and Letters *and* Towards 2000. *Is the kind of bonding you write of in older industrial regions necessarily tied to their particular experience and therefore of only limited general relevance?*

This is very difficult and I admit I'm uncertain. Bonding in traditional societies – as studied anthropologically – is very evident. You can pick out the economic, political and cultural elements of bonding. There is a most complex relationship between socialism and bonding for the following reason. What socialism offered was the priority of one kind of bonding – trade unionism, the class bond – this cancelled all other bonds. This, of course, accounts for the hostility to nationalism and the irrelevance of religious movements, as well as the curious attitude towards the family on the part of some socialists. So there are other bonding mechanisms in reality which are beyond either national consciousness or class consciousness. One crisis for socialism comes from this. Where economic bonding had occurred and socialism had developed to as high a point as was then known, has it always been the case that bonds of other kinds were analytically suppressed? For, historically, it seems to me to be more and more true that where centres of proletarian consciousness developed, their strength really drew from the fact that all the bonds were holding in the same direction. This has become much clearer to me from the experience of the women's movement, where more than one kind of bonding has made for exceptionally penetrative political practice and significant success. Aspects of the peace movement come to mind from a similar nonterritorially particular viewpoint. But to return to your question, there is a possible way out of the analytical problem of an overnarrow emphasis on the bond of economic experience. This was always the specialized version of socialism. A new theory of socialism must now centrally involve *place*. Remember the argument was that the proletariat had no country, the factor which differentiated it from the property-owning classes. But *place* has been shown to be a crucial element in the bonding process – more so perhaps for the working class than the capital-owning classes – by the explosion of the international economy and the destructive effects of deindustrialization upon old communities. When capital has moved on, the importance of place is more clearly revealed.

In writing about 'bonding' you have drawn heavily on the experience of established regional communities such as Clydeside and South Wales. It could be argued that you romanticize proletarian cultures, especially in the light of their subordination of women and often narrow focus on wage struggles. How would you respond to such a criticism?

The old socialism excluded the reality of women and families. Women gave generations of support to their men and received no recognition for it. This must change and the lessons to be learnt from the analyses of the women's movement are that it will change, and if socialists are not to lose a substantial part of their potential constituency they had better come to terms with the problem very quickly.

As far as the wage-bargain is concerned – what elsewhere I've called *militant particularism* – I can see why these men did it. I'll explain why obliquely. I'm doing a new novel at the moment. It starts in the 1930s with a meeting between some Oxbridge socialists and representatives of the Welsh working class, although most of it is set in the postwar period. In researching the novel I came across a quotation from Arthur Horner, the miners' leader from Wales, who said that 'labour is a commodity like any other. Employers have to buy it, so I want to control it.' This is understandable, but of course it reproduces the language of capital. When you're in organized bargaining of this kind it leaves you with no moral basis against, for example, monetarist arguments. Monetarists can say 'Fine, we don't want labour now, and if that's the strong point of your argument, we can steer around it without any difficulty.' Without the first stress being on people rather than money, you have not a strong movement but a shell. So when, as in the 1983 election, the Conservatives said 'there is no alternative', some of their ground had been prepared for them already.

The implication then is that you believe in incomes policy?

There are bound to be incomes policies. Official left thinking has occurred in compartments. Wages policy has been not to have a wages policy. Welfare expenditure cannot somehow rise in a separate compartment. There is an increasing proportion of nonworking population and the unemployed. Policy has to be general – integrated – or it is opportunist. You can't run an economy on a humanized version of market forces, then bring out the welfare policies like Crosland suggested, any longer. I've increasingly taken the view that, at this stage of internationalized production, there's no way that growth is going to produce the satisfaction of people's needs. Simply, some are made affluent by it while others are made poorer. Of course, there's a need for short-term measures to stimulate the economy, but to think that this can be done without attending to the distortions of market relations – in wage as well as other kinds of market exchange – is to think fifty years in arrears.

You clearly see the need for some degree of centralization in aspects of economic management. But what are the mechanisms for gaining mass popular support for socialism, given the diversity of places to which you have drawn attention? Is the cultural level given an added importance now, and what is the nature of a politics of culture?

I'm conscious of this difficulty. What depresses me is that the setting for these ideas is the need for the mobilization of scattered movements and interests. Yet the intellectual Left is concentrated in London – it is distant from these concerns. But when people's ideas move closer on a set of issues, history teaches us that they can be given powerful expression despite geographical and intellectual distance. Ideally, a new movement comes out of new ideas being specified in particular places – then there may be a model being expressed which is adaptable to the interests of other places and scales of operation. These can be ideas relating to long- or short-term real interests and the policies which express them. It is perfectly clear that ideas have to federate – it's in the nature of the analysis. The difficulty comes not least because of the existence of the old Labour Party nationalism, its tradition of metropolitan centralism (what I've referred to in a more general context as *metropolitan provincialism*) and its tradition of short-term electoral politics, and leadership geared to precisely that. It is difficult to produce ideas for a single place; it needs lots of people with skills being brought together. This is very difficult, especially as intellectuals will work in campaigns such as disarmament, the ecological movement and on questions of the economy. But there is little bringing together of these energies. It would happen more quickly – this bringing together – if it happened in a place. There are no shortcuts, but to some extent the Greater London Council has focused this in London. It could be a model.

What do you see as the future for decentralized political mobilization, given the strong centralizing forces operating in such areas as the mass media?

This is difficult. All I'd say is we're entering a phase of cultural politics with both more risks and opportunities. The monopoly of centralized public broadcasting authorities coinciding with current nation-state electoral politics is going to be overtaken by a rough international force with the coming of cable TV. I see the public authorities as the agents of a centralized, perniciously *mass* media as represented in absurdities such as *Nationwide* or *Sixty Minutes*. The operators of cable are not, of course, in the business of decentralized socialism. But there are real possibilities and opportunities for entry into cable at a time when the centralized forces are weakening. Small organizations, parties, interest groups could get time at low cost. The Left has to see this as an opportunity as well as a threat. Greater dispersion does mean the flooding in of foreign material. But in somewhere with a distinctive linguistic and cultural base such as Wales, this happens now anyway. Getting a policy on community cable is acting positively. The Left must move out of its old phase. The new political economy of TV will be smaller audiences, such as Channel 4 experiences, based on communities of interest. If we can work it out, we can connect to these multichannel networks. This is one of the most interesting and possibly rewarding challenges faced by decentralist politics for the future.

7

Redefining Socialist Democracy

The Forward March of Labour Halted?

1981

If it were only a halt in a forward march it would all be very much simpler. People take these figures of speech to make discussion more lively, but the figure of a 'forward march' is from an antiquated kind of military campaign based on the poor bloody infantry. Its only contemporary use is in parade-ground exercises, with sergeant majors bawling their orders. And actually one of these orders is 'Halt!' – to get new orders, to reorganize, to have a bit of a rest. There must still be some people, including some in what is called the leadership, who really do see contemporary politics like this.

The rest of us cannot afford to. What was plain to some from the beginning, and what for very many is now slowly sinking in, is that we have recently lived through a major defeat. We should not hide behind figures of speech. The defeat has happened, and its extent is formidable. Who among us could have believed in 1945 or 1966, or even in 1974, that at the beginning of the 1980s we should have not only a powerful right-wing government, trying with some success to go back to the politics and the economics of the 1930s, but – even worse – a social order that has literally decimated the British working class, imposing the cruelty of several million unemployed?

That figured in nobody's perspectives of a forward march. Now that it has happened it has to be faced in its real terms. Eric Hobsbawm faced some of it in 1978. But because he faced it, not in the easy habit of projection – 'take two deep breaths, spit and say "Thatcher"' – but in the harder spirit of looking at our own organizations, assumptions and ideas, to see how it could be that such openly reactionary forces could, even temporarily, defeat us, he got, from some, little thanks. Ritual spitting, ritual reassurance ('you just wait till next time'), are so much easier to go in for.

He wouldn't claim to have got all the analysis right, but what he said is still a good place to start. I'd come in, first, on an underlying point. To what extent, after the experience of these years, can we still talk, realistically, of a single entity called 'the labour movement'? Most of us know, with Hobsbawm, why our forecasts called it and served it as a *movement*. It was a coming together, under hard conditions, to help each other, to connect immediate struggles, to move through and beyond them to change society. It was a movement rather than just another institution. It organized, but to extend the movement rather than just to sustain an organization.

Of course we must then also say that as it became more successful it made many institutions, was recognized as a set of institutions in modern society, had large and complex organizations to keep going. That is both a fact and a problem. For into these changed conditions the imagery if not always the reality of a movement persisted. There is one strange image that we all grew up with: that of the industrial and political *wings*. Wings of what? Of a bird, of an aeroplane? But then what happens if one of the wings starts seeing itself as 'the natural governing party' in a still predominantly capitalist social order; indeed as independent and autonomous in the sovereignty of parliament? And what happens, further, if the other wing, for its own reasons, starts flapping in the opposite direction? In a bird or an aeroplane that is the moment of nosedive, and you would expect to hear the noise of mutual recriminations on the way down to the crash. Wings? But then where is the body, where is the head? In the period since 1945 we have not faced these underlying problems. Instead we keep saying that the wings must maintain regular contact, must take care to fly together and at the same speed, must flap steadily on to their undoubted common destinations. But that is what now needs questioning. Do these wings, as they now are, even belong to the same body?

In the crudest sense, yes. They are at once the historical creation and the still major organized embodiment of British working people. Everything that Hobsbawm says about the conditions of this creation and embodiment, but also about the really major subsequent changes in social conditions – in part as a result of their success – seems to me to be true. But does he sufficiently distinguish between the effects of the changes on what can still in some ways be seen as a whole movement, and the more differentiated effects on specific elements of the movement and indeed on what have now become, in many respects, independent and largely self-referring institutions?

Consider first the differential effects on trade unions. The factors that Hobsbawm analyses are all historical realities, and so far from being capable of being reversed are in many cases, because of radical changes in the labour processes themselves, virtually certain to intensify. And that they have led to the dominance of certain political tendencies, to the practical habits of what he calls sectionalism and economism, is equally evident.

But we have to pull back beyond this, for on its own it can lead only too quickly to mutual recrimination during the nosedive. Some years ago I described one of the same phenomena as 'militant particularism'; an awkward phrase, but I wanted to get past my simple equation of militancy with *socialism*. Of course almost all labour struggles begin as particularist. People recognize some condition and problem they have in common, and make the effort to work together to change or solve it. But then this is nothing special in the working class. You have only to look at the militancy of stockbrokers or of country landowners or of public-school headmasters. The unique and extraordinary character of working-class self-organization has been that it has tried to connect particular struggles to a general struggle in one quite special way. It has set out, as a movement, to make real what is at first sight the extraordinary claim that the defence and advancement of certain particular interests, properly brought together, are in fact in the general interest. That, after all, is the moment of transition to an idea of socialism. And this moment comes not once and for all but many times; is lost and is found again; has to be affirmed and developed, continually, if it is to stay real.

You can say it was idealism that led to that moment: the vision of a better society. You can say that it was hard bitter learning: that you would lose or only ever partly win particular struggles unless you could generalize and broaden them, and change their underlying conditions. In history, and today, there is plenty of both. But what has to be faced now, honestly and without recrimination, is that the struggle for that moment – the moment of transition to the *idea* of socialism quite as much as of a transition to socialist practice – has been at least temporarily lost. This is so not only in the fact that we have been defeated at the most general level – it is reasonable to argue that we can recover from that. The point is that the struggle has been to an important extent lost inside our own organizations, and that no amount of necessary and militant defence or advancement of our own particular interests will of itself recover it. Indeed, the most shattering fact in our culture is that not only the employers and the rich and their friends and agents believe and say that we are all interested only in selfish advantage: a *majority* in our society believe and say this, including a large and growing number, cynically or angrily, within our own organizations.

Well, it has been said before. We know boss-class propaganda when we hear it. Breathe twice and spit. But it is genuinely more serious than that. Within the culture of poverty, from which by struggle and

organization our forebears led so many of us, the claim that these particular
interests amounted to a general interest had a certain absolute cost. It
could not be right for so many human beings to live like that. So no
matter what those very poor and hard-driven men and women were
actually thinking, even if they had nothing in mind but some temporary
easement, they were in a certain absolute sense right. In fact, even in the
hardest times, some of them were thinking much further. It is often still
so today. It has been true, in recent struggles, of the local authority
manual workers, of the miners, of the nurses: particular claims and true
general interests.

But it can no longer be taken for granted that so absolute a link is
inevitably present, and certainly not that it is magically conferred by the
fact that it is a trade-union action. Just because, with such good other
effects, unionism has developed within relatively comfortable, even
relatively privileged white-collar and even professional occupations, the
older absolute ratification based on poverty and exposure is no longer
there. It is then much more a case of the busy bargaining of interest
groups; is seen like that, most of the time, from inside; is almost always
seen like that from outside, including by many of the other interest
groups. It is indeed, in prevailing conditions, a necessary process. It is
part of the mechanism of a modern capitalist society. Even most modern
capitalists want only to regulate it, and to steer it away from more dangerous ideas like changing the social order or going beyond the mere
bargaining process to direct action.

This is the point at which we can see what has so widely happened.
Other much more powerful interest groups, in the state, in the city, in
the big corporations, are still there, combining, and the rest of us say:
'while they do it, we do it'. But they are not the only people beyond us.
There are the millions of marginal and beyond-the-margin poor in our
own country but also in far greater numbers in many very poor countries
with which we trade. The indifference of modern capitalism to all those
who live beyond the current bargaining terms and procedures is well
known and shameful. But the question then is: do we join that indifference, or do we really try to surpass it?

This is again the moment of socialism: a moment that is more than
some verbal affiliation. It is the moment when we have to show, not only
to our own satisfaction, which is usually easy, but to an effective
majority of others, which is very much harder, that our particular
interests promote, are compatible with, or at least do not damage, the
general interest. And then it is necessary to recognize that within the
terms of ordinary bargaining – the everyday mechanisms of a capitalist
labour market – this is only rarely certain to be the case. Indeed it is only
the bourgeoisie that has ever tried to believe it: that pursuing special

interests ensures the general interest, by a hidden hand. It was the whole mean, false and privileged view of society that first the labour movement, and then more consciously and more effectively the socialist movement, set out to challenge, to destroy, but above all, *to replace.* What we are then saying is that trade unions on their own, acting only as trade unions, cannot change the social order and make a new kind of society. But as they get more powerful they can mitigate its effects, make some changes *inside* it, and in the end even make the existing order relatively unworkable. All this has been happening, but within it for generations much more has been seen and attempted. That was the political effort: founding and funding the Labour Party; seeing it as the way to a new social order.

What Hobsbawm says about the modern Labour Party, and about what I suppose we must still, with an effort, call the Labour Party's governments, seems to me true but very restrained. The process has been an uneven one, and so it's hard to put a date to. But, on the one hand (the one wing), it's been clear for a long time that the Labour Party in parliament has had no intention of changing the social order, though it has made some important reforms inside it. And in the same period, the trade union movement has not really been pressing them to do anything of the kind, though it has supported the reforms and has insisted on particular measures important to the unions as such. This recrimination between the wings is relatively pointless. The timing may often have gone wrong, many details have been argued about, but the long slow flap has been broadly in a common direction: towards what seemed a reasonable future, which we might all have settled for, but which has now, rather suddenly, been cancelled.

This is the present crisis. This is what is wrong with all those ideas of a simple forward march. The underlying perspectives of a reforming Labour Party and of a steadily bargaining and self-improving trade-union movement – a perspective within which so many major gains have been achieved – suddenly look like and are dead ends.

I have then no doubt that, as in every previous period of major change in world history, most existing leaders, still confident inside their powerfully established institutions, will fight like the devil to keep the old perspectives, the old methods, alive. What else, after all, can most of them practically do? It has been, as they say, their whole lives. But then what has happened before is not that the old leaders change, or even that they are quickly replaced by new leaders, with new ideas and new methods. What usually happens first, and it can take a long time, is that the old institutions go on being outwardly powerful and impressive, while they wither from inside: their membership stagnant or declining; full of faction and manoeuvre; a slowly settling mood of resignation and cynicism, since nothing quite works any longer, in the old ways, though inside the institutions most experienced people still say that any new ways are quite impractical. This seems to me the evident condition today of large parts of the Labour Party and of the trade-union movement. Of course, in these circumstances, nobody will be thanked for saying so.

But then what is this so-called major change in world history? Isn't it just (spit) Thatcher, or (spit) Wilson, or (spit) whoever? If that were only so! There is indeed a specific crisis of *British* capitalism, with many special local features. But this crisis has occurred with the massive penetration of British capitalism by a more powerful international (including British) capitalism, and by the politics and culture of an imperialist military and political alliance. Moreover, what we now face is that wider system itself in crisis, amid the powerful consequences of a worldwide movement against imperialism. This has happened in poor countries, determined at last to make their own history. They are trying to advance their particular interests, from within their poverty, as both particular and general human interests. It has happened with much more effect in other, strategically rich countries, able to disturb and permanently alter some of the terms of trade, and thus to shift and threaten to overthrow the general conditions within which those old local bargains were struck. Furthermore, all this is happening within the deadly military confrontation between the imperialist alliance and now powerfully established socialist states, most of these new states not of our own kind of foreseeing or desire. And then, most profoundly underlying these different levels of crisis, there is the newly realized and decisive fact: that we cannot *materially* go on in the old ways; that at key points in our modern labour processes, and especially in inputs of energy, there will be at best radical limitation, at worst absolute shortages, within which, while we stick to the old terms, we shall be able only to scramble and fight for some temporary advantage.

Well, we all know all that. Or do we? On television or in the papers some of us know it. But nobody really knows it until it has been tracked back into everyday life. So we are penetrated by international capitalism? All right, get out (spit) of the Common Market, or put on import controls. But while anybody's even talking about proposals like that, the real world is moving. For capital can pick up and move much faster than any worker. Jobs can be rapidly transferred to where the labour is cheaper or less organized. British capital, to cut its costs and to restore its rate of profit, can move overnight to some flag of convenience. Yet still the rest of us are here, on an island crowded by the success of that now vanishing (vanished?) position of priority and privilege in the world. So shall we become more productive, more efficient? Let British capitalism modernize itself. But at *our* expense? By renegotiating the rate of profit, which over the years, by organization, we have steadily reduced? Not likely, even when the flags of convenience are flying all around us, and the international corporations are getting ready to wave goodbye.

This is the moment of the differential effect. The Labour Party in parliament, taking some of this crisis on board, forgets any new social order, settles for a hopefully new nationalism, finds ways of trying to modernize British capitalism from the public revenue. It is then opposed not only by those who do not want to pay taxes to raise the revenue. Not only by those 'consumers' – and we are all consumers now – who, consulting their particular interests and finding their calculations satisfactory, decide that they 'have no alternative' but to buy foreign manufactures. So watch it with this talk of import controls. But centrally, and critically, opposed by the trade union movement, on its own most necessary ground. For while the process is only the modernization of British *capitalism*, and of analogous state enterprises, it is at every level, from restoring the rate of profit to what is called 'productivity' (which is nearly always, in practice, getting the same output with fewer workers – and, in the necessary new processes, millions fewer) acting against the established and both short- and long-term interests of the working class as a whole.

It's relatively easy, intellectually, when it is the current sort of fight against a Tory government. But during most of the years since 1966 there has been a more shattering inner history: a fight, with truces and with fragile compromises, between essential working-class interests and this now quite separate political programme. And we can't just say that, when we have spat out Thatcher, in fantasy or – with much more difficulty – in fact, we can simply go on as before, in some old perspective. An underlying unity, of interest and purpose, may still survive, subjectively, in many minds. It is honoured in memory and still often active in aspiration. But objectively that unity has gone, or is very rapidly going. And this is the profound reason for the crises, the differential crises, within the labour movement, which Hobsbawm began to describe.

Yet is that, miserably, the end of the story? It certainly could be, unless we are very open and honest with each other, and start to do some new kinds of work. Perhaps what will happen is that the British trade union movement will indeed accommodate, radically, to a Labour government of this type, or to some more openly centrist government. The American, the recent German, the Japanese solution? It would gain some temporary advantages, for an even smaller number of people, but of course that would be the end of the historical labour movement. Yet if not accommodation, will it then be defeat, lasting rather than temporary defeat? That too is possible, if the crisis deepens still further, and if the much more authoritarian solutions that are already being thought about are put into drastic action, isolating and controlling and finally emasculating the unions, with public opinion (already not exactly loath) readily mobilized against them? It couldn't happen here? Some steps in these directions are already well in hand.

So get ready for militant defence? Agreed. But as in most actions we shall need to do more than be defensive. We shall have really to establish, in this actual and rapidly changing world rather than in any historical memory or rhetoric, a necessary and workable settlement between particular interests and the general interest. This will undoubtedly mean changing our minds, in many cases, about the form of our particular interests. And then, since it is bound to be painful, we have the unusually heavy duty – easy to say, very hard to discharge – of really making it equitable. We shall have to learn a whole new kind of negotiation, which the most lively parts of the movement are already approaching, trying to rethink our ideas of work and of the working life, and then as a crucial part of that, the realities rather than the habits of 'income' and 'wages'.

This will do much, but not enough. For what has really failed, inside the movement and inside the whole society, is any valid concept of the general interest. That is why appeals to it are so often resisted or rejected. In the forms in which we have known it – the undifferentiated 'nation', the needs of the 'economy' – it has again and again been a *false* general interest: a label stuck over a radically unequal society, or over a necessarily privileged and exploiting system. But while we have been talking about the failures of the labour movement, we ought to take note of one paradoxical kind of success. By sticking so tenaciously to particular interests, the falsehood of these versions of the general interest has been thoroughly demonstrated. Yet not consciously, not at the level of argument, only really at the level of feeling, of mood. Indeed it has been almost too thoroughly learned. One of the labour movement's central failings, since 1945, has been its quite insufficient attention to, and support of, research, education and popular argument. This failing has been especially painful in a period in which its own members and its own sons and daughters are in a very much better position to do such work. So that, lacking the necessary consciousness and argument, the falsehood of these versions of general interest has been demonstrated only in everyday practice, where they not only don't hold but are visibly not believed, even if everybody, on demand, can intone them, usually against other people.

That is a sort of success, for these versions of the needs of 'the nation' or 'the economy' are indeed in their usual forms false. But it is a dangerous sort of success if all that is then left is the defence and advancement of particular interests, at a time when the earth is visibly shifting under us. There can be no reversion to those old forms, even at their most plausible. However it may be done, in the complexities of politics, and necessarily on a much wider than British scale, the concept of a practical and possible general interest, which really does include all reasonable particular interests, has to be negotiated, found, agreed, constructed.

It can only, I believe, be socialism. But not just the name, or some imported model. We can say that we must march in a different direction, towards a different kind of working democracy, gaining some real and equitable control over these terribly limiting objective conditions. That is indeed the right direction, but it will mean more than marching. It will mean rethinking, practically, every single one of our enterprises, and as part of this the relations between them. It will mean constructing, in convincing detail, from our shared practical experience and from tough intellectual analysis, the general shape of a new social order. Then, as we find agreements, it will mean uniting as far as we can to push through, against real opposition, to start to put it into effect, and probably again and again to amend it.

Wings? We have to put back the body. But the only body that will get anywhere will need a very clear head. So now, urgently, research, information, argument, publication: the conditions of any adequate militancy for a new kind of working class, a new and renewed labour *movement.*

Democracy and Parliament

1982

'Enemies of parliamentary democracy!', the shout goes up. Conservatives, Liberals, Social Democrats, some Labour leaders and a host
of attendant journalists take up the cry and point accusing fingers. We
can look around to see where the fingers are pointing. Is it at certain
judges qualifying the notion of mandate? At the more secretive and
unaccountable parts of the civil service or the military establishment? At
the extra-parliamentry power of the financial and multinational corporations? At the political files of the secret police? Some fingers waver
in those directions. But most of them, with emphatic stabs, swing round
in a single direction: at certain 'new' kinds of socialist Marxists, the
Hard Left.

Cry, what shall we cry? Shall we produce our marked canvass lists,
our envelope rosters, as if they were war medals – evidence of long electoral service? Or shall we catch the habit of stabbing fingers, tracking the
journalists especially to their notably open and democratic institutions?
It is tempting. But the problems of democracy in any modern society are
too serious and too intricate to be reduced to that level of public knock-
about. An important new phase of argument about democracy and
parliament has in fact already begun, for internal reasons within the
political establishment. It is necessary for socialists to intervene in this
argument, in positive ways. If in existing terms we have some different
questions, and some different answers, they must now be carefully put.
Moreover, as socialists, carrying both the inspiration and the burden of
an inherited history, we have very serious questions to put to ourselves,
and difficult answers to find.

256

1. Parliamentary Democracy

The appeal to 'parliamentary democracy', and the allegation that it is now threatened by enemies on the left, require careful scrutiny. To begin with, what sort of definition is 'parliamentary democracy'? Is 'parliamentary' a qualifying adjective, to indicate one kind of democracy but also to admit that there are other kinds? Or is it, in effect, an excluding adjective, to indicate that there is only one real kind of democracy which operates through the procedures of a parliament? This second answer often carries the further implication: that a parliament is not only a necessary but a sufficient condition of democracy. If you have a parliament, you have a democracy.

The difficulty with any such conclusion is, of course, that there have been several kinds of parliament in societies which hardly anyone would consider to be democracies. The English medieval *parlement* or *parliamentum* was a meeting of the king in the council, to which judges were summoned. One of the same words, *parliamentum*, was later applied to what was also called a *colloquium*, a meeting of the king in council, to which peers, or the higher clergy, or representatives of counties and boroughs, were summoned for specific business. Later again, such a *parlement* – still then a general word for a meeting and discussion – became more regular, and was distinguished from the king's council. Eventually there was a definition of two 'houses', of lords and commons, which could enact legislation and pass it to the king's council for assent. All these and later developments are important stages in the movement from an absolute to a constitutional monarchy, but none of them, as yet defined, are or were ever claimed to be elements of a *democracy*.

But if a parliament is not a sufficient condition for a democracy, should the definition then be taken as a whole: *parliamentary democracy* or, as we now often hear, 'parliamentary democracy as we know it'. The crucial condition then becomes a process of *election* of the representatives gathered in a parliament. This is widely and reasonably believed, but the problem is then how we identify and date it. The two elements of the definition, *parliament* and *democracy*, are not only run together but are often confused. Thus 'the English parliamentary tradition' can be given an historical ancestry of some seven hundred years, but the element of 'democracy' has to be given a more arguable but in any case much shorter ancestry: from at most, say, one hundred and fifty years (the Reform of 1832), down to little more than fifty, when all adult women were at last given the vote (1928). The electorate as a percentage of the adult population (over 20) ranged from 4.4% in 1831 to 16.4% in 1868 to 30% in 1914 to 74% in 1921 to 96.9% in 1931.

As matters of history these are important and complex stages, but they are often overridden by a sweeping invocation of 'the tradition of parliamentary democracy', running these diverse and often contrasting elements into a general and even 'immemorial' haze.

But that, it is said, is the past. What is at issue, now, is the system of parliamentary democracy 'as we know it'. Yet this, also, requires scrutiny. Suppose we begin not historically but formally, and define parliamentary democracy and its conditions. 'We must recognize some diversity of arrangements, in different national traditions, but we can probably agree on the most general features. Consider this definition: *A parliamentary democracy is a system in which the whole government of a society is by a representative assembly, elected in secret ballot by all adult members of the society, at stated and regular intervals, for which any adult member of the society may be an open and equal candidate.* All formal definitions have their difficulties, but this seems fairly to represent the general idea of parliamentary democracy which is now current.

We can then ask three questions. To what extent, in the terms of this definition is Britain, today, a parliamentary democracy? More generally, to what extent can any parliamentary democracy be said to determine the whole government of a modern society? Finally, what are the relations between parliamentary democracy, in this agreed general sense, and other actual and possible ideas and institutions of democracy?

Parliamentary Democracy in Britain

It is taken for granted, in current arguments, that Britain is a parliamentary democracy. But this assumption can be shown to depend on running the two elements of the definition together, unargued. We indeed have a parliament. We also have a system of general election, by universal adult suffrage. This system is supported by general customs and conventions of free speech and free assembly. These are very important and valuable conditions of British society. It is necessary to support and defend them, most specifically against those elements of the Right who talk of the society as 'ungovernable' and of the 'crisis of democracy'. Yet to defend the real values which they embody or partly embody, we have to take the claim to 'parliamentary democracy', and especially to 'parliamentary democracy as we know it', at something more than face value.

For, first, the British parliament, strictly speaking, is not an institution but an assembly of three bodies, of which only one is elected. The House of Commons is elected by all adult members of the society who wish to participate, and candidacy to it is (with some marginal exceptions) open to any adult member. It is not in fact elected at stated and regular intervals, but in terms of a maximum duration (five years); the date, of an election, within this limit, is determined not by law but by the political decision of the head of the existing government. Its representative composition is determined by electoral procedures which need not (and in fact normally do not) correspond directly or even closely with the actual distribution of votes. Nevertheless, it is an elected assembly, and is often, as such, called 'Parliament'.

Yet parliament in Britain, both formally and practically, contains only this one elected element. A second house of the assembled parliament, the Lords, is composed by inheritance in certain ranks of the peerage, by appointment to certain state offices, and by royal and political patronage. The distribution of powers between those two houses has a long and contentious history. In the twentieth century the House of Commons has achieved substantial predominance. Yet parliament is still, formally and practically, and for all legislation, these two elements acting together and in relation to the third: 'royal assent' by the hereditary monarch: *Be it enacted by the Queen's most excellent Majesty, by and with the advice and consent of the Lords Spiritual and Temporal, and Commons, in this present Parliament assembled, and by the authority of the same.* Indeed parliament is only fully constituted when it is assembled in this way: the 'Crown in Parliament', as at the 'Queen's Speech', when the Commons are summoned to the Lords to hear the monarch.

It is hardly necessary to argue that this does not sound like the language and procedures of modern electoral democracy. Of course some aspects of this real situation are treated, in practice, as if they were merely ceremonial: what Bagehot called the theatrical elements of the constitution. Certainly some of them are so. It is well known that the 'Queen's Speech' is determined and written by the government which commands a majority in the Commons. The elaborate fancy dress and ceremonies, on such occasions, are also evidently theatrical and decorative. Yet it would be a serious mistake to suppose that this actual constitution of the true parliament is only a picturesque survival. The House of Lords, controlled by heredity rather than by election, is often seen as residual: a contradiction of the ideology of electoral democracy. It is indeed a contradiction of the ideology, but in terms of the actual constitution it may be not the House of Lords but the House of Commons that is anomalous. For the sovereignty of the British state is not in the British people, as in most electoral democracies, but in this special definition of the 'Crown in Parliament'. British adults are not citizens but, legally, *subjects*, in that old term derived from absolute monarchy. The powers of the often unregarded 'third element', in the Palace, and also in the Privy Council, are legally very extensive, though conventionally only exercised formally and in certain limited areas (such as universities).

When the House of Commons is functioning in what have come in the twentieth century to be regarded as 'normal' ways – for example with an evident prime minister with a majority in the Commons – the powers are indeed only formal. But in either of two possible cases, in changing political conditions – failure of parties to agree, in a House of Commons with no single party majority; or a more general state of civil emergency – the powers are there and ready to be exercised.

Such powers are in any case backed by an alternative ideology, which runs in a crazy parallel with the ideology of electoral democracy. For all British ministers are Ministers of the Crown, Her Majesty's Ministers. Even the Opposition is Her Majesty's Opposition: a phrase first used in the nineteenth century as a joke. The state bureaucracy is a Civil Service, the armed forces the Military Services, of this same 'Crown' or 'Crown in Parliament'. The constant reinforcement of this level of authority, locally theatrical but then undoubtedly culturally powerful, can never reasonably be seen as politically neutral. Attempts to assimilate the second chamber to the electoral ideology – for example by a general or Commons vote to abolish or radically reform the House of Lords – would encounter, at every stage of its legislation, the entrenched powers of the legal constitution of parliament, to the point where it could indeed be the case that the electoral process and the elected Commons were seen as anomalous and practically, within existing terms, ineffective. A majority of practising politicians seem already willing to back off when they see this forbidding range ahead of them, for it may in practice be very much easier to override an electoral mandate (the normal ideological appeal for legitimacy) than to sustain a conflict with these entrenched powers.

Thus it matters a good deal, in current arguments in Britain, whether the appeal is to 'parliamentary democracy' or to 'parliamentary democracy as we know it'. For the latter, with its deeply conservative implications, has to be sharply distinguished from the former, as generally understood. Indeed there would seem to be three minimum conditions for Britain to become a modern parliamentary democracy:

(i)   the transfer of legal sovereignty to the people or to their elected parliament;

(ii)   abolition of the second chamber now based on heredity and patronage, and its replacement by a differently constituted body, based on election;

(iii) adoption of an electoral system which would determine the composition of an elected parliament in terms of the actual distribution of popular votes.

It is perfectly possible to argue against any or all of these changes, by other political criteria. What is really disreputable is to argue against any of them in the name of representative or parliamentary democracy. The details of such changes, including the necessary choices between available and possible alternative procedures within these conditions, can be separately argued. But it is necessary at the outset to reject the current orthodox cant and to place the whole argument on its real ground, which is that if Britain wants a system of full parliamentary democracy, it has still some distance to go.

2. 'Parliamentary' and 'Representative' Democracy

The defects of British 'parliamentary democracy as we know it' can be seen as archaic and residual. Yet there is another dimension of argument (often used to defend or rationalize these residual elements) which turns on the broader question of 'representation'; 'parliamentary democracy' then being a special form of the more general principle of 'representative democracy'.

'Representation' is at first sight a very simple idea. In societies which have too many people to be able, practically, to meet together and take decisions, representatives of various localities, various interests, various opinions, are in some way appointed or elected to meet and conduct the necessary business. This is so obviously necessary, in all ordinary contemporary circumstances, that it acquires the status of common sense, and is then used to justify, in what are often very sweeping ways, many kinds of political system which describe themselves as 'representative'. Yet if we look back at the definition just given, and think about it, many problems soon appear. 'Various localities ... interests ... opinions': there, for a start, are three quite different bases of representation. 'In some way appointed or elected': there, in practice, is a diverse and often fiercely contested political history. 'The necessary business': there is the problem of defining the scope and powers of 'representatives'.

Before entering the detail of such problems, it is necessary above all to be aware of the different actual meanings of this important group of words: *represent, representation, representative*. From very early in their history there are two related but distinguishable lines of meaning: on the one hand the process of 'making present'; on the other hand the process of 'symbolization'. The political uses are often confused across this range.

What does it mean, for example, when the successful candidate, in a contested parliamentary election, says, as is now customary after the result, that she or he intends to represent all electors in her or his constituency, and not just those who voted for her or him? This can sound absurd or offensive, especially to those who have just given much time and energy to rejecting him. How can this person whose policies they have bitterly opposed now 'represent' their views in parliament? There is some element of attempted unification and consensus, after the electoral battle, but the main ground of the idea is different and in its own way rational, because it rests on one selected idea of 'representation'. What is being claimed, and is usually honoured in practice, is that the elected person will take up cases and problems on behalf of any of her or his constituents, whether or not they voted for her or him. This is a use very similar to that in 'legal representative', when a competent person acts on another's behalf. Parliamentary representatives, in current practice, act for constituents in a range of dealings with government and public bodies, in which their formal position gives them status or influence, and indeed more widely. It is a useful function; often, paradoxically, because of the distances and intricacies of actual governmental bureaucracy within a parliamentary-democratic governmental system. Yet of course it has very little to do with the central ideas of 'representative democracy', which imply that the elected assembly is a means of representing the diverse political views of all citizens. In practice, in Britain, if we have a local or personal problem with some public body, we write to our elected member and ask her or him to act on our behalf, but if we have a political argument or cause, while we may seek to influence her or him (often knowing in advance that his political views are quite different or are indeed explicitly opposed to our own), we look for other channels to represent ('make present') our views: members elsewhere, in another party, or more general public argument or action.

This familiar problem takes us to the heart of the general question of 'representation'. The notion of responsibility to what members call, with a fine modesty, 'my constituents', rests on the old territorial basis of parliament, in which members were gathered from countries and boroughs, both before and after any electoral procedures. Originally these were 'representative' in a supposed fusion of the two senses of 'represent': they 'made present' a particular locality at the centre of power, and they were able to do this because they were taken to be symbolically 'representative' of that locality as a whole. This latter is in the powerful second line of meaning, as when people speak of a 'representative housewife' or 'representatives of the younger generation':

meaning not 'elected' or 'delegated' or 'mandated' but simply *character-istic, typical.* It is then crucial to maintain a distinction between the two meanings. It is sometimes said, for example, that the House of Lords is in some ways 'more representative' than the House of Commons, since it includes bodies of experience – notably in industry and the pro-fessions, from current direct involvement – which the 'party politicians' of the Commons cannot rival. It is an interesting but deeply confused argument, since the two meanings of 'representative' are made to slip in and out of each other.

Thus if representation were made consciously to depend on typicality – by locality, by gender, by occupation, by age-group – we should have one kind of assembly (not then, in practice, at all like the House of Lords), whereas if it was made consciously to depend on representing a diversity of formed opinions we should have another and very different kind. In practice most 'representative' systems are confused medleys of these different basic principles. If the latter has tended to predominate, through modern party systems which generalize and then usually in practice monopolize the 'diversity of formed opinions', it is significant that it is then almost always (following the main lines of force in whole actual social relations) very 'unrepresentative' in terms of locality, gender, occupation and age group (the real social composition of most elected assemblies, including the contemporary House of Commons, offers glaring examples of this, especially by gender and occupation). On the other hand, the principle used to defend this – the organized repre-sentation of formed opinions, overriding these other differences – is up to a certain point affirmed – the parliament is legitimate because it was elected on these formed and stated opinions – and then beyond this point denied, since most representatives assert other ultimate principles: 'the good of the country as a whole'; 'general public opinion'; 'personal experience'; 'private conscience'.

Of course resolution of these sometimes conflicting points of refer-ence is not easy. What matters is the false ease with which the genuine conflicts are evaded, by moving from one idea of representation to another, as fits occasion or convenience, or, very commonly, by first using and then qualifying the supposedly predominant idea of 'repres-entation' as the representation of 'formed opinions'. The long argument between ideas of a 'representative' and a 'delegate' has to be seen in this light. Election through an organized party system has moved decisively away from the ideas of symbolic or typical representation; formed and stated opinions are presented and voted upon. Legitimacy then neces-sarily depends upon the continued representation – the active presen-tation – of these consciously elected positions. Unforeseen changes of circumstance, or real changes of mind, can lead to difficulties, but by the chosen principle of representation they require either further formal consultation or resignation and new election. Some representatives do this, but most do not, and they justify themselves by moving to another idea of 'representative': an experienced and competent person who acts in his or her own best judgement: the 'representative', we might say, as a *professional* representative.

This idea now has considerable force. In broad terms, a class of 'representatives' has been formed, initially in close relation to bodies of formed opinion, who at a certain point enter personal careers of being representative, in what is really the old symbolic sense. They are persons of political experience and judgement. If they do not already (through some accident of career or election) have anyone or anywhere to 'represent', there is public discussion and private action about 'finding them a seat'. Thus it often happens that there are important political 'representatives' who do not yet represent anybody, in the carefully retained formal sense. Defined in this way, so that being a representative amounts to a career, a position or a job, the actual process of representing formed opinions can be set aside or made subordinate, to the extent that 'failure' to select or reselect such a person can be described as 'sacking' or 'firing' her or him, turning her or him out of her or his 'job'. But this is ludicrous, while the legitimacy of the assembly is still formally derived from open election within the 'diversity of formed opinions'.

There are many problems within the actual procedures of representation and delegation, of mandate and recall, and of the selection of representatives of bodies of formed opinion. These need to be precisely discussed, not only in existing terms, but within the now rapidly changing social and material conditions of public information and communication. Yet little progress can be made in the argument until we have clarified the notion of what it is to represent and to be representative, and then chosen between the now confused and alternative versions.

3. What is Being Represented?

The distinction between 'representative' as actively presenting a formed and agreed position and 'representative' as being more generally characteristic or typical takes us into a profound problem of modern democracy. The simplest version of 'characteristic' representation rests, historically and theoretically, on a view of the social order as constituted by 'estates', from which representatives are summoned. This presupposes a symbolic 'unity in diversity' of the state. In modern conditions, formed bodies of opinion – 'parties' – can be made to resemble 'estates', or, more specifically, social classes, with the same presupposition, however, of 'unity in diversity'. In Britain, in practice, another version of characteristic representation was operated, based not on 'estates' or 'classes' but on territorial localities. Yet although these were naturally diverse, the same principle of 'unity in diversity' – as still in that potent ideological description 'the United Kingdom' – was asserted as governing the character and above all the *function* of represetation. Thus Burke's influential distinction between a 'representative' and a 'delegate' was explicitly based on an idea of national unity: 'parliament is a *deliberative* assembly of *one* nation, with *one* interest, that of the whole'. (This 'whole' includes, for Burke, not only the living but the dead and the unborn!) Equally, from the other end of the political spectrum, the new French constitution of 1791 stated that 'the representatives chosen in the departments shall not be representatives of a particular department, but of the entire nation, and no one may give them any *mandat.*' Yet we can then distinguish between this desire to avoid mere localism and particularism, so as to address the general interest and the Burkean presumption of '*one* nation, with *one* interest', which determines the mode of loose representation rather than specific delegation.

The rhetoric of such a pre-given 'national interest' of course powerfully survives. At its worst, by being presumed, it preempts all basic arguments about what the nation and its interests are and should be. Yet, beyond that, it is clear that there is an immediate difficulty for socialists in the presumption of a unity of interest over and above classes. Much of the practice of politics, on all sides, is the conscious representation of specific social and economic class interests: the details of instruction or mandate may vary, but the consciousness of *interest* – including, very obviously now, the special interests of locality – is openly and obviously there. Moreover, in the modern practice of manifesto which on successful election becomes and is called a *mandate*, the idea of deliberation by loosely characteristic representatives about a presumed and agreed national interest has in practice long been abandoned.

What then actually happens, at the level of ideas, is that on the one hand the Burkean idea is retained for use only when there is some subsequent conflict between elected and electors, or elected and the party through which election has deliberately, on a principle of mandate, been sought; and, on the other hand, there develops a radical challenge to any such idea of characteristic or semi-autonomous representation, and its attempted replacement by the alternative idea of *making present, in continuing and interactive ways,* the views and interests of those who are in this more specific sense represented.

It is significant that it has been mainly in Labour and socialist parties that these alternative ideas have come into open conflict. For the dividing line, very deep in the alternative theories, appears to be between the presumption of a pre-existing common interest, which characteristic and autonomous or semi-autonomous representatives meet to deliberate by their own judgement and conscience, and the presumption of radical *conflicts* of interest, within a state or nation, which representatives of the conflicting interests assemble to negotiate or fight out, the determining criterion then being the formed and stated views of the people and interests being represented, *made present.*

Yet there is also another level of the problem. In conditions of extended or full adult suffrage, representation of either kind is determined by numerical aggregates of individual votes. Even in proportional electoral systems, where all individual votes count (as distinct from 'first-past-the-post', where many individuals are counted and then disregarded; often, in contests with three or more candidates, when those thus disregarded are the majority), the basis of election and mandate is individual. This presumes the sovereign individual making his choice about the whole government of his country, and then all or some individuals being counted. This theoretical presumption of the 'sovereign individual' of course prefigures the sovereign individual 'representative', though then with some obvious confusions. In either case the whole range of social relations is reduced to two entities: the 'individual' and the 'nation'.

But there is then a theory of parliament as the choice of the 'whole people', through which majorities emerge and form governments. It is not a wholly false theory, but it is not wholly true either. For in practice, in other ways, people form active institutions to represent their interests: trade unions, employers' organizations, special-interest campaigns and so on. The theory of parliament indicates that all interests are gathered and represented there, and it is then not easy to say what these other representative forms really are.

One answer is that they 'make representations' to the sovereign parliament, which then decides on the issues. Yet in practice the situation is at once more indirect and more direct. The presumed mandate of a government rests on a majority in the elected assembly, but such a majority, like the original general election, typically rests on a general package of issues, which through the parliamentary-representative system have to be chosen *as packages,* thus leaving much room for actual and subsequent diversity and disagreement. What in practice usually happens is that a government, based on its general majority, actively consults and often negotiates with representative bodies outside parliament; indeed at times more actively than it consults and negotiates with parliament itself, since from its majority in the Commons it has moved to a monopoly of sovereign state power – a monopoly centred on the prime minister – within the old post-feudal 'Crown in Parliament' system. Some such complexities are inevitable, but what they show in practice is that the claims of *parliaments* to monopolize and exhaust the representative process – on which their theory still depends – are in actual conditions unrealizable.

What has then to be faced is the practical coexistence of two different forms of represented interest. At one level the counting of all or some individual votes – at intervals of some years, though the process is periodically mimicked by opinion polls – leads to a representative parliament of some duration, and a government generally dependent on it. It is then already true that representation is both indirect and partial. It is notorious that hardly any modern government, in Britain, has received the positive votes of half or more than half of the electorate, and it is unusual for a government to have received even half of the votes cast. Yet a further distance and attenuation then supervene. The leader of the majority or largest party 'is invited' to form a government: the constitutional interlock with the monarchy. From that point on, the powers of the prime minister are in effect the powers of the whole state. Other ministers are selected by the prime minister and not (even for confirmation) by the elected assembly. There are always some ministers who have been elected by no one. It is necessary for such a prime minister and government to retain the general support of a majority of elected representatives, but in practice they almost at once achieve an effective autonomy. This system, described in *The Long Revolution* as the periodic election of 'a court', has since been described more harshly, from the Right, as an 'elective dictatorship'. The power of the cabinet, and increasingly of minority committees with cabinet authority, is thus of a sovereign kind, derived from the representative process and in the end answerable to the electoral process but, in the crucial space between these, autonomous. Much of the detailed information on which decisions depend is disclosed neither to parliament nor to the public, and some key decisions, on major issues, are not even announced.

What has then happened is the institution of a temporarily absolutist body within the carefully preserved contradictions of the electoral process and the monarchic state. It is defended by the (in itself fair) argument that this body is 'answerable' to parliament and eventually to the electors, but the effective meaning of 'answerable' is always post-dated, thus transferring any substance of representation to the first and last phases of a complex process, with all the intervening phases effectively and deliberately controlled by what is quite properly called a 'cabinet', an inner body of royalist-style state officers (the original *cabinet* was the monarch's private room). In relation to this system, parliament retains a considerable importance, but most observers agree that the dominant system is not parliamentary but cabinet government, within which represented interest has been effectively divided and distanced. This situation was crucially evident in the recent Falklands/ Malvinas crisis, when the complex details of various stages of negotiations to prevent a war were not at the relevant times laid before the House of Commons, which had in part approved the sending of armed forces as a way of backing up these precise negotiations. The limited information both properly claimed and unreasonably extended in respect of actual military operations was justified in this matter of open public importance, in which by definition the details were known to 'the other side', in terms of an effective sovereignty of cabinet government. Fuller information was laid only when the negotiations were ending and military operations were about to begin.

At another level, both as new issues come up and as general policies are made specific, there is an interplay of such a government with other bodies of formed interest and stated views. Of course this is described, sometimes accurately, as 'consultation with those affected'. But much of it is a very different social process, which a certain mystique of parliament disguises. For beyond the theory of sovereign individuals being counted, there are major extra-parliamentary formations of political and economic power. Surely everyone on the Left must see (as the Right always in practice assumes) that the major financial institutions, the great capitalist corporations (including the key multinationals), the capitalist press, play key roles directly and indirectly, in the formation and viability of all major policies. Ironically it is usually the trade unions and the radical campaigns which are identified as seeking to exercise extra-parliamentary power. Yet they are doing no more than join in an already active, powerful and accepted process, in which, by their command of resources, the extra-parliamentary forces of the capitalist system, national and international, now play the dominant part.

If the argument then is that parliament should be defended against these interests, two things must be said. First, that there are honest and dishonest versions of this, and the dishonest version is that which selects trade unions, radical campaigns and party committees as the prime agents of extra-parliamentary pressure. They are at times the most visible, because they usually do not have systematic and therefore often private access, but they are far from the most powerful. Second, and more radically, that it is time to look again at the real processes and institutions of decision-making in large-scale and complex modern societies, and to look beyond the received and often residual definitions of how the system nominally or in part works. This brings us, squarely, to the problem of the relations between socialist ideas of democracy and 'parliamentary democracy as we know it'.

4. Socialism and Representative Democracy

The central socialist objection to existing systems of representative democracy, including 'parliamentary democracy as we know it', is that their claim to constitute the whole government of the society is manifestly false. Certain key political and economic decisions are of course made and contested through such systems, but always within conditions in which control and therefore decision-making in the major economic resources of the country remain firmly in 'private' hands: in fact the hands of national and international capitalist *corporations*. Thus major decisions affecting the lives and livelihood of a majority of (individual) citizens are quite legally made beyond the reach of the system of political 'representation'. Genuine socialist programmes, to extend and achieve economic democracy, as the necessary counterpart to political democracy, are then necessarily centred on measures of public ownership and control. At the same time, such programmes vary in decisive ways. They can lead to public ownership, control or direction in the already constituted sense of 'public' as the state which emerges from the interaction between established institutions and a government derived from political representation. But the lines of control and policy are then so indirect that to speak of them as analogous with political democracy is illusory or deceptive. Moreover, the immediate social relations of decision-making, within such enterprises, are usually in no way changed. The actual socialist claim to economic democracy is very different, centred on the control and management of enterprises by all those working in them, and on specific policies for relating such self-management to more general and more extended interests.

Until economic democracy in this full sense is established, it is necessary for socialists to describe existing representative systems as what they are: bourgeois democracy. The description has been sloganized, but it has a precise meaning: it is the coexistence of political representation and participation with an economic system which admits no such rights, procedures or claims. It is then because this identification is so necessary, as the central issue of modern politics, that socialists have to be very firm not only against their political enemies but also against some of their supposed friends.

For the growth of bourgeois democracy was accompanied and made possible, typically in long struggles, by what is often in practice taken as the true substance of democracy: free speech, free assembly, free candidature, free election. It is then one thing to point out that these are still incomplete in bourgeois democracy, and that the power of 'private' (corporate) money can limit or at times overwhelm them. It is quite another to make a false transfer from the genuinely distinguishing characteristics of bourgeois democracy – the continuing bourgeois monopoly of predominant economic power; the use of this power to influence and at times marginalize political democracy – and then arrive at a classification of rights and procedures which are necessary in any democracy as merely 'bourgeois-democratic'. This line of argument, from a dominant tendency within the countries of 'actually existing socialism', is not only theoretically false. Its practical association with the positive denial or suppression of these rights – most evidently in matters of free speech but just as crucially in matters of free candidature and election – is both a threat and an obstacle to the development of socialist democracy. Moreover, and unforgivably, it lets bourgeois democracy off the hook, allowing it to parade these undoubted if imperfect elements of its own system as a cover for its retention of economic and associated political power over its citizens.

Thus no socialist making the necessary criticism of 'parliamentary democracy as we know it', or of representative electoral systems within still dominant capitalist economies, should delude her- or himself or others by thinking that there is an available practical model – socialist democracy – which can be wheeled up and put into place. Some of the means to socialist democracy are now again being actively explored, but we are still at a relatively early stage, and we have then hard questions to put not only to others but to ourselves.

5. Two Roads for the Left?

What is now most striking, in an exceptionally active and militant Left, is a reliance on two principles which, if not ultimately and necessarily contradictory, are at least not self-evidently compatible. These can be summarized, briefly as (i) a left government in power, and (ii) self-management.

There is obvious need for a left government in power. Our social and economic crisis can only be solved, or even mitigated, by such a government or by one of a much harder right. The problem is then urgent, and one set of democratic proposals is in practice tied to this urgency. Thus the Labour Left proposes a tightly organized mass party – the Labour Party – which arrives through majority decisions by a conference of delegates at 'formed and stated' policies which it campaigns for in a general election, and then carries out in government through representatives who are in a strong (but not the strongest) sense delegates: committed to these policies, subject to questioning on them and to eventual reselection, though not to positive recall. As a radical campaign against familiar evasions of the representative system and against claims to the loosest version of representation by those who have nevertheless ridden and chosen to ride the party machine, this pressure is welcome. But theoretically and then practically it is vulnerable in several respects.

First, the source of legitimacy, in conference, is itself open to most of the objections that can be made against representation in general. This is not only a matter of the version of representation in union block voting, itself variably arrived at but only in a minority of cases based on positive voting by all members who wish to participate, and in none preserving the actual distribution of such votes, or of the more indirect votes of committees and delegates. It is also a matter of the relative indirectness of representation even by party delegates, which again is only rarely based on positive votes by all members who wish to participate, and again fails to preserve the actual distribution of any such votes or more indirect votes by committees and local representatives.

Secondly, what is intended to emerge from such a system is an elected assembly with the retained existing sovereignty and duration. No proposals are made – and indeed such proposals are often resisted – for representation in proportion to the actual distribution of votes. The residual non-democratic assembly – the House of Lords – is correctly identified for necessary abolition, but no proposals are made for any other form of second chamber, in spite of some obvious disadvantages and dangers in unicameral government.

Thirdly, and most fundamentally, connected with the first two points, the proposals can be seen as elements of a *command* programme, in which what are in one sense elements of democratization can be converted into elements of political monopoly, hopefully functioning within the existing sovereignty of the state machine. Since the programme is avowedly socialist, there are then many important questions from our whole critique of bourgeois democracy, and it is here, for honest reasons, that the command element enters. It is reasonable for socialists to believe that only a determined and powerful central government can beat back and overcome the inevitable capitalist resistance to socialist measures: resistance which would typically be made in extra-parliamentary ways, through the money markets and their international alliances and institutions. Clearly the hope is that an elected parliament with a temporary monopoly of political power could use the state machine to overcome this. There are persuasive historical reasons for the *need* for such an attempt, a need which has been the origin of all socialist command economies. Yet it is one thing to identify this need, and to interpret democracy through it, and quite another to use the need to justify – by historical presumption, by theories of a vanguard, or by the fact of *past* decisions or elections – the practical monopoly of political power.

It is then a matter of great urgency to distinguish, within this now active and hopeful movement, between the genuine democratic impulses which are intended to improve and extend parliamentary democracy, and the actual methods proposed, which in their existing form – without shorter parliaments, without proportional representation, without reforms of Conference, without primary democratic selection of all delegates and candidates, without procedures of positive recall, and unicameral – could go as easily in the direction of a command-bureaucratic government as in the direction of socialist democracy ('actually-existing socialist democracy' is of course much nearer the former than the latter).

It is at this point that the second principle is invoked, often by the same people and in the same apparent theoretical position. What will be achieved through the command programme, some say, is self-management: popular democracy, community socialism, workers' control. There are of course others who put their primary emphasis on these means to direct democracy as an *alternative* to representative democracy, representatives then being only those who, for unavoidable physical reasons, make present and report back to the people who retain primary responsibility and can alone make decisions. This whole mode, now attempted and active in our newest social forms – in working co-operatives and collectives – is not likely to be reduced to the status of an intended result within a command-representative system. Yet this, in muddled and generous ways, is where the argument now often rests.

It is my own belief that the only kind of socialism which stands any chance of being established, in the old industrialized bourgeois-democratic societies, is one centrally based on new kinds of communal, cooperative and collective institutions, in which the full democratic practices of free speech, free assembly, free candidature for elections but also open decision-making, of a reviewable kind, by all those concerned with the decision, are both legally guaranteed and, in now technically possible ways, active. This is really the only road which socialists in these countries have left to travel. But it is then necessary to begin a very open and practical discussion about the relations between such institutions and the undoubted need for larger-scale institutions, whether in the unavoidable struggle against major capitalist or external resistance, or in the actual working of a complex and numerous modern industrial society. The existing dominant formula, of the tight party government which will deliver self-management, seems to me at best a pious hope, at worst a pathetic delusion.

6. Institutions of Socialist Democracy

The attraction of self-management, as now commonly foreseen, is its whole and direct democratic character. It is a conscious stage beyond representative democracy, whether in its post-feudal or bourgeois or social-democratic forms. Yet it is clear that most of its projections and experiments assume small-scale enterprises and communities, where its principles are more evidently practicable. What is then left beyond these, on larger scales, is either some vague and general goodwill or ... the socialist command economy.

Some new definitions and principles then need consideration. First, the problem of scale is more complex than the customary contrast of small and large. Thus certain industrial processes are necessarily complex, within both vertical and horizontal divisions of labour, and decision-making in them cannot in all respects be assigned to elements of the enterprise. Similarly, there is a range of social policies from those which affect only the inhabitants of a definable locality to those which affect much wider populations and the relations between localities. Self-management then cannot be confined to isolable enterprises and communities, for which some models exist, but must be taken, as a principle, into what are necessarily more indirect, more extended and therefore more complex forms. This can be defined as the need for many new kinds of *intermediate* institutions, though we must be careful not to accept, uncritically, the received language of the intermediate between the dominant large and the locally autonomous small, which is evident in such terms as 'devolution' and 'decentralization'. The condition of socialist democracy is that it is built from direct social relations into all necessary indirect and extended relations: what is expressed in received language as 'power from the base' or 'starting from the grass roots': each better than 'devolution' or 'decentralization', with their assumption of authentic power at some centre, but in some ways affected by them. The real emphases are better expressed as 'power *in* the base', '*at* the grass roots'. In any event decisions must remain with those who are directly concerned with them.

Yet this returns us to the problem of scale. In fact, here, we can get some help fom the present crisis of local government. What is now being fought out there, and increasingly also thought out, is this precise problem of the definition of an area of responsibility. It is a very difficult problem, as we can all see, especially since it necessarily includes the provision of resources as well as the often simpler provision of services. It is now a matter of urgency to discuss and identify the appropriate scales of decision-making, through a range of size of communities from the parish or ward to the county or city, on through the minority nation or region to presumed national levels, and beyond these again to any wider international community. In practice, in orthodox politics, these scales and levels are being continually negotiated and contested, and there is much available practical experience. But the socialist intervention will introduce the distinctive principle of *maximum self-management*, paired only with considerations of economic viability and reasonable equity between communities, and decisively breaking with the new dominant criterion of administrative convenience to the centralized state. On a range of current issues, from transport policies to rating finance, such an intervention is now already on the agenda, but the full definition must cover the whole ground.

It soon becomes apparent, in such an inquiry, that the scales of relevant community vary, often greatly, according to the interest or service in question. Such variation is additionally necessary in the organization of economic self-management, by the variation of labour processes, by factors of relative monopoly or relative profitability or attractiveness of enterprises, and so on. Once these complex questions are no longer determined by the imperatives of capital or of the centrally-originated plan, new forms of self-management and of cooperative agreements between self-managed enterprises and communities have necessarily to be shaped. In the perspective of socialist democracy, this reality introduces the second redefinition: that we have to move beyond the all-purpose political unit and the all-purpose representative to a range of specific and varying political units and specific and varying representatives. This becomes the full democratic ground for any socialist critique of existing systems of political representation.

It is certain that, in any foreseeable situation, forms of general political representation, at the level of every kind of community, will be necessary, if only as a means of deliberating and negotiating the necessarily complex relations between different forms and areas of self-management. But, in the perspective of socialist democracy, such representatives cannot be seen as all-purpose representatives, who exhaust and dominate all the decision-making processes. Indeed it is a powerful factor against socialism that, even under monopoly capitalism, many economic decisions by non-capitalist citizens have at least some free play, and that it is this which is seen as likely to be reduced or extinguished by an all-purpose socialist representative system which had greatly extended its powers in the economic sphere. Thus there is a both political and ideal need for new kinds of parallel representative institutions.

For example, publicly owned industries and services could not only be reformed by new modes of internal democracy and the election of management and boards, but those thus democratically elected, through these specific institutions, could further associate and elect to form representative industrial councils, which could act and negotiate in parallel with general political representatives, rather than indirectly and divided in relation to ministries. State and other public departments would then become genuinely executive, under the control of the two broad kinds of decision-making, in industrial and political representation. The emergence, through such processes, of alternative forms of general representation, could in turn be related to the emergence of direct representatives of newly autonomous minority nations and regions. These two and other related sources in fact form a shape for a relevant second chamber, in which the democratic process would run equally strongly but along different lines of relationship. This would apply not only at existing 'national' levels, but at all appropriate levels, to be determined by local (which could then also be variable) decision.

The purpose of these redefinitions, which to be given practical detail would require the most careful and widespread inquiry and discussion, is to indicate the shape of a practicable socialist democracy, as distinct both from the model of a centralized command economy and from the developing model of an increasingly fragmented self-management. It cannot be claimed that they do more than indicate a resolution of the tension and confusion between these models, but they are based on the belief that any foreseeable socialist society must have fully adequate general powers, and that at the same time such powers must depend on deeply organized and directly participating popular forces. It is the kind of resolution which is now our central historical challenge. Inspiring modes of direct popular power – none of which, historically, has lasted for long – have to be taken through to new possibilities of endurance by the building of complex interlocking systems which can deal not only with emergency but with continuing everyday life. Break-downs into monopoly (party or bureaucratic) power can be avoided only in this way, by a depth and variability of institutions. Equally, in the old capitalist societies, which have experienced and valued representative democracy, only those processes which increase real representation, and which make this practically open to full and informed participation, can generate the political will to attempt and achieve not only profound transformations but, at this late stage, even limited socialist reforms.

7. Agenda for Research and Discussion

It should then be a political priority to move into all these areas, by practical action and experiment wherever possible, by research, and by a new wide process of discussion. As one contribution to this, a draft agenda for discussion is now proposed.

A)   Interventions in the Argument about Parliament

(i) Sovereignty and Citizenship

Socialists should broaden the dimension of the whole argument by proposing a change of legal status from that of 'British subjects' to 'British citizens'. The principle here is clear, and is both correct in itself and easy to support (and correspondingly difficult to oppose) in terms of the orthodox commitment to a democratic social order. On the other hand it has far-reaching implications for the present constitution of the British state, which thrives on this ingrained contradiction. The constitutional and legal details and proposals require urgent and competent research and discussion.

As a complement to this basic proposal, socialists should propose a redefinition of sovereignty, in terms of a modern democratic social order. In principle this should involve the definition of sovereignty as based collectively in all citizens. The authority of a reformed parliament should be legally defined as deriving wholly from the citizens by election, without separated or reserved state powers of any kind.

These would in practice be major political struggles, but their ground is the belief in a democratic society to which there is already general assent, and it would be important to make the enemies of such apparently obvious changes fight on this apparent common ground or shift to their own real ground.

(ii) Houses of Parliament

Socialists should support current proposals to abolish the House of Lords. But if we are looking for broader rather than narrower democratic government there should be no impatient dismissal of a second chamber. There should be wide discussion of its possible forms. One immediate proposal is that it should be composed of elected minority-national, regional, industrial and professional representatives. If this general direction finds support, there will need to be detailed discussion of the consequent proportions and methods of election.

(iii) Duration of Elected Houses

There is a longstanding claim for annual parliaments, which many socialists still support. Given the complexities of modern legislative and consultative procedures – many of which have substantial democratic importance – this period may be too short. A period of three years can be reasonably supported. In either case, or even if the present duration were retained, there should be a change to fixed dates for general elections, to take this politically important prerogative away from the temporary holders of offices. The right of election at a definite time is intrinsic to democratic practice, and is already widely operative elsewhere in the society. (Note: there are complications about a government resigning or falling before the fixed date. Procedures for such emergency elections, which would not cancel the subsequent fixed dates, remain to be devised, but there are many comparative cases in other societies.)

(iv) Electoral System for House of Commons
Many on the Left still oppose reform of the electoral system, using either traditionalist arguments or calculations of advantages to Labour in the present system. Yet socialists have everything to lose, in the present situation, if they are not in the vanguard of campaigns for an active, fair and rational electoral process. The suspicion of socialist commitment to active popular democracy, as distinct from types of corporate or party democracy, must be overcome in practice if anything else is to be done. Socialists should therefore support electoral reform, preferably in terms of single transferable votes in multi-member constituencies. If this is supported by non-socialists, so much the better.

There should be two further reforms, directly associated with this. The cause of active local responsibility, within representative systems, should be assisted by a new rule – itself again an old radical claim – that all candidates should have regularly resided in their electoral area for at least the preceding three years. There are some disadvantages in this, in modern conditions of mobility, but many more advantages, in its operation amongst the formation and reproduction of a class of permanent professional representatives, who simply alight in real places. At the same time the deposit system for candidacy should be abolished. It operates primarily in the interest of established party machines or the already privileged, and is often in effect a fine on minority opinions.

(v) Selection and Recall of (Left) Representatives
Some real progress has been made recently, in procedures for the reselection of parliamentary Labour candidates. This should now be taken further. All candidates for representative, at whatever level of election, should be selected by primary ballot by all members of the party or organization. It is once again crucial for socialists to support such active popular democracy, as distinct from more limited or delegated or corporate forms. Correspondingly, all representatives should be subject to recall (as a condition contracted by their original offer to be a candidate) upon

a positive vote of more than half the members of the party or organization.

The detailed changes thus far proposed are limited to interventions in the existing mainstream argument, though attempting to build on and transcend it in the interest of an active popular democracy. It is important, however, that socialists should not limit their arguments about democracy to parliamentary and constitutional issues. There is, first, an intermediate range of issues, on the relations between a central parliament and other elected bodies; and second, a crucial set of issues in the active development of general democracy.

B)   Parliament and Other Forms of Government

(i) *'Devolution'*

The first thing for socialists to do with the renewed discussion about 'devolution' is to shift it towards questions of autonomy and of the distribution of power and resources. Thus socialists should propose and begin acting to ensure that minority nations and existing regions prepare, by public commission and enquiry, *their own* proposals for institutions of self-government and representation. Of course these would at a later stage need to be compared and to some extent (though not necessarily uniformly) coordinated, but in this above all political matter there is no case for even the most benevolent plan being handed down.

(ii) *'Local Government'*

The settled assumptions and procedures of British local government – once an all too settled edifice – have been radically disturbed by recent central government policies, to the point of open crisis. Here is a major opening for socialist contribution, drawing on the detailed experience of left councillors. What is needed, as in the case of 'devolution', is that cities and boroughs, counties and districts, should initiate and prepare, including by public inquiry and hearings, their own proposals for democratic reform. The old and new problems of local government will not be solved by any handed-down general reform, which would simply confirm the existing relations of power.

(iii) *Powers and Resources*

At the heart of any socialist changes in 'devolved' or 'local' government is a new set of issues, which need discussion and research at many levels, from the most theoretical to the most practical. It will not be enough to claim new powers, in such institutions, unless there has been

(a)   a provisional listing of those functions in which total autonomy, and those in which partial autonomy, is justified (this will of course draw on experience, but needs to be rethought from the beginning);

(b)   a rationally costed account of the resources required for both wholly and partially autonomous functions, with detailed proposals for their direct or shared provision (these would include local progressive income tax, sales taxes and transfer provisions. The shift of control of taxation resources from the central state machine is now urgent. Property taxes (rates) also need reform).

C)   Development in Democracy

(i)   *Industrial and Professional Democracy*

There is already an important theoretical and practical contribution, by socialists, to new forms of general democracy in working institutions. This should be sustained and developed

(a)   to identify, through trade unions and professional associations, new and precise forms of internal democracy at work, these to include the democratic constitution, typically by election, of management and directorial persons and functions;

(b)   to develop, from such forms of internal democracy in the workplace, associated representative institutions which would be the fibres of new forms of democratic process in economic, industrial, social and cultural policy. It is especially important that self-management should not be limited to any one workplace or industry or profession, though of course that is where it must start. It is necessary to build on such local self-management to the point where it at least stands level with more formal general representative systems, as in the proposal in A (ii) above, and more widely.

(ii)   *Communications Technology*

Socialists should work to keep existing forms of modern technical communication in public ownership (telecommunications); to extend public ownership, of a self-managing kind, to broadcasting; and to place new systems (such as cable and satellite television) in the public service.

But there is also a new range of work, of direct relevance to the development of an active popular democracy, which is already or is about to become technically possible. There should now be active studies and where possible experiments by socialists in the new electronic and especially electronically interactive systems, in such areas as political teleconferencing; transmitted and interactive procedures of mandate, consultation and recall; 'town meetings'; and the presentation and discussion of major policy issues, for example by teletext (as distinct from opinion polling on centrally determined questions). This is an area which socialists will neglect at their peril, for these are the key processes of an emerging 'information society' which will be used either against active democracy or, by thought and effort, for its radical and hitherto inconceivable extension.

Conclusion

The proposals set down in this draft agenda follow from the preceding arguments, but they are of course in their present form incomplete and are in any case only opening bids, as it were, in issues and solutions. They are offered for discussion, argument, amendment and improvement, in the Socialist Society and elsewhere. My argument began with resistance to the forms of the current campaign against the Left in the name of 'parliamentary democracy': a campaign, however, that has to be not only resisted but superseded by a more active democratic campaign (including a campaign for the democratization of Parliament) by all socialists. This includes reexamination of our own ideas, and new constructive contributions. Socialists have many other urgent issues and campaigns, but what is being argued here is that success, or even the avoidance of failure, is going to depend in any field on what happens in the most general democratic processes. We have been learning this, recently, in many hard ways. It is now time for our own initiatives, at this centre of all struggles.

Walking Backwards into the Future

1985

'Let us face the future,' said a famous manifesto. But how exactly, at any actual time, are we supposed to do that? Facing the present is usually quite enough for most people, and even in active politics within the electoral timescale, four or five years is usually as far as the future goes. Most people want to change our present social and economic conditions, but it's noticeable how many of the words we use to define our intentions have a reference to the past: recovery, rehabilitation, rebuilding. In fact ideas of a better past and of a better future have chased each other through all modern political thought. Many early radicals believed that there had been a better and happier time, just before recent disastrous changes, and that was what they had to recover or restore. At the same time, though, others were talking of the much happier future that we could devote our lives to achieving. The morale of generations of struggle was sustained by the belief that the *future was ours.* It is not often like that today. Actual majorities, including very many young people, have lost this conventional hope, from the experience of repeated political failures and long-term economic decline. Our future is now regularly defined in terms of *dangers*; the threat of nuclear war; the probability of large-scale structural unemployment; the steady working through of ecological crisis. Many of us still respond actively, and propose different ways forward. But this change in thinking about the future is taking its toll. Fear and apathy breed in these shadows, and are the grounds for a politics of hard and selfish competitive advantage: the propaganda of the ruling hard Right.

The traditional confidence of socialists has had two sources. The first, more influential than we care to admit, came out of older religious ideas of a millennium: a moment in history when the world would be changed. 'Shall we live to see it?' people could be heard asking, 'shall we live to see socialism?' The way the idea was being used could be most easily recognized in the middle of some discussion of an actual problem, when there was always someone to say 'under socialism it will be different,' though usually in some quite unspecified way. Why was it always *under* socialism, I remember asking, only to be met by the half-pitying, half-contemptuous look reserved for those who lack faith. But the point of 'under socialism' was that it assumed some near-miraculous general condition, within and under which all the irritating practical difficulties would be resolved. Well, we have a millennium coming, in the year 2000. But like many others I can feel the sadness that nothing of that kind is being expected to happen. The second kind of confidence in the future was in some ways similar, in others very different. Modern scientific socialism had discovered the laws of movement of history. From a basis in actual history, epochs were known to succeed each other: notably feudalism, capitalism and then socialism. We have all learned so much from the actual historical analysis that went into this outline that it seems ungrateful to object that all we can know for certain is the succession of actual crises and developments that have already occurred.

There is no problem in following the outline to our own day, in the contemporary crisis of capitalism. Why then is there not the old confidence in the necessary next stage, the socialist future? Is it only that we expect history to move more quickly than it ever can? Is it that we have been in the crisis of capitalism for so long, and seen the damage and danger and confusion so often, that we have reason to doubt whether there can be any peaceful and practical way out of it? Or if we say, as some do, that there are versions of socialism already powerfully in existence, showing that this next stage has been and can be reached, must we not also say that the contemporary struggle between two world-systems – as our time is continually presented to us – is no simple transition from one general stage to another but with the technology of nuclear weapons is as likely to be the end of all the stages: the end of human history itself?

The irony then is that the kinds of thinking about socialism which used to produce a confidence in the future now typically produce, in all but a few of us – stranded utopians and sectarians – the exact opposite, despair and pessimism; the millennium as apocalypse; the final crisis as nuclear holocaust. Some of the best people of our time speak now only in this dark language. Their grave voices have to compete with the jingles of happy consumption, the only widespread form of contemporary optimism. Is it then to these sad warnings, as against those chirpy superficialities, that socialists must settle? In practice, no. What is most surprising about contemporary socialism, haunted as it is by these dark ideas, is the resilience, the energy and in surprising ways the confidence of those most committed to it. The reasons for this are important. The central reason is that however much we may have been affected by these other ideas – of the coming millennium or of a historically inevitable socialism – we have always drawn our real strength from very different sources: from our actual relationships and class experiences in our own lives. To understand this, intellectually, we have to make a difficult distinction between the idea of socialism and the related but still different idea of progress.

The idea of socialism, as the word itself indicates, is based on the idea and the practice of *a society*. This may seem, at first sight, to do nothing to distinguish it from other political ideas, but that is only because we haven't looked closely enough. The very idea of *a society* – that is, a definite form of human relationships in certain specific conditions at a particular moment in history – is itself comparatively modern. *Society* used to mean mainly the company of other people. The idea of *a society* was to distinguish one form of social relationships from another, and to show that these forms varied historically and could change. Thus, in thinking about the longstanding problems of virtue and happiness, people who began from the idea of a society did not immediately refer the problems to a general human nature or to inevitable conditions of existence; they looked first at the precise forms of the society in which they were living and at how these might, where necessary, be changed. The first uses of *socialist*, as a way of thinking, were in deliberate contrast to the meanings of *individualist*: both as a challenge to that other way of thinking, in which all human behaviour was reduced to matters of individual character and more sharply as a challenge to its version of human intentions. Was life an arena in which individuals should strive to improve their own conditions, or was it a network of human relationships in which people found everything of value in and through each other?

This is by now an old argument, but unlike many more marginal definitions its positions, and its challenges, have still a startling contemporary relevance. Of course it was possible, given the idea of a changeable society, to link it up with the idea of progress: conditions could be and were made better. But we have since seen, very clearly, that the two ideas are not necessarily connected. Capitalism, in all its restless stages, has always attached itself to the idea of progress, of course in its own versions. To find more modern ways of making and doing things, to break down the resistance of old customs and settlements, has been a constant theme of capitalism down to our own raucous day.

Working men and women experienced both sides of this process. Cleaner and lighter ways of doing and making things were wholeheartedly welcomed (it was they, after all, who had been closest to the dirt and the darkness). But the *breakdown* of their customs and settlements? That, to this day, is quite another matter. Progress, for the capitalist, is more profitable because of more efficient production, through which selected individuals, perhaps all individuals, can enrich themselves. And for the socialist? For a long time, there seemed no real problem. At the end of the modernization, socialism was waiting, and the fruits of greater production would at last be fairly distributed. Except that along the line of that version of progress a surprise was in store. So much progress could be made, in making and doing things, that there was now no real need of many or even most of the people. And what then should socialists say, socialists who believed that people found everything of value in and through each other?

Modern socialism has been through this process of shock. It found, for example, that an increase in gross national production didn't necessarily, as was once believed, abolish poverty. We had only to look across the Atlantic, at the richest capitalist society, to see how poverty persisted in it, and how some of it was even caused by the very developments that were making others wealthy. Then socialism found, or perhaps is only now really finding, that there were traps waiting as this reality was admitted.

The first trap is very tempting. If improved methods of production make many people redundant, should we not stop looking to improve our methods? It is a difficult question, especially when it is separated out into the many diverse actual kinds of work. But there is no socialist answer on capitalist terms, which tend to abstract *production* as such. Beginning and never shifting from an idea of a society, socialists can not afford an evasion in either direction. We can neither fail to produce enough to keep our whole society well provided. Nor can we agree to kinds of production, and kinds of monetary and trading relationships, which make whole groups of our people, whole regions and communities, redundant. And then it is no use pretending that there are simple answers which fulfil both these aims. The practical transformations that we need are immense, and their procedures will be found only in detailed, informed and fully contemporary analysis. Yet whether we do this analysis, and go on to act on it, still depends on our basic ideas, and on the perspectives that follow from them. It is here that we must re-examine what we still, by habit as well as by conviction, call socialist values.

The central socialist value is an idea of sharing. This follows from the emphasis on the well-being of a whole society. But here too there is a trap. There is an idea of sharing which is based only on consumption. It draws its strength from an idea of fairness, or more traditionally of charity, in the distribution of what has been produced. It is the fairness of the meal after work, the feast after labour. As such we have to hold to it, but all real sharing begins well before that. Neither what is called a welfare state on its own, nor what are called aid and charity to the Third World, begin to measure up to the real challenge of sharing. It is at a much earlier stage, where in certain specific ways the work has to be done, responsibility taken, care given, that the need for sharing really arises. Moreover, if we do not meet this real challenge, capitalist economics and bourgeois society – the most uncaring and irresponsible systems in modern history – can easily pick us off as sentimental idealists and evaders.

That is why there are distinctive socialist forms of the idea of sharing. There are two linked forms – popular democracy and common ownership. These are the only practical means of genuine social sharing. In the language of the old social order, they are the means of sharing power and wealth. In the language of a new social order they are the means of sharing our decisions and our livelihoods. The link between socialism and popular democracy is literally the key to our future. Without it, the practice of socialism can degenerate to bureaucratic state forms or to the political and economic monopolies of command economies. Yet, if socialism is seriously to carry through the idea of sharing, it has to go beyond the limited forms of representative political democracy, which have been, historically, the liberal modifications of absolutist states, and which as such have been properly supported and where necessary defended by democratic socialists. To move on to real sharing in all the decisions that affect our lives, not by some all-purpose mandate to others, but by direct participation and by accountable delegation, is the historic task of socialist democracy.

Socialist democracy necessarily challenges these reserved areas, to give all members of a society a practical share in the most fundamental organization of our common life. In practice this sharing has to begin in the organization of our most basic social forms – those of work and of community. The power of private capital to shape or influence these decisions is replaced by active and often local social decision, in what is always in practice the real disposition of our lives. Within all the arbitrary consequences of large-scale capitalism, and in spite of the confusions by pseudo-socialist state and bureaucratic forms, there is an immense and widespread longing for this kind of practical share in shaping our own lives. It has never yet been fully articulated *politically* and it is our strongest resource, if we can learn to deal honestly with it, for a socialist future. Many of the signs *are* good.

Modern information systems make the processes of common inquiry and decision more practical than they have ever before been (even small-scale face-to-face democracy, in earlier times, was limited only to particular groups). A century of general education, still needing major extensions, has greatly improved the necessary human skills. The social energy that comes through, whenever people now feel that they are organizing something for themselves, has often to be seen to be believed. If, with these historic advantages, socialists fail to push through to a practical working democracy, through attachment to older ideas, or through compromise with the limits of a capitalist state, we shall have no future.

It is still the *ideas* that require our analysis. It is clear that any transition, however limited, from capitalist to socialist forms, requires some strong central organizations – in finance, in external trade, in foreign policy and in the management of existing state forces. These have been the historical justifications for a command economy, and in any transitional period they can not be avoided. At the same time, for the basic purposes of the transition, moves to genuine self-management of workplaces and communities are similarly indispensable. The greatest challenge, now, to democratic socialists is to find the linking and intermediate institutions between these otherwise different forms.

An example can be given at this point. A socialist economy does need a general plan, but there is no socialist reason why this has to be monopolist. Instead of one state planning group there could be alternative public planning centres, offering different analyses and proposals, different mixes of priorities, for public discussion and decision. The immediate defensive functions of centralized power could be retained, but development and growth should be put out, from the beginning, to a wider process of decision, and not about half-formed intentions, but about detailed and costed alternatives. This is what sharing would really mean. Older socialists had a simple equation for planning – rationality plus public interest. This led often to the arrogance of monopoly. For it is a matter of everyday experience that rational people arrive at different conclusions, and that the public interest is not singular but is a complex and interactive network of *different* real interests. A sharing plan begins from this acknowledgement of *diversity*, and encourages the true social processes of open discussion, negotiation and agreement.

It is as well to face the difficulties, but only as a challenge. The future that is otherwise in store for us is, as always, uncertain but can be reasonably predicted. There are major dangers if we continue the reckless exploitation of our natural environment. This case is beginning to be heard. But there are equal and perhaps greater dangers in what is now being done to people: in the cruelties of dislocation and redundancy; in a disruptive poverty; in the simultaneous exploitation and repression of the ways people then react. The social forces now active are so dynamic and so diverse that literally nothing can control them, short of destruction, unless shared popular directions are found.

A sharing socialism is the only probable and hopeful direction. Limited and chastened by disappointments and failures, some socialists, including some socialist leaders, back away from this challenge. Yet, against the odds, there are many signs of a more general resilience, learned more from ourselves under pressure than simply from ideas. In this sense we can face the future as we really get to know ourselves in the present: a confidence in ourselves that is always our leading resource.

Hesitations before Socialism

1986

Every few years some people announce that socialism, finally, is dead. They then read the will and discover, unsurprisingly, that they are its sole lawful heirs. Socialists meanwhile carry on. All too often, indeed, we carry on regardless. We are so used to the parting shots of a long line of careerists and compromisers that we often fail to notice quite different voices which are addressing a genuine crisis: always, in practice, a crisis of change. The parting shots are heaviest when there has been some notable failure. That's it, they say, pointing to Stalin and the Gulag, or to the last three Labour governments. It's as if socialism were some unchanging entity, a perfected and timeless system handed down by its pioneers, and now, look, it has gone wrong and must be abandoned.

But socialism, in spite of some of its propagandists, has never really been of this kind. It has been a movement of many different kinds of people, in very different historical situations. It has repeatedly overlapped with other particular movements: of democratic advance, of social welfare, of national liberation. Its most distinctive analysis has been of the nature of the capitalist system. Its most distinctive vision has been of a society in which people are free to identify and relate, in their own places, beyond the rule of capital and its agents. Yet both analysis and vision have occurred under definite historical pressures and within clear social and historical limits. As these change, the successes and failures within both need to become part of a changing and renewed analysis and vision. Neither apologists for the failures nor cheerleaders for the successes, let alone the simple guardians of an unchanging entity which they have decided to call socialism, have then much to say to our condition.

We can see today in Western Europe, and in Britain as clearly as anywhere, a widespread hesitation before socialism which is different in kind from the rejections of our enemies and from the rationalizations of simple deserters. It is a very complex set of ideas, and an equally complex structure of feelings. No socialist movement can afford to ignore it, let alone patronize it. Millions of people still vote or work for some version of socialism through a whole web of reservations and doubts. As many millions, perhaps, choose different priorities: against the dominant political and social order, but not for socialism.

The many failures and crimes of different socialisms in practice are not enough to explain this. Grave as they are, they are outweighed by the long and persistent infamies of autocratic reactionary regimes, and by the cruel and persistent indifference of those who are moderate only in their ability to recognize the dangers of war, poverty, famine and exploitation. What is in question, however, is not really this comparison. It is whether socialism, as now variously understood, is at least part of the solution, at a time when many are wondering whether it is not also part of the problem.

The unease is often diffused and only partly articulate. In public jousting it competes unfavourably with still confident dogmas and formulas. Yet though it can never be reduced to them, it is identifiable in three kinds of contemporary popular movement: each of which at times overlaps with formal socialist movements yet in each of which, also, there is this significant and principled hesitation before socialism. I will take each of these three in turn.

Popular Planning

It is ironic that the most widespread democratic aspiration – that people should have the power and the resources to manage their own affairs – has come so widely to identify socialism as one of its main enemies. It is a historical irony since the central force of the early socialist movement was an aspiration of this kind. Trade unions and a socialist order were its distinctive means. It is here that the real historical limits and pressures, within which the analysis and the vision were shaped, need precise recognition. Trade unions could only establish themselves against a capitalist resistance which used every kind of displacement, delay, fraud, bribery and violence, by unique forms of discipline: collective disciplines, exercised in crisis by a leadership. Socialist parties, facing more general and certainly more complex resistance, could only begin to change a powerful existing order by forms of public control which were capable of overriding privileged and sectoral interests. Thus into the practical shapes of the democratic aspiration there was built, very early, a drive towards centralizing control.

No serious socialist can overlook the pressures which drove our movements this way. Moreover, in identifiable areas, such disciplines and controls will remain necessary to any genuine socialist project. Yet in their old forms they now repeatedly contradict the still growing aspiration. The strongest single social demand, in our communities and workplaces, is for self-management: still a radical challenge to capital and privileged authority. But we do not live in isolable communities and workplaces. More than ever before, the key decisions affecting our lives are taken over wide geographical and economic areas, often well beyond the old nation-state.

To propose self-management as a simple and direct solution is in these circumstances fantasy. It is a local political or economic democracy which simply asserts its own aspiration, without reference to available resources and effects from elsewhere. On the other hand, to fail to propose self-management – to come back, with a knowing confidence, to centralized, expert, leadership plans and controls – is to lose contact with the only force now capable of changing society. As this dilemma is seen, the hesitations deepen. This now is our crisis: that we have to find ways of self-managing not just a single enterprise or community but a society. We can begin by questioning one old but still current formula: that socialism is the rational use of resources in the public interest. If this were true, the expert plans still proposed would be sufficient. Yet we have learned, the hard way, that 'public interest', in this simple and abstract form, does not exist.

What is rational often becomes problematic. The rationality of the Coal Board, instituted in the 'public interest', is different from the rationality of miners. The rationality of an 'internationally competitive industry' is not the rationality of those who are in these terms uncompetitive. The rationality of the strong is not the rationality of the weak or disabled. Thus we have to go beyond the formula of 'the rational public interest', and face the reality of diverse and, at key points, *conflicting* popular interests. These can either be overridden by some confident central plan, or, alternatively, can become the complex of needs and aspirations from which plans and forms of self-management are negotiated and commonly shaped.

The special case of trade unions, with defensive responsibilities to their members, is crucial in this: not as a veto, but as a source of claims and proposals which must genuinely convince enough others. The case of deprived cities and regions is similarly crucial. A defensive defiance, in either, is repeatedly necessary, but there will only be moves towards socialism if ways can be found of negotiating with all those practical majorities, beyond every special case, which will in the end decide the outcome. Any unreasoning defence of special interests as if they were, unarguably, the 'public interest', only deepens the hesitations of all those who are beyond the internal, self-regarding forms. One key to our advance is revision of the idea of 'the plan'. This can no longer be assumed to emerge from expert rational analysis of a generalized public interest, still less from centralized accommodation to the most pressing special interests.

Every socialist will concede the priority of *defensive* central agencies, in such areas as general finance and international trade, without which capitalist institutions could at once overwhelm all socialist projects. But when it comes to construction, within these defences, plans and programmes need to be built from the ground up: from real places and enterprises. Only this detailed process of shared information and negotiation can hope to establish the outlines of a practicable general interest. Moreover, this kind of popular planning, which would include alternative and costed proposals for further discussion and decision, is now the only force, drawing on the immense aspiration for self-management, capable of politically defending and sustaining the very existence of a socialist government.

Responsible Production

The strongest organized hesitation before socialism is perhaps the diverse movement variously identified as 'ecology' or 'the greens'. It is important for socialists to recognize how diverse this is. It runs all the way from people proposing subsistence agriculture and a craft economy to people repeating, whether they know it or not, some of the classic positions of socialist analysis:

> So to those who clamour, as many now do, 'Produce! Produce!' one simple question may be addressed:– 'Produce what?' Food, clothing, house-room, art, knowledge? By all means. But if the nation is scantily furnished with these things, had it not better stop producing a good many others which fill shop windows in Regent Street? ... What can be more childish than to urge the necessity that productive power should be increased, if part of the productive power which exists already is misapplied?

That is R.H. Tawney, the English socialist, in 1921. But the simple and devastating question can still be addressed to many who in all other respects consider themselves socialists.

There are two reasons why this socialist argument against indiscriminate production – part of its central case against capitalism, which selects not by need but by profit – became weakened in theory and practice. First, that virtually any production, even the production of idleness by intensive domestic service, leads to employment. In times of serious unemployment, even harmful or undesirable production can be justified in this way. This is still a contentious matter in some localities and trades. Yet the socialist response should be clear: that work can be redirected, by overriding the priorities of capital, to the many things that we can generally agree are useful and necessary and that are still often in short supply.

Second, that the socialist and labour movements are the deepest response yet made to poverty, and it can seem commonsense that the only answer to poverty is more and still more production. But this, as we have had many opportunities to learn, is a capitalist answer and, moreover, deceitful. There is obviously a general diminution of poverty, and indeed a notable rise in the general material standard of living, as an economy produces more. Yet we have only to look at remarkably rich and productive economies like the United States to know that increased production on its own does not abolish poverty.

There is ground for reuniting the socialist and what is now the core ecological case. But socialism can, if it clears its own mind, take the argument much further. With its commitment to a whole society, rather than such society as is possible as a by-product of capitalist production, it can steadily transform the whole nature of work and its relations to its actual physical world. Auditing its own real resources, a socialist economy can alter the calculations and the relativities of all production, service and trade, taking the care of its whole land and *its whole people* as the priority to which all economic decisions are *in the first instance* referred.

Internationalism

The causes of war, it used to be said, were monopoly capitalism and imperialism, so that the way to peace was through socialism. Historically, this case is still strong, but in our own world we have to face not only a militarized socialism, under the familiar rationale of 'defence', but also actual wars between socialist states. It is then not surprising that so many people push aside socialist arguments as irrelevant or tendentious, and give all their political energies to direct campaigns for peace and disarmament.

For social-democratic governments in the West, including Labour governments, have in majority chosen to participate in this general militarization and, even worse, in the outlook on the world which supports it. It is a serious weakness if the only socialists who oppose this are apologists for Eastern European practice, for the real case runs much deeper. The worst moment of the 1966 Labour government was its open support of the war in Vietnam: not just its support for an evil military action, but the more basic failure to recognize the nature of a national-liberation and socialist movement of a kind made necessary, in so many parts of the world, by an imperialism in which 'Britain' – that commanding abstraction – had been a leading participant.

It is then useful but insufficient if Western socialist parties identify nuclear weapons, or certain categories of nuclear weapon, for reduction or abolition. The basic campaigns for peace and for socialism will only converge if a clear socialist view of the global political economy comes through in forms that will allow the negotiation not only of general disarmament, but also of a new international economic order, and with that a new information order, which those who should be our comrades in the poorest and most exploited countries now demand.

The constraint, as always, is what passes for 'patriotism'. Too many socialists have competed and still compete with their political rivals for possession of a patriotism drawn in residual imperial and capitalist terms. The love of country which a redefinition of production and trade could make practical – an intense and long-term caring for all our people in our actual land – is entirely compatible with a negotiated equity with other peoples who live by the same concerns. So specific an attachment, from which recognition of the attachments of others most readily follows, is or ought to be natural socialist ground. A patriotism reduced to a Realm in which we are all, factually, not even citizens but subjects, or tendentiously identified with an in fact grovelling military alliance, is no place for socialists.

Other areas can be identified, where people who are now active, or could be active, against the dominant social order hesitate before an affiliation with socialism. There is the whole contentious area of direct democracy, which is what more and more people now want to exercise, as against the limited (and manipulable) forms of representative democracy, in which the selected have privilege to speak and all others have the primary duty of selecting and electing them.

There is the very active area of new practices and definitions of personal relationships, and especially of changing relations between men and women, where socialism even in theory, and notoriously in practice, has not only had little to say but from a residual base in the male worker is often openly obstructive. Yet liberal or psychoanalytic responses to these issues as private are plainly insufficient. Every act of the regulation of employment, every definition of forms of social benefit, every taxing system, joins with specific capitalist economic pressures to shape the social patterns within which personal and family relationships are reproduced or changed.

There is the further set of issues now simplified to 'race', which in a socialist perspective are actually problems of practical social relations and of culture. Yet some very old and some new groupings, under heavy pressure, put their specific needs ahead of existing definitions of the general interest, and will continue to do so if socialism, for them, is only a further form of the nation-state kind of integration, overriding and flattening real cultural diversities and identities.

There are still other areas. But my main point is to explore, through these examples, the underlying political problem. Support for socialism in Britain, however measured, is not only low but much lower than it ought reasonably to be. Under an especially hard capitalist government, negative alliances of many different tendencies and beliefs inevitably form, with useful immediate objectives. Yet those of us who are socialists have still to argue our whole case, since we know that it is the only general and long-term alternative to capitalism. And to do this properly we must continually respond to reasonable and understandable hesitations among those whom we might expect to be our comrades and allies: not in some routine cry to join us, but in any necessary remaking of ourselves and our movements which would make them, for these serious people, worth joining. These significant hesitations mark a genuine crisis, in which socialism will either discover (in some cases rediscover) these broader perspectives, or decline to accommodation or a survival as a mere sect.

Towards Many Socialisms

1985

It is reasonable to begin from what is customarily defined as 'the world-historical development of socialism'. At the most general level this can be more confidently affirmed in these closing decades of the twentieth century than at its beginning. Yet it is a condition of this confidence that in some central ways, and not merely in the admission of certain errors and difficulties, this affirmation has to include changes in the nature of the development itself.

On the one hand the twentieth century has shown us, unmistakeably, that we have to think in world-historical ways. Not only its two world wars, but its effective development of an interacting global economy and its unprecedented development of worldwide communications systems, make this perspective inevitable. Yet on the other hand the language of the 'world-historical' process, and the forms of thinking which are embedded in it, have been in many ways obstacles to analysing the very processes to which they appear to point.

The central reason is that the 'world-historical process', and the forms of socialist thought which developed within its influence, have been typically unilinear and singular. Modelled, as this kind of thought was, on eighteenth-century 'universal histories' of the progress from 'barbarism' to 'civilization', and on pre-genetic versions of natural evolution, this was often a world history only in appearance. Broadly generalized and relatively uniform stages of development were schematically outlined, and to a presumed final stage the names of 'socialism' or 'communism' were confidently attached.

It is now above all this rigid form of thought which underlies what is widely described as 'the crisis of socialism'. Yet it is world history itself, in its actual complexity and diversity, which has shown not only the inappropriateness of the singular and unilinear model but also the underlying truths of the analysis and aspirations which this model had tried to enfold.

This is clear in three ways. First, the received model was markedly Eurocentric, like its eighteenth-century predecessors. Radical differences in the cultures of the world, which within the simple model were at worst classified on the old scale from barbarism to civilization and at best reduced to marginal or superstructural elements, in fact came through, in the real world history, as major factors of social development, always interactive with more general economic processes. Second, the central agency of the transition to the socialist phase was at times monopolistically identified with forms of the European industrial proletariat at a definite (and now radically changing) stage of what were in fact imperialist-based forms of industrial production. In the real world history, the actual agencies have been more complex and more diverse, including both national and rural formations. The simple projection of a universal industrial proletariat has been repeatedly shown to be inadequate. Third, the essential components of socialism were schematically defined as a combination of economic rationality with a majority class public interest. This was inadequate, in the real world history, in several ways. There is indeed a fundamental irrationality in capitalism, but at the level of *instrumental* rationalities it has been and remains a formidable competitor for this limited title. Again, the simple notion of a majority public interest has to contend, in practice, not only with the complexity and diversity of actual social classes, but with the facts of contradictory interest not only between the surviving classes but even within the working class itself, in its different working sectors and especially between its industrial and rural producers. Moreover the regime which was offered to express or achieve a resolution of this complex of class and popular interests was primarily projected from the pre-existent model of development, with too little analysis of its own possible forms and at first with little reference to the wide diversity of inherited state forms and institutions which stood ready to influence, direct and in some cases contain it.

It must then be repeated that what this actual history has shown is not, as some would have it, the impossibility or the undesirability of socialism, but the inadequacies of what have been some of its directive definitions. The deepest irony of the history of this unilinear, singular and Eurocentric model is that in these last decades of the twentieth century it is above all in Europe (in capitalist Western Europe especially but also with some signs in Central and Eastern Europe) that a significant desertion from socialism has been expressed in terms of an abandonment of its own former model.

Indeed this is what is now at stake in an intense and at times desperate battle of ideas. On the one hand, if the model is retained unamended, or is simply propagated from elsewhere or in residual formations as an undeviating and timeless truth, the strength of socialist forces in actual world history will be significantly reduced. On the other hand, if it goes into simple disintegration, lacking rigorous theoretical argument within the socialist movement, it will be ever more widely replaced by apparently sophisticated accommodations to capitalism and imperialism.

This is not to say that the decisive encounters, into the twenty-first century, will be within Europe. That would be to repeat one of the errors of the model. But, first, it is in Europe that there is now the most terrifying concentration of mutually confronting nuclear-armed forces: the one active force of world history that could end the whole socialist project. The intense argument about the nature and possibility of socialism is in practice a major factor in this confrontation and cold war. Then, second, Western Europe shares with North America and Japan a wholly disproportionate influence in the world trading economy, in monetary systems and in the powerful sector of new communications technologies and cultural forms. The significant recruitment of failed socialists into the institutions and ideologies of this aggressively dominant and still expanding international capitalism is more than any of us can afford.

It is then the central duty of socialists in these countries of advanced capitalism to weaken and work to end these dominant forms. This will not be done for them by others, in the actually existing socialist countries or in the so-called Third World, though what happens in either will have major effects. Some still interpret this duty through the received singular model. They are matched by others who, having reduced socialism to the model, are equally tireless in propaganda against it. Meanwhile the real task, which should be within the capacity of a still intensely active and notably exploratory Marxism, is to distinguish the actual world history, and our diverse positions and relations within it, from the schematic and overconfident model which is at the root of so many contemporary problems.

If we are looking for one position from which this work of struggle and renewal has already begun, it is this: that *since there are many peoples and cultures, there will be many socialisms.* What is happening is still, in this sense, a world-historical process, but it is visibly escaping from the old singular and unilinear model. There is then, however, a complementary danger: that socialism may become, may already be becoming, whatever any temporarily dominant ruling group or militant tendency chooses to call it. Indeed this is a main source of resistance from adherents of the old model, who are in the rhetorical position of being able to call all others revisionists, and who are not easily persuaded that their own inherited versions are themselves revisions and reductions of the long struggles and aspirations of the labour, democratic and national-liberation movements of the real history. Yet, their only respectable position is wariness of the renaming and relabelling which are now so prolific.

Significant theoretical discussion has then to move quite quickly beyond such over-generalized controversies. It has to identify the central issues around which the name-calling occurs. As a preliminary contribution to this identification I will discuss three issues: first, the problem of the general relations between socialist planning and self-management; second, the interactions of advanced capitalism with liberalism and social democracy; and, third, the matter of contemporary anti-capitalism, which is often not specifically socialist but which is a large and growing social and intellectual force. For reasons of space and experience, I shall give most emphasis here to this third issue: not because it is more important than the others, but because it is less often discussed and is in any case, in its contemporary forms, especially complex and original.

Planning and Self-Management

On the question of the relations between planning and self-management, I have three points to make: each of them as a way of moving beyond the singular and unilinear mode. These points are:

1. the inherent diversity of rational planning;
2. the variant meanings of 'market';
3. the material and practical inequalities of actual work processes, leading to complex problems of transfer both within and beyond social class.

It is strange that towards the end of the twentieth century we should still have to argue that all reasonable planning has to be diverse. Of course this does not mean that decisions do not have to be taken, and priorities assigned. But the strongest intellectual influence of the singular model was on the singular plan. This derives from the unexamined assumptions of an evident rationality of development and a self-evident general interest. But then it is not only from the experiences of the socialist economies, it is also from the records of capitalist corporations and of reforming bourgeois governments, that we are forced to learn the unreasonableness of these assumptions. For even when, as too rarely, and in the plans of capitalist corporations not at all, the plan is put out for more general discussion and even possible amendment, it is clear that there is little room for analysis at the most basic level, at which forms of desirable development are built in, usually without significant argument.

This comes out in some spectacular cases: the decision to give heavy industry a radical priority over food production; the decision to orient industrial production to an export market; the decision to base energy supply on oil rather than coal. I deliberately take examples from different societies and plans, because my point is general. There were in each case (as in the Soviet Union, Italy or Poland, Great Britain) major pressures, needs and constraints towards which these versions of planning were oriented, but what was wrong in each case was that there was insufficient discussion, indeed planning at the stage of decisive initial assumptions.

It is then more than a matter of collecting examples of failed plans. The genuine social and material difficulties of all human societies make the mere cataloguing of errors unhelpful or even cynical. The central point is intellectual and theoretical. In all actual analysis of real resources and their possible uses the record of serious scientific work is a record of diversity. It is only from the intellectual presumptions of the singular model that it is supposed that the planning process must be singular. It is then at these earliest and most fundamental stages of planning that the need for varying and alternative plans, brought to a stage of specificity where they can be rationally assessed and compared, is evident in any but especially in a socialist economy. Capitalist planning, though carried out technically by comparatively similar groups, has elements of practical competition between alternative plans built in at a later stage, in which particular corporations succeed or fail, often with arbitrary advantage or damage to the people and regions over whom these decisions have been taken. Similarly, in capitalist economies with contested electoral systems, there are elements of competition between alternative plans and kinds of plan.

It is then a special weakness of the idea of socialist planning, which is intended to move beyond the recklessness and arbitrariness, the dislocating fluctuations, of bourgeois economies and societies, if 'competition' between plans is seen as ruled out by the singular model. It is often falsely argued that the basic alternatives in planning are no more than the expression of conflicting class interests, but while this is undoubtedly often so there are also material and social variables which, in almost all situations, require the preparation of genuinely alternative *socialist* plans. Moreover, since in all foreseeable situations effective central planning is going to be necessary, it is important to transcend the merely negative critique of planning and to move towards this kind of positive critique. It would indeed make a significant difference to the prospects of socialism if in every socialist country and party there were publicly recognized alternative planning groups, able to present their analyses and proposals at an early stage for democratic discussion and decision. There is nothing utopian in this, for in the end, in the real world, consequences disclose themselves, and it is more important to analyse these in their real terms than to displace them to the struggles of intra-party groups or, even worse, to lie and go on lying about them.

The special importance of this question is in its current interlock with the variable meanings of 'the market'. It is clear that certain crude and singular forms of planning failed in one especially damaging respect: that they were arrived at without any serious attempt to discover what the people in whose names they were being promulgated actually needed or wanted. A vast amount of anti-socialist feeling has built up around these failures, which are in any case easily exploited by those who never wanted anything of the kind to succeed. But there are theoretical dangers in supposing that the lesson of such failures is closer attention to an unanalysed 'market'. Those of us who have really experienced the capitalist version of the market, determined as it is by the power of pre-existing capital and by highly developed forms of persuasion, know or should know how disastrous any unexamined move to what are loosely called 'market forces' would be. In the simplest kind of direct supply, of many foods, most clothing, and a host of small personal articles and services, the responsiveness of an explicit market – including but not confined to a competitive market – is evidently a factor of efficiency: not only, as it is put within capitalism, in satisfying that curious construction the 'consumer' but as a key flow of information in useful production. In these sectors especially it has manifest advantages over the imposed plan.

On the other hand, even in these sectors, and then much more seriously in the case of durables and of large-scale services, the inherent organization of corporate capitalism produces a market which is only by analogy, and in an ideological coincidence of name, of this direct kind. The profound distortions of advertising, shifting information from product or service to a relatively arbitrary and invariably deceptive association with some other object of desire, are only the most visible effects. For advertising rests on an ideological form of market research, in which apparent choices are structured by predetermining corporate interests and intentions. It is very similar in this respect to electoral opinion-polling, which largely grew out of it, in which 'public opinion' is indeed classified and counted, but on a set of questions and within assumptions and exclusions which effectively limit both choice and informed choice.

It is easy to understand why socialists, faced with the errors and indifferences of the cruder kinds of plan, can talk naively about the advantages of at least some 'market forces'. But that ideological phrase fuses and confuses a range of practices from useful flows of direct information and interaction to very crude domination or even cancellation of markets by large-scale and paranational manipulation. It is characteristic that the ideologists of 'market forces' now quite openly use the significant terms 'aggressive marketing' and 'market penetration', and this is not only an economic but a political operation, directed at other kinds of society and at the socialist countries themselves. What has then to be said, however, is that this cannot be defeated by adherence to the rigidities of the one-way plan. What is actually needed is the transformation of market research in the popular rather than the corporate interest. Not only would its results be made open, as elements in decisions on planning, but crucially, as the special instance of a higher form of socialist society, full information would be a major input, as in all real research. Consider the changes in research on food preferences if genuine dietary information were made simultaneously available. This is only a relatively simple example of the full and *connected* supply of information which a socialist society could make practical. There are equally great if less obvious needs at the other end of the productive scale, in the new high technology of personal machines. In this as in many other respects the socialist of the twentieth century can leap over the apparent advantages of advanced capitalism and convert them to real advantages.

This movement from the plan to the presumed public interest to actual and complex participatory planning marks the change that is coming: from the idea of socialism as a rationally simplified economy to the idea of a more complex political economy which can actually achieve rationality. For the complexity necessarily occurs within conditions which, for historical reasons, the old singular unilinear model insufficiently recognized. To end exploitation by a capitalist order is to remove one major source of inequality, but even in its most ideal realization substantial inequalities remain, for hard material reasons. The earth itself is diversely endowed. Beyond class, it is where the oil and coal are, the arable land, the reliable rainfall, the fish, the forests, that inscribes practical inequalities. Moreover, and in complex interactions with class, the evident needs for certain kinds of work, and rewards that follow them, do not necessarily correspond with longer-term or less evident needs, which require different scales of assessment. It is in this respect that advanced capitalism, with its overwhelming orientation to evident short-term needs, is already dislocating its richer societies and profoundly damaging the poorer.

Then, if these two facts – the material diversities and inequalities of the earth; the complex scale of human needs – are brought together, it should be clear why there can be no simple reaction from the singular plan either to 'the market' or to the socialist idea of self-management. The materially endowed and the most evident providers have no difficulty with the idea of self-management: it is an immensely attractive alternative to corporate capitalism, and is already appearing, in small ways, within capitalist economies, in cooperatives and similar enterprises. But for socialists this form is only a partial solution. The radical inequalities that can persist and even be sanctioned by it are dislocating in any whole society, and are a major source of political conflict and, between societies, as so often historically, of wars.

Thus the socialisms of the twenty-first century will need to be a set of very complex systems which, while based on the greatest possible self-management enterprises, will have created institutions capable of effecting necessary social and economic transfers and of guarding longer-term and less evident needs. It is in these areas, already, that the socialist economies have moved beyond the human perspectives of capitalism, but still enormous tasks lie ahead. Indeed it is not too much to say that the possibility of successful democratic socialisms, and beyond that achievement of an equitable and peaceful international order, will be decided in our degree of success in building these complex and flexible institutions. It is not only a major institutional problem, given the variety of specific solutions that will be necessary. It is also a major political problem, because the making of such institutions is the point at which the struggle for socialism passes beyond national and class and sectoral interests and offers to establish and embody a general human interest. The simple claim that the proletariat, in liberating itself, would liberate all others still has some rhetorical force. But it will be a deceptive and counter-productive rhetoric unless in several decisive areas – the inequalities of women, the deprivations of badly endowed lands, the structured inequalities between 'developed' and 'underdeveloped' economies, the inequalities between regions of a country, the differentials between attractive or profitable and dirty or boring but necessary work – there are in practice effective and open institutions directed towards transfer and equity. Thus not only in general ways, but for these specific social purposes, planning of a transformed kind, in its methods but also in its objectives, will be the lasting condition of any socialist society.

Advanced Capitalism, Liberalism and Social Democracy

It is one of the major problems of our time that the ideological contrast between socialism and democracy, so often heard in capitalist societies but increasingly also beyond them, cannot be reduced to its ideological components alone. Certainly there are several obvious replies. The 'free world' factually includes military dictatorships and other repressive non-electoral regimes, provided their economies are capitalist or open to capitalism. Freedom, there, is a capitalist-trading rather than a democratic-political quantity. Again, though now entering more difficult ground, even serious uses of 'democracy', in a contrast with 'actually existing socialism', are unreasonably restricted to particular forms, notably that of 'representative' government. It is a fact that the phrase and idea of 'representative democracy' was introduced, in the late eighteenth century, as a ruling-class alternative to direct popular democracy. There are certainly institutions other than parliaments and national assemblies in which democracy can be practised, and it is significant that in the current crisis of late capitalism there are simultaneous moves to destroy or limit the powers of more local assemblies and to shift effective power from increasingly nominal parliaments to state administrations. Further, the means of democracy – in access to public information and in civil rights – are under heavy pressure, direct and indirect, even in societies with long liberal traditions.

But these are still responses rather than answers to the real problems. The central historical fact is that most socialist revolutions occurred in societies which had no long and substantial experience of bourgeois democracy. The result has been that in both argument and apology, to say nothing of simple lying propaganda, the complexities of bourgeois democracy have been simplified to mere appearance and deception. Paradoxically this then actually weakens the socialist case against bourgeois democracy, because it succeeds in incorporating the long liberal and social-democratic experience, with its achievements in struggle against bourgeois state and economic power, as part of the unanalysed case for corporate capitalism. It is bad enough to have to listen to an authoritarian government, elected on a minority vote, combining with paranational corporations and foreign military establishments to say that it represents Democracy. But it is even worse when from some actually existing socialist country, in which there are unarguable denials of the most general civil rights, to say nothing of the admitted cases of the worst kinds of repression, there is the same old reduction of 'bourgeois democracy' to its capitalist components and limits. Indeed this has reached the point where in countries with long liberal and social-democratic traditions there is no possibility whatever of socialism unless it can be shown, in practice, that socialist democracy would be a qualitative advance on bourgeois democracy, not only in the economic fields, where this is relatively more accessible, but also in the broadest political fields, where experience of democratic achievements, even sharpened by phrases of their limitation or denial, is too strong to be renounced. While corporate capitalism retains that constituency it will continue to dominate not only its own societies but large parts of the rest of the world.

Thus, in the international socialist movement, it is necessary to resume, and in many cases to begin, the long and difficult search for a practical socialist democracy. Here what has been proposed as the law of the twenty-first century is especially relevant: since there are many peoples and cultures there will be many socialisms. Specific institutions and practices can be expected to vary. But we need decisive moves beyond the inherited models in which, for the defeat of capitalism and then for defence against it, power moves to the party which has substituted for the class and which is in turn often substituted by, or transforms itself into, the state machine. The duties of defeating capitalism, and of defending even a limited socialism, are indeed heavy. They are still being carried out in exceptionally difficult conditions. But even in the simplest strategic sense, it is crucial, in the perspective of the twenty-first century, that the alliance between corporate capitalism and liberal democracy should be broken, by surpassing both. It is from that alliance that powerful political, economic and military obstacles to socialism are now being erected. But it can only be broken if what is real in liberal democracy is at last taken seriously, in socialist theory and practice.

Thus the idea of a free press is not only of a capitalist press. Nor is the fact of capitalist ownership a total cancellation of open public argument. Political democracy is not only the competition of bourgeois parties. Nor is the competition of bourgeois parties a mere illusion of public choice. In a hundred such cases, what we need to look for is a way beyond such simplifying dichotomies. Many examples might be given, but the most interesting area can be related to what has already been argued about the nature of planning and self-management.

The singular unilinear model of socialism, based on a particular historical class at a particular stage of economic development, is at its most distorting in the matters of public information and argument. Even where the class has not been substituted for by a party and then by a state machine, the deep formation imposes only one classification of argument: for or against this class. There is thus only, in theory, the class and its enemies, and in practice this is supported by the fact that both are still real. Yet as a basis for public argument and decision-making this is radically insufficient. Significant numbers of people are outside this class, in its ordinary residual terms, without in any predetermined way being its enemies. This is evident in the sexual division of labour, now being so widely challenged and questioned. It is inevitable in the cases of the elderly and the old, and in trainees and students. There are then significant divisions of interest within the class itself, even in its most ideological interpretation. Quite apart from the increasing numbers of professional and scientific and educational work, where immediate interests are often different from those of direct producers, there is a major growth of every kind of service, still quite falsely classified as tertiary (falsely because it is in itself diverse and because what is being 'produced', in such services as health and recreation, is in socialist terms real production, of human beings and their welfare, as distinct from capitalist restriction of production to commodities). Through and beyond all these diversities of condition there are the hard material inequalities of the earth, often finding, in default of developed socialist analysis, alternative expression in nationalist and regionalist forms.

It should then be clear that the basis for a socialist democracy is the authentic diversity and complexity of any people. The complex bonds and alliances which offer to negotiate this diversity are not reducible to simplified projections of class which confer legitimacy on only one version of one generalized sector. Certainly the conflicts of interest have to be resolved, and in difficulties there have to be priorities. But nothing is gained by pushing a residual version of political monopoly so hard that the only place for others to go is into faction and enmity, or into an equally damaging apathy and cynicism.

The experience of liberal democracy is relevant here. The adversary parties of a bourgeois electoral system are in practice based on sectors and regions of the same general class. Social-democratic parties, with a different initial class basis, are in part always drawn into the limited terms of this intra-class contention. Yet at their best they have moved beyond it, only to be often pulled back by the relative rigidities of official party formations. Thus the party, in that relatively fixed sense, is typically a simplification of a relative complexity of interests. Moreover, in bourgeois democracies, it becomes increasingly defined by highly generalized electoral contests, often losing significant alternative substance, to the point where the party system as a whole can fail to involve and represent the diverse people and interests which are really at issue.

But this is only the negative side of liberal democracy. Its positive side, in many of its early stages and in the continually active formation of new campaigning groups, is that its practice creates conditions for the expression and negotiation of real diversities, and of genuinely alternative responses to a more general situation, in ways from which the socialism of the twenty-first century can substantially learn. The authentic inheritors of liberal democracy have now to work within systems determined by corporate capitalist power, but this is a power with variable and often significant and indispensable tolerances. Socialist power, in its very early and most defensive stages, may impatiently reject this version of democracy, but in development it is required both to learn from and to go beyond it. In the points made earlier about participatory popular planning, based on open public alternatives and on much higher levels of accessible and useable public information, the socialism of the twenty-first century has begun to define its directions.

But the case goes well beyond the economic field. In some matters, in some periods, certain relatively large-scale decisions have to be arrived at. This is the force of the singular unilinear model. But in other matters and in other periods, and in some matters always, the object of a socialist process cannot and should not be a singular solution. The phrases 'building socialism' and 'making the new socialist man' have in this respect often misled us. In thousands of everyday matters, and not merely in some folkloric margin, a diversity of resolution is necessary to any actual human liberation. We cannot yet say how far these may go, within recognizable socialisms. But it is the emphasis that now matters. Democracy, in the socialism of the twenty-first century, will need to go beyond the honourable slogans of 'Power for the People' and even 'Power to the People'. It will become the practical everyday exercise of powers by people. Even the ancient dream of direct face-to-face democracy, thought to be limited to very small communities, can be in some new ways achieved in larger societies, using the new interactive communication and information technologies which a socialist emphasis can turn to full human uses.

The Matter of Anti-Capitalism

For the last hundred-and-fifty years it has been necessary, but often difficult, to distinguish between socialism and anti-capitalism, as political and intellectual tendencies. For my present purpose, in a forward-looking perspective, it is necessary to note only that the problem of distinction is now exceptionally complex. Within the singular and unilinear model of socialism it was customary to patronize 'anti-capitalism' as an immature or romantic stage, which needed to be completed and hardened by scientific socialist theory and practice. At times the critique went further, dismissing the whole tendency as a form of petty-bourgeois sentimentality. These responses can still be heard, but the fact now is that the content of anti-capitalism, some of it continuous with those earlier phases, is a major element, at once of difficulty and of possibility, in the contemporary renewal of socialist perspectives.

Anti-capitalism is that element of the critique of a bourgeois-industrial social order which is not turned or confined to advocacy of a pre-bourgeois or pre-industrial order. It is true that there are many penetrating rejections of capitalism which have no social perspective other than some form of return to an idealized earlier order: typically classical Greek, medieval European or pre-industrial. But these can at best find only a literary foothold, and in their simplest forms they are also explicitly anti-socialist. Indeed socialism is seen, not only here but in a wider anti-capitalist tendency, as simply one of the forms – in some arguments one of the worst forms – of a social order which is defined as alienated, instrumental and inhumane: a mechanical industrial order shot through with cultural degeneration and with manipulated mass democracy.

What is important then, in our own time, is to see and understand the overlap between these earlier positions, including but not confined to those hostile to socialism, and certain very active contemporary propositions, in the ecological movement, in critiques of industrial labour, in new emphases in personal and especially sexual relationships, and in certain kinds of opposition to nuclear-weapons systems and computerized war. It can of course still be said that these are mainly tendencies among the young – especially the middle-class young – in the capitalist world, though if that incomplete analysis is accepted it should be added that within capitalist societies they constitute, between them, the most active and effective opposition. But there is then not only the problem of how these movements relate to the received bases of socialist organizations, in organized labour movements. There is also the problem of how these tendencies bear on the underlying and still dominant socialist model, of a singular and unilinear kind.

We need take only the most obvious point of difficulty. A large part of the earlier socialist critique of capitalism was that it was incapable of expanding production to satisfy all human needs. Indeed in periods of capitalist crisis and depression this was often the major content of the socialist project: to release new forces of production to end poverty. The position would in any case be more difficult to maintain now. There have been spectacular revivals of capitalist production, and no simple relationships between socialism and economic growth. But that earlier position was always a reduction of the necessary socialist analysis. It was never only a matter of increasing production, in familiar capitalist terms, but of social instead of capitalist controls on what was produced and of altered social relationships which changed the real distribution of an otherwise merely aggregated product.

Yet the rhetoric of increased aggregate production, as such, took a powerful hold on the socialist movement, even tempting it to competition with capitalism in this limited respect and on these terms. It is then not surprising that old socialist questions – about what kinds of things were to be produced, for what uses and with what effects, as distinct from generalized statistical aggregates – were often left to be picked up by movements which not only did not begin from socialism but which could include much socialist practice as a similar kind of misdirection. These questions were then made more powerful by newly measurable objective effects of certain kinds of production: widespread pollution and in some cases destruction of physical environments; new forms of stress and bodily damage to workers in certain processes and to those living in or near their places of production. It has become especially clear in capitalist societies that this kind of reckless and now objectively predictable damage is being done by the large industrial corporations and by agribusiness, which have also worked hard, politically, to minimize or evade necessary social controls. In this central respect, the most serious oppositional campaigns could not fail to become anti-capitalist. But would they become socialist? The problem is that there seems to be no solid reason, either in socialist practice or in the still dominant theory, why in these ways socialism must be qualitatively different.

But then to give good socialist reasons means, yet again, to move beyond the singular and unilinear model. The question of production has to be taken back to the deepest elements of the socialist project, as a way of getting beyond its more recent, temporary and misleading formations. In fact historical materialism is the clearest way of understanding these now complex and dynamic developments, for its whole emphasis is on the changing forms of labour within an unarguably physical environment. The various ideologies which have overridden this emphasis – the reduction of a physical world and physical human beings to the triad of raw materials, capital and disposable labour; the triumphalist celebration of maximum exploitation of all three or of any two – are hostile to socialism, whatever their nominal forms. In the labour movement, close to the real ground, it has always been known that a relentless exploitation of raw materials involves also the exploitation of labourers as mere human raw material. Moreover this fact can persist through changes in property relations, while the same essential drive is maintained. It is one thing, faced by absolute or relative poverty, to mobilize all possible human and physical resources to overcome it. But it is quite another thing to reify this as abstract production, or to suppose that we have reformed this when we have taken out the single element of alienated profit. It is then in new socialist definitions and redefinitions of production that the central perspective of the socialism of the twenty-first century must be open.

For anti-capitalism, left to itself, even in its most humane forms, cannot meet the constructive challenges of ending both exploitation and poverty. Certain forms of the proposition of 'zero growth', and virtually all forms of the proposition of ending industrial production and reverting to crafts and subsistence agriculture, are not only fantasies; in the world as it now is they can become cruel deceptions, readily accommodated within a so-called 'post-industrial' capitalism which will continue to be possible only on the basis of its imperialist and neo-colonialist exploitation of the rest of the non-socialist world. On the other hand, any simple re-emphasis of a merely abstract 'socialist production' will fail to answer the crucial underlying questions, and will be increasingly vulnerable to the genuinely transforming changes now occurring within the labour processes themselves.

Thus socialism has to propose not only the ending of labour as a commodity; it has to propose, in practical ways, the end of using the earth as mere raw material for commodities. This involves replacing the capitalist terminology of 'products' and 'by-products', by a new emphasis, from historical materialism, that *both* are production, in any selected form, and that the human and physical effects of the selected products and types of work are unavoidable parts of a whole social and material process. It is in these ways that socialists can redefine what is abstractly known as 'the crisis of resources', for this can never be only a quantitative question; it is, from the beginning, a qualitative social and material question. The crude responses of 'zero growth' or 'ending industrial production' can then be replaced by discriminating assessment and monitoring in what is still a process of human intervention in an inseparable physical world: interventions which simultaneously create altered social and physical worlds.

The socialist forms of such intervention will of course begin from the most general human needs, but we shall specify, in contemporary terms, the facts that Marx emphasized: that different kinds of need are themselves socially and materially created; that responses to need create new situations and relationships; that a socialist society, therefore, is a continually observing, reflecting and reassessing social order, as distinct from the capitalist drive to increase profitable aggregate production, and from the more general industrialist drive (which has included much early socialist construction) to produce as if this were a specialized and isolable activity. It will be one decisive sign of an advanced socialist society that it will have integrated, practically, the now separated sciences of economics and ecology, and will have been able to do this within a material social science.

We are as yet far from that, but the perspective is compelling. It will be not only in this field of production and resources, but in the understanding of human work itself, that the changes will come. For in the long domination of capitalist versions of production and then of work, vast areas of human work have been practically excluded, and this has taken one special form in the exploitation of women. It is at present impossible for women campaigning against this fundamental exploitation, as well as against more specific inequalities, to believe that the dominant socialist model is wholly on their side. But this difficulty is occurring within a transformation of simple productive processes, in which production can be increased with significant reductions of labour and labour time, with the result that much more energy is available for those other kinds of social production, in the care of people, that had been specialized to women and then arrogantly excluded from 'productive work' and from social and material recognition and respect.

This will not be the only or indeed a sufficient change in the relations between men and women. Nor, however, will a socialist society look for singular solutions in new forms of these relations. Here, if this is to be genuine liberation, there will be radical diversity both within and between societies. But if there has been danger for socialists in failing to answer contemporary anti-capitalist ecological questions, there is at least equal danger in failing to answer – or indeed, in old ways, from the dominant model, even offering to answer, as if to claimants or petitioners or an excluded interest group – the fundamental questions about relations between men and women which even at its best the socialist tradition has never taken seriously enough.

Yet another perspective of the socialism of the twenty-first century will be a remaking of its understanding and practice in culture and communications. The most immediate task is to end the stifling orthodoxy which continues to produce its 'correct' definitions of cultural production and communications practice. Here the matter of anti-capitalism is especially complex, since it has penetrated and in some areas been absorbed by especially dynamic forms of capitalism itself. The most vital cultural production of the twentieth century has in fact originated either in repressed popular forces or in small and relatively isolated oppositional and marginal formations. Capitalism, of course, has busily traded in both, in ways that have transformed what was once known simply as 'bourgeois culture', work of and for that class. But here, especially, socialism has offered few alternatives. It is ironically more successful than capitalism in maintaining and respecting traditional work, and it has made positive contributions in resisting what is genuinely inhumane and self-destructive – more significant socialist terms than 'decadent' – within the torrent of new cultural production. But while it offers only, against these, its 'correct' projections from its singular model, or at best its support for older traditional and popular forms, it is not only inadequate for any general liberation; it can often be identified as a force offering only to control it, as against the reckless vitality of the capitalist exploitation.

By the beginning of the twenty-first century the whole body of cultural and communicative relations will have in fact been transformed. New technology will provide both more individual and self-selected access and vastly extended and more diverse transmission and opportunities for production. In its negative aspects, this is already a moment dangerous to socialism. International capitalist production of every kind, including skilful mixes of entertainment, sport and propaganda, is reaching out to remake consciousness in its own images, and is scoring many successes. No policy of mere defensive exclusion can stand against this. Only the positive recovery, development and open exploratory use of the new forms and technologies by actual societies, for their own diverse purposes, can make new socialist cultures. Thus socialists everywhere must support the demand for a new international information order, beyond the controls and influences of Western capital. But this will not be achieved by some simple reversal to a singular alternative model. It is from within actual societies, and then not only from their elites, that new and diverse work should come, capable of hospitable exchange but controlled neither by orientation to the international market nor to some internal and globally distributed singular model. In practice we are already further along, in this new cultural perspective, than in either politics or economics, yet the pace of technological change is producing no simple line of development but a dynamic complex of new dangers and new opportunities.

This is not, moreover, as in the old model, a merely 'superstructural' field. On the contrary, what now happens and can happen in culture and communications is profoundly inseparable from world economic and political and perhaps especially military problems. The guidance systems which have already transformed warmaking, at levels even more fundamental than those of nuclear weapons themselves, have their technically linked counterparts in the unprecedented exposure of most modern societies to versions of the character and intentions of other societies and peoples. The struggle for socialism is now going on at least as intensively in this area of information and ideas and images as in directly political, economic and military ways.

It is a condition of any socialism, indeed of any civilization, in the twenty-first century that actual war, at this rapidly developing technical level which has already converted it to generalized massacre, should be both directly avoided and in its waste of preparatory resources pushed much further away. Yet here is another interlock with a form of anti-capitalism which does not arrive at, indeed can become equally hostile to, socialism. Some contemporary peace movements, correctly identifying modern military systems as fundamentally alienated from effective democratic controls, have gone on to see no difference, in a wider respect, between capitalist and socialist systems. But this position cannot be brusquely dismissed by reassertion of the essentially peaceful character of socialism, or by an identification – in itself largely correct – of the causes of war in the capitalist system and in the imperialist offensive against the socialist societies and against popular and revolutionary movements elsewhere. These points modify the wilder assertions, but they do not meet the underlying questions: that the advanced military systems themselves are incompatible with any form of full political democracy, so that only their abolition can release new forces of liberation; and that in their currently defensive stages, under vast pressures, actually existing socialist societies have not only been subject to some explicit militarism but in some tragic cases have not even been able to keep the peace between themselves.

Thus the rhetorical production of 'socialism' as the way to lift the threat of war is unconvincing. The real socialist position is the kind of total analysis which, in placing the complex causes of war within the long crises of the imperialist and capitalist systems, is sufficiently open and undogmatic to recognize three important contradictions in the relations between socialism and peace. These are:

(i)   that the very fact of imperialist resistance to popular and revolutionary movements, and its attempted destabilization of socialist societies, lead many socialist and national-liberation movements not only to the acceptance but often to the initiation of armed struggle;

(ii) that especially in post-colonial societies, but also in other cases, the history of imperialist and other foreign domination has left a confusion of peoples and arbitrary frontiers which are bound to generate disputes and can in some cases lead to wars between newly liberated and/or socialist countries and peoples;

(iii) that the long stance of defence against aggression and destabilization has produced within many socialist and newly liberated societies a set of formations, centred on military and security forces, which always contradict and can long distort the general social and economic formations appropriate to socialism, leading in the worst cases to its frustration or actual repression.

It is of central importance that these issues should be frankly discussed within the international socialist community: not only because in practice everything must be done to avoid or reduce any scale of war, but also because at the level of theory there is danger in relying on any simple residual equation of socialism with peace, which would evade our actual historical situations. Moreover, because the question of war and peace is that which will decide whether there is to be social construction of any kind in the twenty-first century, all our other analyses and struggles are dependent on clarity and understanding in this.

The Practice of Possibility

1987

Terry Eagleton[1]: *You retired from the chair of drama at Cambridge University in 1983, after a long career on the political Left which still continues. You fought Fascism in Europe, and took a major role in the creation of the early New Left and the early years of CND. Since then you've been involved in a whole series of socialist interventions, both inside and outside the Labour Party, and your intellectual work – what you've come to call 'cultural materialism' – has transformed the thinking of generations of students and workers in the cultural field.*

It would have been nice to have been able to present you on your retirement, not with a gold clock, but with a socialist society. It's arguable, however, that such a goal is now as remote, if not more so, as at any time in your political career. Instead we are witnessing the most viciously anti-working-class regime of most people's political memory, the laying of the groundwork of a police state, and an apparently baffled left opposition. Militarily speaking we live in the most terrible danger. Could I ask you, then, whether after so long a struggle you now feel in any sense disillusioned? What are your political thoughts and hopes, immediately after the election of a third Thatcher government?

Raymond Williams: Disillusionment, not at all; disappointment, of course. Yet looking back it seems to me I absorbed some of these disappointments quite early on, so the recent ones didn't come as so much of a surprise. Indeed I was so thrown out of my early expectations, as a young man and a soldier in the war, by the events of 1947 that I went into a kind of retreat for a year or two, trying to work out a different

---

1. Terry Eagleton is Lecturer in Critical Theory at the University of Oxford and a Fellow of Linacre College. The interview took place in July 1987. [Ed.]

kind of intellectual project, which also involved a sense of what a different political project might be. This was a time, remember, when the expectations of a Labour government, which had been the whole perspective of my childhood, had been not just disappointed but actively repulsed: the priority of the military alliance with the USA over Labour's quite real achievements in welfare, the use of troops against groups of striking workers and so on. So the crisis for me was an early one; and perhaps this partly explains why the crisis of 1956 didn't come as so much of a shock for me as it did for some of those intellectuals who had stayed in the Communist Party. There was then a sense of reinvigoration in the late 1950s, which carried on throughout the sixties in the various attempts at some new gathering of left forces. When that went down, in 1970, there was of course a sense of setback and defeat; but I think that whole history had prepared me emotionally and intellectually for the failures which the Left was then to go through.

When all of this passed into the period of open reaction of the Thatcher governments, it seemed to me that the Left was repeatedly trying to reconstitute the very limited kind of hope that I'd repeatedly seen fail. The rhetoric of victory in 1945 is in a sense fair enough, but it shouldn't convince anyone unless it is immediately qualified by the realities of 1947-48. The rhetoric of the (supposedly) successful Labour governments of the 1960s is for me similarly qualified by the events of 1968 – that very confused time in which the attempt to feed new currents of ideas and feelings into the labour movement was not merely ignored but, again, actually repulsed.

Today, it's clearer to me than ever that the socialist analysis is the correct one, and its correctness has been in my view repeatedly demonstrated. But the perspectives which had sustained the main left organizations were simply not adequate to the society they were seeking to change. There was always the attempt on the left to reconstitute old models: the notion of 'uniting Britain', to take an example from recent electoral rhetoric, or of an autonomous sovereign economy – as if what's happened in international capitalism over the past forty years simply hadn't happened. When they fight in these terms, what can and should be fought for becomes much more difficult to define.

What then should be fought for? Are you suggesting a wholly different strategy for the Left?

The strategy is all still to be found, but what blocks it, I'm saying, is this old model of creating a relatively powerful, united Britain with a 'successful' sovereign economy. That, I think, is what history has ruled out. And one consequence of this has been a retreat to certain areas, traditional strongholds of labour: Scotland, Wales, the north of England. But the shape of a genuine strategy would be to pass beyond this idea of altering such situations only in Britain. To adopt at least a West European perspective, where there are many people and regions in similar situations, penetrated and distorted by international capitalism and the military alliance. Any useful strategy would involve a great building up of autonomy in such regions in Britain, but instead of orienting that to the British state, looking out for the connections which can be made to Western Europe, at least in the first instance.

The obvious block to this is the electoral system which imposes the need for a national party – 'national' on this superannuated model of the British state. There follows the necessity for a coalition of left forces which everyone knows is impossible to sustain honestly. The range of opinion from liberal to far left is just too broad. Socialists want to take part in defeating something uniquely vicious, and so must be friendly to the Labour Right, or to Liberals, Social Democrats, even progressive Tories; but if you do so pretending that you share their perspective then you fail in one of your most basic duties: telling the truth as you see it.

Meanwhile a major obstacle to any socialist strategy is that the Left makes repeated attempts to remake the whole Labour Party in its own image, as distinct from maintaining, within present constraints, a socialist element. In practice, this has prevented the Labour Party from achieving the kind of unity it needs for the limited jobs it has to do. But it also means a limitation on the amount of absolutely straight socialist argument and propaganda, under the pretence of consensus. When one hears a Labour candidate, as mine did, talking about loyalty to NATO, building up a fine fleet and the rest, one knows one simply isn't living in the same world with people with whom otherwise one's prepared to be comradely and cooperative, for specific objectives. Yet while the Left still sees the wholesale conversion of a social democratic party to a socialist party as its objective, there's an important sense in which it silences itself.

If we had proportional representation, what we would rapidly get is a realignment of the centre. People talk of a realignment of the Left, but what's already beginning to happen is actually a realignment of the centre. Now such a realignment of the centre, which I think is bound to happen, just isn't the Left's business. Socialist analysis and propaganda must be made in its own terms. If there *was* a realignment of the centre which took the Labour Party into some unambiguous social-democratic phase, there would be in altered electoral conditions a space for some federation of socialist, Green and radical nationalist forces. This would not be insignificant electorally, and above all it would be able to speak up without equivocation for its view of the world, which at present doesn't get through politically very far. It would be dreadful for the Left in the Labour Party to try to break it up, weaken it even further, and there's no simple question of a breakaway. But in the situation I'm describing, there will be a possibility of the Left speaking in its own voice; and in a political situation as hard as this, that's not to be discounted.

Indeed; though as the crisis of capitalism has tightened, we've been witnessing a steady haemorrhage of intellectuals from the far Left. Individuals, groups, journals, whole parties have moved inexorably to the right, and this at a time – a bitter irony – when in a sense there's never been so obviously, so devastatingly what one might describe as a 'total global system', which demands an appropriately radical response. To affirm such a truth in an age of postmodernist fragmentation, however, is becoming increasingly unfashionable. To mention social class in certain so-called left circles is to be unceremoniously shown the door. Defeatism and adaptation, however 'dynamically' and modernistically tricked out, seem instead the order of the day. I once heard you refer in a nicely sardonic phrase to those who 'make long-term adjustments to short-term problems'. I wonder whether it was this treason of the clerks that you had in mind?

Well, the strength of our enemies isn't to be doubted; yet the most intelligent operators of the system itself know just how profoundly unstable it is. The whole future of a US-led, anti-Communist, anti-Third-World alliance is coming under pressure, if only from its own internal divisions and the increasing inability of the USA to dominate it. The international financial system is a helter-skelter economy based on frightening credit expansion and credit risk, which would have terrified an earlier generation of orthodox bankers and financiers. To say this, of course, isn't to advocate some policy of waiting for the crash; for one thing such crashes aren't automatic, and for another thing they're just as likely to produce a hard Right well beyond anything we've seen so far – those who talk of the hard Right in Britain haven't really seen one. But if the system is that unstable, this clearly isn't a world to adjust to. It's not a world in which one has to settle for belonging to an eccentric minority who believe there are old socialist texts and ideas which must be kept alive, in an all too powerful and successful system. Powerful, yes; successful, no.

Meanwhile what's happened in so-called 'actually existing socialism' in Eastern Europe has done the Left more damage than can be properly accounted for. It's been a key feature in many intellectual desertions, and one difficult to argue against since of course one endorses the denunciation of terror, while recalling that such terror is in fact historically outweighed by the long, systematic terror of the Right. If it were a reason to desert socialism, because such terrible things have happened in its name, it would be a reason to desert every system we know. The Eastern European societies, however, aren't going to remain in their present condition; they know they can't sustain themselves without radical change. And this will be a positive factor for socialist intellectuals in the West.

It would sometimes seem today that a commitment to class struggle on the one hand, and a celebration of difference and plurality on the other, have been lined up on opposite sides of the left political fence. Yet both ways of thinking would seem to have subtly coexisted in your own work almost from the beginning. You've always deeply suspected closed, monolithic theories and strategies, and from the outset your socialism has stressed difficulty, complexity, variety; yet, not least in your development over the past decade or so, in the very period of some other left intellectuals' sail-trimming or simply renegacy, you would seem to hold firmly to a class perspective. How do you see the relation between these two emphases?

I've always been very aware of the complicated relationships between class and place. I've been enormously conscious of place, and still get an extraordinary amount of emotional confirmation from the sense of place and its people. Now the key argument in Marxism was always whether the proletariat would be a universal class – whether the bonds it forged from a common exploitation would be perceived as primary, and eventually supersede the more local bonds of region or nation or religion. On the one hand the recognition of exploitation continually reproduces class consciousness and organization on a universal basis. On the other hand, I don't know of any prolonged struggle of that kind in which these other issues haven't been vital, and in some cases decisive. So I'm on both sides of the argument, yes: I recognize the universal forms which spring from this fundamental exploitation – the system, for all its local variety, is everywhere recognizable. But the practice of fighting against it has always been entered into, or sometimes deflected, by these other kinds of more particular bonds.

Which of course vitally include gender. In your book The Long Revolution, *right back in 1961 and long before the resurgence of the contemporary women's movement, you identified what you saw then as four interlocking systems within any society, and named one of them as the 'system of generation and nurture'. Yet your theoretical work would seem to have preserved a relative silence on those issues; instead, perhaps, they*

have tended to take up home in your fiction, in which the family, gen-
eration and their connections to work and politics have figured prom-
inently.

That's true. It's really all in my second novel, *Second Generation*; that's
what it was really all about. But at about the same time I was writing *The
English Novel from Dickens to Lawrence*, where I describe the Brontë
sisters as representing interests and values marginalized by the male
hegemony. Not only that, however, but representing human interests of
a more general kind which showed up the limits of the extraordinary
disabling notion of masculinity. I remember how I used to embarrass
students in my lectures – you will doubtless remember this – by suggesting it would be interesting to locate the historical moment when men
stopped crying in public. The suppression of tenderness and emotional
response, the willingness to admit what isn't weakness – one's feelings in
and through another; all this is a repression not only of women's experience but of something much more general. And I suppose I found it
easier to explore that in more personal terms, in my novels. That's no
real excuse; I ought to have been doing this in my other work too; but by
the time I came to understand it in that way it was already being done by
a lot of good people who were no doubt making more sense of it than I
could have done.

*The media, or communications as you prefer to call them, have long
formed a centrepiece of your work. Although the whole concept of
'media' is surely much too passive to convey the enormous power of these
institutions. The editors of the* Sun, Mail *and* Express *were surely
infinitely more important to Thatcher in the election than any members
of her inner circle, and ought to be buried in Westminster Abbey. I mean
as soon as possible. How are we to go about combatting this formidable
source of political power?*

Well, one can talk of course of education – of arming people's minds
against that kind of journalism. But there's now been a sustained cultural attempt to show how this manipulation works, which has hardly
impinged on its actual power. I don't see how the educational response
can be adequate. The manipulative methods are too powerful, too far
below the belt for that. These people have to be driven out. We have to
create a press owned by and responsible to its readers. The increasing
concentration of power in the media has been a process strangely unre-
sisted by socialists, by the labour movement as a whole, who have actually let go of key sectors. When I was concentrating on this kind of
cultural analysis in the 1950s I was sometimes told by good Marxist

friends that it was a diversion from the central economic struggle. Now every trade union and political leader cries 'the media, the media'. It was correctly foreseen that this, in electoral politics, was where the battle would be fought, but the response to that was very belated. The proposals which I put forward in my book *Communications* in the early 1960s, for a democratic control of the media, still seem to me a necessary programme.

You have turned increasingly to Wales both in your fictional and political work; you still have close, active relations, personally and politically, with Wales. Is this marginality a source of strength in your work? Or is it simply convenient to have, so to speak, a different passport and identity when one sallies forth among the middle-class English natives?

I think some of my Welsh friends would be kind enough to say that if I have some importance for them it's precisely because I came out – because I went among the English, and got a hearing, even recognition, in their own institutions. When you're part of one of these disadvantaged nationalities you can be very bitter about people who have gone off and made it elsewhere, but it can be different if you also know they still relate to you, even if one has crossed the border rather than remained inside it. In that sense I don't altogether regret crossing the border, though there are times when I do. Coming from a border area of Wales in any case, the problem for me has always been one of what it was to be Welsh – I mean in some serious sense, rather than in one of the exportable stage-Welsh versions. I suppose there was some group I thought of as the *real* Welsh, secure in their identity, who would come out in force and flail this returning migrant with all his doubts.

The response I've had, especially from young Welsh people, has been precisely the opposite: thank God someone has come out and asked who are we, what are we? All my usual famous qualifying and complicating, my insistence on depths and ambiguities, was exactly what they already knew. And this experience of ambiguity and contradiction hasn't only equipped us in Wales to understand our own situation better; it's also equipped us, emotionally and intellectually, to understand the situation of increasing numbers of people – including the once so self-assured, confident English. It's easier for us, in other words, to put questions to those simple, confident, unitary identities which really belong to an earlier historical period.

Let me return finally to where we began, with the question of disappointment or despondency. What you say about the need to reject any kind of disillusion strikes me as absolutely right. Your work has always seemed to me distinguished by a kind of steady, profound humanism, which it would be too facile to describe as optimism. Beneath your political writing has always run this confident trust in human capacities – capacities so steadfast and enduring that not to see them finally triumph in some political future would seem not only unthinkable but, as it were, blasphemous. Perhaps I share that belief; but let me put it to you, in the spirit of devil's advocacy, an alternative scenario. The historical record shows that such capacities have so far always been defeated. History, as Walter Benjamin might have put it, is more barbarism than progress; what you and I might consider moral and political virtue has never ruled any social order, other than briefly and untypically. The real historical record is one of wretchedness and unremitting toil; and 'culture' – your and my speciality – has its dubious roots in this. How then are we to undo such a history with the very contaminated instruments it has handed us? Is socialism, in other words, anything more than a wishful thinking which runs quite against the historical grain? To put the point more personally: how far is your own trust in human creative capacities in part the product of an unusually warm and affectionate working-class child-hood, of which it's in some sense the nostalgic memory?

It's true that much of my political belief is a continuation of a very early formation. I can't remember any time when I haven't felt broadly speaking as I do now, except for the period of retreat I mentioned in the 1940s, which in a sense was a kind of cancellation of the certainties I'd assumed in childhood. I ceased then to be simply a product of that culture. I don't know what I became a product of, since I couldn't accept the offered alternatives. Out of that period of radical dislocation was rebuilt what was, and I think still is, an *intellectual* conviction. Though of course it can't ever be only that. The crisis which came to me on the death of my father, who was a socialist and a railway worker – I haven't been able to explain this to people properly, perhaps I explained it partly in my novel *Border Country* – was the sense of a kind of defeat for an idea of value. Maybe this was an unreasonable response. All right, he died, he died too early, but men and women die. But it was very difficult not to see him as a victim at the end. I suppose it was this kind of experience which sent me in the end to the historical novel I'm now writing, *People of the Black Mountains*, about the movements of history over a very long period, in and through a particular place in Wales. And this history is a record of all you say: of defeat, invasion, victimization, oppression. When one sees what was done to the people who are physically my ancestors, one feels it to be almost incredible.

What do I get from this? Simply the confidence of survival? Yes, that in part. There's been a quite extraordinary process of self-generation and regeneration, from what seemed impossible conditions. Thomas Becket once asked a shrewd, wordly-wise official on the Marches about the nature of the Welsh. 'I will show you the curious disposition of the Welsh', said the official, 'that when you hold the sword they will submit, but when they hold the sword they assert themselves.' I like the deep, poker-faced joke of that. The defeats have occurred over and over again, and what my novel is then trying to explore is simply the condition of anything surviving at all. It's not a matter of the simple patriotic answer: we're Welsh, and still here. It's the infinite resilience, even deviousness, with which people have managed to persist in profoundly unfavourable conditions, and the striking diversity of the beliefs in which they've expressed their autonomy. A sense of a value which has won its way through different kinds of oppression in different forms.

If I say, estimating, for example, whether we'll avoid a nuclear war, 'I see it as 50-50', I instantly make it 51-49, or 60-40, the wrong way. That is why I say we must speak for hope, as long as it doesn't mean suppressing the nature of the danger. I don't think my socialism is simply the prolongation of an earlier experience. When I see that childhood coming at the end of millennia of much more brutal and thoroughgoing exploitation, I can see it as a fortunate time: an ingrained and indestructible yet also changing embodiment of the possibilities of common life.

Raymond Williams: Select Bibliography

Culture, Communications, Politics

Culture and Society 1780–1950 (London 1958)
The Long Revolution (London 1961)
Communications (Harmondsworth 1962; 3rd edn with afterword 1976)
May Day Manifesto, ed. (Harmondsworth 1968)
Television, Technology and Cultural Form (London 1974)
Keywords (London 1976; enlarged 2nd edn 1984)
Problems in Materialism and Culture (London 1980)
Culture (London 1981)
Towards 2000 (London 1983)

Literary Criticism and Theory

Modern Tragedy (London 1966; revised edn with afterword 1979)
Drama from Ibsen to Brecht (London 1968)
Orwell (London 1971; 2nd edn with afterword 1984)
The English Novel from Dickens to Lawrence (London 1970)
The Country and the City (London 1973)
Marxism and Literature (Oxford 1977)
Cobbett (Oxford 1983)
Writing in Society (London 1984)
The Politics of Modernism (London 1989, forthcoming)

Fiction

Border Country (London 1960)
Second Generation (London 1964)
The Fight for Manod (London 1979)

The Volunteers (London 1978)
Loyalties (London 1985)
People of the Black Mountains (London 1989, forthcoming)

Interviews

Politics and Letters: Interviews with *New Left Review* (London 1979)

Index

DATE DUE

DE 17 '06			